Thoughtfulness and the Rule of Law

Thoughtfulness
and the **RULE OF LAW**

JEREMY WALDRON

HARVARD UNIVERSITY PRESS

Cambridge, Massachusetts, and London, England · 2023

First printing

Cataloging-in-Publication Data is available from the Library of Congress

ISBN: 978-0-674-29077-8 (alk. paper)

For the memory of
Marshall Sanger (1923–2004)
Colonel, US Army (retired)
with love and gratitude

Contents

Introduction   *1*

1   Thoughtfulness and the Rule of Law   *11*

2   The Concept and the Rule of Law   *35*

3   How Law Protects Dignity   *75*

4   Self-Application   *96*

5   Vagueness and the Guidance of Action   *120*

6   The Rule of Law and the Role of Courts   *145*

7   The Rule of Law and the Importance of Procedure   *159*

8   Stare Decisis and the Rule of Law: A Layered Approach   *179*

9   Legislation and the Rule of Law   *208*

10   Rule *by* Law: A Much-Maligned Preposition   *235*

11   The Rule of Law in Public Law   *256*

Notes   *271*

Acknowledgments   *315*

Index   *319*

Thoughtfulness and the Rule of Law

Introduction

What is the rule of law? No definition commands universal assent—there's a lot to disagree about—but basically it amounts to a requirement that our social, political, and economic life together should be governed by law. Law, not people, should rule, and any ruling *we* do should be conducted under the auspices of law. This places a special burden on the institutions and individuals entrusted with the making and finding of law, with its administration, and with the upkeep and repair that's necessary for a legal system to remain in good condition. And it also burdens those who seek and exercise power. It's their job to find the law and follow it, not brush it aside or neglect it in their enthusiasm for their own ideals.

Even this much is enough to generate controversy. Where does law come from, if not from the rule of people? How can there be one without the other? What if the laws we have inherited embody rules, procedures, or forms of authority that no longer command respect? What if they prohibit us from focusing our intelligence directly on some urgent problem? Does the rule of law rule out discretion? Even discretion that is framed and authorized by law? How important are rules? Are rules all there is to law? What *is* law? What is it, exactly, that is supposed to rule over us—statutes, codes, case law, constitutions, doctrines written down in treatises?

Questions like these challenge us, they shake us up in our understanding of the rule of law, and—thankfully—they stop us from getting bogged down in some ossified definition. Different answers push us in different directions, and we actually find ourselves enriching one another's understandings when one set of answers collides with another. I have argued elsewhere that the rule of law is an essentially contested concept.[1] This does not mean that it is hopelessly confused. It means that the use and application of the concept in question is actually enhanced by constant controversy about its meaning: arguing about it has always been part of the heritage that the rule of law brings with it. You don't understand the rule of law if you don't understand the parameters of the argument.

All that said, if I were looking to go further than the "definition" we've just considered, I would add a few things along the following lines. I would say:

1. The rule of law requires people in positions of state authority to exercise their power within a constraining framework of public norms rather than simply on the basis of their own personal or political preferences.
2. There have to be rules or standards laid down clearly in advance—norms whose public presence enables people to figure out what is required of them, what the legal consequences of their actions will be, and what they can rely on so far as official action and assistance is concerned.
3. Courts are a key part of the rule of law—independent institutions that operate according to recognized standards of procedural due process, which offer an impartial forum where disputes can be resolved, and which allow people an opportunity to present evidence and make arguments before independent adjudicators to challenge the legality of official action, particularly when it impacts on their interests in life, liberty, or economic well-being.
4. The rule of law requires legal equality: a principle that ensures the law is the same for everyone, whatever our other differences; that everyone has access to the courts; and that no one is above the law.

All this—or something like it—is part of what people mean when they say we are committed to the rule of law.

Whether we agree on a definition or not, my aim in these essays is to enrich our understanding of this problematic ideal. We know the rule of law is not the only principle that governs our politics. It is but one star in a constellation of political ideals: others include democracy, human rights, social justice and economic freedom. No doubt there are connections between these various ideals. But I think we should try to enrich our understanding by probing the distinctive character of each one. Rule of law, democracy, human rights, social justice, economic freedom—these are *all* important values, but they are different from one another, and nothing is gained by erasing the boundaries between them. Trade-offs are sometimes necessary, and we need to understand what's at stake when rule of law has to be balanced against democracy or when either of them has to be traded off against human rights. I have written a lot about the other values—democracy, human rights, and so on.[2] But what I want to do in *this* book is deepen our engagement with values and principles that only the rule of law can convey. Everything written here is imbued with a firm understanding that the rule of law makes a *distinctive* contribution to the constellation of ideals we bring to our politics, and that we should explore that distinctive contribution for what it is, so we don't lose sight of it in our (perhaps justified) enthusiasm for the other values I have mentioned. To repeat: they are *all* important—the rule of law, in its distinctiveness, no less than any of the others.

Some will see nothing but formalism in this approach: "Everything is what it is and not another thing." But part of my reason for working this way is to show that treating the rule of law as a distinctive value need not lead to an impoverished understanding. I hope we will see how the riches open up as we begin to explore the rule of law as a distinctive part of our heritage of political philosophy.

To this end, I have woven a number of very general themes into these essays. They include the following:

The importance of standards. I want to think through the role of standards, as well as rules, under the rule of law. Standards are norms that in their use of terms like "reasonable," or even other, more specific value terms, seem to require judgment on the part of those who apply them. F. A. Hayek said in *The Road to Serfdom* that "one could write a history of the decline of the rule of law . . . in terms of the progressive introduction of these vague formulas [like 'fairness' and 'reasonableness'] into legislation and of the increasing arbitrariness and uncertainty that results."[3] I want to show that he is wrong, and that there is nothing antithetical to the rule of law and certainly nothing that promotes arbitrariness in the deployment of such norms, whether they are found in common law, in statutes, or in constitutional provisions.

The value of dignity. Plainly, the rule of law is a value-laden concept—though which values it embodies is something worth exploring. There are certainly connections with liberty, in its establishment of a legal environment that is safe for individual freedom. But in addition, the rule of law expresses a powerful commitment to dignity and respect for the dignity of human agency in the forms and procedures it requires for law. I want to explore the understanding of dignity expressed in these commitments, and the implications of this value loading for our overall approach to the concept of law.

Principles of procedure. As a third theme, I am going to emphasize again and again institutional and procedural values as well as the values of juridical form that have dominated academic discussions of the rule of law in the wake of Lon Fuller's work.[4] I will insist that we focus, for example, on procedural due process, not just clarity, generality, and prospectivity. Also, we need to look at imperatives governing the institutions that administer the law—independence of the judiciary, the responsibility of the legal profession, and the care and impartiality with which courts approach questions of evidence, argument, and proof. The propositional form of the legal norms themselves is no doubt important, but as we shall see in these essays, our understanding of the rule of law is greatly enhanced when we take on board the procedural and institutional elements as well.

The essays that follow are freestanding, though they secure a modicum of unity by engaging the three themes I have mentioned. Here's how they play out:

1. The piece that gives this book its title, Chapter 1, is an attempt to revive the ancient connection between the rule of law and reason, and to push back against attempts to associate rule of law with legal forms that dictate a sort of mechanical and implacable certainty in their application. For many jurists, the rule of law is associated with the precision and determinacy of legal rules, and the predictability of the environment that rules provide. But it is not supposed to turn us into machines. We should think also about the ways in which law helps make us more thoughtful and reflective, governing us through standards and principles rather than the robotic precision of rules. Whether in private law (e.g., with standards of reasonable care) or in human rights law (e.g., with norms prohibiting inhuman and degrading treatment), law sometimes invites its subjects to make thoughtful judgments about their behavior or about the situations that they face, prompting, struc-

turing, and channeling that thoughtfulness in various ways that are explored in detail in Chapter 1.

2. I also want to explore the relation between the rule of law and the work we do in general jurisprudence on the concept of law. In Chapter 2, I consider the values that underpin our commitment to the rule of law—respect for liberty and our dignity as agents—and the relation of this value loading to our overall understanding of law in the positivist tradition. Chapter 2 argues in favor of a more demanding understanding of what law is than most positivists offer. I argue against what I call "casual positivism," which takes almost any instance of centralized command and control as a legal system. Positivity remains a key feature of law—law is something people make, and the positivists are right that there is no guarantee that it is good and just even when, by formal and procedural standards, it is well made and properly applied. But although the conditions of its making and application do not clinch the issue in favor of its substantive merits, these formal and procedural aspects of the rule of law and the values that support them still matter enormously for our understanding of law and our understanding of what it can contribute *just qua law* to the pursuit of the common good.

3. Chapter 3 takes up in more detail the claim that our commitment to the rule of law is underpinned by the value of human dignity. Insisting that we be ruled under the auspices of law is a sort of tribute to our dignity as agents. As Lon Fuller put it, "Every departure from the principles of law's inner morality"—which is what he called the rule of law—"is an affront to man's dignity as a responsible agent."[5] In the way law operates, in the way it presents its requirements, in the way law expects its requirements to be taken on board and observed by those to whom such requirements are primarily addressed, in the procedural way it organizes hearings, in the way that it sponsors argumentation, even in the way it arranges for coercion—in all these ways, law treats humans as dignified agents, capable of self-control, with a sense of themselves and their interests that commands attention and respect and with the ability to respond intelligently to its demands. I know law is sometimes brutal and degrading in its application. Aspirations don't equal reality. But Chapter 3 argues that it is part of law's inherent aspiration to deal with human persons as dignified agents. A failure to do this should always be seen as a betrayal, even among those who disagree

about the substantive merits of the law being enforced. This aspiration and the extent to which it is honored is a large part of what distinguishes legal forms of control from other modes of governance.

4. My discussion of self-application in Chapter 4 takes up a particular aspect of the engagement of law with our agency. In their book *The Legal Process,* Harvard law professors Henry Hart and Albert Sacks discussed what they called the technique of self-applying regulation.[6] What they meant by this is that in most cases, officials are not the first appliers of the law. The individuals to whom legal norms are addressed have the initial task of applying the norms. In most cases, official application is not necessary. Officialdom comes into the picture only when there is some problem with or dispute about what the primary norm subject has done. Hart and Sacks maintained that overwhelmingly the greater part of the general body of the law is self-applying, and they said that this is of enormous significance alike in the theory and the practice of social orderings. In Chapter 4 I explore this idea of self-application. I consider the reasons we have, in some areas of law, for not using this technique. The law relating to divorce is one example: you can't just use criteria laid down in general norms to declare yourself divorced, without an official determination. I discuss self-application by officials as primary addressees (in constitutional law, for example) as well as by firms and citizens. And I consider also the self-application of what we call standards as opposed to rules.

5. This last point is taken up yet again in Chapter 5. I said earlier that the use of standards in the law is a recurring theme of this collection. Rules give us determinacy and clarity. But the rule of law should not be construed as demanding determinacy and clarity at all costs; it should not always be conceived as the rule of rules (as opposed to the rule of standards or principles). Now some jurists object to standards because their use of predicates like "reasonable" or "excessive" gives relatively little guidance to those to whom they are addressed, leaving the individual unclear about what to do or where she stands so far as the law's application is concerned. And this is thought to be an affront to the rule of law. In Chapter 5, I address this objection, using as a paradigm the "reasonable speed" statute considered in an old Ohio traffic case.[7] I argue that standards *do* provide guidance for action: they guide the use of our practical reasoning to figure out what kind of action is appropriate in varying circumstances. In that sense, they are every bit as respectful of our capacity for agency as rules are (though in a different

way). I also consider issues about fairness and the possible chilling effect of using standards, taking my lead from a comment of the court in the traffic example that it was in fact precisely the *intention* of the Ohio statute to chill the enthusiastic and aggressive driving of (what the court called) "the reckless, wanton speed maniac."

6. And then we switch gears to consider what the rule of law requires in the way of institutions and institutional oversight. In Chapter 2, I emphasized the importance of institutional procedures in enriching both our conception of law itself and our understanding of the rule of law. And in Chapter 6 we ask: What role do courts play in advancing or upholding the rule of law? Does the rule of law require that courts should have authority over all other branches of government, including the legislature?[8] Or does it only require judicial review of executive action, leaving judicial review of legislation an open question? To the extent that it does empower courts, does the rule of law impose constraints on the sort of reasoning and decision-making that courts engage in? Chapter 6 explores an array of possible answers to these questions. It considers the possibility that the ascendancy of courts in a constitution may represent a form of judicial supremacy that looks remarkably like the uncontrolled rule of men, which the rule of law is supposed to supersede. To preclude that possibility, it is particularly important for courts to recognize that any authority they have is limited in scope and should not be guided by any overall political program other than that of seeing that limited constitutional constraints on government are upheld.

7. Proponents of the rule of law argue incessantly about whether that ideal should be conceived formalistically or in terms of substantive values. Formalistically, the rule of law is associated with principles like generality, clarity, prospectivity, consistency, and so on. Substantively, it is associated with market values, with constitutional rights, with democracy, and with freedom and human dignity. In Chapter 7, I argue for an additional layer of complexity: the *procedural* aspect of the rule of law; principles that have to do with natural justice and procedural due process. These I believe have been neglected in the jurisprudential literature devoted specifically to the idea of the rule of law, and they deserve much greater emphasis. Moreover, procedural values go way beyond elementary requirements like the guarantee of an unbiased tribunal, the liturgy of a hearing, and the opportunity to present and

confront evidence. They include the right to argue in a court about what
the law is and what its bearing should be on one's situation. As we see
also in Chapters 1 and 2, the provision that law makes for argument is
necessarily unsettling, and so emphasis on this facet of procedural
rule of law highlights the point that predictability cannot be regarded
as the be-all and end-all of the rule of law.

8. Still working in the realm of courts, I have endeavored also to
ascertain the rule-of-law principles that support the practice of following precedent. Chapter 8 explores the relation between stare decisis and the rule of law, in a layered way, relying not so much on a
predictability rationale but on the rule-of-law principles that enable
expectations to emerge in the first place. The chapter looks first at the
rule-of-law constraints that affect the initial decision of a judge whose
ruling might possibly generate a precedent. Such a judge has an obligation to try to phrase her ruling as a general principle, and any subsequent judge, faced with a similar question, has an obligation to play
his part in crediting the principle the first judge uses as a source of
law. That is how it comes about that subsequent judges are bound by
rule-of-law principles of constancy once a precedent has emerged.
We first explain the emergence of a principle and then ascertain the
extent to which it is binding. Chapter 8 argues that it is important to
distinguish these various layers so that the account of precedent does
not already assume what we are trying to establish. So it is generally
the importance of being ruled under the auspices of general principles as much as the more familiar idea of predictability that explains
the principle of stare decisis.

9. I don't want the rule of law to be associated exclusively with
values on display in a courtroom. We should also look at legislative
values, and I consider them in Chapter 9. This task is all the more
important because in certain circles, the rule of law is associated with
an antilegislative mentality, such as an identification of rule by legislation with rule by men, or, worse still, with a frank antipathy in the
name of the rule of law toward majoritarian democracy. To combat
this set of prejudices, it is important to find ways of crediting, under
the auspices of the rule of law, the desire of the inhabitants of a society
to use legislation to govern the conditions of their life together. Such a
desire may seem perverse from the point of view of an outside investor. But for the people concerned, there is nothing more natural,

and proponents of the rule of law should not be in the business of disparaging this impulse. The rule of law does not require that law remain static. True, it calls for a modicum of constancy so that legal rights and legal duties can provide a solid framework for our life together. But it is part of the wisdom of human affairs that conditions change, that there is progress in matters of value as well as in matters of science, and that a society needs to be equipped with procedures for modifying its laws when circumstances require—even when we disagree about it, even when change seems costly and disconcerting. All this calls for careful thought about the relation between rule of law and democracy. The two values are not the same, but they are not necessarily in opposition, either. Democracy is the means by which we effect change in our social arrangements; law frames the processes of change, as well as imbuing what we decide on with the necessary authority to coordinate and govern our affairs.

10. Similar themes are taken up in Chapter 10, where I consider the distinction between the rule of law and the idea of rule *by* law. Commentators working in the law-and-development field distinguish between the rule of law and rule by law, with the latter being treated as an authoritarian caricature of the former. Under rule by law, a regime may use law and legal institutions to control its population, but it will not allow law to be used to control the regime. There are also a number of other understandings of rule by law, most notably a conception that associates it ideologically with enacted law, as opposed to autonomous law (law that can somehow be thought of as emergent rather than enacted, rather in the way the common law is supposed to have emerged from thousands of individual cases). Bearing all this in mind, Chapter 10 reexamines the idea of rule by law and suggests that if that phrase is taken at face value, it may involve the admirable willingness of a regime to submit itself to the discipline of legality that I have spent most of this volume defending. It should not be disparaged, and indeed, we can see that (like the rule of law itself) it admits of a spectrum of applications, some of them quite demanding.

11. The themes of these last few chapters come together one more time in Chapter 11, which considers whether the rule of law should be thought of as privileging private law over public law. I argue that we should not understand it in this way, but equally, we should not think of the rule of law as an abstract or anodyne conception that is supposed

to apply indiscriminately to all areas of governance. Instead, we should develop an account of the rule of law that takes the mission of public administration seriously and seeks to establish it on a footing of legality rather than managerialism, while at the same time acknowledging that sometimes private interests do have to give way to the interests of the public. In earlier work I spoke of "the dignity of legislation," intending that as a necessary corrective in legal philosophy to the disparagement of majoritarian lawmaking.[9] This final chapter, and indeed the book as a whole, can be seen as a way of standing up for the respectability of ruling through legislation. I do not want to deny that the rule of law governs the development of law through courts. But legislation is important too, along with the forms of administration that it makes possible, and we need to have a good sense of its necessity under the rule of law and an understanding of the rule of law that makes it clear how public administration can be held to standards of legality without betraying its mission.

1

Thoughtfulness and the Rule of Law

1. Law's Obtuseness

We want to be ruled thoughtfully. Or, to put it in a democratic idiom, we want our engagement in governance to be thoughtful and reasoned, rather than rigid or mechanical. Thoughtfulness—the capacity to reflect and deliberate, to ponder complexity and confront new and unexpected circumstances with an open mind, and to do so articulately (even sometimes argumentatively) in the company of others with whom we share a society—these are some of the dignifying attributes of humanity, men and women at their best in the governance of their society.

But does the quest for thoughtfulness in government mean endorsing what used to be called the rule of men (now the rule of people—thinking people) rather than the rule of law? To be ruled by laws rather than by men has been an aspiration, indeed an imperative, of the Western political tradition since the time of the ancient Greeks. But it was the Greeks (or some of them) who noticed that rule by law might be something opposed to thoughtfulness in government. Law, said Plato's visitor in *The Statesman*, "is like a stubborn, stupid person who refuses to allow the slightest deviation from or questioning of his own rules, even if the situation has in fact changed and it turns out to be better for someone to contravene these rules."[1] Thoughtfulness—when we get it—is an attribute of human rulers, of people (the few or the many) participating in government. And maybe it is one of the things we turn our back on when we say we want to be ruled by laws—categorical inflexible laws (laid down, in many cases, centuries ago)—rather than ruled by men. For the sake of the benefits that the rule of law provides, we swallow the costs of a certain diminution of intelligence in government.

Of course, in many ways, this distinction between rule by men and rule by laws is a false contrast. Laws are human artifacts. They are made by men (made by people), interpreted by people, and applied by people. Rule by law seems to be rule by people all the way down. And in some of those capacities human thoughtfulness *is* paramount. Lawmaking, when it is done explicitly, is a thoughtful business, and often it represents a paradigmatic exercise of reason in policy conception, in drafting, and even (sometimes) in legislative deliberation. Though all legislators no doubt hope their works will endure, the legislative mentality at its best represents the agile and flexible application of human intellect, on a collective scale, to the shifting problems and challenges faced by a society. That's what I have argued in *The Dignity of Legislation* and elsewhere.[2]

Historically, though, proponents of the rule of law have tended to be suspicious of legislation for that very reason. It is too clever by half, particularly in democratic politics; it changes too quickly; in an assembly of representatives, said Hobbes, it changes haphazardly with every variation in the political composition of the legislature—different men, different laws.[3] If the idea of the rule of law is to be credible, law needs to be relatively constant in the face of changes of personnel among those who are thinking about how the society is governed.

The same point was made thirty years ago by the Supreme Court of the United States in 1992 in the great case of *Planned Parenthood v. Casey.*[4] What would happen, it was said in the plurality opinion, if precedents changed as often as changes in personnel on the court? Wouldn't people infer that this was rule by those who happened to be judges rather than rule by law? We can't go around overturning our past decisions too often, said the Court, certainly not our important decisions. (They were talking about *Roe v. Wade,* which some of them had previously disclosed a thoughtful inclination to revisit.)[5]

> There is . . . a point beyond which frequent overruling would overtax the country's belief in the Court's good faith. . . . There is a limit to the amount of error that can plausibly be imputed to prior Courts. If that limit should be exceeded, disturbance of prior rulings would be taken as evidence that justifiable reexamination of principle had given way to drives for particular results in the short term. The legitimacy of the Court would fade with the frequency of its vacillation.[6]

With that sort of changeability, it would be less convincing for a thoughtful Court to present itself as guardian of "the character of a . . . people who aspire to live according to the rule of law."[7]

In any case, whether or not laws are made and changed thoughtfully, there is still the issue of thoughtlessness in the way they are applied. Intellectual agility in the making of law is one thing; intelligence in its application is another. I said a moment ago that laws don't interpret and apply themselves; it is people who interpret them and people who apply them, and if we are looking for thoughtfulness in that process, it might well seem that we are looking for something other than the rule of law. Many would say that the discipline of the rule of law aims to ensure that law is applied with as little independent input from the judge as possible. Whether she is thoughtful or not, she is not supposed to bring her subjective views into play; she is supposed to be bound rigidly and mechanically by the literal text in front of her.

Indeed, our law schools are full of people who say that the only way to respect the thoughtfulness of our lawmakers is to be literal-minded in the way we apply their work product to changing circumstances. In the United States, this reaches its apogee in constitutional originalism. We celebrate the thoughtfulness of the Founding Fathers—James Madison, Alexander Hamilton, and so on, all very thoughtful men—but we do so, 240 years later, either by substituting what we know of their eighteenth-century thoughtfulness for our twenty-first-century kind, or by sticking rigidly to the text that they produced, even though we know that its calligraphy was framed for utterly different circumstances (a few colonies clinging to the edge of a largely unexplored continent with a population less than half that of modern New Zealand).

Even if it is today's legislation that is being interpreted, the textualists among us insist that judges cannot be trusted with adding independent input. And a connection is made between not just thoughtfulness and change, but also thoughtfulness and variability, maybe even thoughtfulness and subjectivity. Different people think in different ways. And we say "subjective" because we want to emphasize the point that one thoughtful judge may come up with conclusions that are quite different from those that another thoughtful judge comes up with. One man's thoughtful judge is another man's partisan of a rival set of ideals. The rule of law is supposed to mean that a party coming to law can expect to have his fate determined by the law itself—the law the legislature has enacted—and not by the vagaries (even the thoughtful vagaries) of whoever is wearing a wig in the courtroom he happens to be assigned to.[8]

2. Clarity and Certainty in the Rule of Law

Law can be obtuse, rigid, stubborn, and in its application, mechanical. But, people will say, at least it is *predictable;* at least we know where we stand with a law that does not often change and which is applied constantly and faithfully, whatever the subjective opinions of the judiciary. And this, it is said, is not just an *effect* of the rule of law—many will say that it is as close as we can get to the *essence* of the rule of law. "The rule of law," said Thomas Carothers, "can be *defined* as a system in which the laws are public knowledge, are clear in meaning, and apply equally to everyone."[9] There is a tradition of trying to capture the essence of the rule of law in a laundry list of principles: Dicey had three, John Rawls four, Dick Fallon five, Cass Sunstein came up with seven, Lon Fuller has eight, Joseph Raz eight, John Finnis eight, and Lord Bingham eight in his excellent book *The Rule of Law* (I don't know why eight is the magic number, but it's a slightly different eight in each case).[10] Robert Summers holds the record, I think, with eighteen rule-of-law principles.[11]

At the top of Lord Bingham's list we find a principle that seems incontestable in what it requires: "The law must be accessible and so far as possible intelligible, clear and predictable." Who could disagree with that—accessible, clear, predictable? The rule of law has consistently been associated with the value of predictability in human affairs. The most important thing that people need from the law that governs them, we are told, is predictability in the conduct of their lives and businesses. Tom Bingham quoted Lord Mansfield: "In all mercantile transactions the great object should be certainty: and therefore it is of more consequence that a rule should be certain, than whether the rule is established one way rather than the other."[12] And Bingham went on to observe in his own voice that "no one would choose to do business, perhaps involving large sums of money, in a country where parties, rights, and obligations were undecided."[13]

Lord Bingham does not speak of F. A. Hayek in his book, but in many ways Hayek's work—especially his early work on the rule of law—has been decisive in pushing this element of predictability to the fore. "Stripped of all technicalities," said Hayek in chapter 6 of *The Road to Serfdom*, the rule of law requires that "government in all its actions [must be] bound by rules fixed and announced beforehand, rules which make it possible to foresee with fair certainty how the authority will use its coercive powers in given circumstances and to plan one's individual affairs on the basis of this knowledge."[14] It is a passage that has been quoted in many studies since, notably at the beginning of Joseph Raz's discussion.[15] This element of predictability, this ideal of "formal rules [which] tell people in advance what action the state will take in certain types of situation, defined in general terms, . . . provided as a means for people to use in making their own plans"—it is this aspect of the rule of law that has been most prominent in law-and-development studies, with the World Bank and other global institutions treating it as indispensable for the creation of a secure environment for investment in developing countries.[16]

Philosophically, the idea here—again, elaborated most thoroughly by Hayek—is that there may be no getting away from legal constraint in the circumstances of modern life, but freedom is possible nevertheless if people know in advance how the law will operate and how they have to act if they are to avoid its application. Knowing in advance how the law will operate enables one to make plans and work around its requirements.[17] It creates a stable and calculable environment for business and investment. Not only that, but predictability is the basis of security: whether we think of personal rights or property rights, determinate legal rules applied according to their terms are supposed to give each citizen certainty as to what she can rely on in her dealings with other people and the state.

Accordingly, the rule of law is supposed to highlight the role of rules rather than standards (I am thinking of Justice Scalia's famous article, "The Rule of Law as a Law of Rules"), operationalized determinacy rather than open-ended language, literal meanings rather than systemic inferences, direct applications rather than arguments, closure rather than continued deliberation, and ex ante clarity rather than labored interpretations.[18]

The rule of law is violated, on this account, when the norms that are made public to the citizens do not tell them in advance precisely what to expect in their dealings with officialdom. It is violated when outcomes are determined thoughtfully by official discretion rather than by the literal application of rules with which we are already familiar. And it is violated when the sources of law leave us uncertain about what the rules are supposed to be. Lord Bingham's book has a useful discussion of the problem posed by multiple judgements in the House of Lords in a single case (and presumably, this continues to be an issue in the UK Supreme Court also)—dissents and concurrences that can leave people unsure about what principle of law has actually emerged from a given case.[19] If discretion, vagueness, and uncertainty become endemic in our system of government, then not only are people's expectations disappointed, but increasingly they will find themselves unable to *form* expectations on which to rely, and the horizons of their planning and their economic activity will shrink accordingly.

So there you have it: a dominant conception of the rule of law that seems to cherish values and features of law and legal administration like certainty and predictability, and a conception of thoughtfulness, which seems likely to disrupt that. The contrast is clearest, of course, in the continuing debate about the relation between law and discretion; and since Dicey, the rule of law has been viewed as an antidiscretion ideal, attacking and discrediting the proliferation of discretionary authority in the agencies of the modern administrative state. There is a lot to be said in defense of discretion, and a lot of it has been said over the years in the response to Dicey's work, not least in the excellent critique of Dicey's argument in Kenneth Culp Davis's book, *Discretionary Justice,* first published in 1969.[20] But that is not where my argument today is located. Instead of defining the need for discretion against the claims of the rule of law, I want to indicate ways in which predictability conceptions sell short the idea of the rule of law itself. There is more to law, and more to what we value in legality under the heading of the rule of law, than regularity, rules, determinacy, closure, and certainty. That is what I want to argue.

Normally, when people say that, what they are promising to do is to develop a more substantive conception of the rule of law, imbued perhaps with convictions about substantive justice held by them and their friends. Predictability is associated with a formalist conception of the rule of law, so thoughtfulness must be associated with a substantive conception of the rule of law entangled with substantive justice.[21] That is *not* my approach. No doubt there is a debate to be had about whether the rule of law should include a substantive dimension: Lord Bingham is unashamed about including fundamental human rights under the auspices of the rule of law in chapter 7 of his book. But before we even get to that, there are important formal features and particularly procedural features of the rule of law that are much more amenable to legal thoughtfulness than the predictability conceptions would indicate. It is these formal and procedural aspects of legal thoughtfulness that are my subject today.

3. Lay, Academic, and Professional Views

I am conscious that in talking about these features of the rule-of-law ideal, I am referring primarily to a body of academic literature written by scholars who are detached from the actual practice of law but detached, to a certain extent, from the way in which the rule of law circulates outside legal philosophy, in the populace at large.

This does not mean, by the way, that academic studies have no influence. Let me give one example. In recent years, scholars have turned their attention to the possible application of the rule of law to international governance, meaning not just the presence and importance of international law, but the suggestion that international law and international lawmaking should be subject to rule-of-law requirements. The whole area remains undertheorized, but I am afraid that a great deal of the work that has been done on it simply adopts uncritically the perspective of those who say, at the national level, that the rule of law requires clarity, predictability, and determinate rules. And people working in the international area might be impressionable enough to be bullied into accepting this, even though as lawyers they know very well that there is a lot more to law and legal practice than this. For example, they might be overly impressed by a report that Simon Chesterman produced, titled *The UN Security Council and the Rule of Law: The Role of the Security Council in Strengthening a Rules-Based International System,* which in my view, with its exclusive emphasis on rules, is way too narrow a conception to develop in this area.[22]

I have written elsewhere about the dissonance between academic and lay understandings of the rule of law.[23] The pages of the law journals devoted to this often read like a set of footnotes to the scholarly work of Lon Fuller, and they emphasize the formal features that Fuller drew attention to: clarity, constancy, prospectivity, consistency, practicability, and generality.[24] It is understandable that philosophers will focus on these formal attributes; it enables them to show off their special talents in abstract, analytic argument. But important as they may be, the formal ideas are not always what ordinary people, newspaper editors, and politicians have in mind when they clamor for the rule of law. Often, what they are concerned about are procedures and institutions. When people demanded a restoration of the rule of law recently in Pakistan, their concern was for the security and the independence of the judiciary. When US and foreign lawyers demand the rule of law for detainees at Guantánamo Bay, what they are calling for is not clarity or prospectivity, but an adequate system of hearings in which detainees would have an opportunity to confront and examine the evidence against them, such as it is. It is wrong to neglect these procedural and institutional aspects of the rule of law, and they are key to the case that I want to develop in this chapter.

The gap between academic and practitioners' understandings of the rule of law is also troubling. Though practitioners will often join in the demand for certainty and predictability of legal rules, they know very well that anything approximating "mechanical jurisprudence" is out of the question. Law is an exceedingly demanding discipline intellectually, and the idea that it consists or could consist in the thoughtless administration of a set of operationalized rules with determinate meanings and clear fields of application is of course a travesty. It is curious that we philosophers underestimate both the technicality and the effort of intricate thought that mastery of the law represents, and practitioners and judges reading this may feel amused as a legal philosopher struggles to find a home within an overly abstract account of the rule of law for an acknowledgment of the thoughtfulness that is required to fulfil the intellectual demands that law makes on its real-world practitioners—a fine example of what Jeremy Bentham once called "a grandmother egg-sucking instruction." All I can say is, bear with me if I am stating the obvious, because it is important to state it clearly in the environment in which the principle of the rule of law is reflected on and made explicit.

So, what are the more thoughtful aspects of the rule of law? There are many things we could consider. There is space here to focus on only three aspects of modern legal practice that are, I think, wrongly neglected or denigrated in philosophical discussions of this ideal. The first is the use of standards, as opposed to rules, to occasion and channel thoughtfulness in the application of law. The second is the way in which the rules of legal procedure—the rules of adjudicative procedure in particular—sponsor and orchestrate forms of *argumentative* thoughtfulness. And the third is the way in which stare decisis provides something like shared premises, or a way of arriving at shared premises, for the sort of thinking-in-the-name-of-us-all that distinguishes legal thinking from, say, the tendentious and partisan thinking of an individual participating in politics. So: standards, procedures, and precedents. These are my headings.

4. Rules versus Standards

Cass Sunstein once remarked that "law has a toolbox, containing many devices," and it is probably a mistake to identify the rule of law with the use of
just one kind of tool.[25] Rules, with their strict logic and their descriptive and
numerical predicates specifying ex ante the outcome for cases that fall under
them, are one kind of tool; standards, which use value terms like "reasonableness" or in some other way call for judgement in the course of their application, are another. There is no particular reason to associate law or the
rule of law with the former category only, as though, for example, in the
US Constitution, the Eighth Amendment were less truly law than, say, the
Article II rule that says the president must be at least thirty-five years old.

When we distinguish rules from standards, we sometimes say that the difference is that a standard is a norm that requires some evaluative judgment of
the person who applies it, whereas a rule is a norm presented as the end
product of evaluative judgments already made by the lawmaker. A posted
speed limit of 70 mph represents a value judgment made in the legislature that
that speed is appropriate for driving in the designated area. A legal requirement to drive at a "reasonable" speed, by contrast, looks for a value judgment
to be made downstream from the legislature; it indicates that the legislature
has decided not to make all the requisite value judgments itself, but has left
some to be made by the law applier. Now, by "the law applier" I do not just
mean the police and the magistrate (the police officer who pulls the driver
over and gives him a ticket, and the judge in traffic court who decides whether
or not to enter a conviction); I mean in the first instance the subject himself
who is tasked under the standard with figuring out what a reasonable speed
will be and monitoring and modifying his behavior accordingly.[26]

In New Zealand, where I learned to drive, there used to be things called
"limited speed zones" (LSZs), where there was no fixed speed limit lower
than the general speed limit but where the LSZ sign alerted drivers to the
variability of local circumstances and instructed them to proceed at a speed
appropriate to the conditions. Some jurisdictions eschew speed limits altogether and just tell their drivers to proceed at a reasonable speed. A conviction entered in Montana against a driver who went 80 mph on hilly country
road was struck down in 1998 on the grounds that the relevant statute was
void for vagueness, since the array of traffic statutes offered no guidance
at all as to appropriate speed.[27] But other courts in the United States have

upheld the use of standards rather than rules in other circumstances where there are background speed limits but where conditions in a particular area defy easy classification, so that at some times of day a patch of road is like an urban street and at other times it is like a rural highway.[28] On highways, perhaps, we can vary the speed limit with digital signs, but not on every country lane. Anyway, the traffic example is just an easy paradigm; much more important cases concern the imposition of duties of care in tort law, where a requirement of reasonable care is imposed on potential tortfeasors or human rights provisions that deploy complex value terms like "dignity" or "inhuman and degrading treatment" rather than telling us directly what we are or are not allowed to do.

What people sometimes say in the rule-of-law tradition is that norms that use terms like "reasonable" or value terms like "cruel" or "inhuman" suffer from a deficit of clarity—"The desideratum of clarity," said Lon Fuller, "represents one of the most essential ingredients of legality."[29] Therefore, we are told, the standards that embody them detract from or undermine the rule of law, because they don't let people know in advance exactly where they stand, they don't offer determinate guidance, and they empower those entrusted with the application of the law to impose their own judgments in a way that is not legally controlled, or at least not tightly controlled by law. People then seem to be at the mercy of the value judgments (i.e., the discretion) of officials and courts, second-guessing their own futile attempts to figure out how these norms will be authoritatively applied. It is Hayek's opinion, expressed in *The Road to Serfdom,* that "one could write a history of the decline of the rule of law . . . in terms of the progressive introduction of these vague formulas [like 'fairness' and 'reasonableness'] into legislation and of the increasing arbitrariness and uncertainty that results."[30]

But if we are supposed to infer from this that when standards are in play, we might as well not have law at all, or if the implication is that the thoughtfulness that is sponsored in the use of standards represents the opposite of the rule of law, then I beg to differ. It is a mistake to regard these norms as simply blank checks for discretion, as though the most they told the person they were addressed to was to prepare yourself for the arbitrary imposition of a value judgment by those in power. In fact, the use of standards clearly represents an exercise in legal guidance. Think back to our Limited Speed Zone sign. Is it really the case that it gives the driver no guidance? Only in the crudest behavioral conception of what it is to guide someone's action. Having one's action guided by a norm is not just a matter of finding out the

norm and conforming one's behavior to its specifications. It can involve a
more complex engagement of practical reason than that. The use of a standard credits a human agent not just with the ability to comply with instruc-
tions, but with the capacity to engage in practical deliberation. The sign that
says drive at a reasonable speed in the circumstances tells the driver that *now*
is the time to check the weather and the road conditions and relate that
information to your speed and moderate your behavior accordingly. *Now* is
the time to focus on this and do the thinking that the application of the
standard requires. It mobilizes the resources of practical intelligence possessed by the norm subject—a mobilization that might not take place if the
lawmaker had not promulgated the standard. It guides the subject's agency
in that way, even if it leaves it up to her to determine the appropriate behavior.
It is law that requires and triggers thoughtfulness, rather than law that super-
sedes thoughtfulness.

And sometimes, standards channel our thoughtfulness as well as trig-
gering it. A standard that prohibits "inhuman" and "degrading" treatment
requires, it is true, an exercise of judgement, value judgement on the part of
those who apply it: the legislators and officials to whom it is directed in the
first instance, and the judges who are called on to review their compliance.
But it does not require an all-purpose evaluation. "Inhuman" and "degrading"
have specific meanings. They require assessment of a practice or a penalty
in some dimensions and not others. And so, depending on the particular
thick predicate that is used, the standard directs our practical reasoning to
a particular domain of assessment. So these norms, too, guide the practical
reasoning (and action based on that reasoning) of those to whom they are
addressed: they provide structure and channeling for the thoughtfulness they
are designed to elicit.

Let me pursue this one step further.[31] There is a temptation among
scholars to think that when faced with something like, for example, the Article 3 prohibition in the European Convention on Human Rights (ECHR)
of "inhuman and degrading treatment," the task of the courts is in effect to
replace the standard with rules developed through a succession of cases. In
other words, we treat the standard as an inchoate rule, formulated in half-
baked fashion by the lawmaker, awaiting elaboration and reconstruction as
a set of determinate rules by the courts. If the courts decide that solitary confinement is inhuman, then we can treat the standard prohibiting inhuman
treatment as including a rule prohibiting solitary confinement. If they
decide that shackling prisoners is degrading, then we take the provision

prohibiting degrading treatment as comprising a rule that prohibits shack-ling. As the precedents build up, we replace vague evaluative terms with lists of practices that are prohibited, practices that can then be identified descriptively rather than by evaluative reasoning. In time, the list usurps the standard; the list of rules becomes the effective norm in our application of the provision; the list is what is referred to when an agency is trying to ensure that it is in compliance.

All this might make law more manageable, but I fear it detracts from the sort of thoughtfulness that the standard initially seemed to invite. Article 3 of the ECHR invites us to reflect on and argue about the ideas of degrada-tion and inhumanity, which are moral ideas. But if we follow the suggestion set out in the previous paragraph, we will be tempted to simply consult the precedents and the set of rules they generate, abandoning any of the guid-ance in our evaluative thought that these particular moral predicates might provide.

By the way, none of this is new. I am really just elaborating some points made by Ronald Dworkin in a body of insight ranging from his discussion of what he called "weak discretion" in a famous article from 1967 to his more recent advocacy of what he calls "the moral reading" of terms like these in the constitution of the United States.[32] Actually, I hope it is clear that a lot of what I am doing in this chapter is inspired by insights and arguments that have been prominent in Dworkin's jurisprudence.

5. Formal Procedures

A second regard in which law as such might be associated with thoughtful-ness has to do with procedural due process—the highly formalized proce-dures that structure the judicial hearings in which official legal determina-tions are arrived at. I worry sometimes that our philosophical conceptions of law and the rule of law do not pay nearly enough attention to procedural as opposed to formal aspects of the rule of law.[33] For the rule of law is not just about the formal characteristics of the norms that we apply; it is about the processes by which they are applied, and those processes involve not just an official with a power of decision, but a whole elaborate structure in which evidence is presented and tested and legal arguments are made.

I have discussed the difference between lay, professional, and philosoph-ical images of law. For most lay people, law and the workings of law are represented by the courtroom—the dramatic and almost ritualistic way in which opposing bodies of evidence and opinion confront each other in court. Think of the influence of the ubiquitous US television show, *Law and Order*. It is a mistake to think of this as the whole of legal practice: most lawyers are not litigators, and a lot of them never see the inside of a working courtroom from one year to the next. But the public are right to assign it an important role nonetheless, because an awful lot of legal business is conducted in the shadow of due process, and with a view to (or a dread of) legal proceedings, even if it does not actually take place in the courtroom itself.

So let us think about the way we structure judicial or quasi-judicial hearings. By "hearings," I mean formal events like trials, tightly structured in order to enable an impartial tribunal to determine rights and responsibilities fairly and effectively after hearing evidence and argument from both sides. Those who are immediately concerned have an opportunity to make submissions and present evidence, and to confront, examine, and respond to evidence and submissions presented from the other side. Not only that, but both sides are listened to by a tribunal that is bound to respond to the arguments put forward in the reasons that it eventually gives for its decision. We tend to think of due process primarily in terms of fairness, but we can think of it also as a way of maximizing the role of reason and thoughtfulness in the settlement of disputes.

Here I draw on the work of Lon Fuller in a long essay published posthumously in 1978 in the *Harvard Law Review,* called "Forms and Limits of Adjudication." It is an irony, which Nicola Lacey has written about, that in the work of his that is most cited in the rule-of-law tradition (and in his famous 1958 dispute with H. L. A. Hart), Fuller focused mainly on formal elements to the exclusion of procedural elements, whereas he was in fact one of our deepest thinkers on matters of procedure.[34] The quality of his work in this essay is light years beyond anything you find in Hart's writings on procedure. Fuller said this about adjudication: "The distinguishing characteristic of adjudication lies in the fact that it confers on the affected party a peculiar form of participation in the decision, that of presenting proofs and reasoned arguments for a decision in his favor."[35] It is, he said, "a device which gives formal and institutional expression to the influence of reasoned argument in human affairs." Fuller did not think that the distinguishing characteristic of courtroom process was the impartial office of judge, because there are all sorts of judging functions, where impartiality is at a premium, that do not involve the presentation of reason and argument at all—Fuller mentions umpiring in baseball or judging in an agricultural fair. He says, "What

distinguishes these functionaries ... from courts, administrative tribunals, and boards of arbitration is that their decisions are not reached within
an institutional framework that is intended to assure to the disputants an
opportunity for the presentation of proofs and reasoned arguments."[36]
Again, one might object to Fuller's characterization that there are opportunities to present reasoned arguments in all sorts of contexts—in election
campaigns, for example. But, says Fuller, "This objection fails to take account of a conception that underlies the whole analysis being presented
here, the conception, namely, of a form of participating in a decision that is
institutionally defined and assured."[37] And how is it assured? Among other
ways, by the requirement that judges or arbitrators give reasons for their
decisions. This is not just because we want judges to be thoughtful (though
we do). It is rather, Fuller says, because without such reasoned opinions, the
parties would have to just "take it on faith that their participation in the
decision has been real, that the arbiter has in fact understood and taken
into account their proofs and arguments."[38]

I know that courtroom process can seem cumbersome. And to someone
in the grip of an image of thoughtfulness that privileges the relatively
unstructured working of the human intellect—spontaneity and flashes of
insight—the laborious ritualized proceedings of the courtroom may seem the
antithesis of the sort of thoughtfulness we are looking for in government. And
in some areas, that may be right: I am reminded of Fuller's caution against
over-insisting on the use of judicial procedures: "As lawyers we have a natural
inclination to 'judicialize' every function of government. Adjudication is a
process with which we are familiar and which enables us to show to advantage our special talents. Yet we must face the plain truth that adjudication is
an ineffective instrument for economic management and for governmental
participation in the allocation of economic resources."[39]

We need not deny this point in order to recognize that, nevertheless,
where it is used, law in its intricate and formal proceduralism does do
the work of structuring and channeling argumentation. Even if it is not
the form of thoughtfulness we always want from the agencies of the modern
administrative state, still it needs to be credited for what it is: a mode of
thoughtfulness that allows rival and competing claims to confront and engage
with one another in an orderly process, where the stakes are high indeed, often
deadly, without degenerating into violence or an incoherent shouting match.
Like parliamentary procedure, it is one of the ways in which we get thoughtful
together, even when my thoughtfulness is the adversary of yours.[40]

There is much more to be said on this, and I can't say it all here. If I could, I would want to refer to the dignitarian aspects of due process as well, in the work that people like David Luban and Frank Michelman have done (and some work that I did in my Tanner Lectures in 2009) on the dignity of the opportunity to present oneself before an official who has the power to impose binding decisions, to present oneself directly or through a legal representative as someone with a view of one's own on the matter that the public is addressing and a conception of one's own of the elements of the public good that are at stake—a view and a conception that the decision maker is required to listen to and take into account.[41]

Let me take the analysis in a slightly different direction. The institutional and proceduralized character of legal process makes law a matter of *argument*. Law presents itself as something one can make sense of. The norms administered in our legal system may seem like just one damned command after another, but lawyers and judges try to see the law as a whole, to discern some sort of coherence or system, integrating particular items into a structure that makes intellectual sense. And ordinary people take advantage of this aspiration to systematicity and integrity in framing their own legal arguments—by inviting the tribunal hearing their case to consider how the position they are putting forward fits generally into a coherent conception of the spirit of the law. In this way, too, then, law conceives of the people who live under it as bearers of reason and intelligence. Even in conflict, they are conceived not as mad dogs at each other's throats, but as rival bearers of reason and intelligence, thinking adversarially about the basis of social order.

Now, of course, this does bring us slap-bang up against conceptions of the rule of law that are preoccupied with predictability. Argumentation of this sort can be unsettling, and the procedures that we cherish often have the effect of undermining the certainty that is emphasized on the formal side of the rule-of-law ideal. An argument may bring something new into the world, a new way of looking at things, and for all we know, a panel of judges may be persuaded by it. The upshot of argument is unpredictable, and to the extent that legal process sponsors argumentation, it sponsors uncertainty in the law.

Still, there is no getting away from it. This is not the rule of law versus something else. As the late Neil MacCormick pointed out, law is an argumentative discipline, and no analytic theory of what it is and what distinguishes legal systems from other systems of governance can afford to ignore this aspect of our legal practice.[42] A fallacy of modern positivism, it seems to me, is its exclusive emphasis on the command-and-control aspect of law, without any reference to the culture of argument that a legal system frames, sponsors, and institutionalizes. The institutionalized recognition of a distinctive set of norms may be an important feature. But at least as important is what we do in law with the authoritative norms we identify. We don't just obey them or apply the sanctions they ordain; we argue over them adversarially, we use our sense of what is at stake in their application to license a process of argument back and forth, and we engage in elaborate interpretive exercises about what it means to apply them faithfully as a system to the cases that come before us. And legal procedure facilitates and sponsors that form of argumentativeness.

I know the demand for clarity and predictability is made in the name of individual freedom—the freedom of the Hayekian businessman in charge of his own destiny who needs to know where he stands so far as social order is concerned. And he may be disturbed—his investment plans may be disturbed—by the unsettling and unpredictable consequences of adversarial argument in law. But think about it: with the best will in the word and the most determinate seeming law, circumstances and interactions can be treacherous. From time to time, the free Hayekian individual will find himself accused of some violation or delict. Or his business will be subject—as he thinks, unjust or irregularly—to some detrimental regulation. Some such cases may be clear; but others will be matters of dispute. An individual who values his freedom enough to demand the sort of calculability that the Hayekian image of freedom under law is supposed to cater to is not someone we can imagine always tamely accepting a charge or a determination that he has done something wrong. He will have a point of view on the matter, and he will seek an opportunity to bring that to bear when it is a question of applying a rule to his case. And when he brings his point of view into play, we can imagine the plaintiff or prosecutor who opposes him responding with a point of view whose complexity and tendentiousness matches his own. And so it begins: legal argumentation and the facility that law's procedures make for the formal airing of arguments.

Courts, hearings, and arguments—those aspects of law are not optional extras; they are integral parts of how law works, and they are indispensable to the package of law's respect for human agency. To say that we should value aspects of governance that promote the clarity and determinacy of rules for the sake of individual freedom, but not the opportunities for argumentation that a free and self-possessed individual is likely to demand, is to truncate what the rule of law rests on: respect for the freedom and dignity of each person as an active intelligence.

6. Premises

I cannot cover every aspect of this topic; it is as wide as legality itself. But a third thing I want to emphasize is the way law provides not only the occasion for thoughtfulness and the terms that channel it, and not only the procedures that structure it in formal settings, but also the premises with which it works.

In our individual political thinking, in our moral deliberation, we are privileged as autonomous beings to choose our starting points and argue from whatever set of premises we find compelling. Some begin with God, others with utility, others with some idea of self-fulfillment, and still others with some ancient conception of virtue. And as we proceed from our different starting points, our arguments are something of a cacophony as people talk across each other, following different and often mutually unintelligible trajectories of thought. This is the problem of public reason that has exercised John Rawls and his followers.[43]

Law, on the other hand, sponsors a mode of argumentation in which premises are to a very large extent *shared,* and pathways of thought are charted out on a common basis, at least in their initial stages. The point is obvious enough in the case of constitutional and statutory provisions, where the text of an enactment provides all of us, grappling with a given issue, with the same point of departure in our interpretive arguments. It is less easy, but no less important, to see how this works in the case of precedents too. This is the last topic I want to address in this chapter.

When jurists defend stare decisis—the idea that we should respect and be constrained by norms laid down in previous decisions—the defense is usually in terms of predictability. We enhance the certainty of the law, it is said, and the determinate guidance afforded to those who live under it by insisting that courts must regard themselves as bound in most cases by the principles of their own earlier decisions in similar cases. As I said earlier, the argument is about not just respecting the expectations that may have been invested in a particular decision or line of decisions, but also allowing sufficient stability so that expectations can actually form in the first place.

But it can't just be a matter of making legal outcomes more predictable. Once again, we owe to Ronald Dworkin (this time, the Dworkin of *Law's*

Empire) the observation that predictability—in the straightforward sense of allowing us to predict legal outcomes reliably in advance—can hardly be regarded as the ground of our interest in precedents, because in the practice of law we worry away at the meaning of precedents, their interaction with one another, and their bearing on the cases we are currently dealing with, long after any element of real-world predictability has evaporated. The predictability account cannot explain what Dworkin called "the constant and relentless concern judges show for explicating the 'true' force of a . . . precedent when that force is problematical."[44] He says that our judges actually pay more attention to precedents than the expectations theory would dictate. Indeed (and I am paraphrasing now), we would expect judges to lose interest in precedents once their holding or their bearing on future cases became difficult or controversial, because then we should not suppose that any settled expectations had formed around them. "The general power of precedents to guide behavior will not much be jeopardized if judges refuse to follow them when the advice they give is garbled or murky."[45]

True, certain precedents—you might think of them as super-precedents—contribute powerfully to legal predictability by pinning down *major* major premises of law in particular areas. This has been pointed out by scholars like Richard Fallon and Henry Monaghan in the debate about stare decisis in US constitutional law.[46] The background here is that—motivated largely by concern about the continuing authority accorded to the abortion decision in *Roe v. Wade* (in the days before *Dobbs*)—some conservative law professors have suggested that stare decisis should have less force in constitutional law, where serious individual rights or other constitutional values may be betrayed by sticking with a constitutional precedent that is mistaken, and such a betrayal could not possibly be justified by the pragmatic considerations that are associated with certainty and predictability.[47] In response, Fallon and Monaghan reminded their readers of how much US constitutional law is structured by precedent and how much of the legal framework structuring modern governance in the United States might unravel if old precedents were always up for grabs. The cases they cite include the prospect of revisiting the holdings that established things like the application of the Bill of Rights to the states and the constitutionality of the use of paper money. What these precedents do is limit the range of what can be up for grabs in legal argument; they specify outer limits on where legal argument can go, even while they do not themselves directly determine the result of any litigation that is likely to come before a modern court.

With more mundane precedents, however, it seems to me that the role of established case law is not to determine outcomes in cases with any degree of certainty, certainly not in appellate cases, but rather to provide substantive points of departure that people can use when they argue those cases through. I say "points of departure" rather than "major premises." Unlike statutes and the provisions of written constitutions, cases do not easily disclose the principles of their decision. Often, we have to first argue our way upward through the cases themselves to arrive at the principles they stand for, before we can do anything like treating those principles as major premises and arguing downward from them in a syllogistic fashion. Still, we share starting points in this dynamic of argument. We argue on the same page, even when we are adversarially opposed to what someone else is making of a given line of cases.

I will have much more to say about precedents in Chapter 8. For now, my concern has been to emphasize ways in which the establishment of precedents frames and facilitates thoughtful argument in the law. It doesn't just invoke predictability.

One final point. I suppose someone obsessed with intellectual autonomy might worry about forms of thoughtfulness that take their premises as given. That may seem, in Kantian terms, *heteronomous* thoughtfulness, not partaking of—indeed, compromising or undermining—the intellectual autonomy that is human thinking at its best. But many modes of thought are like this. Theological argument proceeds in this way, by reference to certain inescapable creedal and biblical commitments; but it remains a domain of thoughtfulness. Creedal propositions (of the Nicene Creed, for example) do not determine the outcome of theological argument. But still they constrain and direct it, providing inescapable starting points, axioms, and a good number of theorems that are to have a non-negotiable presence in any respectable argument. And scientific argument is sort of like law, too, in this regard: one proceeds within the framework of existing scientific consensus, building one's own work on the accepted results that have come in from other laboratories, so that scientists can pursue their results and findings as a community, not just as an array of intellectually autonomous thinkers.

7. Picking Up the Threads

Let me now draw some of these threads together. I have mentioned three main ways in which law sponsors and facilitates public thoughtfulness: first, in its use of standards rather than rules as the norms that govern behavior; second, in the procedural structuring of public adversarial argument in court hearings; and third, in providing through texts and precedents many of the axioms and theorems that enter into legal reasoning.

These are not marginal characteristics of law. They are central to it—business as usual in the law—though it is my lament that none of them is made prominent in the most influential jurisprudence of our day, which in many law schools in the United States and in the United Kingdom remains positivist and analytical. Legal positivism in the tradition of Hart remains committed to viewing law as a system of rules; it gives scant consideration to procedural aspects of legal practice; and it says next to nothing about the importance of stare decisis. More generally, it treats disagreement about the law and inconclusive legal argumentation as a marginal phenomenon, stemming mostly from the accidental use of terminology too vague to determine hard cases.[48]

8. Modes of Thoughtfulness

The modes of thoughtfulness I have alluded to are not the only forms of thoughtful deliberation that a society needs; legalistic thinking is not the only desirable mode of thoughtfulness in government.

We do need what is often excoriated as discretion—thoughtful discretion, sometimes technical expertise, sometimes policy oriented either as a matter of implementation or in an awareness of what is politically and administratively possible, sometimes value oriented in the choice of policy. We need discretion in all these senses, in the hands of administrative agencies and their coteries of expert and experienced officials. And that, I concede, is *not* what the rule of law can supply.

Some think that the mission of the rule of law is to stamp that out and minimize such discretion, replacing it at every turn with clear and determinate rules administered by courts, or at the very least, cultivating a posture of suspicion toward it. Maybe. On the other hand, as Professor Davis pointed out, administrative discretion is here to say.[49] And law has a role to play in authorizing it, channeling it by providing criteria, and bounding its outer limits with basic constraints of justice. My point is that even that role for law is played out as a form of legal thoughtfulness—legal thoughtfulness constraining a different form of administrative thoughtfulness—rather than in terms of the rule of law imposing on a recalcitrant administrator a set of mechanically applied determinate rules. Sometimes the role of courts here is simple deference to administrative decision-making, but when administrative decision-making is called into question, it is important that we have thoughtful rather than mechanical ways of challenging it under the auspices of the rule of law. The modes of argumentation that I have been discussing here are crucial for that.

The other distinction that I think is important is between legalistic thoughtfulness and the broader style of political deliberation needed in the public realm of a flourishing democracy. Some have toyed with the prospect of seamless continuity between the two. Ronald Dworkin said once that "when an issue is seen as constitutional,"—he was speaking of the United States, for example—"the quality of public argument is often improved," because the terms of legal argumentation inform the terms of public discussion "in newspapers and other media, in law schools and classrooms, in public meetings and around dinner tables."[50] I guess this is part of the process that Alexis de Tocqueville referred to when he remarked that "there is hardly a political question in the United States that does not sooner or later turn into a judicial one." Tocqueville went on to suggest that as a result,

> parties feel obliged to borrow legal ideas and language when conducting their own daily controversies. . . . Judicial language thus becomes pretty well the language of common speech; the spirit of the law starts its life inside schools and courtrooms only to spread gradually beyond their narrow confines; it insinuates itself, so to speak, into the whole of society right down to the lowest ranks until, finally, the entire nation has caught some of the ways and tastes of the magistrate.[51]

I am not as enthusiastic about this as either Dworkin or de Tocqueville. Public debate often does perfectly well without a forensic structure.[52] In many ways, legalistic pathways of thought are too stilted for the purposes of general civic deliberation. My point throughout this chapter has been that legal pathways and legal structures make a particular contribution in the work that the rule of law has to do, not that they epitomize every kind of thoughtfulness that we need in politics. Even when we need formality in public debate, what we sometimes need are the rather differently shaped procedures of parliamentary deliberation, rather than forensic procedure. And there is a further problem, which I cannot discuss in this chapter, of how to relate that legislative discourse to the broader, looser, and radically less structured mode of deliberation that we hear (and that we need) in civil society, among political parties, in social movements, on the streets, and in the media.

Anyway, from the fact that legalistic thoughtfulness is no substitute for the thoughtfulness we need in public political discourse, it does not follow that legalistic thoughtfulness is unimportant. For in the areas and to the extent that we want to insist on government constrained by law, or in the areas and to the extent that we want a social and economic environment structured by law, we need to understand that constraint and that structuring as being done by law in the thoughtful ways that law operates, rather than mechanically and thoughtlessly in the service of some exalted ideal of predictability.

Let me say, finally, that I don't want to denigrate predictability values altogether. In my discussion here I have tried to redress a balance, not strike the other side out. Elements of clarity and certainty are often important in the law, but nowhere are they all-important, and such importance as they have does not justify sidelining or ignoring other more thoughtful aspects of legal practice in our conception of the rule of law.

Can the two sides perhaps be reconciled? In his later writings, particularly in his trilogy, *Law, Legislation and Liberty,* F. A. Hayek announces that he was turning his back on thirty years of "deeply rooted prejudice"—his own deeply rooted prejudice—that clear codified legislation would increase the predictability of the law. He speculated that judicial decisions may in fact be more predictable if the judge is also bound by generally held views of what is just, even when they are not supported by the letter of the law, than when he is restricted to deriving his decisions only from among those accepted beliefs that have found expression in the written law.[53]

Thinking through the abstract issue of what a fair order of mutually adjusted intentions would involve so far as the settlement of the instant cases is concerned may enable the judge to come up with a result more congruent to the expectations of the parties than his application of some enacted rule according to its terms. I cannot go into Hayek's argument in any detail here, but it's a challenging possibility, and well worth the attention of those who continue to cite Hayek as a philosophical authority for associating the rule of law with a rule-based conception of predictability.

In the end, though, it is a matter of tension and balance within the rule of law. I don't think what I am doing is introducing a rival political ideal to compete with the rule of law—in the way that, say, democracy might sometimes compete with the rule of law. Of course, we must bear in mind Joseph

Raz's dictum: the rule of law is not the sum of all good things.[54] As I said in the Introduction, the rule of law is but one star in a constellation of ideals that dominate our political morality; the others are democracy, human rights, social justice, and economic freedom. We want societies to be democratic; we want them to respect human rights; we want them to organize their economies around free markets and private property to the extent that this can be done without seriously compromising social justice; and we want them to be governed in accordance with the rule of law.

Even considered as a limited concept—one star among others—the rule of law is a contested concept, and this chapter is intended to contribute to that contestation.[55] Also, "law" connotes many different things; as I said, there are many tools in law's tool box. Different things may come to different people's minds when we imagine the rule of law. For some, it may be the rule of a constitution that has been in place for decades or even centuries. For others, it is the rule of a recently enacted statute. For others still, it is the rule of common law. Aristotle famously remarked that "a man may be a safer ruler than the written law, but not safer than the customary law."

I have tried not to rely on newfangled ideas intended to transform the rule of law out of all recognition. I have tried to limit myself to elements centrally and incontestably associated with the core of legal practice—elements (like due process) whose absence from contemporary positivist jurisprudence and from recent philosophical accounts of the rule of law looks, in retrospect, curiouser and curiouser. I have been offering not just a theory of thoughtfulness in government (and then calling that "the rule of law"), but an account of the way in which practices and institutions—which everyone recognizes as legal—help to sponsor, channel, and discipline that thoughtfulness. That is why I was so anxious to distinguish this form of thoughtfulness from other notions of thoughtfulness that we need.

9. Conclusion

Aristotle exasperated generations of readers of his *Politics* when he inserted this observation into his discussion of the rule of law: "He who bids the law rule may be deemed to bid God and Reason alone rule, but he who bids man rule adds an element of the beast; for desire is a wild beast, [and] the law is reason unaffected by desire."[56] It is a challenging observation (to say the least), and in the past when I have taught the history of the rule of law to law students, I have tended to pass over it in silence.

Some formalists I know—some of the Toronto formalists—say that what is crucial here is that law must be articulated without reference to the substantive quality of the ends or policies that are being pursued—that's desire—and they are hoping to sponsor an account of legal argument unaffected by desire.[57] If I had more space here I would question the austerity of that sort of formalism on grounds of basic sanity. But it is Aristotle's connection of law to reason that intrigues me, for it is not primarily a natural lawyer's connection between law and the eternal verities of rationality, but a connection between law and the godlike activity of reasoning. We reason together using the forms, channels, and points of departure that law provides, and when we celebrate being ruled by law, what we are celebrating in large part is that sort of influence of reason in human affairs.

2

The Concept and the Rule of Law

1. Introduction

The rule of law is one of the most important political ideals of our time. It is one of a cluster of ideals constitutive of modern political morality, the others being human rights, democracy, and perhaps also the principles of free market economy. Open any newspaper and you will see the rule of law cited and deployed—usually as a matter of reproach, occasionally as an affirmative aspiration, and almost always as a benchmark of political legitimacy. Here are a few examples, plucked at random from the world's press:

- In November 2007, when then-president Pervez Musharraf of Pakistan fired the chief justice of the Supreme Court of Pakistan and had him placed under house arrest, his actions were seen around the world as a crisis of the rule of law. Law societies and bar associations all over the world protested, and, in Pakistan itself, thousands of judges and lawyers demonstrated in the streets. Hundreds of them were beaten and arrested.[1]
- In 2005, the *Financial Times* lamented that the "absence of the rule of law undermines Russia's economy."[2] Specifically, the British newspaper associated the absence of the rule of law with the irregularity of Vladimir Putin regime's proceedings against Mikhail Khodorkovsky.[3] But the newspaper also offered the more general suggestions that "no prosperous market economy or fair society can flourish without the rule of law" and that this is "a lesson [that] foreign investors must heed."[4]
- In the years after 9/11, practices and policies associated with the war on terrorism were constantly being evaluated and found wanting

against the criterion of the rule of law. The most prominent, of course, was the incarceration of hundreds of detainees by the United States at Guantánamo Bay in Cuba. A few days after the publication of the article I just mentioned on Russia and the rule of law, the *Financial Times* thundered again: "Military tribunals are not the way: Guantánamo is beyond the rule of law and should be shut."[5]

- Some readers will remember that during the electoral debacle in Florida in 2000, the rule of law was invoked at each stage on all sides of every issue, culminating in the famous dissent by Justice Stevens in *Bush v. Gore:* "Although we may never know with complete certainty the identity of the winner of this year's Presidential election, the identity of the loser is perfectly clear. It is the Nation's confidence in the judge as an impartial guardian of the rule of law."[6]

Thousands of other examples could be cited. The rule of law is seen as a fragile but crucial ideal, and one that is appropriately invoked whenever governments try to get their way by arbitrary and oppressive action or by short-circuiting the procedures laid down in their countries' laws or constitution. Interfering with the courts, jailing someone without legal justification, detaining people without any safeguards of due process, manipulating the constitution for partisan advantage—all of these are seen as abuses of the rule of law.

In this chapter, I want to consider the role of the rule of law in general jurisprudence—that is, in the conceptual work that we do in legal philosophy when we try to explain what "law" is.[7] I shall put forward two propositions. First, I shall argue that our understanding of the rule of law and our understanding of the concept of law ought to be much more closely connected than they are in modern jurisprudence. Second, I shall argue that our understanding of the rule of law should emphasize not only the value of settled, determinate rules and the predictability that such rules make possible, but also the importance of the procedural and argumentative aspects of legal practice. I shall argue, moreover, that these two propositions are connected. Grasping the connection between the rule of law and the concept of law is much easier when we understand the rule of law at least partly in terms of procedural and argumentative themes rather than purely in terms of determinacy and predictability. The procedural aspect of the rule of law helps bring our conceptual thinking about law to life, and an understanding of legal systems that emphasizes argument in the courtroom as much as the existence and recognition of rules provides the basis for a much richer understanding of the values that the rule of law comprises in modern political argument.

2. What Is the Rule of Law?

The rule of law is a multifaceted ideal. Most conceptions of this ideal, however, give central place to a requirement that people in positions of authority should exercise their power within a constraining framework of public norms, rather than on the basis of their own preferences, their own ideology, or their own individual sense of right and wrong. Beyond this, many conceptions of the rule of law place great emphasis on legal certainty, predictability, and settlement; on the determinacy of the norms that are upheld in society; and on the reliable character of their administration by the state. Citizens—it is said—need predictability in the conduct of their lives and businesses. There may be no escaping legal constraints in the circumstances of modern life, but freedom is nevertheless possible if people know in advance how the law will operate, and how they must act to avoid its having a detrimental impact on their affairs. Knowing in advance how the law will operate enables one to plan around its requirements.[8] And knowing that one can count on the law to protect certain personal rights and property rights enables each citizen to deal effectively with other people and the state. On this account, the rule of law is violated when the norms that are applied by officials do not correspond to the norms that have been made public to the citizens, or when officials act on the basis of their own discretion rather than norms laid down in advance. If actions of this sort become endemic, then not only are people's expectations disappointed, but they will increasingly find themselves unable to form any expectations at all, and the horizons of their planning and their economic activity will diminish accordingly.

A conception of the rule of law like the one just outlined emphasizes the virtues that Lon Fuller discussed in *The Morality of Law:* the prominence of general norms as a basis of governance; the clarity, publicity, stability, consistency, and prospectivity of those norms; and congruence between the law on the books and the way in which public order is actually administered.[9] On Fuller's account, the rule of law does not directly require anything substantive; for example, it does not require that we have any particular liberty. All it requires is that the state should do whatever it wants to do in an orderly, predictable way, giving us plenty of advance notice by publicizing the general norms on which its actions will be based, and that it should then stick to those norms and not arbitrarily depart from them, even if it seems politically advantageous to do so. Requirements of this sort are sometimes described as procedural, but I think that is a misdescription. They are formal and structural in character: they emphasize the structures of governance and the formal qualities—like generality, clarity, and prospectivity—that are supposed to characterize the norms on which state action is based.

There is, however, a separate current of thought in the rule of law tradition that does emphasize procedural issues. The rule of law is not just about general rules; it is about their impartial administration. For example, one of the great nineteenth-century theorists of the rule of law, Albert Venn Dicey, placed at least as much emphasis on the normal operation of the ordinary courts as he did on the characteristics of the norms they administered.[10] A procedural understanding of the rule of law requires not only that officials apply the rules as they are set out; it also requires application of the rules with all the care and attention to fairness that is signaled by ideals such as "natural justice" and "procedural due process." Thus, if someone is accused of violating one of the general norms laid down, they should have an opportunity to request a hearing, make an argument, and confront the evidence before them prior to the application of any sanction associated with the norm. The rule of law is violated when the institutions that are supposed to embody these procedural safeguards are undermined. In this way, the rule of law has become associated with political ideals such as the separation of powers and the independence of the judiciary.

For the most part, these two currents of thought sit comfortably together. They complement each other. Clear, general public norms are valueless if they are not properly administered, and fair procedures are no good if the applicable rules keep changing or are ignored altogether. But there are aspects of the procedural side of the rule of law that are in some tension with the ideal of formal predictability. The procedural side of the rule of law presents a mode of governance that allows people a voice, a way of intervening on their own behalf in confrontations with power. It requires that public institutions sponsor and facilitate reasoned argument in human affairs. But argument can be unsettling, and the procedures we cherish often have the effect of undermining the predictability that is emphasized in the formal side of the ideal.[11] By emphasizing the legal process rather than the formal attributes of the determinate norms that are supposed to emerge from that process, the procedural aspects of the rule of law seem to place a premium on values that are somewhat different from those emphasized in the formal picture. Instead of the certainty that makes private freedom possible, the procedural aspects of the rule of law seem to value opportunities for active engagement in the administration of public affairs. On both sides, the rule of law condemns official behavior that treats individual agency as something of no consequence. On one side it is private agency in civil society that is respected, while on the other side it is private agency exercised within the context of the institutions of the state.

If you were to ask which current of thought is more influential in legal philosophy, most scholars would say it is the one that is organized around predictability and the determinacy of legal norms, rather than the procedural current. It has received a great deal of attention in connection with Lon Fuller's argument in *The Morality of Law*. But it is quite striking that in the popular and political deployments of the rule of law, of which I gave a few examples at the beginning of this chapter, it is the procedural current that tends to be emphasized. When people say, for example, that the rule of law is threatened on the streets of Islamabad or in the cages at Guantánamo, it is the procedural elements they have in mind, much more than the traditional virtues of clarity, prospectivity, determinacy, and knowing where you stand. They are worried about the independence of the Pakistani courts and about the due process rights of detainees in the war on terror. I will come back to this disparity between what legal philosophers emphasize and what ordinary people expect from the rule of law several times in what follows. But the main point of this section has been to identify these two currents in the rule-of-law tradition and to understand both how they work together and the tensions that exist between them.

3. The Rule of Law and the Concept of Law

Suppose for a moment that the rule of law does represent a more or less coherent political ideal. How central should this be to our understanding of law itself? What is the relation between the rule of law and the specialist work that modern analytic philosophers devote to the concept of law, and to the precise delineation of legal judgment from moral judgment and legal validity from moral truth?

Grammar suggests that we need to understand the concept of law before we can understand the rule of law. "The rule of law" is a complex phrase, and the word "law" is only one of its components. Just as we cannot understand a phrase like "the protection of human rights" unless we understand the smaller component phrase "human rights," so it might appear that we cannot understand the meaning of "the rule of law" unless we already grasp the concept of law. But I disagree. I think the surface grammar is misleading, and we cannot really grasp the concept of law without at the same time understanding the values comprised in the rule of law. I do not mean to say that we must understand the concept of the rule of law first, and then go on to conceptualize law itself in a way that is derivative from that understanding. Instead, I think we should understand these terms as a package, rather than understanding one as a separable component of the other. It is, after all, an accident of usage that the particular phrase "the rule of law" is used for this ideal. Some theorists use the term "legality" or "principles of legality" instead, and there is no grammatical or logical difficulty in supposing that law and legality need to be understood together, rather than law being understood first and legality second.[12]

This issue about the priority of conceptual understanding is not just verbal. Joseph Raz offers a powerful version of the claim that law must be understood first. In a 1979 essay, he argues that the rule of law is intended to correct dangers of abuse that arise from law as such:

> The law inevitably creates a great danger of arbitrary power—the rule of law is designed to minimize the danger created by the law itself. . . . Thus the rule of law is a negative virtue . . . the evil which is avoided is evil which could only have been caused by the law itself.[13]

This implies that before you even get to the rule of law, you must understand what law is and the dangers to which it gives rise. I think Raz is wrong about this. The rule of law is an ideal designed to correct dangers of abuse that arise in general when political power is exercised, not dangers of abuse that arise from law in particular. Indeed, the rule of law aims to correct abuses of power by insisting on a particular mode of the exercise of political power: governance through law. That mode of governance is thought to be more apt to protect us against abuse than, say, managerial governance or rule by decree. On this account, law itself seems to be prescribed as the remedy, rather than identified as the problem that a separate ideal—the rule of law—seeks to remedy.

There is a broader version of the claim that an understanding of the rule of law presupposes an understanding of law. It has to do with the priority of what Jeremy Bentham called "expository jurisprudence" over what he termed "censorial jurisprudence."[14] It is said that if we do not maintain a bright line between expository and censorial jurisprudence, then our legal exposition will be contaminated by moralistic or wishful thinking and our moral evaluations will be confounded by a sense that nothing wicked can be law and nothing legal can be wicked.[15] On this account, the rule of law should be placed firmly on the censorial—rather than the expository—side of this division, since it is undoubtedly an evaluative ideal. And since philosophical inquiry into the nature of law is conceived as a conceptual prelude to the expository side, it follows that the rule of law can have little bearing on that philosophical inquiry.

What should we make of this argument? It is certainly true that we need to understand the facts of political life and the reality of the way in which power is being exercised before we can deploy the rule of law as an evaluative ideal. And we need all the conceptual apparatus that this descriptive or empirical task presupposes. But it begs the question to say that the concept of law must be regarded as part of that descriptive or empirical apparatus, or that we cannot perform the descriptive or empirical task without it. In my view, to describe an exercise of power as an instance of lawmaking or law application is already to dignify it with a certain character; it is already to make a certain assessment or evaluation of what has happened. We look for certain patterns and features that matter to us when we are looking to characterize something as "law." It is not a term we use to capture, at the most basic descriptive level, the empirical reality of what is going on. Even in positivist jurisprudence, "law" is not a fundamental descriptive category. Calling something "law" supervenes on our being able to describe what is happening in other ways—in terms of practices, habits of obedience, dispositions to comply, and so on. So on all accounts, there is a layer of description beneath the level at which we use the term "law," a layer of descriptive inquiry that everyone agrees needs to be conducted clear-headedly before we can begin the process of evaluation. That descriptive inquiry gives us the data for our evaluations. On the positivist account, a category like "law" is simply a way of sorting that preliminary data before we begin to evaluate it; on the account that I favor, however, it is a way of beginning the process of evaluation. This dispute cannot be settled by simply reiterating the claim—with which everyone agrees—that we need to know the facts before we can begin evaluating.

4. Against Casual Positivism

I said at the beginning of this chapter that the rule of law—like democracy—
is one of our most prominent political ideals. Clearly there are important
connections between the two ideals, and these might be worth exploring
on another occasion. For now, however, I would like to propose an analogy
between the way we use the term "law" (particularly in the sense of legal
system) and the way we use the term "democracy."

During the Cold War, we did not take seriously the titles that certain
societies gave themselves, such as "German Democratic Republic" (GDR).
We knew that the GDR was not a democracy and we were not fooled by its
title. Just because something called itself a democracy did not mean that it
actually was a democracy. We do not pander to authoritarians. For us to recognize a system as a democracy, the system has to satisfy certain substantive criteria. For example, it has to be a system that allows political dissent
and organized opposition, and that conducts free and fair elections—with
universal adult suffrage—on a regular basis.

I believe we should be similarly discriminating about how we use the
term "law" (in the sense of a legal system). Not every system of command
and control that calls itself a legal system *is* a legal system. We need to scru-
tinize it a little—to see how it works—before we bestow this term.

I worry that modern students of jurisprudence—particularly modern legal
positivists—are too casual about what a system of governance has to be like
in order to earn the appellation "law." If it calls itself a system of law, they are
very reluctant to question that self-characterization. But even if the starting
point is not the self-characterization of actual systems of governance, the
legal positivists' own specifications for what it takes to count as a legal system
are overly generous in my view: basically, any well-organized system of centralized order using articulate and identifiable prescriptions and prohibitions
counts as law, provided that elite participants in the system can distinguish
prescriptions and prohibitions coming from the center from other norms
that may be circulating in the society. This is the positivism of H. L. A. Hart
and his modern followers.[16] In this regard, it really is not much different from
the positivism of earlier generations of jurists stretching back through John
Austin and Jeremy Bentham, all the way to Thomas Hobbes: law is any system
of command with the power to dominate all other systems of command in a
given society, where the chain of effective command can be traced to a single
politically ascendant source.[17] I call this "casual positivism." On this account,

the regimes of Kim Jong-Il in North Korea and Saddam Hussein in pre-2003 Iraq are legal systems. I propose that a philosophy of law should be less casual, less accommodating than this.

Historically, the opponents of casual positivism have presented us with a richer array of positions. Some classical theorists—like Cicero, Augustine, and Aquinas—argued that a system of rule that calls itself law may fail to qualify as law because of its injustice.[18] That is a substantive critique of casual positivism, and of course it amounts to a "natural law" critique of the positivist position itself. Other forms of opposition are structural rather than substantive: I have in mind the body of medieval English theory— culminating in the work of Sir John Fortescue—distinguishing between political forms and royal forms of kingship, and the philosophy of John Locke, which denied that an absolute monarch could be said to share a legal system with his unfortunate subjects.[19]

In the twentieth century, there were theories of this kind that were formal as well as structural. For example, there was the jurisprudence of the highly original Bolshevik thinker Evgeny Pashukanis, who honorably insisted— possibly at the cost of his life—that socialist legality was a contradiction in terms and that it was important to distinguish between law and the sort of social ordering that might characterize the management of an industrial enterprise or the timetabling of a railroad or the internal workings of an army.[20] Pashukanis warned against using the word "law" to refer to a system of social regulation simply on account of its effectiveness. He said that "the attempt to make the idea of external regulation the fundamental logical element in law leads to law being equated with a social order established in an authoritarian manner."[21] He believed that law was a particular and distinctive form of social ordering, organized around the coordination and empowerment of private, independent agents. Accordingly, he believed there was no future for law under communism.[22]

There is also the work of Lon Fuller, who famously insisted on distinguishing law as a mode of social ordering from the Nazi model of rule by terror, as well as from various forms of economic management and psychiatric manipulation.[23] In chapter 2 of *The Morality of Law*, Fuller entertained his readers with a little fable about a king, King Rex, who ruled his country incompetently by issuing decisions and commands that were ad hoc and inconsistent, secret or unintelligible, retroactive and impracticable, and changing so constantly that the social environment they defined was completely unpredictable. Do you remember how the fable ends? His subjects' constant complaints about these defects in governance led Rex to an embittered and premature death. Fuller tells us: "The first act of his successor, Rex II, was to announce that he was taking the powers of government away from the lawyers and placing them in the hands of psychiatrists and experts in public relations."[24] Should we say that Rex II tried a different kind of law? No, I think we are supposed to infer that Rex II tilted away from the legal enterprise altogether. Henceforth, his subjects would be manipulated, treated, and ordered about in a way that would not involve the distinctive techniques, skills, structures, and constraints of law. In chapter 4 of his book, Fuller considers a number of trends in social control in modern societies that remind us of his fantasy about Rex II's regime. He mentions the contemporary US narcotics control regime and alludes to the increasing use of actuarial techniques to regulate social intervention in the lives of ordinary people.[25] He also argues that to the extent that methods of social control such as therapy, conditioning, and psychological manipulation of deviants become standard, we will not just have changed the laws or amended our procedures; rather, we will have abandoned the idea of a legal order because it will have come to seem archaic and troublesome—just as it seemed to Rex II.

Fuller's concerns about nonlegal modes of governance are associated by many legal philosophers with his particular characterization of Nazi Germany and his participation in the debate about whether the Nazis really had or made law. His position was that for the most part, they did not. From a jurisprudential point of view, what was wrong in Germany from 1933 to 1945 was not so much that the Nazis used their power to advance oppressive and genocidal aims (though of course that is what matters in the broader scheme of things).[26] What was wrong in terms of law and legality was that they systematically undermined the formal and procedural conditions associated with the very existence of a legal system: they used retroactive directives, rumors of secret decrees, and verbal orders that could override formal statutes.[27] They also intimidated judges with a general requirement that courts not apply any standards or directives that conflicted with Nazi race ideology— which they treated as natural law—or with the interests of the party or the German people. Further, they maintained facilities for concentrating and murdering large numbers of people—facilities that were free from anything other than industrial constraints. To call this a system of law would make a mockery of the term, according to Fuller. Rule by this sort of terror is not rule by law, and we need to make sure that our concept of law is not such as to preclude us from making that point. I believe that this claim by Fuller needs to be confronted whether or not we also agree with his further claim that a genuine system of law is less likely to engage in Nazi-style wrongdoing than any other system of governance.

I mentioned the Rex II example, however, to indicate that Fuller pursued his distinction between legal and nonlegal modes of rule on a much wider front than was necessary to sustain his points about the extreme regime maintained in Germany by the Nazis. Placing the powers of government in the hands of psychiatrists and public relations experts is different from Nazi-style terror, both morally and formally. Fuller is prepared to accept that in some regards, it may even be desirable; even where it is desirable, however, he still wants to say it is not rule by law.[28]

There are features of Pashukanis's jurisprudence and of Fuller's jurisprudence that make them unattractive to many modern legal philosophers: Pashukanis's Marxism, of course, and Fuller's overstated claims about the connection between "the internal morality of law" and substantive justice. But they are both right about the need to overcome casual positivism—to keep faith with a richer and more discriminating notion of law.

5. The Essence of a Legal System

So how do we escape from casual positivism? Let me return to my democracy analogy. We should not call a system of governance a democracy if it does not regularly hold free elections to determine who occupies the highest political offices. Is there an equivalent for law? In other words, are there institutions or practices whose absence would decisively disqualify a system of rule from being regarded as a legal system, in the way that the absence of regular and free elections would decisively disqualify a system of governance from being regarded as a democracy?

I am going to make a number of suggestions about the elementary requirements for a system of rule to qualify as a legal system. You may be irritated by how obvious my suggestions are, but I hope you will redirect some of that irritation toward the philosophical theories of law—particularly positivist theories—that largely ignore or downplay these elements in contemporary jurisprudence.

(a) Courts

First and foremost, I do not think we should regard something as a legal system absent the existence and operation of the sort of institutions we call

courts. By "courts," I mean institutions that apply norms and directives established in the name of the whole society to individual cases, that settle disputes about the application of those norms, and that do so through the
medium of hearings—formal events that are tightly structured to enable an
impartial body to fairly and effectively determine the rights and responsibilities of particular persons after hearing evidence and argument from
both sides.[29]

It is remarkable how little there is about courts in the conceptual accounts
of law presented in modern positivist jurisprudence. The leading source is
H. L. A. Hart's magisterial work, *The Concept of Law*. Hart conceives of law
in terms of the union of primary rules of conduct and secondary rules that
govern the way in which the primary rules are made, changed, applied, and
enforced. He certainly seems to regard something like courts as essential;
when he introduces the concept of secondary rules, he talks of the emergence of "rules of adjudication" in the transition from a pre-legal to a legal
society—"secondary rules empowering individuals to make authoritative determinations of the question whether, on a particular occasion, a primary
rule has been broken."[30] But this defines the relevant institutions simply in
terms of their output function—the making of "authoritative determinations
of the question whether . . . a primary rule has been broken."[31] There is
nothing on the distinctive process by which this function is performed.[32] A
Star Chamber ex parte proceeding—without any sort of hearing—would satisfy Hart's definition, as would the tribunals we call "kangaroo courts" in
the antipodes, and as would a minister of police rubber-stamping a secret
decision to have someone executed for violating a decree.

Much the same is true of Joseph Raz's view about the importance of what
he calls "primary norm-applying organs" in *Practical Reason and Norms*.[33]
Raz believes that norm-applying institutions are key to our understanding
of legal systems, much more so than legislatures. There are all sorts of institutionalized ways in which norms may be applied, according to Raz, but
"primary norm-applying organ[s]" are of particular interest.[34] Raz describes
their operation as follows: "They are institutions with power to determine
the normative situation of specified individuals, which [institutions] are required to exercise these powers by applying existing norms, but whose
decisions are binding even when wrong."[35] He tells us that courts, tribunals, and other judicial bodies are the most important examples of primary organs. In his abstract philosophical account, however, the operation of primary norm-applying institutions is understood solely in terms

of output (and in terms of what is done with their output). Again, there is nothing about mode of operation or procedure. Secret military commissions might meet to "determine the normative situation of specified individuals . . . by applying existing norms," in the absence of the individuals in question and without affording any sort of hearing. The impression one gets from Raz's account is that a system of rule dominated by institutions like that would count as a legal system. Of course, Raz would criticize such institutions, and he might use the ideal of the rule of law to do so; in his writing on that subject, he suggests that requirements of "open and fair hearing, absence of bias, and the like are obviously essential for the correct application of the law and thus . . . to its ability to guide action."[36] But he seems to suggest that this is relevant to law only at an evaluative level, rather than at the conceptual level.

There is a considerable divergence here between what these philosophers say about the concept of law and how the term is ordinarily used. Most people, I think, would regard hearings and impartial proceedings—and the accompanying safeguards—as an essential rather than a contingent feature of the institutional arrangements we call legal systems. For most people, their absence would be a disqualifying factor, just as the absence of free and fair elections would be in an alleged democracy.

I do not want to be too essentialist about details. The nature of electoral arrangements varies from one democracy to another, and equally, the nature of hearings and the procedures used differ between one legal system and another. But the essential idea is much more than merely functional, applying norms to individual cases. It is also partly structural, involving Martin Shapiro's idea of the triad structure: a first party, a second opposing party, and above them, an impartial officer with the authority to make a determination.[37] Most importantly, it is procedural: the operation of a court involves a way of proceeding that offers those who are immediately concerned an opportunity to make submissions and present evidence, such evidence being presented in an orderly fashion according to strict rules of relevance and oriented to the norms whose application is in question. The mode of presentation may vary, but the existence of such an opportunity does not. Once presented, the evidence is then made available to be examined and confronted by the other party in open court. Each party has the opportunity to present arguments and submissions at the end of this process and reply to those of the other party. Throughout the process, both sides are treated respectfully and, above all, listened to by a tribunal that is bound to attend to the evidence presented and respond to the submissions that are made in the reasons that are given for its eventual decision.[38]

These are abstract characteristics—and it would be a mistake to get too concrete, given the variety of court-like institutions in the world—but they are not just arbitrary abstractions. They capture a deep and important sense associated foundationally with the idea of a legal system—that law is a mode of governing people that treats them with respect, as though they had a view of their own to present on the application of a given norm to their conduct or situation. Applying a norm to a human individual is not like deciding what to do about a rabid animal or a dilapidated house. It involves paying attention to a point of view and respecting the personality of the entity one is dealing with. None of this is emphasized in the dominant positivist account; all of it, I submit, should be regarded as an essential aspect of our working conception of law.

(b) General Public Norms

A second feature is suggested by the way I have characterized courts. I argued that courts are institutions that apply norms established in the name of the whole society through the medium of tightly structured proceedings. It is essential to our understanding of a legal system that there are such norms and that they play a central role in the legal system, a role to which almost all its defining features are oriented. A system of political rule is not a system of law unless social order is organized around the existence of identifiable norms issued for the guidance of conduct.

Two things about these norms are particularly important. First, they are general in character. As such, they form the basis for all the particular legal orders issued and enforced in the society, including the particular orders of courts. Some positivists see the generality of law as a pragmatic matter: Austin observed that "to frame a system of duties for every individual of the community, [is] simply impossible: and if it were possible, it [would be] utterly useless."[39] Hart said that "no society could support the number of officials necessary to secure that every member of the society was officially and separately informed of every act which he was required to do."[40] But I think the generality of law is not just a contingent matter—as though a society with a sufficiently large coterie of officials could in principle be governed entirely by ad hoc decrees and still be said to have a system of law. Definitionally, the word "law" is associated with general, as opposed to particular, statements: consider its use in "laws of nature" or "lawlike" statements in science, or "moral law" in Kantian ethics. Our concept of law in jurisprudence embodies this meaning and the principles of impersonality and equality that it conveys.

Second, to play this central role in a legal system, the norms must be not only general but also public. They must be promulgated to the public—those whose conduct will be assessed by them and those whose interests their application is supposed to affect. The public existence of such norms is to be contrasted with a situation where there are no abiding points of reference in one's relations with state authorities, where significant portions of the population are kept in the dark as to what is expected of them, and where the tribunals—whose job it is to resolve particular disputes—apply secret directives that are neither known to nor knowable by the non-state parties affected. Such a system of secret norms is not a legal system, for it lacks the dimension of publicity that most people associate with law.

The identifiability of law is one of the leading themes of modern positivism. The idea of a rule of recognition—a way of determining whether a given norm has the status of law—is crucial to positivist jurisprudence, but this tradition has not emphasized *public* identifiability. Modern positivists follow H. L. A. Hart in basing the identification of norms as law on the existence of an accepted rule of recognition practiced among the elite members of the society, notably the judges. Hart asserts that in a modern system of government, "a great proportion of ordinary citizens—perhaps a majority—[will] have no general conception of the legal structure or of its criteria of validity."[41] He acknowledges that such a conception is consistent with the regime of secret rules that I mentioned earlier. Again, I think Hart is wrong about this. It is a mistake to think that a system of rule could be a legal system if there were no *publicly accessible* way of identifying the general norms that are supposed to govern people's behavior. I do not mean that a legal system may be said to exist only when knowledge of the law and how to find it is disseminated in detail among every last member of the community. The norms should be public knowledge in the sense of being *available* to anyone who is sufficiently interested, and available in particular to those who make a profession of being public-norm detectors (lawyers, as we call them) and who make that expertise available to anyone who is willing to pay for it. More generally, the public character of law is a matter of the abiding presence of certain norms in a given society. They present themselves as public-standing norms—settled and calculable features of the social landscape—norms

that are not necessarily immune from change, but which are not expected to
have such ephemeral half-lives that would make it not worth anyone's while
to figure out what they are and what they require.

The publicity of these norms is also not just a matter of pragmatic administrative convenience along the lines of its being easier to govern people
if they know what is expected of them. It embodies a fundamental point
about the way in which the systems we call "legal systems" operate. They operate by using, rather than suppressing and short-circuiting, the responsible agency of ordinary human individuals. Ruling by law is quite different
from herding cows with a cattle prod or directing a flock of sheep with a
dog. It is also quite different from eliciting a reflex recoil with a scream of
command. The publicity and generality of law look to what Henry Hart and
Albert Sacks called "self-application"—that is, to people's capacities for practical understanding, for self-control, and for the self-monitoring and modulation of their own behavior, in relation to norms that they can grasp and
understand.[42] Even when the self-application of general norms is not possible and institutional determination is necessary, either because of disputes
about application or because application inherently requires an official determination, the particular orders that are eventually issued still look toward
self-application. Unsuccessful defendants in private law litigation are expected to pay the decreed damages themselves; rare is the case where bai-
liffs have to turn up and take away their property. I do not mean to deny the
ultimately coercive character of law. But even in criminal cases—where the
coercive element is front and center—it is often the case that a date is set for
a convict to report to prison of his own volition. Of course, if he does not
turn up, he will be hunted down and seized. Still, the law strains as far as
possible to look for ways of enabling voluntary application of its general
norms and many of its particular decrees.

I believe this pervasive emphasis on self-application is definitive of law
and that law is therefore sharply distinct from a system of rule that works
primarily by manipulating, terrorizing, or galvanizing behavior.[43] Lon
Fuller has argued that this emphasis embodies law's respect for human
agency: "To embark on the enterprise of subjecting human conduct to the
governance of rules involves . . . a commitment to the view that man is, or
can become, a responsible agent, capable of understanding and following
rules, and answerable for his defaults."[44] Many positivists would agree with
him; they accept that law's function is to guide action. But they do not

make the connection between this function and the definitive feature of publicity that I have emphasized. For example, Jules Coleman takes pains to argue that the action-guiding function of law is not necessarily expressive of a dignitarian value.[45] In my opinion, however, this argument is motivated more by a dogmatic desire to resist any connection between the concept of law and substantive values like dignity than by any real insight into the distinctiveness of an action-guiding rather than a purely behavior-eliciting model of social control. I believe that the action-guiding character of law—with its emphasis on self-application and its reliance on agency and voluntary self-control—furnishes a second dignitarian theme in our understanding of law.[46] At the end of my discussion of courts, I suggested that law is a mode of governance that deals with people on the basis that they have a view of their own to present on the application of the norm to their situation; it respects their dignity as beings capable of explaining themselves. We can now complement that with the idea that law is inherently respectful of persons as agents; it respects the dignity of voluntary action and rational self-control.

(c) Positivity

General norms of the kind that I have been talking about are often associated with the existence and operation of something like a legislature. The legal norms that govern our actions are not just discovered; they are man-made. Of course, legislation is not the only way in which laws are made and changed. International law emerges by treaty and custom, and in municipal legal systems, courts often play a major role in the development and growth of the law. Courts, however, perform their lawmaking function nontransparently—under cover of a pretense that the law is being discovered, not made or changed—and through processes that are not organized as legitimate lawmaking processes.[47] Legislation, by contrast, conveys the idea of making or changing law explicitly, in an institution and through a process publicly dedicated to that task.

Modern legislatures are set up as large representative assemblies. Ideally, they are established on a democratic basis and organized in a way that is supposed to ensure that they are responsive to as many interests and opinions as possible. It is probably a mistake to identify these features of legislation as definitive of our modern concept of law, though some political theorists have done so. However, at least one prominent jurist, Joseph Raz, has maintained that legislatures are not essential to a system of law.[48] But this turns out to mean only that Raz can *imagine* something like a legal system operating without a legislature, though he cannot point to any actual example of this. This possibility is similar to his suggestion that the imagination need not balk at the idea of a legal system without sanctions.[49] In the real world, sanctions and the deliberate and public activity of legislatures are both definitive features of law. Their prominence—respectively, among the explanation of compliance and the basis of legal change—may vary from system to system, but their presence is indispensable to the ordinary notion of law.

The existence of such public law-producing processes reminds us of law's positivity, of its being something that people have made and people can control. Law is a man-made institution, and its central norms are human artifacts. True, we talk readily enough of divine law—God's law—so there are senses of the word "law" that do not have this connotation of being manmade.[50] But when we think of law as a mode of governance, we think of it as something humans have set up—sometimes using the image of the deliberate actions of a founding generation, sometimes using the image of the accretion of customs and practices over generations. To understand law in this way is not to beg any questions against natural law jurisprudence. Jurists in the natural law tradition do not deny the positivity of human law; indeed, they often talk about it much more sensibly than self-styled positivists do. The distinctiveness of their position consists of a particular view about the relation between God's law and human law, or between the moral law and human law—not in any denial of the positivity of human law.

Positivity is partly a matter of what law is: it is human, it is contingent, it is the product of historical processes. But it is also a matter of how people understand it. Those who are ruled by law understand that they are ruled in an order that is susceptible to change and modification. The norms by which they are ruled could be otherwise. It is only our decision to have them and keep them as a basis of governance that explains why *these* norms, and not some others, are law. The idea of law, therefore, conveys an elementary sense of freedom, a sense that we are free to have whatever laws we like. Of course, the "we" in that sentence does not mean that any one of us is free to have whatever laws they like, nor does it necessarily imply any idea of democratic control. The "we" is bound up with whatever system of human power is in place in a given community. Still, law's positivity underwrites the use of imagination and creative thought in regard to law: the norms we are governed by could be different. A demand that the law should be different may be impracticable from a political point of view, but it is not inherently futile (as it would be in the case of the laws of nature).

(d) Orientation to the Public Good

I have mentioned a number of regards in which law is essentially public. It is made known to members of the public as a basis on which they may organize their expectations, and it is made, changed, and administered in the public proceedings of institutions like courts and legislatures. There is also an additional sense of publicness relating to the way in which law is oriented to the good that it serves.

We recognize as law not just any commands that happen to be issued by the powerful, but also norms that purport to stand in the name of the whole society and to address matters of concern to the society as such. We recognize institutions as part of a legal system when they orient themselves in their public presence to the good of the community—in other words, to issues of justice and the common good that transcend the self-interest of the powerful. It strains our ordinary concept of law to apply it to norms that address matters of personal or partial concern, or to institutions that make no pretense to operate in the name of the whole community, presenting themselves as oriented instead to the benefit of the individuals who control them.

That law presents itself in a certain way—as standing in the name of the public and as oriented to the public good—seems to me to be one of its defining characteristics. I do not mean that nothing counts as law unless it actually promotes the public good. Jurists used to ask—in the vein of Saint Augustine—"What is the difference between a system of laws and a set of commands issued by a band of robbers?"[51] One answer might be that the robbers' commands do not promote the public good; they are simply for the advantage of the robber band. That is something like a strong natural law position, however, and it is not what I am suggesting here. Positivist answers to Augustine's question have tended to revolve around issues of effective institutionalization; the order constituted by the power of the robbers would not be effective enough nor be sufficiently institutionalized to call for the use of the concept of law in all its complexity.[52] There might be an intermediate position, however. Instead of saying that nothing is law unless it promotes the public good, we might say that nothing is law unless it *purports* to promote the public good—that is, unless it presents itself as oriented in that direction.[53] This is an aspirational or orientational idea, not a substantive one. But it is nevertheless very significant.

(e) Systematicity

The fifth defining feature of law that I want to mention is much harder to label than the others. I call it "systematicity," though it is predicated on another closely related feature, which may be called the "cumulative" character of law.

A legal system builds on itself. Though it is always possible for a law to be amended or revoked, it is not usual for each new legislature to wipe the slate clean of the work of its predecessors. Instead, what legislators do—and what courts also do in their lawmaking capacity—is add to the laws already in existence. That is what I mean by law's cumulative effect. Even when there is a radical change of personnel in the political system—with liberals replacing conservatives—indeed, even when there is a revolution, we hardly ever see a return to "Year Zero" so far as the law is concerned. Instead, law grows by accretion, so that new liberal legislation takes its place alongside old conservative legislation—or at least alongside the old conservative legislation that has not been explicitly repealed.

On the other hand, a legal system is not just a succession of legislated norms—like the common view of history in Toynbee's phrase, "just one damned thing after another." In the simplest command model, particular laws come into existence by virtue of particular commands. The strongman in charge of a society issues one command; the next day, he issues another command; and so on, until there is a whole heap of commands. In the crudest positivist understanding, that is what the law of the society amounts to—a heap of commands—whether or not anyone can make sense of them all together. But I do not think we would call that a legal system, or regard the unrelated and unreconciled heap of commands as a system of laws, if it was not thought appropriate to try to introduce some organizing system into the accumulation.[54] Legal norms present themselves as fitting or aspiring to fit together into a system, each new ruling and each newly issued norm taking its place in an organized body of law that is fathomable by human intelligence. Positivists like Raz have emphasized law's coherence as an institutional system.[55] Law is not only a system in an institutional sense, however, but in a sense relating to logic, coherence, and perhaps even what Ronald Dworkin has called "integrity."[56] At its most modest, this feature of systematicity amounts to something like Lon Fuller's requirement of consistency: people must not be confronted by the law with contradictory demands—for example, with rules that require and prohibit the same conduct at the same time and in the same circumstances.[57] Legal systems satisfy this demand with the use of maxims like *lex posterior derogat priori*. Beyond that, there is a felt requirement essential to law that its norms make some sort of sense in relation to one another; even apart from formal consistency, we should interpret them so that the point of one does not defeat the point of another. That is why the use of analogy is appropriate in legal argument; it builds on a sense that individual norms are not self-contained and that the point of any one of them may have some bearing on how it is appropriate to think about any other. This broader sense of the systematicity of law helps explain why we think of a body of law as consisting of not just legislation and decisions in particular cases, but also principles whose content reflects powerful themes that run implicitly through the whole body of law and that are reflected in various ways in its explicit norms. The principles of a legal system are not part of its enacted law or its formal holdings, but they represent the underlying *coherence* of its enacted laws and its formal holdings.

The making of law is often thought of as embodying a principle of will rather than reason. In the legislative process, something becomes law for no other reason than that someone wills it to be so. But legislation is not just the addition of a rule to the heap of laws; it is a modification of the corpus juris. That is why legislating is in part a technical task: each bill must be framed in a way that pays attention to the juridical (as well as the social and economic) environment in which it is to operate. Also, it is striking the extent to which particular legislative measures present themselves not just as peremptory fiats, but also as small-scale normative systems, with an array of provisions dealing with interpretation, application, exceptions, and so on. (The extreme case, of course, is legislation that sets out explicitly to codify a given area of the law.) This systematicity also affects the way law presents itself publicly. Finding out what the law is consists of finding out how the accumulating system of norms has been modified.

Judges like to pretend that they are not making law in the willful way that legislators make law. Even when their conclusions are new, they present them as the product of reasoning rather than will. The systematicity of law helps explain this. The process by which courts make law involves projecting the existing logic of the law into an area of uncertainty or controversy, using devices such as analogy and reference to underlying principles.

Courts would have to operate in quite a different way—and the pretense that they are really just finding the law rather than laying down new law would be much harder to sustain—were it not for the systematicity of the existing body of norms that they manipulate.

Above all, law's systematicity affects the way that law presents itself to those it governs. It means that law can present itself to its subjects as a unified enterprise of governance that one can make sense of. I do not just mean that one can make sense of each measure, as one might do on the basis of a statement of legislative purpose. I mean that one can make sense of the "big picture," with an understanding of how the regulation of one set of activities relates rationally to the regulation of another. This is another aspect of law's publicness. The law's susceptibility to rational analysis is a public resource that members of the public may make use of—not just as an intellectual exercise, but in argument. In court, for example, the submissions that may be made on behalf of each party are not limited to a view of the facts and the citation of some determinate rule. They can also be a presentation of the way in which the antagonists take their positions to fit generally into the logic and spirit of the law. In this way, the law pays respect to those who live under it, conceiving them now as bearers of individual reason and intelligence.

Again, the theme of dignity is important. Earlier, we considered the way in which law respects the dignity of individual agency by relying largely on the self-application of general norms. Now we see that it also respects the dignity of reasoning and even argumentativeness. The individuals whose lives law governs are thinkers who can grasp and grapple with the rationale of that governance and relate it in complex but intelligible ways to their own views of the relation between their actions and purposes and the actions and purposes of the state.

6. A Narrow Concept of Law

I am unsure whether we should say that the five features I have considered provide the basis of a positivist account of law. The positivity of law is emphasized in my third feature, but—as I noted—it is also recognized by jurisprudential theories opposed to positivism. It is certainly not a purely descriptive account.[58] Shortly, we will consider the significance of the fact that all five of these features are, to a greater or lesser extent, value laden. Even if they do provide the basis of a positivist account of law, it is no longer casual positivism of the sort we considered in section 4, above. It defines a distinctive mode of governance that is worth having and worth distinguishing from other modes of governance.

The mode of governance that is properly called law is quite common in the world today, but we should not infer from this that just any mode of governance necessarily conforms to it. There have been and are societies that are not ruled in this way. They may be the "pre-legal" societies of pure custom without institutions that H. L. A. Hart discussed in *The Concept of Law*.[59] They may also be modern tyrannies or totalitarian societies that do not use any institutional process recognizably like that of a court and that base their rule on a haphazard array of secret decrees issued at the whim of a strongman and known only to the officials charged with enforcing them. In societies like these, it will be regarded as at best a puzzling naïveté and at worst a fatal insolence to demand one's day in court, to attempt to present any sort of reasoned argument about one's own view of one's obligations, or to insist on knowing in advance and in stable and general terms what is required of one so that one can organize one's life accordingly.

The commands and decrees imposed in such a society may be *called* "laws" and the institutions that administer them may *describe themselves* in terms appropriate to a legal system. If someone wants to insist on these descriptions, we will not be bewildered; we will understand what is going on. The use of a concept does not always involve all of its meaning or resonance, and the use of complex and important concepts is often crude and peremptory, as people use them roughly to cover anything that they think is analogous to their proper or central application.[60] But those who use language so loosely should also not be surprised when others withhold the relevant terms, insisting on a more rigorous and specific meaning.

This is particularly the case when terms have an important appraisive or accreditive function. Consider terms like "doctorate" and "master's degree." When someone says that they have a doctorate in physics or a master's degree in political science, I think we are entitled—conceptually—to expect that these terms refer to accredited qualifications from a proper university, with all the attributes and orientations that graduate education at a university involves. It may not be Harvard or Oxford, but we would expect it to be an institution of a certain kind or character.

Yet, we know there are dubious institutions that offer "degrees" on the basis of programs that do not conform to anything recognizable as advanced university education. Imagine receiving a spam email that reads: "Too lazy to attend exam or classes? We have Diplomas and Degrees—Masters' or Doctorates—to choose from in any field of your interest. Only two weeks required to deliver the prestigious, nonaccredited university's paper to your doorstep. Do not hesitate to give us a call today! 1-555-693-8861." In this scenario, the company is not promising to send a Harvard doctorate in the mail. There is no element of misrepresentation. Degrees are relative to institutions: some people (after years of study) can put "PhD (Harvard)" after their name, while others (two weeks after dialing 1-555-693-8861) can only put down "PhD (Flybynight U.)." Anyone who orders a degree from this company knows what the degree will be worth. On the other hand, if I were insisting that *conceptually* a doctorate must be a qualification based on a serious program of advanced study, I do not think that I should be embarrassed by this email as a counterexample. We all know what is going on. We know there can be unsophisticated uses of sophisticated concepts, and we can recognize this example as such. Certainly, it would be a mistake to insist that since this email represents an intelligible use of the word "doctorate," our analysis of the concept of a doctorate must be relaxed enough to accommodate it. We can have a more stringent analysis than that, while still understanding the temptations and conveniences of using "doctorate" in this particular way.

The same is true of democracy in the analogy we have been using. We know what people were getting at when they described the United States in 1918 as a democracy, even though women were not guaranteed the right to vote; even apartheid South Africa might have been called a democracy—on account of universal adult white suffrage—to distinguish it from countries that were ruled by a king or a dictator not subject to the votes of ordinary people at all. And if elections are infrequent or corrupt, we may still understand what the supporters of a regime are doing when they call it a "democracy." Even so, our ability to understand any of these uses does not mean that a proper account of the concept of democracy requires that it be extended to cover them.

Similarly, a secret edict issued by a dictator to the effect that the assets of anyone who fails to display sufficient enthusiasm for the dictatorship are forfeited to members of the dictator's family can be called "law," if you like. We know what someone would mean by calling it the law of pre-invasion Iraq in 2003. But this usage need not embarrass us in our account of law's essential features, for our account is not promising to say what is conveyed by every intelligible use of the word "law." It is an explication of the central concept of law that needs to be understood in itself as background to our necessarily more jaundiced understanding of these other degenerate, exploitative, and backhanded uses of the term.

In *The Concept of Law,* one of the grounds on which Hart defended a fairly relaxed (if not casual) form of positivism was that any more restrictive use of the term "law" would not isolate a distinctive phenomenon worth separate study. "Nothing is to be gained," he said, "in the theoretical or scientific study of law as a social phenomenon by adopting the narrower concept [of law]."[61] Hart argued that any proposal to leave to another discipline the study of systems that did not satisfy the more restrictive test would simply invite confusion. Note, however, that Hart was not talking about any of the five characteristics of law that I have mentioned, but instead about the traditional natural law view that certain edicts are too wicked to be called laws. And he may have been right about the idea of separating the "scientific" study of such edicts into a discipline separate from the study of laws that are just. But I do not think his argument applies to the case that has been made in this chapter.

Though there is a discipline devoted to the study of all forms of political order—namely, political science—a lot can be gained from defining a subfield that would concentrate on systems of governance that exhibit the five characteristics I have mentioned. Legal systems have structure and complexity, and they engage the consciousness and agency of their subjects in ways that starkly distinguish them from other forms of rule. They are likely to exhibit patterns of growth and decline and to generate certain outcomes under certain conditions that are worth studying as a matter separate from the patterns of growth and decline and the outcomes under similar conditions of dictatorships or "pre-legal societies." Just as political scientists make a study of electoral politics, which is distinct from forms of study that include, say, Kremlinology, so the study of how legal systems (in my sense) operate in the real world may well generate a body of research and literature that is not readily applicable to the behavior of other sorts of political systems where quite different types of institutions are involved and quite different modes of interaction and expectation exist between rulers and ruled.

Let me turn now to the evaluative dimension of my account. The features that I have suggested are definitive of law are formal, structural, institutional, and procedural in character. They are not substantive features, though they are not without moral significance. I think they define something worth treasuring as well as something worth studying. We have noted various ways in which these characteristics define a mode of governance that takes people seriously as dignified and active presences in the world—persons with lives of their own to lead, with points of view about how their lives relate to the interests of others, and with reason and intelligence to exercise in grasping their society's system of order.

I am sure that my defining features can be stated in purely descriptive terms (if anyone wants them characterized in that way). But let us be clear: these features are morally motivated—just as, in our analogy, the insistence on free and fair elections for a democracy is a morally motivated criterion. When we say that there cannot be a democracy unless there are elections, it is because democracy is something that we care about and the idea of elections goes to the heart of what matters to us. We could phrase this definitional requirement in purely descriptive terms, but in doing so, we would sell it short in our account of its importance and the connection between it and the overall value of democracy. Similarly, the criteria for law that I have identified—criteria like courts, with their characteristic modus operandi; governance by general norms in a way that respects people's dignity as agents capable of autonomous self-government; law as representing a way in which a community takes public control of the conditions of its collective life; and law's amenability to reason—all of these go to the heart of what we value about law. They explain in evaluative terms why the distinction between legal systems and other types of systems of governance is important to us. Their definitional connection with law is not just a semantic point; it is a substantive moral thesis.

Hart addressed this aspect of the matter as well. He worried that a narrow value-laden definition of law might confuse the issue of whether people should obey a law that they perceive to be iniquitous. That issue, he worried, might become equivocally poised between the judgment that "this is law; but it is too iniquitous to be applied or obeyed" and the judgment that "if this were as iniquitous as I think it is, it would not properly be regarded as law."[62] Hart went on to argue that

what surely is most needed in order to make men clear-sighted in confronting the official abuse of power, is that they should preserve the sense that the certification of something as legally valid is not conclusive of the question of obedience, and that, however great the aura of majesty or authority which the official system may have, its demands must in the end be submitted to a moral scrutiny. This sense, that there is something outside the official system, by reference to which in the last resort the individual must solve his problems of obedience, is surely more likely to be kept alive among those who are accustomed to think that rules of law may be iniquitous, than among those who think that nothing iniquitous can anywhere have the status of law.[63]

A fair point. But plainly, this is an argument only against a definition of law whose implicit values are supposed to clinch the issue of obedience. It is not an argument against a definition of law whose implicit values are relevant to, but far from determinative of, the overall question of obedience. The values that support my account of law's distinctive features are not the sort of values that can settle what we should do when faced with an edict that appears unjust or harmful to the public good. We may ask: Is it at least publicly presented in a way that is oriented to the public good? Is it administered through courts with familiar procedural safeguards? Has it been made available as a basis on which people might organize their lives, applying it themselves to their own conduct? Is it administered as part of an intelligible system? The answers to these questions may affect our overall moral estimate of the situation, but they still leave the crucial question of obedience unsettled. Thus, they do not give rise to the concern that Hart expressed.

Let me return to my democracy analogy to make another point. Elections in the real world are seldom perfect, even in the countries—like the United States—that we regard as paradigms of democracy. Electoral systems are flawed, registration and turnout are low, systems of recording and counting votes are often chaotic and vulnerable to manipulation, and so on. "Free and fair elections" is a matter of degree, and when we call it a defining feature of democracy, we may have in mind a fairly low threshold compared with what a perfect system would offer. The same is true of law: all five criteria that I have mentioned are matters of degree. A particular directive may be more or less stable, more or less well publicized, enforced through more or less scrupulous procedures, and integrated more or less fully into a coherent system of norms. I think we call something a legal system if it satisfies a recognizable minimum along these five dimensions, at least to the extent that it pays credible tribute to the concerns that underlie each of the criteria. We may not have a precise sense of what that minimum is; there may be gray areas around the threshold that will likely generate dispute about whether a problematic case qualifies as a legal system. This is also true of democracy. It means that both the disciplinary boundaries we are imagining and the morally motivated conceptual distinctions that we want to draw in these respective fields are not crisp, but only blurred and uncertain.

Not only are our defining criteria matters of degree, but they are matters of degree in several dimensions. One important dimension not mentioned so far is the extent to which recognizably legal institutions and requirements actually impact the way society works. Law is not a game. There might be a set of norms and institutions that exhibit all of the characteristics I have mentioned but which apply only to a very small subset of social, economic, and political interactions and regulate both public and private power to an inconsiderable extent. I do not think we should call such a system the legal system of a society if it is confined to an obscure corner in this way. It is part of our idea of law that even if it does not regulate everything, it must be effective in governing many—if not most—of the more important interactions and conflicts in a given society. It must apply to the main ways in which ordinary people and businesses are subjected to and affected by the exercise of power in society (certainly by the exercise of public power and maybe by big centers of private power as well). And, it must effectively control, direct, govern, and, where appropriate, restrain the exercise of political power in ways that people can count on.[64]

7. From the Concept of Law to the Rule of Law

I said at the outset that one of my aims in this chapter is to argue for a closer connection between the concept of law and the rule of law. Those who are familiar with the rule of law will have noted that what I have called the defining characteristics of law are also among the most prominent requirements of that ideal. The requirement I mentioned at the end of the previous section is a version of Lon Fuller's principle of congruence.[65] And of the five defining ideas explored in section 5, three are intimately connected with rule-of-law requirements: (1) systematicity is associated with the rule-of-law requirement of consistency or integrity;[66] (2) the existence of general norms is associated with the rule-of-law requirements of generality, publicity, and stability; and (3) the existence of the distinctive institutions we call courts is associated with the rule-of-law requirement of procedural due process.

Much like the criteria I used for specifying what we mean by "law," the requirements associated with the rule of law are all matters of degree. They are matters of degree because first, a system of governance may satisfy the rule of law in some areas of governance and not others; second, the rule of law comprises multiple demands, some of which may be satisfied while others are not; and third, a particular norm or directive may be more or less clear, more or less stable, more or less well publicized, and enforced through more or less scrupulous procedures. Moreover, this feature of the rule of law seems essential to the work that it does as a political ideal. We use it to make nuanced and qualified assessments as well as all-or-nothing condemnations or commendations of systems of governance. We do sometimes say that there is a catastrophic failure of the rule of law (like the Nazi Germany of Fuller's characterization).[67] But mostly we talk about "departures" from the rule of law, or actions that "undermine" the rule of law to a certain extent, or the "weakening" of the rule of law, or we talk of particular—though not necessarily systemic—violations of the rule of law, and so on.

I believe that one can understand these two sets of criteria—for the existence of law and for the rule of law—as two perspectives on the same basic idea. The very idea of law is a demanding concept, and there are two ways of thinking about its demanding-ness. We can think of the demands as being incorporated into the meaning of law itself, placing limits on our use of this term. Or we can think of the demands as being aspirations embodied in an ideal associated with the operation of a legal system—the rule of law. John Finnis brings the two perspectives together when he says, in his discussion of the rule of law in *Natural Law and Natural Rights,* that "the rule of law" is "the name commonly given to the state of affairs in which a legal system is legally in good shape."[68] A legal system can be in better or worse shape, but after a point it can be in such bad shape that it does not satisfy the criteria for being a legal system at all.

But even if it is recognizable as a legal system, we may still demand more from that system on any or all of these dimensions. The fact that we work with a roughly defined threshold for a system of governance to count as law does not mean that we rest satisfied with these minimum credible achievements. There is always room for improvement, and there is also danger of deterioration. The criteria I have outlined make themselves available as sources of continuing normative pressure to reach higher up each scale and to resist the downward pressure that other exigencies of politics inevitably generate.

For example, on the issue of courts, there is pressure to improve procedural due process and to resist the tendency to replace adjudicative hearings with other types of process. Regarding norms, there is a continuing campaign against retroactivity, failures of generality, vagueness, and other vices specified in Lon Fuller's "inner morality of law." With systematicity, there are arguments for codification and for the promotion of a greater element of what Ronald Dworkin has called "integrity" in both legislation and common law.[69] With the control of power, there may be a continuing aspiration to bring more and more of the discretion that characterizes the administrative and welfare state under the control of legal norms and institutions, particularly forms of discretion that impact directly and deleteriously on individuals' lives, liberties, and property.

These demands can be characterized in a number of ways. If the problems with a particular system of governance are deep, multifaceted, and endemic, we may understand the pressure for improvement as a demand that the system become a less marginal case of a legal system—more evidently and less controversially an example of the operation of law. Using our analogy again, it is like insisting that elections in Zimbabwe be free and fair, and uncontaminated by violence, so that the country can be regarded as a more definite case of a democracy rather than as the degenerate mixture of democratic forms and rule by fear that it became in the mid-2000s. Even if a country is undoubtedly a democracy—such as the United States—one may still put pressure on its institutions to be more truly democratic. Whether this pressure is characterized in terms of the concept of democracy or some aspirational democratic ideal may be a matter of choice in the way that the demand is presented. Similarly, a system of governance that is undoubtedly a legal system may be reproached for occasional lapses into retroactivity, or for occasional failures to control bureaucratic power. Such reproaches may be phrased either in terms of the concept of law—"Let us make this a less marginal example of a legal system"—or in terms of the rule of law—"Let us apply the rule-of-law ideal more rigorously to this legal system." In both phrasings, there is an evaluation and a degree of categorization going on.

Usually, a reproach in terms of the concept of law indicates that we may be in danger of falling short of some minimum threshold, while a reproach in terms of the rule of law represents continuing upward pressure along each of these defining dimensions. Different people in various circumstances will use the terms differently, so there will be ample room for disagreement about whether a given case should be regarded as a poor example of a legal system, as opposed to one that does not score as highly on the rule-of-law requirements as it should. For instance, Jeremy Bentham might denounce the system of English common law as not really law at all, while more moderate thinkers might say that it is a system of law—just one where there is massive room for improvement along rule-of-law dimensions.[70] Each side can see what the other is getting at, however, and each side can understand the looseness in the use of this common terminology.[71] In addition, the existence of multiple criteria on both sides—in our definition of law and in our understanding of the rule of law—means that there is even more room for variation and indeterminacy. This is exactly what we should expect of a complex evaluative concept. It is what we have in our analogous case of democracy, and I suggest that it is what we should also expect for law.

8. Disputes about What the Law Is

The word "law" is sometimes used in the sense of legal system and sometimes in the sense of legal proposition. In this chapter, I have focused mostly on law in the sense of legal system. But what about law in the sense of legal proposition? We say, for example, that it is the law that you must pay your taxes by April 15. How is this second usage to be understood in the framework I am proposing?

A crude understanding might relate the two senses of law in the following way. Law in the first sense requires the existence of certain general norms that serve as a basis of orientation for people's behavior, as well as a basis for decision by the courts. That was our second defining element of law in section 5. Maybe this second sense of law is just a way of talking about those general norms; whether something is the law may simply be a matter of whether it can be found in the array of publicly promulgated general norms that I mentioned.

Unfortunately, this account is too crude, for a couple of reasons. First, we will want to include among the possible values of the predicate "__ is the law" not only the identifiable general norms of the society, but also the particular decisions of courts. Once we do that, we are bound to feel some pressure to extend it to comprehend the basis on which courts make their decisions. If the courts seem to be establishing certain ways of understanding the general norms, or if the courts seem to be articulating certain principles of decision that are intermediate between the enacted general norms and the decision of particular cases, then it may be appropriate to describe such modes of interpretation and such intermediate principles as law, too.

Second, the emphasis placed on the systematicity of law and its penetrability by human reason in section 5 may also mean that we must give the term "law" a broader extension. Occasionally, counsel or a judge may argue that people ought to be able to rely on some lawlike proposition, even though that proposition has been neither adopted explicitly in legislative form nor articulated (until that moment) by a court. Nevertheless, we might say that since the proposition can be inferred from existing legal materials that already carry legal authority, it also should be accorded authority. It is a distinctive feature of legal systems that they set up institutions—courts—that are required to listen to submissions along these lines. These are not just arguments about what the law ought to be—made, as it were, in a sort of lobbying mode. They are arguments of reason that maintain competing contentions about what exactly the law is. Inevitably, the line between characterization and normativity in these arguments will be blurred. One party will argue that a particular proposition cannot be inferred from the law as it is; the other party will respond that it can be inferred if we just credit the law with more coherence than people have in the past. Our account of what the law is, then, is not readily separable from our account of how the law aspires to present itself. Our response to the pressure for coherence may well alter our sense of what the law already contains.

It follows from this that the determination of whether something is law or not may sometimes—perhaps characteristically—be a matter of doubt and contestation. Such contestation can be explained by the interaction of some of the features emphasized in this chapter: the invocation of clear public norms, on the one hand, and argumentation on the basis of coherence and systematicity, on the other. Both are practices to which the formalities of the courtroom are hospitable, and together they explain why people often disagree about what the law is.

Some lawyers will be troubled by the resulting indeterminacy. They will ask, "How can it be so unclear what the law is?" But the approach I have indicated here has the descriptive advantage of explaining the disagreements about law that actually occur in legal practice. At times, of course, the law is clear. There is no controversy about the speed limit on Route 316 heading west out of Athens, Georgia, toward Atlanta. But in many other cases, the existence of disagreement about how to establish the truth of some legal proposition is undeniable. The account given here draws heavily on the recent work of Ronald Dworkin, who insists that our concept of law must be able to make sense of the disagreements we often have about how to determine what the law on a particular topic is.[72] Moreover, it must be able to explain this disagreement not just as a jurisprudential puzzlement or pathology, but as a distinctive aspect of legal practice.[73]

Dworkin has his favorite cases to cite on this point. He mentions the 1978 US Supreme Court case of *Tennessee Valley Authority v. Hill,* where it was argued that the Endangered Species Act required halting the completion of a vast dam in its final stages of construction, at a huge waste of public funds.[74] The act requires that once a species has been identified as threatened with extinction in a particular habitat, no governmental action may be taken that might jeopardize the continued existence of such endangered species or result in the destruction or modification of its habitat.[75] At the time the act was passed, the Tellico Dam in Tennessee was already partially built. In the late stages of its construction, however, a small species of fish—the snail darter—was identified as endangered by the project. An immense amount of money had already been spent on the dam, but more work needed to be done to complete it. The question was whether the statute required work on the dam to be halted immediately for the sake of the snail darter, or whether the Endangered Species Act should be read in a commonsense way that would not prevent the completion of projects initiated long before its enactment. Is the law that governs this case the literal text of the statute or the statute read in a way that avoids alarmingly costly and counterintuitive results? Any plausible account of what went on in this case shows the two sides disagreeing about how to infer legal requirements from the same mass of legal materials.

Another example of legal disagreement cited by Dworkin is the 1980 decision of the California Supreme Court in *Sindell v. Abbott Laboratories,* addressing the allocation of tort liability on the basis of market share.[76] Where a plaintiff has used a product—such as a pharmaceutical drug—supplied by a number of different manufacturers and has suffered harm as a result of negligence in the manufacture of the product, is it right to assign liability to each manufacturer on the basis of market share without proof that any particular defendant caused the harm that the plaintiff actually suffered? The plaintiff might argue that this is the fairest resolution, one that is consonant with what we might think of as the moral tenor of the background law. On the other hand, the defendant might argue that the law cannot countenance liability in this case because there is no legislative enactment or judicial precedent directly authorizing the imposition of this sort of liability absent proof of actual causation.

I think Dworkin is right to observe that those who disagreed in each of these cases disagreed not just about what to do, but about what it meant to *abide by the law* when deciding what to do. There was no disagreement about the facts in these cases, or the terms of any statute or precedent, or the contents of the opinions in the array of relevant precedents. What was in contention was what to make of all these agreed upon facts—physical and juridical—so far as the legal disposition of the cases was concerned. If there were no law to distract us, it might be obvious what the sensible or fair solution in each case would be. (We should finish constructing the dam and make each pharmaceutical company pay Mrs. Sindell a fair measure of damages.) But in a system of law, the pragmatic pursuit of good outcomes is sometimes constrained by statutes, precedents, principles, and doctrines. In each of these cases, there was plenty of material to establish a sense that the law placed *some* constraint on what should be done; the contention was only about what that legal constraint amounted to.

If it is not unnatural to say that the two sides in *Tennessee Valley Authority* and the two sides in *Sindell* disagreed about what the relevant law was, then it is also not unnatural to say they disagreed about what the rule of law required for the disposition of each case. This is because the rule of law is also a highly contestable idea. Jurists disagree about whether the rule of law requires rule by anything other than rules; they disagree about whether rule by judicial decision represents the rule of law or the rule of men; they disagree about whether statutory law, common law, customary law, or constitutional law should be taken as a paradigm for the rule of law; they disagree about whether the rule of law is conceived as a way of framing moral and political arguments in a community, or as a way of settling these arguments; and they disagree about whether or not the exercise of official discretion should be regarded as consistent with the rule of law when it is framed and authorized by statute.

In the name of legality, one side in *Tennessee Valley Authority* urged submission to the literal terms of the enactment, insisting that it was not for the courts to form any "individual appraisal of the wisdom or unwisdom of a particular course consciously selected by the Congress," while the other side insisted that legality required the exercise of intelligence and common sense when selecting among possible interpretations of the statutory text.[77] Similarly, the parties in *Sindell* disagreed about the constraints the rule of law imposes on one's thinking about a good—or fair or appropriate—solution to a public policy problem. According to one view, legality requires courts to limit liability on the basis of fundamental and long-established rules about causation. Under the prevailing view in *Sindell*, however, it would not be incompatible with the rule of law for courts to adapt existing principles to the realities of contemporary complex commercial society in a thoughtful and consistent way (consistent with the spirit of their previous application). So there is disagreement about what the rule of law requires as well as disagreement about what the law is.

It is Dworkin's view—and I think he is right—that disagreements about what constitutes law in these cases and about what the rule of law requires amount to the same disagreement.[78] We cannot sensibly drive a wedge between the claim that the judges disagreed about what the rule of law—or, as it is sometimes called, legality—required in these cases and the claim that the judges disagreed about what the law required. In *Sindell,* for example,

> we can sensibly think that though the law rejects [the plaintiff's] claim for damages according to market share, justice supports that claim. Or (less plausibly) the other way around: that though the law grants her that claim, justice condemns it. But it would be nonsense to suppose that though the law, properly understood, grants her a right to recovery, the value of legality argues against it. Or that though the law, properly understood, denies her a right to recovery, legality would nevertheless be served by making the companies pay.[79]

It is evident in these cases, and thousands more, that there is intense disagreement among judges and lawyers about what it means to solve certain problems legally—as opposed to pragmatically—and what it is to constrain one's moral or pragmatic solutions on the basis of what the law requires. Since this disagreement exists anyway, we should not be upset by any complaint about the introduction of contestability into the law on the account that I have given. Law is *already* contestable in cases like *Sindell* and *Tennessee Valley Authority,* and so the best way to characterize that contestability is to accept that disagreements about the implications of the rule of law are bound up with the very concept of law itself.

9. Process and Settlement in the Rule of Law

I stated in section 2 of this chapter that most conceptions of the rule of law emphasize the importance of determinacy and settlement. For these, the essence of the rule of law is predictability—people want to know where they stand. Accordingly, such conceptions highlight the role of rules rather than standards, literal meanings rather than systemic inferences, direct applications rather than arguments, and ex ante clarity rather than labored interpretations. Conceptions of this kind are very popular. So, it is natural to think that the rule of law must condemn the uncertainty that arises out of law's argumentative character.

But I also said in section 2 that there was another current in our rule-of-law thinking that emphasizes argument, procedure, and reason, as opposed to rules, settlement, and determinacy. This theme sometimes struggles to be heard. But, as I argued at the end of section 2, it is often quite prominent in public and political use of the rule of law ideal. The most common political complaint about the rule of law is that governments have interfered with the operation of the courts, compromised the independence of the judiciary, or made decisions affecting people's interests or liberties in a way that denies them their day in court—their chance to make an argument on their own behalf.

Here is my claim: if we understand the relation between the concept of law and the rule of law in the way that I have urged us to understand it, then the importance of the second procedural current is obvious. No conception of law will be adequate if it fails to accord a central role to institutions like courts, and to their distinctive procedures and practices such as legal argumentation. Conceptual accounts of law that only emphasize rules and say nothing more about legal institutions than that some institutions make rules and some apply them are way too casual in their understanding of what a legal system is; they are like understandings of democracy that neglect the central role of elections. A philosophy of law is impoverished as a general theory if it pays no attention to the formalized procedural aspects of courts and hearings, or to more elementary features of natural justice like offering both sides an opportunity to be heard. Failing to capture this in abstract terms, or regarding it as just a contingent feature of some legal systems and not others, and therefore beneath the notice of general jurisprudence, can make conceptual analysis in jurisprudence seem empty and irrelevant. Even if one could defend focusing solely on the rules themselves, a philosophy of law is still impoverished if it pays no attention to the defining role of law's aspiration to achieve coherence among the norms that it contains and to the forms of reasoned argumentation that are involved both in maintaining consistency and in bringing it to bear in the application of norms to particular cases.

Neil MacCormick has pointed out various ways in which law is an argumentative discipline, and I am greatly indebted to his account.[80] No analytic theory of what law is and what distinguishes legal systems from other systems of governance can afford to ignore this aspect of our legal practice and the distinctive role it plays in a legal system's respect for ordinary citizens as active centers of intelligence. The fallacy of modern positivism is its exclusive emphasis on the command-and-control aspect of law, without any reference to the culture of argument that it frames, sponsors, and institutionalizes. The institutionalized recognition of a distinctive set of norms may be an important feature, but at least as important is what we do in law with the norms that we identify. We do not just obey them or apply the sanctions that they ordain; we argue over them adversarially, we use our sense of what is at stake in their application to license a continual process of argument, and we engage in elaborate interpretive exercises about what it means to apply them faithfully as a system to the cases that come before us.

When positivists in the tradition of H. L. A. Hart pay attention to this aspect of interpretation and argument, they tend to treat it as an occasional and problematic sideline. The impression given is that in most cases, the authoritative identification of legal norms using a rule of recognition is sufficient; once it is recognized, a legal norm can become a straightforward guide to official action. Occasionally the language is unclear, however, because words have open texture or because our aims are indeterminate, or because for some other reason there is a hiccup in the interface between words and the facts to which they apply. Unfortunately, we are then left with no choice but to argue the matter through. And usually, the positivist will add, the upshot is that the court will just have to cut through the Gordian knot of argumentation and make a new rule, which can be recognized and applied more readily without any attendant controversy.[81]

But this account radically underestimates the point that argumentation—about what this or that provision means, or what may be the effect of a given array of precedents—is business as usual in law. We should be uneasy about counting as a legal system a system that did not exhibit such argumentation and make routine provision for it. And since it is a central part of our understanding of what a legal system is, it should also play a significant role in the ideal of the rule of law—as Finnis puts it, in the account we give of "the state of affairs in which a legal system is legally in good shape."[82]

In this chapter, I have contrasted two views of the concept of law and two views of the rule of law. So far as the concept of law is concerned, we have what I call the "casual positivism" of Hart and his followers, contrasted with the richer account that I developed in section 5. The former emphasizes rules—primary rules identified by a secondary rule of recognition, together with a minimalist account of the institutions that produce and apply them. The latter pays more attention to the distinctive institutional features of a legal system and to the practices and modes of argumentation that they sponsor and accommodate. So far as the rule of law is concerned, we have one conception that emphasizes the determinacy of enacted norms and the predictability of their application, and another, richer conception that also emphasizes procedural due process and the presence and importance of formally structured argument on behalf of ordinary citizens.

These might be regarded as separate controversies, but I believe they are intimately connected with one another. There is a natural correlation between a conceptual account of law (COL_1) that emphasizes rules and a rule of law ideal (ROL_1) that concentrates on their characteristics like their generality, determinacy, and so on. Additionally, there is a natural correlation between a conceptual account of law (COL_2) that focuses not just on the general norms established in a society but on the distinctive procedural features of the institutions that administer them, and an account of the rule of law (ROL_2) that is less fixated on predictability and more insistent on the opportunities for argumentation and responsiveness to argument that legal institutions provide. Conceivably, this correlation could be shaken loose by an insistence that the concept of law and the rule of law are to be understood quite independently of each other. Then, we might imagine someone acknowledging the need to move from COL_1 to COL_2 while still sticking with a conception of the rule of law (ROL_1) that does not go beyond the formal characteristics of rules. Or, we could imagine a positivist adhering dogmatically to COL_1, but acknowledging the importance of a separate rule of law ideal that emphasizes procedural and argumentative values. But these combinations seem odd; they treat the rule of law as a rather mysterious ideal—with its own underlying values, to be sure, but quite unrelated to our understanding of law itself. It is simply one of a number of ideals (such as justice, liberty, or equality) that we apply to law, rather than anything more intimately connected with the very idea of law itself.

I have argued, on the contrary, that the rule of law as a normative ideal arises out of our understanding of what law is. It represents a natural trajectory of normative thought projected out from the normative significance of law's defining features. It seems to follow that just as a conception of law would be impoverished if it emphasized only the existence of rules and the bare minimum of institutions necessary to apply them, so, too, would a

conception of the rule of law be impoverished as an ideal if it (1) emphasized only the clarity that crisp and determinate rules provide and the settlement and predictability that follow from their straightforward application, and (2) neglected (or, even worse, denigrated) the value we should
give to law's procedural, rational, and argumentative aspects.

Whether we end up with an impoverished conception of law itself, an
impoverished version of the rule of law, or—more likely—both, the damage
to our understanding of the distinctive value of law is likely to be considerable. The concept of law will end up accommodating, and the rule of law
will end up idealizing, aspects of governance that look quite demeaning and
unpleasant from the point of view of what we value in legal practice—indeed,
demeaning and unpleasant even from the point of view of those who
extol ROL$_1$.

Let me explain. I do not think that a conception of law or a conception of
the rule of law that sidelines the importance of argumentation can really do
justice to the value we place on requiring governments to treat ordinary citizens with respect as active centers of intelligence. The demand for clarity
and predictability is commonly made in the name of individual freedom—the
freedom of the Hayekian individual in charge of his own destiny who needs
to know where he stands so far as social order is concerned. But with the
best will in the world, and with even the most determinate-seeming law, circumstances and interactions can be treacherous. From time to time, the
free Hayekian individual will find himself charged or accused of some violation, or his business will be subject—as he thinks, unjustly or irregularly—
to some detrimental rule. Some such cases may be clear, but others may be
matters of dispute. An individual who values his freedom enough to demand
the sort of calculability that the Hayekian image of freedom under law is supposed to cater to, is not someone who we can imagine always tamely accepting a charge or determination that he has done something wrong. He
will have a point of view on that, and he will seek an opportunity to bring it
to bear when there is a question of applying a rule to his case. And, when he
brings his point of view to bear, we can imagine his plaintiff or his prosecutor responding with points of their own. And so it begins—legal argumentation and the use of the facilities that the law creates for the formal airing
of arguments.[83] Courts, hearings, and arguments are not optional extras; they
are integral parts of how law works and they are indispensable to the package
of law's respect for human agency. To say that we should value aspects of
governance that promote the clarity and determinacy of rules for the sake

of individual freedom, but not the opportunities for argumentation that a free and self-possessed individual is likely to demand, is to truncate what the rule of law rests on: respect for the freedom and dignity of each person as an active center of intelligence.

The rule of law and the concept of law can inform each other and protect each other against the prospect of that impoverishment. Our conception of what law is is our best guide to what matters about law, and a full understanding of how the legal system matters to us is our best guide to what is distinctive about legal as opposed to nonlegal modes of governance. The alternative, I fear, is an impoverished concept of positive law, which emphasizes nothing more than the existence of two kinds of rules, and an impoverished account of the rule of law, which treats everything besides the determinacy of the rules as though it did not matter.

3

How Law Protects Dignity

1. Legal Rights to Dignity

The most obvious way in which law protects dignity is by proclaiming and enforcing specific norms that prohibit derogations from or outrages upon human dignity. Some of these norms are explicit, like Common Article 3 of the Geneva Conventions, which prohibits "outrages upon personal dignity." Implicitly, dignity is protected also by prohibitions on degradation like those we find in Article 7 of the International Covenant on Civil and Political Rights (ICCPR) and Article 3 of the European Convention on Human Rights (ECHR).

Many pages have been devoted to the question of what these provisions mean.[1] In this chapter, I want to talk about a less obvious way in which law protects dignity, but a way that is deeper, more pervasive, and more intimately connected with the very nature of law. For when we consider Article 3 of the ECHR or Common Article 3 of the Geneva Conventions, it may strike us as a matter of contingency that dignity is protected under these provisions. Maybe any worthwhile bill or charter of human rights should regard human dignity as something worth protecting, but it is notorious that at the level of positive law, many bills of rights omit things that ought to have been included. There is no mention of dignity in the US Constitution, for example, and to the extent that the ideal has had any influence at all in US constitutional jurisprudence (and it has—for example, in Eighth Amendment jurisprudence),[2] it has had to be imported as judge-made doctrine. And that, too, is historically contingent, not to say vulnerable to passing fads and fashions. So there's our question: Are there connections between law and dignity that are less contingent than this?

2. Dignity as the Basis of Rights

Some have suggested not only that dignity ought to be protected as a human right, but that dignity is itself a ground of rights, perhaps *the* ground of rights. The ICCPR begins its preamble with the acknowledgment that the rights contained in the covenant "derive from the inherent dignity of the human person." And some philosophers say the same thing.[3] Even if this is not a connection between dignity and law as such, it certainly purports to identify a wholesale connection between dignity and the branch of law devoted to human rights.

Others remark (more skeptically) that "dignity" is just a sonorous word we use whenever we are engaged in human rights talk, so it is no accident that it turns up all over the law in this area. In a 2008 paper, Christopher McCrudden remarks that that "dignity" operates mostly as "a place holder for the absence of agreement" in human rights discourse, used when people want to sound all serious and philosophical but are not sure what to say.[4] That may be overly pessimistic, but it does alert us to the fact that dignity may not necessarily be a load-bearing idea. A term that is pervasive is in danger of platitude, and if we are tracking the pervasiveness of "dignity" in law, we must take care that we are not just on the trail of some embedded rhetorical bombast.

3. The Meaning of "Dignity"

So what do I mean by "dignity"? What is it that we are tracking in the law? Dignity, in my view, is a sort of status-concept.[5] It has to do with the *standing* (perhaps the formal legal standing or perhaps, more informally, the moral presence) that a person has in a society and in her dealings with others. So what I mean by the term, when I ask about the various ways in which law protects, recognizes, vindicates, or promotes human dignity, is something like this:

> Dignity is the status of a person predicated on the fact that she is recognized as having the ability to control and regulate her actions in accordance with her own apprehension of norms and reasons that apply to her; it assumes she is capable of giving and entitled to give an account of herself (and of the way in which she is regulating her actions and organizing her life), an account that others are to pay attention to;

and it means finally that she has the wherewithal to demand that her agency and her presence among us as a human being be taken seriously and accommodated in the lives of others, in others' attitudes and actions towards her, and in social life generally.

As a general point, it is likely that a being with these capacities will have a status in law that is different from the status of a being (such as a non-human animal) that lacks these capacities. But people try to do all sorts of things with power, and one of the things they sometimes try to do is to treat certain people as having a status that is lower than this or treat people as though the capacities I have mentioned are unimportant and have no implications for the way those people are ruled. Because this is possible, dignity has to function also as a normative idea: it is the idea of a certain status that ought to be accredited to all persons and taken seriously in the way they are ruled.

I am not *stipulating* this as a definition of dignity. I believe that the definition I have given captures much that is already present in our ordinary usage of "dignity." But it is controversial; and other accounts are different. I am using dignity as a status idea rather than a value idea (as it is used by Kant, for example, in the *Groundwork of the Metaphysics of Morals,* where it refers to a certain kind of precious and nonfungible value).[6] Twelve years after the publication of the *Groundwork,* Kant wrote again about dignity in "The Doctrine of Virtue," which is the second part of his late work, *The Metaphysics of Morals,* and there he spoke of it much more as a matter of status. He spoke of the respect that a person can "exact" as a human being from every other person, and that respect is no longer simply the quivering awe excited in a person by his own moral capacity (which is what you find in the *Second Critique,* for example) but a genuine making-room for another on a basis of sure-footed equality and acting toward another as though he, too, were one of the ultimate ends to be taken into account. The later discussion preserves the element of infinite value but presents it much more in the light of this status idea.[7]

My conception does not directly capture all the work that "dignity" does in law. Rules against "degradation" and "outrages upon personal dignity" are sometimes used to vindicate the human interest in elementary aspects of adult self-presentation (care of self, taking care of elemental physical needs) and to protect against forms of humiliation impinging on this interest. This is a cognate idea, connected with my conception via the idea of being recognized and treated as a being capable of self-control. So, consider the requirement in ECHR jurisprudence that it is degrading to parade criminals or suspects in shackles (unless they pose a clear and present danger to themselves and others).[8] This requirement is connected to the idea that humans are capable of self-control. They are not just wild animals to be leashed. And they are not to be exhibited as such.

There are many aspects of our proper moral treatment of humans that have little directly to do with dignity. I believe that our basic duty to respect and sustain human life, for example—important though it is—is not really connected to dignity. The preciousness or sacredness of human life is not really a dignitarian idea. I know that in Roman Catholic literature and in some bioethics literature, human dignity is used just in this sense of the special worth or sacredness of human life.[9] In my view, the problem with this account is not that it has strong theological foundations, but that it appropriates the term "dignity" to do work that "worth" or "sacred worth" might do as well. But there is much more to be said—unfortunately elsewhere—about some of the indirect connections between this use of dignity and the use that I am insisting on.[10]

When you hear my definition, the sense in which law inherently promotes dignity begins to become apparent. For it is easy to get the impression, from the way I set this out, of a person appearing on their own behalf before a public tribunal, say, and demanding to be listened to, demanding indeed that their view of things be taken account of before any public decision is made (for example, any public decision about what is to be done with them). This is evidently a legal idea, and it is arguably noncontingently so, in the sense that it is not a matter of the lawmaker having just decided to promote dignity (in the way that the framers of Common Article 3 of the Geneva Conventions decided to promote dignity). Dignity seems to hook up in obvious ways with juridical ideas about hearings and due process and status to sue. And the basic aim of the rest of this chapter is just to elaborate these connections and make them explicit.

4. Dignity and the Form of Rights: Hart, Feinberg, and Dworkin

Here is a preliminary foray. At the beginning of this chapter, I considered the idea of a specific right to dignity. A few lines later, I considered the idea—commonly expressed in the preambles of major human rights instruments—that dignity might be at the ground of every human right. A third possible connection—which we should explore now—is that the very form and structure of a right conveys the idea of the right-bearer's dignity.

This is familiar to us in the "choice theory" or "will theory" of rights, once advanced by H. L. A. Hart. In an essay published in 1955, Hart said that having a legal or a moral right was not just a matter of being the object of legal or moral concern. He rejected what is sometimes known as the "benefit theory" or the "interest theory" of rights. He favored instead the description of the right-bearer as having the power to determine what another's duty should be (in some regard): "Y is . . . morally in a position to determine by his choice how X shall act and in this way to limit X's freedom of choice; and it is this fact, not the fact that he stands to benefit, that makes it appropriate to say that he has a right."[11] Y (the right-bearer) can make a sort of demand on X that X is required to pay attention to, and it may be that this is what his dignity amounts to. Hart developed this argument first for natural rights, but he thought (at least for a while) that it was true of legal rights too.[12] Something similar can be found in Joel Feinberg's work on rights as claims: to have a right in law is to possess the dignity of a recognized claimant entitled to push his case before us and demand that it be considered.[13] To the extent that rights are pervasive in law, the recognition and respect that claimants are entitled to elicit is going to be a pervasive aspect of law's commitment to dignity.

It is sometimes said that we can imagine law without rights. If that means we can imagine law without any of the elements discussed in this section, I think that is false. Even if Hart is wrong about rights generally, law will nevertheless characteristically (not just contingently) establish and respect positions that have the features that Hart's choice theory attributed to rights: for example, law will recognize potential plaintiffs and defer to their dignity in allowing *them* to make the decision whether some norm violator is to be taken to task or not. It is even more evidently false if Ronald Dworkin is right in the basic "rights thesis" he set out years ago in *Taking Rights Seriously*.[14] Dworkin argued that anyone making a case of any sort in law makes it in the tones and language of rights, in the mode of entitlement rather than request or lobbying. (This applies whether it is formally a case about human or constitutional rights or just an ordinary action in, say, tort or contract.) A party in law does not phrase his argument in terms of its being *a rather good idea* to require a defendant or respondent to pay such-and-such a sum of money; he stands on his rights and in recognizing this standing the law accords him the dignity of a right-bearer. So that is worth bearing in mind.

Still, I think it is worth pursuing the possibility of even more direct connections than this. Even if the rights thesis proves a red herring or takes us down a jurisprudential cul-de-sac, is there nevertheless a conceptual connection between dignity and the very idea of law?

5. Fuller and the Dignity of Self-Application

Famously, in the book based on his 1963 Storrs Lectures, *The Morality of Law,* Lon Fuller developed an account of what he called the "inner morality of law": the formal principles of generality, prospectivity, clarity, stability, consistency, and so on whose observance is bound up with the basics of legal craftsmanship.[15]

Positivist legal philosophers (beginning with H. L. A. Hart) sometimes expressed bewilderment as to why Fuller called these internal principles a "morality."[16] I think this bewilderment is disingenuous, and I said so in an article published in the *New York University Law Review* in 2008.[17] Fuller called these internal principles a "morality" because he thought they had inherent moral significance. It was not just that he believed that observing them made it much more difficult to do injustice, though this he did believe.[18] It was also because he thought observing the principles he identified was itself a way of respecting human dignity. Fuller said this in *The Morality of Law:*

> To embark on the enterprise of subjecting human conduct to rules involves of necessity a commitment to the view that man is, or can become, a responsible agent, capable of understanding and following rules, and answerable for his defaults. Every departure from the principles of law's inner morality is an affront to man's dignity as a responsible agent. To judge his actions by unpublished or retrospective laws, or to order him to do an act that is impossible, is to convey to him your indifference to his powers of self-determination.[19]

These are not just platitudes. Fuller is referring here to a quite specific aspect of law—its general reliance on what Henry Hart and Albert Sacks in *The Legal Process* called "self-application"—that is, people applying officially promulgated norms to their own conduct, rather than waiting for coercive intervention from the state.[20] Self-application is an extraordinarily important feature of the way legal systems operate. They work by using, rather than short-circuiting, the agency of ordinary human individuals. They count on

How Law Protects Dignity   81

people's capacities for practical understanding, for self-control, for self-monitoring and modulation of their own behavior in relation to norms that they can grasp and understand.

All of this—as I said in Chapter 2—makes ruling by law quite different from, say, herding cows with a cattle prod or directing a flock of sheep with a dog. It is quite different, too, from eliciting a reflex recoil with a scream of command. The pervasive emphasis on self-application differentiates law sharply from systems of rule that work primarily by manipulating, terrorizing, or galvanizing behavior. It represents a decisive commitment by law to the dignity of the human individual. There is something of this recognition, too, in Joseph Raz's famous article from 1977 on the rule of law, where he connects the rule of law to law's action-guiding character and relates that, in turn, to the idea of dignity: "Observance of the rule of law is necessary if the law is to respect human dignity. Respecting human dignity entails treating humans as persons capable of planning and plotting their future. Thus, respecting people's dignity includes respecting their autonomy, their right to control their future."[21]

Other positivists have indicated a reluctance to pursue the implications of law's commitment to human dignity. Jules Coleman takes pains to argue that the action-guiding function of law is not necessarily expressive of a dignitarian value. He tries to separate the issues in this way:

Law just is the kind of thing that can realize some attractive ideals. That fact about law is not necessarily part of our concept of it. . . . If one is moved by the moral ideals of autonomy and dignity, then one can see how the elements of my analysis constitute a thing (law) that has the capacity for accommodating those ideals in ways that other forms of governance cannot. . . . But autonomy [and] dignity . . . do not enter at any point into the analysis that I offer. . . . These ideals are external to the concept of law; law happens to be the kind of thing that can serve them well. The capacity to do so is, in a metaphysically innocent sense, an inherent potential of law. This implies nothing about how the analysis of law must proceed.[22]

Coleman is surely right to emphasize that not every potential of a practice is part of its concept. Let me illustrate with some analogies. Religion has the potential to stir up murderous passions, yet this is not in any way definitive of religion. Other cases are more difficult. It is part of our concept of democracy to embody a principle of political equality. But is it also part of our concept of democracy to diminish violence by facilitating peaceful transitions from one regime to another? Joseph Schumpeter thought it was, but others have argued that this is a fact about democracy rather than a conceptual truth.[23] It is hard to see how one would decide this. It is certainly a notable fact about democracy. And equally, the commitment to dignity in the use of self-application is also a notable fact about law. I suppose the argument the other way is that the choice of this definitive legal method of governance (as opposed to some other way of governing) might be merely a matter of efficiency; it does not necessarily betoken a moral commitment to human dignity, however minimal. On its own, that may be a plausible position. But in the following sections, as we consider other ways in which law also protects dignity, we will be less patient with Coleman's view. We might suspect that it is motivated more by a doctrinaire desire to resist any connection between the concept of law and values like dignity than by any real insight into the distinctiveness of an action-guiding rather than a purely behavior-eliciting mode of social control.

One other point: it is tempting to say that law can guide conduct only if it is determinate—that is, only if it is cast in the form of clear rules. But it is remarkable that law often presents itself in the form of *standards,* such as the standard of reasonable care in tort law. Some theories of legal process suggest that law can be self-applying only if the indeterminacy of these standards is reduced through official elaboration.[24] But in many areas of life, law actually proceeds without such definitive elaboration. It evinces faith in individuals' abilities to think about and proceed with the application of standards without any assurance that any two applications to similar circumstances will yield exactly the same result.[25]

I believe that this feature of law also presupposes a commitment to human dignity. Law assumes that ordinary people are capable of applying norms to their own behavior, and it uses this as the pivot of their being governed. Ordinary people are capable of acting like officials—recognizing a norm, apprehending its bearing on their conduct, making a determination, and acting on that.

6. Procedure

A second way in which law respects the dignity of those who are governed is in the provision that it makes for trials or hearings in cases where an official determination is necessary. These are cases where self-application is not possible or desirable, or where there is dispute about the application of norms that requires official resolution.

A legal system is not just a set of general norms, officially recognized and applied to individual cases. We call a mode of governance "law" on account of the distinctive way in which official applications are conducted. Law is applied by courts, by which I mean institutions devoted to settling disputes about the application of norms and directives established in the name of the whole society to individual cases. And I mean institutions that do that through the medium of hearings, formal events that are tightly structured procedurally in order to enable an impartial tribunal to determine the rights and responsibilities of particular persons fairly and effectively after hearing evidence and argument from both sides.

It is remarkable how little there is about courts in the conceptual accounts of law presented in modern positivist jurisprudence. In *The Concept of Law*, H. L. A. Hart conceives of law in terms of the union of primary rules of conduct and secondary rules that govern the way in which the primary rules are made, changed, applied, and enforced. When he introduces the concept of secondary rules, he does talk of the emergence of "rules of adjudication" in the transition from a pre-legal to a legal society: he says these are "secondary rules empowering individuals to make authoritative determinations of the question of whether, on a particular occasion, a primary rule has been broken."[26] But that account defines the relevant institutions simply in terms of their output function—"the making of . . . authoritative determinations . . . of whether a primary rule has been broken." There is nothing on the distinctive process by which this function is performed. Outside the halls of academic legal positivism, I suspect most people would regard hearings and impartial proceedings, and the safeguards that go with them, as an essential rather than as a contingent feature of the institutional arrangements we call legal systems. It should certainly be treated as an essential rather than incidental aspect of the rule of law.[27]

Of course, we should not be essentialist about details. In general jurisprudence (the study of law as such), our concept of a court and a hearing is necessarily rather abstract. The nature of hearings and the procedures that are used differ between one legal system and another. It would be wrong, however, even in general jurisprudence, to abstract away from the elements of process, presentation, formality, impartiality, and argument. The basic idea is procedural: the operation of a court involves a way of proceeding which offers to those who are immediately concerned an opportunity to make submissions and present evidence (such evidence being presented in an orderly fashion according to strict rules of relevance oriented to the norms whose application is in question). The mode of presentation may vary, but the existence of such an opportunity does not. Once presented, the evidence is made available to be examined and confronted by the other party in open court. And each party has the opportunity to present arguments and submissions at the end of this process and answer those of the other party. In the course of all of this, both sides are treated respectfully and above all, listened to by a tribunal that is bound in some manner to attend to the evidence presented and respond to the submissions that are made in the reasons it eventually gives for its decision.[28]

These are abstract characteristics. But they are not arbitrary abstractions. They capture a deep and important sense associated foundationally with the idea of a legal system, that law is a mode of governing people that acknowledges that they have a view or perspective of their own to present on the application of the norm to their conduct and situation. Applying a norm to a human individual is not like deciding what to do about a rabid animal or a dilapidated house. It involves paying attention to a point of view and respecting the personality of the entity one is dealing with. As such, it embodies a crucial dignitarian idea: respecting the dignity of those to whom the norms are applied as beings capable of explaining themselves.

7. Legal Argument

Indeed, it is not just a matter of hearing both sides of the story. I think it is part of our concept of law that legal positions are sustained or defeated as a matter of argument—argument by counsel for each side and responsive argument (rather than just peremptory decision) at the level of the tribunal making a determination. This, I believe, contributes yet another strand to law's respect for human dignity. Let me explain.

Law presents itself to its subjects as something that one can make sense of. I do not just mean that one can make sense of each measure, as one might do on the basis of a statement of legislative purpose. I mean that a person can try and make sense of the "big picture," understanding how the regulation of one set of activities relates rationally to the regulation of another. Though individual pieces of legislation and particular precedents add to law in a piecemeal way, lawyers and judges characteristically try to see the law as a whole; they try to see some sort of coherence or system in it, integrating particular items into a structure that makes intellectual sense. This is the stuff of codification and restatements. But it is also a resource and an opportunity in ordinary litigation. It is open to people when they are confronted with law's particular demands to take advantage of this aspiration to systematicity in framing their own arguments, by inviting the tribunal to consider how the position a given party is putting forward fits generally into a certain conception of the logic and spirit of the law.

In this way, law respects the people who live under it, conceiving them as the bearers of reason and intelligence. The individuals whose lives law governs are treated by it as thinkers who can grasp and grapple with the rationale of that governance and relate it in complex but intelligible ways to their own view of the relation between their actions and purposes and the actions and purposes of the state. This, too, in its way, is a tribute to human dignity.

The price of this strand of dignitarian respect is undoubtedly a certain diminution in law's certainty. Occasionally, an argument will be made, by counsel or by a judge, to the effect that the impact of the law on a particular type of event or transaction should be treated as embodied in some proposition, even though that proposition has not previously been explicitly adopted in legislative form or explicitly articulated (until this moment) by a court. The claim may be that since the proposition can be inferred, argumentatively, from the mass of existing legal materials, it, too, must be accorded the authority of law. It is a characteristic feature of legal systems that they set up institutions—courts—which are required to listen and respond in detail to submissions along these lines. These are not just arguments about what the law ought to be, made, as it were, in a sort of lobbying mode. They are arguments of reason presenting competing arguments about what the law *is*. Inevitably, of course, the arguments are controversial: one party will say that such-and-such a proposition cannot be inferred from the law as it is; the other party will respond that it can be so inferred if only we credit the law with more coherence than people have tended to credit it with in the past. And so, the determination of whether such a proposition has legal authority may often be a matter of contestation.

Law, in other words, becomes a matter of argument. This may seem to be at odds with the first dignitarian strain we identified: respecting people enough to entrust them with frontline self-application of legal norms. How, it will be asked, can we maintain this mode of respect if law becomes contestable in the way I have outlined? As I said in my brief discussion of standards, the self-application idea does not rigidly presuppose that law has the form of determinate rules. The act of faith in the practical reason of ordinary people may be an act of faith in their thinking—for example, about what is reasonable and what is not—not just in their recognition of a rule and its mechanical application. And so, it may also be an act of faith not just in their ability to apply general moral predicates (such as "reasonable") to their actions, but also to think about and interpret the bearing of a whole array of norms and precedents to their conduct, rather than just the mechanical application of a single norm.

Courts, hearings, and arguments—those aspects of law are not optional extras; they are integral parts of how law works, and they are indispensable to the package of law's respect for human agency. To say that we should value aspects of governance that promote the clarity and determinacy of rules for the sake of individual freedom, but not the opportunities for argumentation that a free and self-possessed individual is likely to demand, is to slice in half, to truncate, what law and legality rest on: respect for the freedom and dignity of each person as an active intelligence.

8. Rank and Equality

Let me turn now in another direction for a different sort of link between dignity and our modern notion of law. In an article published in 2007, I argued that we should pay attention to the ancient connection between dignity and rank.[29]

In Roman usage, *dignitas* embodied the idea of the honor, the privileges, and the deference due to rank or office. And in English, this was the original meaning of dignity, as when the 1399 statute taking the crown away from Richard II stated: "Ye renounced and cessed of the State of Kyng, and of Lordeshipp and of all the Dignite and Wirsshipp that longed therto."[30] Some have suggested that this old connection between dignity and rank was superseded by an originally Stoic and then Jewish-Christian notion of the dignity of humanity as such.[31] I am not convinced. As I argued in "Dignity and Rank," I think that what happened was a generalization of high rank—a sort of leveling up—rather than the abandonment of one (hierarchical) notion and its replacement by another (egalitarian) one.[32]

The idea is that the modern notion of *human* dignity does not cut loose from the idea of rank; instead, it involves an upward equalization of rank, so that we now try to accord to every human being something of the dignity, rank, and expectation of respect that was formerly accorded to nobility. (I got this idea from Gregory Vlastos, and James Whitman has also pursued in his work the idea of "an extension of formerly high-status treatment to all sectors of the population.")[33] I believe this is true also of the status-concept that I have been trying to elaborate here in connection with the institutions, processes, and practices distinctive of law.

One can imagine—historically, of course, one can actually trace—systems of governance that involved a radical discrimination among different sorts of rank. High-ranking persons would be regarded as capable of participating fully in something like a legal system. For example, they would be trusted with the voluntary self-application of norms; their word and testimony would be taken seriously; and they would be entitled to the benefit of elaborate processes. If they were coerced, they would be dealt with under the auspices of a quite respectful mode of coercion quite different from, and much less brutal than, those applying to members of other strata of society. If they were executed, even, there were special methods of noble execution: beheading rather than hanging, for example. At the other extreme, there might be a caste or class of persons who were dealt with purely coercively by the authorities: there would be no question of trusting them or anything they said; they would appear in shackles if they appeared in a hearing at all; their evidence would be required to be taken under torture; and they would not be entitled to make decisions or arguments relating to their own defense nor to have their statements heard or taken seriously. They would not have the privilege of bringing suit in the courts, or if they were, it would have to be under someone else's protection; they were not, as we sometimes say, sui juris. Slave societies were like that, and many other societies in the past with which we are uncomfortably familiar evolved similar discriminating forms that distinguished between, if you like, the legal dignity of a noble, the legal dignity of a common man, the legal dignity of a woman, and the legal dignity of a slave, serf, or villein. I think it is part of our modern notion of law that all such gross status differences have been abandoned (though there are relics here and there). And the equalization has been an upward equalization, which is why I think it is a matter of dignity.

Consider this incident. In 1606 in London, a carriage carrying Isabel, Countess of Rutland, was attacked by sergeants-at-mace pursuant to a writ alleging a debt of £1,000:

The said serjeants in Cheapside, with many others, came to the countess in her coach, and shewed her their mace, and touching her body with it, said to her, we arrest you, madam, at the suit of the [creditor] and thereupon they compelled the coachman to carry the said countess to the compter in Wood Street, where she remained seven or eight days, till she paid the debt.[34]

The Star Chamber held that "the arrest of the countess by the serjeants-at-mace . . . is against law, and the said countess was falsely imprisoned" and "a severe sentence was given against [the creditor], the serjeants, and the others their confederates." The court quoted an ancient maxim to the effect that "law will have a difference between a lord or a lady, &c. and another common person," and it held that the person of one who is a countess by marriage or descent is not to be arrested for debt or trespass; for although in respect of her sex she cannot sit in Parliament, yet she is a peer of the realm, and shall be tried by her peers.[35] There are two reasons, the court went on, why her person should not be arrested in such cases—one in respect of her dignity, and the other in respect of the law's presumption "that she hath sufficient lands and tenements in which she may be distrained." In light of this presumption of noble wealth, the seizing of her body could not legally be justified as the seizure of a common debtor could be justified, in those days, to recover and secure his assets.

Today, we apply the first point to all debtors: no one's body is allowed to be seized; no one can be held or imprisoned for debt. We have evolved a more or less universal status—a more or less universal legal dignity—that entitles everyone to something like the treatment before law that was previously confined to high-status individuals.

True, we might still use the term "legal system" to describe the highly stratified society I have been imagining, with some members having legal dignity and being sui juris and others not. But it would be much in the way that we describe ancient Athens, nineteenth-century Britain, or apartheid South Africa as "democracies": they had sort of gotten hold of the idea of democracy—governance through the participation of the common people rather than oligarchic elites—but had failed to extend that to all the common people in the society, excluding large sections of the population such as women, slaves, nonwhites, and so on. They had a proto-democracy, not a true democracy. And in a similar way, I am inclined to say that the idea of law or of a legal system now embodies the assumption that everyone in a society ruled by law is treated as sui juris, as having full legal dignity in the sense that I have been discussing. A system that embodied radical differences of legal dignity might be a sort of proto-legal system, but we should no longer call it a true system of law.

9. Dignity and Representation

Obviously, the sense in which we all have equal access to the law, participate equally in its proceedings, and enjoy the benefits of its confidence is somewhat fictitious. Most ordinary people are not in a position of straightforward familiarity with law; most law is technical and forbidding and takes years of study to master. And, as Max Weber was famous for pointing out, this is getting worse, not better.[36] Moreover, law often still excludes and denigrates some of those it deals with, still discriminates in favor of the rich and powerful.

These are fair points. We have to come to terms with the normative rather than the purely descriptive character of equal legal dignity. Even if it is conceived as a response to the objective moral facts of inherent human dignity, still, *legal* status—equal legal dignity—has to be understood as a constructed human artifice, with all the fragility, bad faith, and ramshackle character of human constructions. Moreover, as I said at the beginning of this chapter, the artifice is a normative one, and like all norms, honored often in the breach. And even at its best, it has to deal with descriptive inequalities among people using a variety of practices and techniques to create something like a rough and artificial equality in standing before the law.

The primary technique we use is the artifice of legal representation. David Luban has developed a persuasive account along these lines, building on some philosophical insights of Alan Donagan.[37] Forgive me if I quote Professor Luban at length, but he makes exactly the points I want to make. He asks why litigants should have professional representatives:

> The answer that, over the years, has appealed to me the most rests on a principle stated by the late philosopher Alan Donagan: "[N]o matter how untrustworthy somebody may have proved to be in the past, one fails to respect his or her dignity as a human being if on any serious matter one refuses even provisionally to treat his or her testimony about it as being in good faith." An immediate corollary to this principle is that litigants get to tell their stories and argue their understandings

of the law. A procedural system that simply gagged a litigant and refused even to consider her version of the case would be, in effect, treating her story as if it did not exist, and treating her point of view as if it were literally beneath contempt. Once we accept that human dignity requires litigants to be heard, the justification of the advocate becomes clear. People may be poor public speakers. They may be inarticulate, unlettered, mentally disorganized, or just plain stupid. They may know nothing of the law, and so be unable to argue its interpretation. Knowing no law, they may omit the very facts that make their case, or focus on pieces of the story that are irrelevant or prejudicial. They may be unable to utilize basic procedural rights such as objecting to their adversary's leading questions. Their voices may be nails on a chalkboard or too mumbled to understand. They may speak a dialect, or for that matter know no English. None of this should matter. Human dignity does not depend on whether one is stupid or smooth. Hence the need for the advocate. Just as a non-English speaker must be provided an interpreter, the legally mute should have—in the very finest sense of the term—a mouthpiece. Thus, Donagan's argument connects the right to counsel with human dignity in two steps: first, that human dignity requires litigants to be heard, and second, that without a lawyer they cannot be heard.[38]

The account that I gave in sections 6 to 8 might have seemed rather rosy and utopian, especially the account of process and argumentation. It becomes a little less so when we realize that law does not just throw us back on our own natural resources in this regard. It sets out to create the equal legal dignity that it is committed to.

10. Dignified Coercion

Some will be tempted to complain that I am making law seem too "nice," and that all this emphasis on dignity obscures the ultimately power-ridden, violent, and coercive character of law.[39] Law kills people, ruins them, beats them up, spoils their reputation, locks them up and throws away the key. And these are not aberrations; this is what law characteristically does. Where, it might be asked, is the dignity in that?

In *The Morality of Law,* Lon Fuller seemed to suggest that we have to choose between definitions of law that emphasize coercion and definitions of law that emphasize the sort of dignitary considerations I have been explaining. I think this is a mistake. It is because law is coercive, because its currency is ultimately life and death, prosperity and ruin, freedom and imprisonment, that its inherent commitment to dignity is so momentous. Fuller actually recognizes this when he observes that the "branch of law most closely identified with force is also that which we associate most closely with formality, ritual, and solemn due process."[40] Law is a mode of governance, and governance is the exercise of power. But that power should be channeled through *these* processes, through forms and institutions like these, even when that makes the exercise of power more difficult or requires it occasionally to retire from the field defeated, is exactly what is exciting about rule by law.[41]

That is a wholesale answer to the objection. We might also give some retail responses. The coercive character of law manifests itself in a number of ways: (1) law presents its norms as categorical and non-negotiable demands; (2) law is committed, in extremis, to doing what it takes to see that its orders are obeyed and its demands complied with; (3) law imposes punishment; and (4) law has and exercises the power to hold persons against their will and sometimes uses force to tightly control their behavior. These four points are undeniable. But in each case, there is a strong dignitarian strand in the *manner* in which law exercises its power.

(1) I have already mentioned (in section 5) the importance of self-application so far as the administration of law's demands is concerned. Law looks wherever possible to voluntary compliance, which of course is not the same as saying we are free and never coerced, but which does leave room for the distinctively human trait of monitoring and applying norms to one's own behavior. This is not a trick; it involves a genuinely respectful mode of coercion, even though the coercive element is not dispelled.

(2) Max Weber is famous for observing that although "the use of physical force is neither the sole, nor even the most usual, method of administration," still, "the threat of force, and in the case of need its actual use, is the method which is specific to political organizations and is always the last resort when others have failed."[42] But it would be wrong to infer from this that law uses any means necessary to get its way. The use of torture, for example, is now banned by all legal systems. Elsewhere, I have argued that modern law observes this ban as emblematic of its commitment to a more general nonbrutality principle:

> Law is not brutal in its operation; law is not savage; law does not rule
> through abject fear and terror, or by breaking the will of those whom
> it confronts. If law is forceful or coercive, it gets its way by methods
> which respect rather than mutilate the dignity and agency of those who
> are its subjects.[43]

People may fear and be deterred by legal sanctions; they may on occasion
be literally forced against their will by legal means or by legally empowered
officials to do things or go places they would not otherwise do or go to. But
even when this happens, they are not herded like cattle or broken like horses
or beaten like dumb animals. Instead, there is to be an enduring connection
between the spirit of law and respect for human dignity—respect for human
dignity even in extremis, even in situations where law is at its most forceful
and its subjects at their most vulnerable.

No one denies that law has to be forceful. But forcefulness can take many
forms, and not all of it involves, for example, the savage breaking of the
human will, or a regression of the subject into an infantile state where the
elementary demands of the body supplant almost all adult thought, which
is the aim of torture. The force of ordinary legal sanctions and incentives does
not work like that, nor does the literal force of physical control and confinement. For example, when a defendant charged with a serious offense is
brought into a courtroom, he is brought in whether he likes it or not, and
when he is punished, he is subject to penalties that are definitely unwelcome
and that he would avoid if he could; in these instances, there is no doubt
that he is subject to force, that he is coerced. But in these cases, force and
coercion do not work by reducing him to a quivering mass of "bestial des-
perate terror," which is the aim of every torturer.[44] If something cannot be
done without torture, law generally accepts that it cannot be done at all.

(3) Law punishes, but again, there is a sense that we work with modes of
punishment that do not destroy the dignity of those to whom it is being administered. Some of this is the work of the external dignitary provisions I
noted at the beginning of this chapter. Provisions like ICCPR Article 7 and
ECHR Article 3 impose a requirement that any punishment inflicted should
be bearable—should be something that a person can endure without abandoning his elementary human functioning. One ought to be able to do one's
time, take one's licks, while remaining upright and self-possessed. Even
going to one's own execution is something that a human can do, and to the
extent that these provisions affect the death penalty, there is an implicit re-

quirement that it be administered in a way that enables the persons to whom it is applied to function as human beings up until the point at which their lives are extinguished.

(4) Even in circumstances where behavior is very tightly controlled by law (e.g., the behavior of a person in custody), there is an assumption that people will stand upright and move in response to commands rather than being dragged as though they were incapable of self-locomotion. And the commands will be given rather than screamed at them, Nazi-style. These may seem trivial matters. I have hard-ass colleagues who say that if someone is about to be killed, who cares how he gets from his cell to the execution chamber? If someone is under tight custodial control, who cares whether he is dragged into and out of a courtroom or allowed to walk in under his steam? Who cares about the tone of voice in which coercive commands are issued? They say these are just matters of sentiment. Once we have abandoned negative freedom, all the rest is detail. I disagree. For one thing, the individuals concerned do seem to care greatly about these things, however dismissive legal scholars may be. Also, we know from the case law on degradation that things sometimes do come down to details like this, and that in the extreme situation of custody such details loom large for human dignity. Dignity has long had a connection with something like physical bearing: standing upright suggests a sort of moral orthopedics.[45] We have an idea, too, that *in*dignity on these "trivial" matters may presage much more substantial affronts. Is it an accident that at the beginning of the war on terror, Guantánamo Bay detainees did not walk to their interrogations but instead were carried to and fro in wheelbarrows like scarecrows? Those who take what I am calling the "hard-ass line" on custodial control often also take the hard-ass line on abusive interrogation.

11. Aspiration and Reality

The point just mentioned reminds us that various systems of power that call themselves legal systems fall often short of this respect in one way or another. The discipline of dignity is a normative discipline, and as such, it is a costly and demanding discipline. It presents itself on the one hand as an aspiration, and on the other hand as a reproach to our shortcomings— shortcomings that sometimes come close to a betrayal of the whole idea. Add to that the fact that any actually existing legal system has to cope with the burden of its own history, which may not always have been a history of respect for human dignity, and we can see how complicated and controversial the characterization I have given in this chapter might become.

The United States illustrates a number of these points. It is burdened by a history of slavery and racism, which particularly affects the law; it is notable, for example, that the Thirteenth Amendment that abolished slavery did not do so unconditionally, but made an exception for the treatment of prisoners.[46] Critics have observed that in regard to the dignitarian aspect of its treatment of prisoners, the United States remains an outlier compared to, say, Western European systems of penal law.[47] And so, too, with some of the other aspects I have mentioned. Defendants are sometimes kept silent and passive in US courtrooms by the use of technology that enables the judge to subject them to electric shocks if they misbehave.[48] Reports of prisoners being "herded" with cattle prods emerge from time to time.[49] Conditions in our prison are de facto terrorizing and well known to be so, even if they are not officially approved, and we know that prosecutors (who pride themselves on their righteousness) feel free to make use of defendants' dread of this brutalization as a tactic in plea bargaining. Some would say, too, that the use of the death penalty represents a residuum of savagery in our system that shows the limits of US adherence to the principles that I have been talking about—though, as indicated, I think everything depends on the way it is administered. In recent years, too, we have seen the United States tempted away from dignitarian ideals in a number of important regards—in its attempt to establish a form of legally unreviewable detention at Guantánamo Bay, for example, and in its recent use of torture. Other examples, and examples from other countries (e.g., France, the United Kingdom, Russia, Israel) could be multiplied. All have fallen short of the characterization given in this chapter.

A legal system is a normative order, both explicitly and implicitly. Explicitly, it commits itself to certain norms, to the rules and standards that it says publicly it will uphold and enforce. Some of these it actually upholds and enforces, but for others, in certain regards, it fails to do so: the law says that the state should pay a pension or should pay compensation to Smith, but Smith does not receive it. The explicit content of the legal system provides us with a pretty straightforward basis for saying on these occasions that the legal system has fallen short of its own standards.

Less straightforward is the case where a normative commitment is embodied implicitly in the institutions or traditions of a system of governance. But I believe a very similar logic obtains. The commitment to dignity that I think is evinced in our legal practices and institutions may be thought of as immanently present, even though we sometimes fall short of it. Our practices sometimes convey a sort of promise.[50] And, as in ordinary moral life, it would be mistake to think that the only way to spot a real promise is to see what undertakings are actually carried out. Law may credibly promise a respect for dignity and yet fall short of that in various respects. Institutions can be imbued in their structures, practices, and procedures with values and principles that they sometimes fall short of. In these cases, it is fatuous to present oneself as a simple cynic about their commitments or to neglect the power of imminent critique as the basis of a reproach for their shortcomings.

Of course, the interesting thing, now, about law's commitment to dignity is that the promise is embodied institutionally in both the ways we have been describing. It is there, internally or inherently, in the tissue of our practice and institutions, but it is also present in rules and standards that we have explicitly committed ourselves to (like the Geneva Conventions or Article 7 of the ICCPR or, in Europe, Article 3 of the ECHR). The two sorts of commitment reinforce each other. This is not unusual in regard to legal ideals. Think of an analogy: Article I, Section 9 of theUS Constitution states that "no Bill of Attainder or ex post facto Law shall be passed," but many people would say that this is also a definitive feature of the rule of law as such. We didn't need the provision of positive constitutional law to know that retroactive laws were an abomination; we knew that anyway. Still, the combination of an explicit standard and an implicit principle represent an abundance of riches. And just as it would be quite wrong to infer from the fact that Article I, Section 9 might have been different that law is only contingently committed to prospectivity, so it would be quite wrong to infer from the fact that the ICCPR or Geneva Conventions might have been different that law is only contingently committed to the protection of dignity. There is an implicit commitment to dignity in the tissues and sinews of law—in the character of its normativity and in its procedures—and we do well not to sell this short by pretending that dignity is a take-it-or-leave-it kind of value.

4

Self-Application

1. Introduction

Legal norms, we say, are applied by officials to individual cases—by inspectors and police officers, ultimately by judges. But usually, and long before any officials get involved, individuals have the task of applying norms to themselves. Our law largely uses what Henry Hart and Albert Sacks call "the technique of self-applying regulation." (They discuss this in their "Legal Process" materials, set out and circulated in the 1950s but published formally only in 1994.)[1] Indeed, self-application in this sense is all that is necessary in the overwhelming majority of cases, and to a very large extent, it is all that is possible.

A norm is formulated, enacted, and publicized. Individuals take note of what it says (or their legal advisers draw it to their attention). They note the conditions of its application and the consequences that are supposed to follow when those conditions obtain. And they apply the norm to their own behavior as appropriate. In a few instances, officials (or sometimes bystanders or competitors or others affected by the behavior in question) might decide to challenge an individual's self-application of the norm. That is when the matter might come before a court; that is when a judge might have to decide on an authoritative application and apply sanctions to failures of individual application or to misapplications by individuals. In most cases, however, there is no challenge, no second-guessing, no need for authoritative intervention. Each individual applies the law to his or her own situation, and that is that.

In this chapter I would like to consider the process of self-application in more detail, specifically its place in our jurisprudence and its implications for legal theory. I particularly want to consider the self-application of what we call standards as opposed to rules—avowedly indeterminate directives, as they are sometimes called (150). I would also like to discuss whether the use of the technique of self-applying regulation reflects any sort of strong valuation of individual autonomy or dignity. These issues will be addressed toward the end of the chapter, in section 7 for the self-application of standards and section 8 for the questions about liberty and respect. However, a large part of what follows between now and then will be devoted to matters of definition and analytic exploration.

2. Begin with a Traffic Example

Let's begin with a couple of easy examples, taken from the traffic laws in the state where I reside (New York):

> Section 1180(b) . . . No person shall drive a vehicle at a speed in excess of fifty-five miles per hour.
> Section 1129(a) The driver of a motor vehicle shall not follow another vehicle more closely than is reasonable and prudent, having due regard for the speed of such vehicles and the traffic upon and the condition of the highway.

Road traffic could not move safely in New York State unless drivers were able routinely to apply norms like these to their own conduct—and apply them continually—without any official intervention.

Drivers need to know roughly how fast they are traveling so they can comply with the first of these norms; they look at instruments that monitor their speed and they can moderate it when it creeps above 55 mph. In some areas, they are permitted to drive faster. On parts of the New York State Thruway, for example, they can drive at 65 mph. In urban areas, they must drive more slowly than the standard speed limit given in Section 1180(b). These variations are posted, and, again, citizens are expected to apply these changing limits to their own driving without official intervention.

The second norm I quoted—Section 1129(a), concerning following distances—is more complicated than the speed limit. Drivers need to be able to make judgments about prudent and reasonable following distances in order to comply with Section 1129(a), and they have to monitor and moderate their own driving on the basis of these judgments in relation to the vehicles around them. The lawmaker has identified a salient type of circumstance (traffic ahead of the driver moving in the same direction) and has indicated that some adjustment of behavior may be appropriate when that circumstance obtains. The law that has been made—Section 1129(a)—purports to focus each driver's attention in these circumstances on considerations of reasonableness and prudence so far as following distance is concerned, having particular regard to the factors mentioned at the end of the regulation.

Officially applied sanctions are of course not out of the question for either provision. In both cases, the lawmaker has indicated by penal provisions attached to these regulations that drivers need to take seriously this whole business of speed and following distances. But mostly, drivers have to do it all for themselves, because there are nowhere near enough state troopers to patrol the speed of every vehicle or to control every situation in which one vehicle is following another, indicating to each driver what a reasonable following distance would be. Drivers are occasionally pulled over by the police for speeding or for following too closely. And these challenges no doubt have some deterrent effect. But the number of such incidents of official intervention is many orders of magnitude fewer than the number of situations in which application of these norms is called for. People mostly apply the law to themselves; regulations like the ones I have mentioned are mostly self-applying. Traffic law is an exemplar of the technique of self-applying regulation.

3. Disambiguation

Before going any further, I have to hold things up with some disambiguation. It is important to distinguish Hart and Sacks's idea of self-application from a couple of different ideas that are sometimes conveyed using the very same phrase.

(a) Rules That Apply Themselves

"Self-applying" is a term sometimes used to describe the possibility that norms might apply themselves to situations without the need of any human intervention. Those who use the term in this way do it in order to mock and disparage that possibility, which they associate with formalism or other discredited versions of traditional jurisprudence. For example, Margaret Radin says this: "In the traditional conception of the nature of rules, a rule is self-applying to the set of particulars said to fall under it; its application is thought to be analytic."[2] It is not at all clear what this is supposed to mean—that the rule lights up in the presence of the things it applies to?—but whatever it is, Professor Radin is against it. She thinks that the failure of self-application in this sense undermines the rule of law: "The point of 'the rule of law, not of individuals' is that the rules are supposed to rule. The easiest (most 'natural') way to achieve that . . . is to assume that rules apply to particular cases in an analytical or self-applying way."[3] But she does not think this is possible. Even the best-drafted rule cannot apply itself. If our belief in the rule of law is to be credible, says Radin, we have to accept a greater role for humans in the application of rules than this.

What distinguishes the idea of self-application that is under attack in this article by Radin from the idea that I want to consider is the reference of the term "self." In the usage Radin is discussing, the term "self" refers to the rule—the rule applies itself (whatever that means). In the Hart and Sacks idea, by contrast, the term "self" refers to the person who is the subject of the rule. The rule is directed at the conduct of a person (or class of persons) and such person applies it to their own situation. This is what is envisaged in the examples I gave from the traffic code: the speed limit doesn't apply itself in Radin's sense; but the drivers to whom it is addressed are supposed to apply it to themselves—that is, to their own driving—without any official guidance.

It is surprising to me how common the Radin use of "self-applying" is and how strident legal theorists think they have to be in insisting that it is a complete nonstarter. For example, in some work on judging, Kenneth Karst deems it necessary to remind us that "the impartiality we can fairly demand is not devotion to some self-applying principle that eliminates judgment from judging."[4] Others tell us that "rules are not self-applying but are wielded by people acting as decision makers," that "laws are not self-applying, and there will always be close, uncertain cases," that "norms are not always self-applying; they often underdetermine the outcome of specific disputes and therefore sometimes must be shaped in the course of their application," and that "the text of the Constitution is neither self-applying nor self-interpreting."[5] Me, I can't imagine anyone denying any of this, which makes the triumphalist tone in which such statements are put forward in the critical legal studies (CLS) tradition slightly odd. There is nothing wrong with this use of the term "self-application." CLS scholars may use the phrase to make fun of traditional jurisprudence if they like. But it is a different idea from the one that I want to consider in this article.[6]

I find it necessary to repeat all this because I wager that two out of three of my readers thought immediately of this other idea of self-application—and what was wrong with it—when I first mentioned the term. But the fatuous impossibility of self-applying law in Radin's sense or that of the other authors I mentioned in the last paragraph has no bearing at all on the discussion I am undertaking in this paper. In particular, the possibility that individuals might self-apply legal norms (i.e., apply them to their own situation) should not be thrown in doubt by the fact that the norms are not capable of applying themselves. Indeed, self-application in the sense I am discussing is *necessarily* a counterexample to the silly idea that rules might apply themselves, since my use explicitly refers to human involvement in the application—namely, involvement by the very person who is the subject of the norm.[7] At the same time, one of the purposes of this chapter is to insist that norms that are *obviously* not self-applying in the Radin sense— standards like Section 1129(a) that use evaluative terms like "reasonable," "prudent," and "due regard"—are as capable of successful self-application in the Hart and Sacks sense as a numerical speed limit like Section 1180(b).

(b) Private Ordering

Another idea sometimes confused with self-application in Hart and Sacks's sense is the idea of *private ordering*—individuals agreeing among themselves (for example, in a contract) on the norms that will govern their conduct in some area of interaction. This confusion is partly explained by the fact that private ordering is also an important theme in Hart and Sacks's *Legal Process* materials (6–9, 183ff.). Generally speaking, a contract is a private ordering; so is a will. But a private ordering is not necessarily self-applying. Most contractual provisions are. However, wills generally are not: probate has to be sought, and it is individually administered by officials. Also. a great many regulatory schemes are self-applying in the Hart and Sacks sense, even though they do not involve private ordering at all. Neil Duxbury unhelpfully runs the two ideas together. He writes:

> One of the primary institutional distinctions to be highlighted, according to Hart and Sacks, is that which exists between public and private government.... The state may, for example, adopt a "hands-off"

strategy so that the resolution of a particular problem is left to the process of private ordering. Indeed, private ordering, the use of "self-applying regulation" by private individuals in the government of their own activities, is the principal method of social control in a democratic society.[8]

This is just confused. Professor Duxbury is right that the idea of private ordering is very important in Hart and Sacks's scheme of things. And so, as we will see, is self-applying regulation. But they are quite different phenomena.

Many cases involving self-regulation are hybrid cases of public and private ordering: public regulations provide a framework within which private contracting operates, and they determine some of the terms of private agreements. Hart and Sacks's famous case of the spoiled cantaloupes is an example (10–67). A shipment of cantaloupes was consigned to a fruit wholesaler (Joseph Martinelli & Co.), but the wholesaler refused to accept the shipment (abandoning it, in effect, to the railroad) because the cantaloupes were spoiled. The shipper of the cantaloupes sued for the agreed price (less what the railroad was able to raise on the fruit). It succeeded. A federal appeals court held that, given the terms of the contract as governed by the relevant regulations, Martinelli ought to have accepted the shipment, sold it for what it could raise, and then sued the shipper for breach of contract if that could be shown.[9] Unfortunately, Martinelli had not read the situation that way: its view was that it was entitled to reject the shipment, notwithstanding the "rolling acceptance final" term in its contract, once it became clear that the cantaloupes were not as described at the time of shipment.

The "self-application" of law is one of many things this case is used to illustrate in the Hart and Sacks *Legal Process* materials. The relevant regulations (determining the meaning of contractual terms in this business) envisaged that the consignee would have to make an immediate decision about accepting or rejecting the cantaloupes when they arrived—by itself, without recourse to a court or an official determination. But Martinelli misread the relevant regulations and misapplied them to its case. So this is a case of failed self-application: "The regulation which told Martinelli that it had no right of rejection on a 'rolling acceptance final' purchase was self-applying—that is, Martinelli could have complied with it without the necessity of any official intervention" (121). It is conceivable that the whole process could have been conducted by the parties acting pursuant to the relevant regulations and contractual terms: Martinelli would accept the fruit, noting its condition; it would then try to sell the fruit for what it could raise; it would complain to the shipper; the shipper would accept the complaint; the shipper would pay damages or accept less than the agreed price. The parties need never go near a court. But in the scenario that Hart and Sacks describe, the process fell apart at the first step because Martinelli failed to apply the correct legal norm to the choice that it faced when confronted with the spoiled cargo. People sometimes make mistakes in self-application, and officials or counterparties or others who are affected will call them on it.

4. Individually Administered Regulation

Most law is addressed to private persons or businesses, and they are supposed to go ahead and apply it correctly and dispositively to their own actions or situations (120). "Under such a scheme of control," say Hart and Sacks, "only . . . trouble cases come before officials, and these only after the event" (121).

But not all regulatory arrangements operate in this way. Some regulatory arrangements are "individually administered." The law of divorce is an example. To change one's status from married to divorced, "an official determination—an individualized settlement of the matter [by officials or by a court]—is necessary." One cannot, as a married person, say to oneself, "Such and such has happened, and that man or that woman is no longer my spouse" (120–21).[10] In other areas of law, too—bankruptcy, for example— an official determination is also required, though of course there are norms that the subject must comply with himself before there is any question of an official declaration of bankruptcy. And that illustrates an interesting point: as Hart and Sacks put it, "Almost every scheme of individualized regulation includes some self-applying elements" (847). Indeed, in some areas of law, the individualized administration of regulations is nominal only. In the United States, tax authorities "accept" your income tax return. A few are checked—there are algorithms for checking—and many fewer still are singled out for audit. In most cases, the acceptance of tax returns is automatic. Also, although officially, tax *refunds* are individually administered, again, the refund process is mostly automatic once returns are filed.

Is it possible to say anything at a general level about what distinguishes cases where individualized administration is necessary or desirable—anything that will help us understand the distinctive nature of self-application? Toward the end of their materials, Hart and Sacks say this: "However great the advantages of the technique of self-applying regulation when it can be made to work successfully, it has severe limitations. It is an inherently loose form of control and looseness on occasion may be a fault rather than a virtue" (846). They mention medical competence as an example:

> If society is really in earnest about having its doctors competent, for example, it is hardly likely to trust to a general definition of competence, coupled with a prohibition against practicing medicine unless you can satisfy it, to be applied by the would-be doctors themselves, subject only to an after-check. In this and many other situations, what is felt to be needed is an individualized, case-by-case application by officials. (846)

One might say that licensing laws of all kinds are individually administered. That is the very nature of licensing. The state maintains an interest in satisfying itself that an individual taking on a dangerous or socially important function is competent or in other respects a fit and proper person for the function.

Individually administered regulation is generally less efficient administratively than self-applying regulation, but it may be thought superior nonetheless when officials have better access to the relevant facts, or when socially significant discretion has to be exercised (847). It may also be important where the application of the regulation in question is necessary to protect particularly vulnerable interests; that's why the law of adoption, for example, is individually administered rather than self-applied. Or it may be important whenever there is a great temptation to elevate self-interest too far above the interests of others. (Is this why the law of bankruptcy is self-administered? And probate?) Conversely, self-application is superior (when it is) not just for reasons of efficiency, but because individualized application would often involve an unacceptable level of intrusion into the conduct of private life.[11]

I should emphasize again that the technique of self-applying regulation does not preclude individualized application by officials—in problem cases, for example. This can lead to a difficulty. Norms intended for self-application have to be taken on board by the individuals to whose conduct they apply. But regulations formulated in a way that is ideal for this purpose may not be regulations whose formulation is ideal for the work of officials. There may therefore be some discrepancy between the ideal content of conduct rules and (official) decision rules in regard to the same subject matter.[12] And this dissonance may expand, the more courts are involved in applying the rules. The operation of stare decisis may yield a body of law that conceals the norm originally intended for self-application, for in the nature of things, stare decisis is often oriented to the elaboration of decision rules for courts rather than conduct rules. It is one of the virtues of Hart and Sacks's analysis that they emphasize the importance of courts' focusing on the exigencies of future self-application by citizens as they consider the norms that come before them.[13]

However, we should not infer from this that there is no parallel difficulty with regulations that are individually administered from the outset. Even if there is no question of formally specifying conduct rules, subjects still are entitled to know the norms that will be applied to their conduct, so that they can organize their lives accordingly. (People need to know what the grounds of divorce are, even if divorce law is individually administered.)

5. Officials and Organizations as Initial Addressees

Much of what has been said so far about self-application refers to individuals—ordinary people whose conduct is subject to legal norms.[14] However, we should not neglect self-application by organizations like firms and businesses. Here, we have to deal with routinization and institutionalization. Organizations may well institutionalize the application of the norms that apply to their conduct, with offices inside the organization (like human resources offices or compliance offices) set up specifically to monitor the conditions under which legal norms are supposed to apply to activities of the kind that the organization typically performs, and to make provision for, to organize, and to check their application.

What about self-application by officials of the state? It is tempting to say that this takes us into the realm of decision rules rather than conduct rules. I guess decision rules just are conduct rules for officials. And the second-guessing of the self-application of conduct rules by ordinary citizens and businesses requires the self-application of decision rules by the relevant officials. (And the self-application of these decision rules may be checked by still other officials, and so on.)

Some legal norms are directly and primarily addressed to officials. Constitutional norms are an example. Consider:

Congress shall make no law respecting an establishment of religion, or prohibiting the free exercise thereof.

Excessive bail shall not be required, nor excessive fines imposed, nor cruel and unusual punishments inflicted.

The former provision is directed in the first instance to a legislature (the federal legislature); the latter to officials of all sorts involved in the criminal justice system, including legislators. We expect the relevant officials (legislators and others) to self-apply these regulations to their own policy and legislative decisions.[15] As in cases of private conduct, the self-application of such norms can be checked and second-guessed by courts. Only, it is usually private citizens or civil society groups, rather than officials, who complain about such problematic self-applications and bring them to the attention of the courts.

For some reason, Hart and Sacks seem uninterested in cases of this kind. In *The Legal Process,* they say that "the term self-applying regulation is confined to regulatory arrangements which are initially addressed to *private persons*" (120–21; original emphasis). I don't think this is a sensible restriction on the meaning of the term. I see no reason for it, except to avoid confusion with the cases alluded to in the second paragraph of this section. Other scholars have not followed Hart and Sacks in this regard. Henry Monaghan talks cheerfully about the self-application of criminal justice norms by law enforcement officials. He writes: "In both *Miranda* and the lineup cases, the Court was exercising, in a constitutional context, a traditional judicial function—protecting individual rights threatened in circumstances not foreseen by statute by providing guidance to primary actors (law enforcement personnel in these cases) in terms sufficiently specific to allow 'self-applying regulation.'"[16] Monaghan makes explicit reference in a footnote to the passages by Hart and Sacks that we have discussed, and he indicates the importance of focusing, for this sphere, both on the potential benefits and the challenges that the technique of self-applying regulation requires. (For example, he observes that "the official must be aware of what is required of him in sufficiently concrete terms that he may be able to comply," and he points out that "the generalized rules of interpretation we generally associate with constitutional construction . . . will frequently be inadequate for such a task.")[17]

I think it is a pity that Hart and Sacks did not pursue their idea of self-applying regulation into this area of the legal control of the state and its officials.

6. Microjurisprudence

In their *Legal Process* materials, Henry Hart and Albert Sacks say that "over-whelmingly the greater part of the general body of the law is self-applying, including almost the whole of the law of contracts, torts, property, crimes, and the like" (121). They maintain that this is "of enormous significance alike in the theory and in the practice of social orderings."

Enormous significance in theory—so is this something philosophers of law should be writing about? They mostly haven't. My view is that they should. Though it seems banal, the idea of self-application raises a number of interesting issues. So let's focus on its significance for jurisprudence. I should warn the reader that this is not going to be exciting jurisprudence; it doesn't concern the intersection of law and justice or Robert Cover and violence or anything like that (though there will be some swirly stuff at the very end). It is not arterial legal theory; it is about the way we conceive of a legal system's capillaries.[18] We might call it "microjurisprudence"—the analytic study of the details of the way in which laws actually operate. (Over the years, microjurisprudence has included such things as Jeremy Bentham's definition of command, Oliver Wendell Holmes's "bad man" theory of the law, H. L. A. Hart's account of the internal aspect of rules, Joseph Raz's analysis of norms and reasons, and Scott Shapiro's conception of law in terms of planning.)[19]

Self-application seems to be a feature of normative systems generally. It applies to a great deal of religious law.[20] In the absence of any moral officialdom, it applies comprehensively to morality.[21] As for the rules of games, penalties and scores are mostly administered by officials on an individualized basis, as are balls and strikes in baseball. But sometimes in cricket, a batsman is criticized for not "walking" spontaneously when it is clear that he is out (caught or leg before wicket) and standing his ground instead to await the umpire's determination. And some sports are played without officials at all.[22] For a clear case of sporting self-application, consider this incident at the 2016 US Open golf tournament, as reported in the *New York Times:*

> Shane Lowry placed the putter behind his golf ball on the 16th green Saturday to line up a long birdie putt. He then saw the ball move ever so slightly backward. No one else saw the ball change positions. But Lowry knew it was a rules violation, and he acted immediately. He

called a penalty on himself even though he knew that lost stroke could topple him from the upper echelon of the leaderboard in the second round at the 116th United States Open. . . . Lowry, however, never wavered on his decision and never considered doing anything else. "I had to penalize myself," he said.[23]

Rule 18-2 provides that "a player, partner or caddy who moves or causes his ball to move while at rest generally incurs a one-stroke penalty." Shane Lowry became aware that he had moved his ball indiscernibly while addressing it for a putt. Without the need for any official intervention, he applied Rule 18-2 and added a stroke to his score. Of course, the tournament officials had to register the extra stroke that Lowry assessed on himself, but the point is that the matter was settled by the golfer applying the rule to his own conduct. The rule has a roughly "if . . . then . . ." form. He determined that the "if" clause (the condition) was satisfied, and so he applied the "then" clause to his score.

Let me turn back to law now, and to some issues in microjurisprudence posed by the technique of self-applying regulation.

(a) Self-Application and Compliance

Does the idea of self-application comprehend anything more than the simple expectation of *compliance*? Law lays down certain requirements for our conduct, and we are expected to abide by those requirements. That's all that seems to be going on in our initial speed-limit example. We are told to drive no faster than 55 mph, and we comply with that instruction. And the same is true in criminal law. We are told not to kill one another, and we comply with that instruction too, settling our disputes in nonhomicidal ways. Is this all that self-application amounts to?

Well, yes and no. Simple compliance can be a response to a particularized command. One hears the drill sergeant's cry of "Attention!" and one stands to attention. This does not seem to be what Hart and Sacks have in mind. I suppose one could call the parade-ground command a limit case of the self-application of law. The most fundamental characteristic of self-application is the law's reliance on individual agency, and even a reflex response to a command is different from being literally forced into a certain movement.

My reason for hesitation is not that laws cannot be particular. Certainly, their paradigm is generality. But as Joseph Raz points out, the rule-of-law principle of generality requires not that there be no particular legal commands but that "the making of particular laws should be guided by open and relatively stable general rules."[24] Still, the most interesting cases of self-application do involve open and relatively stable general rules, which have the character of standing orders, and which subjects are expected to either internalize in advance or otherwise have access to, so that they can be applied in the appropriate circumstances.

Equally, talk of self-application can make sense with regard to a general norm that is simple and categorical: "Thou shalt not kill." One self-applies this prohibition to one's own conduct. But again, the theoretically interesting cases are conditional norms of the form "In circumstances C, action A is required." The distinctive thing about norms of this kind is that one does not wait for *an official* to determine that one is in circumstance C so that now action A is to be performed; *one judges for oneself* that one is in circumstance C, and one goes ahead with action A on that basis. It is still ultimately a matter of compliance, but it is also a matter of self-applied judgment as to when compliance is required. That is, as I say, *interesting* because of the law's investment in the subject's judgment as well as in her agency.

I emphasize this because, for my money, the most interesting cases of self-application are those that involve conditional standards as opposed to conditional rules. New York State traffic law requires headlights to be used whenever windscreen wipers are being used to clear rain, sleet, or snow.[25] That is a conditional rule, and its application by a driver is fairly straightforward: when she turns on one function of the automobile, she must turn on another. A conditional standard would be a norm requiring headlight use whenever the driver's view is otherwise not reasonably clear. Those are the most interesting cases of all, and in section 7 I shall argue against the common view that they are, by virtue of their vagueness, problematic rather than paradigmatic cases of self-applying regulation.

As I have said, self-application is envisaged as a mode of compliance without the benefit of specific directions from officials. Officials may be nowhere to be seen: day after day, I drive the New York State road system without coming across a police officer. Yet, in all my driving activity, I am constantly self-applying traffic norms—and not just rules (like the speed limit) that apply across the board, but also norms that only come into force, as it were, under certain conditions and whose conditions and requirements call for interpretation by the norm subject. It is for me (the driver) to identify those conditions, and it is for me to make a judgment, guided by the terms of the norm, about the specific line of action that it requires. All in an official vacuum. *That* is what's interesting about self-application.

The other reason for distinguishing between self-application and mere compliance is that it is possible to comply with a legal norm without having any explicit thought about the norm. Compliance is just a matter of behavior corresponding to the content of a norm. Self-application, by contrast, involves some sort of reference to the relevant norm in one's decision-making. Mostly, the law is satisfied with compliance as such. It does not require people to comply for the right reason or for any particular reason; the mere fact of behavioral conformity is enough. People may not know what the law is, but in many areas they are able to comply with it nonetheless, mainly because it never occurs to them to do the things that in fact it prohibits, or not to perform the things that in fact it requires. The distinction is blurred, however, by the fact that a law, once internalized, can come to seem like second nature and be applied intuitively without any conscious reference to its content.[26] Such "unthinking compliance" with the rule may still count as self-application if it is the case that when challenged, the subject would cite the rule to explain and justify her behavior.

(b) Self-Application and the Guidance of Action

As these comments indicate, self-application is partly a matter of what H. L. A. Hart calls the "internal aspect" of a rule.[27] Talk of the internal aspect of a rule means that explicitly or implicitly, an attitude toward the rule— an attitude such as its acceptance as a norm for behavior—features in the best explanation for the subject's action. The subject's behavior doesn't just correspond to the norm; the norm guides the subject's action.

Like almost everyone writing in jurisprudence today, I accept that guiding action (or guiding conduct or guiding behavior) is the mode of governance distinctive to law. Modern legal theorists, following H. L. A. Hart, say that it is characteristic of law that it *guides the action* of those to whom it is addressed. Stephen Perry goes further; he claims that according to Hart, the *function* of law is to guide action.[28] I am not sure that Hart ever says that. In my view, this common formulation makes no sense. Guiding action (as opposed to other relations to behavior, like manipulating action, or galvanizing behavior or eliciting it by terror) is a modal idea, not a functional one.

Guiding action is the way in which law carries out whatever functions it has: it is its mode of operation, not its telos.[29]

Is "self-application" just a way of talking about the guidance of action, understood from the point of view of the person addressed by the law? Is it a helpful gloss on the idea of guidance?

Again, the answer is yes and no. Broadly speaking, yes—the technique of self-applying regulation uses the formulating and promulgation of norms to guide the action of the subjects concerned. This means that such norms have to comply with those aspects of the rule of law that are best understood in terms of making the guidance of action possible. We owe a lot here to Joseph Raz's account of the point of the rule of law: "This is the basic intuition from which the doctrine of the rule of law derives: the law must be capable of guiding the behavior of its subjects."[30] Raz uses this idea to explicate key formal aspects of the rule of law such as the requirements of prospectivity and clarity, as well as procedural aspects like access to courts and the independence of the judiciary.[31]

However, sometimes the guidance of action is understood in a way that distorts the idea of self-applying regulation. Many jurists imagine that action can be guided only by clear rules; guidance by standards is always something of an anomaly, because the actions required and the conditions under which they are required are not properly specified. Later (in section 7), I shall argue that this is a mistake. For now, let me just observe that there are nonmechanical as well as mechanical senses of "guidance," and not every notion of the guidance of action involves rules or the rigid and implacable specification of the detail of behavior.

(c) H. L. A. Hart on Self-Application

H. L. A. Hart (Herbert Lionel Adolphus Hart) is not the same as Henry Hart, but the former was influenced by the latter during his visit to Harvard Law School in the late 1950s. (I shall refer to H. L. A. Hart as HLA in what follows.) HLA's work in *The Concept of Law* discloses something very like the Hart and Sacks idea of self-application, even though he doesn't introduce that phrase explicitly as a term of art. HLA begins with the basic idea of guidance and the primacy of conduct rules:

> The principal functions of the law as a means of social control are not
> to be seen in private litigation or prosecutions, which represent vital

but still ancillary provisions for the failures of the system. It is to be seen in the diverse ways in which the law is used to control, to guide, and to plan life out of court.[32]

He then talks about areas where "we seek to regulate, unambiguously and in advance, some sphere of conduct by means of general standards to be used without further official direction on particular occasions."[33] HLA talks also about "rules the application of which individuals can see for themselves in case after case, without further recourse to official direction or discretion."[34] And he discusses difficulties with this technique of self-applying regulation, based on the open texture of language, our relative ignorance of facts, and our indeterminacy of aim.

> Uncertainty at the borderline is the price to be paid for the use of general classifying terms in any form of communication. . . . It is, however, important to appreciate why, apart from this dependence on language . . . with its characteristics of open texture, we should not cherish, even as an ideal, the conception of a rule so detailed that the question whether it applied or not to a particular case was always settled in advance, and never involved, at the point of actual application, a fresh choice between open alternatives. . . . It is a feature of the human predicament (and so of the legislative one) that we labour under two connected handicaps whenever we seek to regulate . . . some sphere of conduct by means of general standards to be used without further official direction on particular occasions. The first handicap is our relative ignorance of fact: the second is our relative indeterminacy of aim. If the world in which we live were characterized only by a finite number of features, . . . then provision could be made in advance for every possibility. We could make rules, the application of which to particular cases never called for a further choice.[35]

But the world of modern law is not like that.

> In fact all systems, in different ways, compromise between two social needs: the need for certain rules which can, over great areas of conduct, safely be applied by private individuals to themselves without fresh official guidance or weighing up of social issues, and the need to leave open, for later settlement by an informed, official choice, issues

which can only be properly appreciated and settled when they arise in a concrete case.[36]

In his way, then, HLA also identifies an interesting aspect of the relation between conduct rules and decision rules in self-applying regulation, alluded to above in section 4.

I have quoted these passages from HLA's writings because even though the term is not used, they evidently contain a great deal about self-application. I think it is a pity that more attention has not been paid to this overlap between the microjurisprudence of *The Concept of Law* and that of *The Legal Process*.[37] Too often, we see the relation between these two bodies of legal theory purely in the antagonistic light of the so-called Hart-Fuller dispute.[38]

Believe it or not, everything so far has been preliminary. I now want to turn to a couple of larger issues about the Hart and Sacks idea of self-applying regulation. The first issue (in section 7) is about the self-application of standards (or what Hart and Sacks also call "avowedly indeterminate rules"). The second issue (in section 8) is about the overall implications for liberty and dignity of this way of regulating behavior.

7. The Self-Application of Standards

Self-application is no doubt important for categorical prohibitions and requirements. But it is very important also for norms that have a conditional structure—for their self-application involves a determination by the individual that she is in the situation that the norm condition specifies and a determination by her of the conduct that is required (or prohibited) in that circumstance.

It is also important for standards—that is, norms that use value predicates or other predicates whose application involves judgment, either in the norm condition or the norm consequence or both. I gave an example earlier from the New York State traffic code:

Section 1129(a) The driver of a motor vehicle shall not follow another vehicle more closely than is *reasonable* and *prudent*, having *due regard* for the speed of such vehicles and the traffic upon and the condition of the highway.

The words and phrases I have italicized are what make Section 1129(a) into a standard rather than a rule.

But can Section 1129(a) be self-applied by drivers? It doesn't specify any particular following distance or any formula for calculating a minimum distance based on speed and road conditions and weather. It leaves it up to the driver to make a determination of what is reasonable, which is what he would be morally required to do if there were no legally enacted norm. A number of legal philosophers have taken just this approach to "reasonableness" norms. John Gardner, for example, sees this as an instance of law "passing the buck" to morality.[39] He says that

> when the law directs us to rely for some purpose only on "considerations which ordinarily regulate the conduct of human affairs" it purports to leave us, for that purpose of that law, in just the same position we would be in if that law had not existed. It says to its addressee: "In the following respect, do (decide, think, etc.) what you should do (decide, think, etc.) anyway, what you should do (decide, think, etc.) even if this law did not exist."[40]

Likewise, Joseph Raz argues that we always have a background or default moral obligation to act reasonably, and law really only plays a role when it authoritatively requires us to do something other than what morality or reason by itself would dictate.[41] The conscious formulation of a standard indicates that the law expects morality to take over (or, rather, that the law is no longer blocking morality's application). That's what is supposed to happen with the deliberate use of words like "reasonable." The inadvertent use of vague or ambiguous language, on the other hand, represents a failure to provide the guidance that a legal norm purports to provide *in lieu of morality*. This, says Raz, is why clarity is required by the rule of law: "An ambiguous, vague, obscure, or imprecise law is likely to mislead or confuse at least some of those who desire to be guided by it."[42]

I am not convinced by this approach. For one thing, the law does not entirely pass the buck to morality; it enforces the reasonableness standard and stands ready to second-guess the subjects' judgment. This is not entirely an exercise in legal deregulation.[43]

Second, I believe drivers *are* actually guided by Section 1129(a) and that they self-apply it to their driving, rather than move away from it altogether, resorting instead to moral norms of reasonableness. After all, a norm like

Section 1129(a) doesn't just say, "Do the right thing (when following another vehicle)." It mentions a number of factors to be taken into account: "the speed of such vehicles and the traffic upon and the condition of the highway." And the terms "reasonable," prudent," and "due regard" do have some cognitive content. To a certain extent, they channel the evaluative judgment that is to be made in certain directions and not others. This is clearer in cases using more obviously thick moral predicates like "cruel," "inhuman," and "degrading." The elaboration of such provisions is not a matter of nudging them into a rulelike form; it is a matter of eliciting the specific content they convey, such as it is.[44]

Third, Section 1129(a) has a kind of "now is the time" character. It does not just demurely efface itself in favor of morality, as the Gardner / Raz position implies; it indicates affirmatively that following another vehicle is (and legally must be) the occasion for serious thought about reasonableness, prudence, and so on. In this sense, it guides action, by guiding the application of practical reason on the part of the driver. The driver might have treated following distances casually. But instead, self-applying Section 1129(a), he takes them seriously, regarding them as an occasion for serious thought and for acting on the upshot of such thought.[45]

By the way, I am not saying that what a norm like Section 1129(a) instructs drivers to do is pull over and ponder. Those who propounded the norm do not care what sort of thinking process a driver actually goes through, provided its upshot is that he follows other vehicles at a prudent and reasonable distance. Practical reason can be exercised in all sorts of ways, some of them quick and implicit, some of them sustained and reflective. Sometimes, explicit deliberation is called for. In section 5, I mentioned the Eighth Amendment, which offers itself for self-application by legislatures. The appropriate way to respond to that institution is for legislatures to include debates about cruelty and excessiveness in their deliberations on penal laws, and the point of the constitutional requirement is, in the first instance, to see that they do this. Other times, and in our example for experienced drivers, the relevant thinking is almost second nature. Either way, the norm calls for something—practical reasoning—and in self-applying it, we respond to that call.

I sometimes get the impression that jurists think of standards as somehow defective as guides, by virtue of their vagueness or indeterminacy, and that the best thing that law can do is to quickly elaborate them so they become more like rules. In *The Legal Process,* Hart and Sacks talk about the "reasoned elaboration of purportedly determinate directions" in this way (145 ff.).

The point is to eliminate any confusion that might flow from the ambiguity of some term such as "vehicle" in a speed statute such as Section 1180(b) above.

> The statute is self-applying, and needs to be read so as to facilitate accurate self-application and tentative official application. If a motorcycle were sometimes a [vehicle] in the courts of the state and sometimes not, motorcyclists and enforcement officers alike would be reduced to a state of angry confusion. (145)

But Hart and Sacks also have the category of "avowedly indeterminate directions"—

> The framers of a general directive arrangement may not think it wise, or they may not be able, to give it even the degree of definiteness of the speed statute. They may find that it is not feasible ... to reduce their directions to the form of rules ... which are sufficiently definite to eliminate the need for discretion in filling out their meaning. (150)

And that is certainly the case with Section 1129(a). Websites and driving-school manuals may give examples and rules of thumb, but basically, the flexible discretion exercised by drivers and those who watch over them better fulfills the lawmakers' intention than the reduction of the relevant norm to a mechanical rule. We don't want Section 1129(a) to evolve into a rule; we want it to stay as it is, directing the self-application of a standard.

Reasoned elaboration of the standard may still take place, but it is not reductive elaboration. The character of the standard qua standard is maintained; the courts respect the legislature's use of regulatory device. What's more, there is no reason to think that such elaboration only takes place when the question (of following distances, in our example) comes before a court. Leaving the matter mostly for the norm's subjects to deal with means that patterns of acceptable behavior may emerge as people police their own and each other's driving.[46] There will be a certain amount of adjustment, coordination, and interaction. In other cases, where a standard purports to regulate industrial and commercial activity, patterns of self-application may result in the emergence of best-practice ideas and so on. Lawmakers can learn from the results of self-application just as much as norm subjects can learn from officials' second-guessing of their decisions.

8. Liberty and Respect

So far as it concerns private individuals, is the technique of self-applying regulation more favorable to liberty than individualized administration? We saw Hart and Sacks alluding to the restriction of the freedom of private action as a disadvantage of the individualized application of norms (121). Is the expectation of self-application more inherently respectful of the individuals to whom the relevant norms are addressed? Or is there no particular advantage so far as these values are concerned?

In Chapter 3, on the relation between law and human dignity, I made a big deal about self-application. I said that self-application is an extraordinarily important feature of the way legal systems operate. They work by using, rather than short-circuiting, the agency of ordinary human individuals. They count on people's capacities for practical understanding, for self-control, for self-monitoring and modulation of their own behavior in relation to norms that they can grasp and understand. I said that this makes ruling by law quite different from, say, herding cows with a cattle prod or directing a flock of sheep with a dog. The pervasive emphasis on self-application is, in my view, definitive of law, differentiating it sharply from systems of rule that work primarily by manipulating, terrorizing, or galvanizing behavior. There is a modicum of dignity and respect for the norm subject in the technique of self-application. The point is recognized obliquely by Lon Fuller in some reflection on his own rule-of-law principles (what he called the "inner morality" of law), which can be justified as ways of securing the possibility of successful self-application:

> To embark on the enterprise of subjecting human conduct to rules involves of necessity a commitment to the view that man is, or can become, a responsible agent, capable of understanding and following rules, and answerable for his defaults. Every departure from the principles of law's inner morality is an affront to man's dignity as a responsible agent. To judge his actions by unpublished or retrospective laws, or to order him to do an act that is impossible, is to convey to him your indifference to his powers of self-determination.[47]

On the other hand, use of the technique of self-applying regulation does not detract from the point that law is still ultimately coercive. One is required to abide by the appropriate norm, and one's application of it to one's own conduct may be reviewed by the police or by a court, and ultimately the court's view will prevail, through sanctions and / or force. Even if she internalizes it, the norm that the subject self-applies is often not a norm she would have chosen; she may not agree with it in general or in its application in a particular instance. There is nothing about self-application or its connection with what HLA called the internal aspect of rules that reconciles law with individual autonomy. In some cases, the subject may indeed agree with the law. In other cases, her willingness to self-apply it is still, in the final analysis, a matter of duress. (We should not forget that even a bandit relies on something like self-application when he says to his victim, "Hand over your money!")[48]

Indeed, I have heard people say that the prevalence of self-application might betoken an even deeper mode of coercion or oppression, as law insinuates itself into and takes possession of one's very soul. There is no better form of slavery, they will say, than one in which the slave internalizes the function of master, anticipating and applying the master's commands to his own conduct. Self-application is a slave master's fantasy. This point may be overblown, but it shouldn't be neglected.

But it is only one nightmare. We can also imagine a tyranny in which people are shadowed by state officials, who—on every occasion when some change in behavior is deemed necessary—seize the subject and force her into the movement or posture that the authorities require. Or, only slightly less oppressive, a society of nothing but particular commands screamed at subjects to elicit their compliance, without any sense of there being standing rules that subjects can use in their own practical thinking and judgment to apply to their own behavior from time to time without further guidance. Of course, both dystopias would be hopelessly inefficient, hopelessly demanding of official resources. As HLA remarks, "no society could support the number of officials necessary to secure that every member of the society was officially and separately informed of every act which he was required to do."[49] But it's a mistake to think that this lack of resources would be the only objection to such techniques (compared to other more respectful modes of coercion).

Or think of another dystopia, paraded as a first-best ideal in Bruce Ackerman's 1980 book, *Social Justice in the Liberal State*.[50] Ackerman invited us to think about social justice using the model of a spaceship full of colonists approaching an uninhabited planet. The commander of the spaceship gathers the colonists all together and tells them that they will not be allowed to land on the planet until they settle among themselves the principles that are going to govern their life together down there and the division of the resources (mainly "manna") that the planet is known to contain. It's a sort of "original position." Various constraints of neutrality, reasonableness, and rationality are to be placed on the conversation that ensues. For our purposes, however, the most striking thing about Ackerman's model is that the spaceship is imagined to have the technological wherewithal to enforce any principles that we agree on. There are ray guns and force fields that will uphold the distribution and sustain the institutions that the application of principles of justice involves. As we orbit the planet, we know that the ship's "ray guns can be costlessly transformed into a perfect police force, giving constant and infallible protection to whatever distribution of manna we think right."[51] This, says Ackerman, "permits the polity to focus clearly on the question of ultimate objectives."[52] Proceeding on this basis, we do not waste the time allocated to the issue of justice "by talking about important, yet ultimately secondary issues of implementation."[53] As Ackerman reflected in a later article, it was the aim of his "ideal theory" to focus steadfastly on the choice of principles "by introducing a temporary conversational stop upon all questions involving implementation."[54] He suggested that the perfect technology of justice might better have been described as an "ideal legal system."[55]

There are all sorts of things wrong with Ackerman's perfect technology idea. One, he assumes that the norms that the colonists come up with will be all mechanically administrable rules rather than standards that machines like ray guns can administer. Two, he is asking us to imagine the choice of principles of justice in light of the availability of literally unlimited resources to enforce them.[56] This premise takes us so far from the circumstances of justice—particularly moderate scarcity—as to call into question the interest of principles chosen against this assumption. Ackerman rejects both David Hume's assumption of the easy movability of resources from one person to another ("the instability of their possession") and HLA's postulate of our mutual vulnerability (put forward as a part of "the minimum content of natural law") as presuppositions of all realistic talk about justice.[57] And three, quite apart from the analytics of justice, there is a question about whether we should be comfortable faced with a state in possession of these resources. What other uses might they be put to?

More than all this, there are questions about the allegedly ideal character of Ackerman's first-best fantasy. Would *our world* be a better world if walls were so high, barbed wire so sharp, force fields so impenetrable, ray guns programmed so perfectly, that no one could ever violate another's rights or deny the claims that justice supports? People snarling and muttering at one another in aggressive frustration from outside each other's force fields? Is this something to which, in any sense, we should aspire as a means for realizing liberal ideals? Is it a matter of regret that in the real world we have to rely on each other—on self-application—for the implementation of most social norms and principles of justice?[58]

Ackerman's conception seems to be innocent of any awareness or valorization of the way in which laws in modern democracies actually work. True, there is policing and there are technologies like locks and closed-circuit cameras. The southern border may get its wall. But the main burden of the application of the legal norms that our society requires falls on the routine voluntary acts and judgments of individuals. Modern societies depend—and I think any just society *should* depend—largely on the willingness of their members to bear with and work within basic institutions. So much is the self-application of law taken for granted in society that we tend not to focus on its significance for political philosophy. But as Hart and Sacks saw, it is an important aspect of the presence of legal norms and institutions in our lives. To imagine away the necessity for widespread voluntary self-application, as Ackerman does, is to imagine a form of life together that is utterly different from our own.

5

Vagueness and the Guidance of Action

1. Introduction

"The desideratum of clarity," said Lon Fuller, "represents one of the most essential ingredients of legality."[1] And Joseph Raz gives us the reason: "An ambiguous, vague, obscure, or imprecise law is likely to mislead or confuse at least some of those who desire to be guided by it."[2] Raz lists clarity as one of the key principles of the rule of law, and he associates it (as he associates all such principles) with what he calls "the basic intuition from which the doctrine of the rule of law derives: the law must be capable of guiding the behavior of its subjects."[3]

Like Fuller, Raz thinks that this commitment to *guiding action* and the requirement of clarity that is founded on it are not just technical or formalistic ideas. They are ways of respecting human dignity. Instead of manipulating a person psychologically or securing a reflex recoil with a scream of command, they approach governance in a way that takes seriously the capacities associated with ordinary human agency—capacities for practical reasoning by reference to norms that the agent can grasp and understand. Law, as H. L. A. Hart acknowledged, "consists primarily of general standards of conduct communicated to classes of persons, who are then expected to understand and conform to the rules without further direction."[4] Fuller's position is that embarking on this "enterprise of subjecting human conduct to rules involves . . . a commitment to the view that man is . . . a responsible agent, capable of understanding and following rules."[5] And Raz agrees:

A legal system which does in general observe the rule of law treats people as persons at least in the sense that it attempts to guide their behavior through affecting the circumstances of their action. It thus presupposes that they are rational autonomous creatures and attempts to affect their actions and habits by affecting their deliberations.[6]

The question I would like to consider is whether the presence in the law of provisions that may be described as vague or unclear or imprecise is necessarily at odds with this commitment.

2. *State v. Schaeffer*

An old case from Ohio, *State v. Schaeffer,* gives us a couple of examples from traffic law to work with.[7] We are told in this case that in 1917, the Ohio General Code contained the following provision:

> Section 12604: Whoever operates a motor cycle or motor vehicle at a greater speed than eight miles an hour in the business and closely built-up portions of a municipality, or more than fifteen miles an hour in other portions thereof, or more than twenty miles an hour outside of a municipality, shall be fined not more than twenty-five dollars.

But it preceded that with a provision of quite a different character:

> Section 12603: Whoever operates a motor vehicle or motorcycle on the public roads or highways at a speed greater than is reasonable or proper, having regard for width, traffic, use and the general and usual rules of such road or highway, or so as to endanger the property, life or limb of any person, shall be fined not more than twenty-five dollars.

The difference is stark—Section 12604 worked with precise numerical speed limits: 8 mph in some areas, 15 mph in other areas, and 20 mph on the open road. The limits strike us as absurdly low, but this was 1917—and at least drivers knew what was expected of them. However, Section 12603 approached the matter in an entirely different way. It did not use numerical speed limits; instead, it spoke of "a speed greater than is reasonable or proper." Compared to Section 12604, Section 12603 is imprecise, and because of that it seems likely, in Raz's words, "to mislead or confuse at least some of those who desire to be guided by it." True, Section 12604 is not a paragon of precision. The phrase "in the business and closely built-up portions of a municipality" is not a precise

specification of a zone of application for the 8 mph limit; those who know anything about urban geography know that business districts have vague edges,
and the term "built-up" has its own vagueness. Section 12603 avoids those
forms of vagueness by applying universally to any public road or highway, but it
more than makes up for that in the imprecision of the speed limit it lays down.

A driver—a Mr. E. E. Schaeffer—ran over and fatally injured a three-
year-old boy known as Buley Csaki who was playing in the street in a
built-up area with a large number of other children. The state said he was
driving at 25 to 30 mph; Schaeffer denied this, saying he was going no faster
than 8 mph (221–22). Perhaps to avoid the factual issue, the state proceeded
against him with a manslaughter charge based on an alleged violation of
Section 12603. Schaeffer was convicted, and on appeal, he complained "that
section 12603 . . . is unconstitutional and void, for the reason that it is too
indefinite and uncertain in its terms." His claim was that

> the words "reasonable" and "proper" are so general, comprehensive,
> and variable that it would be impossible for the defendant to know, or
> for the jury to fairly determine what was a violation of the statute; that
> juries in one case would hold a speed to be reasonable, while the same
> speed under the same circumstances might be held by another jury in
> the same county, at the same time, to be unreasonable. In short, it is
> urged that the statute should definitely fix what is a reasonable speed
> and a proper operation of a car. (228–29)

Constitutional doctrine provided then, as it provides now, that statutes can
be struck down as void for vagueness, either because they fail to comply with
the US Constitution's Sixth Amendment requirement that the accused "be
informed of the nature and cause of the accusation" or because their vagueness represents a failure of due process.

But the Supreme Court of Ohio unanimously rejected this complaint,
and Mr. Schaeffer's conviction was upheld. I believe it was rightly upheld.
More important, I think the Ohio court's reasoning in its vindication of
Section 12603 helps us see the complicated ways in which a vague or imprecise provision can still succeed in guiding the actions of those subject to
it. What the court said was this:

> The Legislature . . . in this instance, saw fit to fix no definite rate of speed
> for the car. . . . Some statutes have undertaken to fix a rate of speed

which would be prima facie dangerous, but a rate of speed dangerous in one situation would be quite safe in another situation, and if the rate of speed were definitely fixed, naturally it would have to be the minimum speed at which cars might be safely driven, because that speed would have to be a safeguard against every possible situation which would be perilous even at a speed of six or eight miles an hour. There is no place in all the public [roads] where a situation is not constantly changing from comparatively no traffic to a most congested traffic; from no foot travelers to a throng of them; from open and clear intersections, private drives, and street crossings, to those that are crowded; from free and unobstructed streets to streets filled with crowds of foot travelers and others getting off and on street cars and other vehicles. In order to meet these varying situations, and impose upon the automobilist [*sic*] the duty of anticipating them and guarding against the dangers that arise out of them, this statute was evidently passed in the interests of the public safety in a public highway. (225–26)

The court went on to say that it is precisely the statute's "adaptability to meet every dangerous situation" that commends it as a valid enactment:

Absolute or mathematical certainty is not required in the framing of a statute. Reasonable certainty of the nature and cause of the offense is all that is required. Some offenses admit of much greater precision and definiteness than others; but it is quite obvious that in the case at bar the statute must be sufficiently elastic and adaptable to meet all the dangerous situations presented, to adequately safeguard the travelling public, whether foot passenger, horse, or motor vehicle. Section 12603 is as definite and certain on the subject-matter and the numerous situations arising thereunder as the nature of the case and the safety of the public will reasonably admit. (236)

The court was not convinced by the complaint that different juries might apply Section 12603 in different ways; this, it said, "is inevitable under any system of jurisprudence on any set of facts involved in a criminal transaction." In all sorts of areas of the law, courts use what is called "the rule of reason"—from *reasonable doubt* in the ordinary charge to a jury in criminal cases to *reasonable grounds for believing that one is in danger* in a case of self-defense. And the Ohio court added this about the provision in question:

The careful, conservative driver need have no fear of it. The reckless, wanton speed maniac needs to be kept in fear of [§ 12603]. The life of the humblest citizen must be placed above the gratification of the motor maniac, who would turn the public highways into a race course. (236)

This last point is well worth emphasizing, indicating as it does that there are different postures a person can strike, different attitudes one can have, toward the sort of guidance offered by law.

In the sections that follow, I want to consider these issues in a more abstract way; I want to explore the complexity of the idea of a legal provision guiding the action of those subject to it. Like almost everyone writing in jurisprudence today, I accept that *guiding action* (or *guiding conduct* or *guiding behavior*) is the mode of governance distinctive to law. It is the distinctive way in which law performs whatever functions are given to it by lawmakers. But I believe we need to approach the question of unclarity, vagueness, and imprecision in law with a more sophisticated notion of guidance than the one we often use.[8] Having one's action guided by a norm is not just a matter of finding out about the norm and conforming one's behavior to its specifications. It can involve a more complex engagement of practical reason and practical deliberation than that.

3. The Model of Rules

Let us begin with a simple question about the ordinary case. What is it for action to be guided by a rule? On the most straightforward model—a model corresponding roughly to the last part of Ohio's Section 12604—the action of a person P is guided by a legal provision L_1, when the following conditions are met:

Model (i)

(1) L_1 contains a requirement that some type of behavior B_1 is to be performed (in some type of circumstance C_1).
(2) P is capable of understanding and remembering L_1.
(3) At any given time, P is capable of noticing whether he is in a circumstance of type C_1.
(4) When P notices that he is in circumstance C_1, he is capable of monitoring his behavior to see whether he is performing B_1 or not.

(5) If he finds that he is not, he is capable of modifying his behavior
    so that he is performing B_1 in circumstance C_1.

In the case of Ohio's Section 12604, circumstance C_1 might be "driving outside of a municipality," and behavior B_1 might be "driving no faster than
20 mph." P's action can be guided by this ordinance in a way that is perfectly
familiar to every driver. We keep an eye out for where we are (in the country
or in the city, for example), we pay attention to traffic signs, we glance at our
speedometer, and we slow down or speed up accordingly. By its presence,
by our understanding of its provisions, and through the connection between
that understanding and our own practical agency, the traffic law guides our
actions.

    Notice that this model of action-guiding is quite different from any idea
of P's simply responding to, as though galvanized by, a command to do B_1.
Model (i) highlights distinctive features of human agency: the ability to
internalize a norm and to monitor and control one's behavior on the basis
of that norm, and the ability to notice the features of one's environment
and circumstances and relate those to the other abilities just mentioned in
the service of compliance with the internalized norm.[9] Possession of
these capacities is an important aspect of human dignity; Fuller and Raz
both emphasized this, and I have tried to give it prominence in my own
recent writings about the connection between dignity and the rule of law.[10]
Though model (i) uses the term "behavior" to characterize what is required
of P, it is not a "behaviorist" model; it takes seriously the mental and epistemic aspects of full-blooded human agency. And it does seem to presuppose a clarity requirement. The kind of self-monitoring and self-control
indicated in conditions (3), (4), and (5) assumes that P has a clear sense of
the circumstances that L_1 makes salient and the form of behavior that L_1
seeks to elicit in those circumstances. P is supposed to be able to match his
perception to the clear indication from L_1 that it matters whether he is in
circumstance C_1 (as opposed to some other circumstance); and he is supposed to be able to match the monitoring and control of his behavior to
the clear indication from L_1 that it matters whether he is performing B_1 in
that circumstance or not. With the best will in the world (by which I mean
the best attitude toward law and its requirements), he may be in difficulty
so far as the relation between the law and his agency is concerned if the
specification of the relevant circumstance or the specification of the required behavior is indeterminate.[11]

4. The Model of Standards

Though the simple model I have just given indicates ways in which the imposition of straightforward legal requirements respects human agency, the capacities that model (i) presupposes are not the only practical capacities that individuals have. Consider a more complicated model, corresponding to Ohio's Section 12603:

Model (ii)

(1) L_2 contains a requirement to the effect that there should be some appropriate modification of one's behavior whenever circumstance C_2 occurs.

(2) P is capable of understanding and remembering L_2.

(3) At any given time, P is capable of noticing whether circumstance C_2 has occurred.

(4) When P notices that circumstance C_2 is occurring or has occurred, he is capable of considering what behavior is now appropriate.

(5) Pursuant to that judgment, P is capable of monitoring his action to determine whether he is behaving in what he judges to be an appropriate way in circumstance C_2.

(6) If he judges that he is not behaving in an appropriate way in circumstance C_2, P is capable of modifying his behavior so that it does become appropriate for circumstance C_2.

In our example, C_2 may be any of the factors alluded to in Section 12603, such as the narrowness of the roadway, the amount of traffic, or the presence of other factors (such as small children playing on the road), which may make one's ordinary driving—one's usual speed, for example—a potential danger to life or property. And the legal provision requires us to drive at a speed no greater than is "reasonable or proper" for those circumstances.

What is distinct about this model is the failure to *specify* the action that is to be performed when P is in the new circumstance C_2. It is up to P to figure out what action is appropriate. For example, traffic laws often require drivers to lower their speed below the posted speed limit when bad weather (a blizzard or a severe rainstorm) strikes the roadway or when they become aware that an accident has taken place ahead of them. The legislature may not specify a lower speed limit for these circumstances, because what is an appropriate speed may vary so much depending on what else is going on (how much traffic there is, for example, or how bad the accident is) that it makes more sense for drivers to be left to figure this out for themselves. This does not mean that the law endorses whatever the driver decides to do; P may still be cited for driving at an unreasonable speed in the circumstances because a police officer judges that P's calculation at step (4) is culpably mistaken; and he may be convicted if a judge accepts that view. But just because he can be second-guessed by a police officer does not mean that one might as well specify a speed limit for C_2; all it means is that the particularized calculation required at step (4) is capable of being assessed by law.

Like the Ohio Supreme Court, I believe that L_2 guides action in model (ii). True, it does not do so by precisely specifying an action to be performed, but it offers input into P's agency nevertheless, directing his practical reason to a problem to which the law draws his attention, and requiring him to come up with and implement a solution.

We sometimes say that what distinguishes model (ii) from model (i) is that in (ii) the legal provision is presented in the form of a standard rather than a rule. And when we distinguish rules from standards, we sometimes say that the difference is that a standard is a norm that requires some evaluative judgment of the person who applies it, whereas a rule is a norm presented as the end product of evaluative judgments already made by the lawmaker. A posted speed limit of 55 mph represents a value judgment already made by the legislature that that speed is appropriate for driving in the designated area. A legal requirement to drive at a "reasonable" speed, by contrast, looks for a value judgment to be made downstream from the legislature; it indicates that the legislature has not decided to make all the requisite value judgments itself, but has left some to be made by the law applier. That characterization of the difference between rules and standards is helpful here, but only if we remember that the first law applier is not the police officer who pulls the driver over and issues a citation or the judge in traffic court who decides whether or not to enter a conviction. The first law applier is P, the driver himself. Aware of the norm, he takes it on board—internalizes it—and makes for himself the evaluative judgment that the norm requires him to make, and monitors and modifies his behavior accordingly. He may do so well or badly, and if he does it badly, he may be liable to citation, conviction, and penalty; and this, too, he is aware of. All of this adds up to the distinctive way in which P's action is guided by L_2 in model (ii).

Notice that the mode of action-guidance in model (ii) is also compatible with the commitment to dignity that I mentioned in section 1 and at the end of section 3, and to forms of governance that respect human dignity and take seriously the agency of those to whom legal norms are addressed. The dignity of a human agent does not just consist in his estimable capacities for normative comprehension, self-monitoring, and the moderating of his own behavior; it also consists more broadly in his capacity for practical deliberation in both structured and unstructured ways. An open-ended standard of the kind we are considering invokes that capacity and relies on it. It credits the subject with the sophisticated ability to adapt his agency to his own practical thinking when this is required of him, and it indicates the kind of circumstance in which that ability is required. Such a requirement may be more onerous than a simple requirement to comply with a numerical rule, but it certainly treats people as having the dignity to respond positively to this task.

By the way, I am not saying that what L_2 instructs P to do is "pull over and ponder" (so to speak), as though it were dictating the actual implementation of P's engagement of his powers of practical reasoning. The authorities do not care what sort of thinking process P actually goes through or how long it takes him; what they want him to do is drive at a reasonable speed. They expect that he will respond to this instruction using his powers of practical reasoning oriented to the circumstances he is in. But practical reason can be exercised in all sorts of ways, some of them quick and implicit, some of them sustained and reflective. (In everything that follows, I am using "practical reason" in a way that reflects the force of this point.)

5. Judgment and Guidance

I can imagine a pedant saying that my analysis of model (ii) unhelpfully elides the distinction between judgment (of what action is appropriate) and the guidance of action on the basis of that judgment. Inasmuch as the law requires the former, it is not *action* that it is guiding. The pedant may bolster this position by developing the following contrast with model (i): model (i) assumes that the legislature has reached a value judgment about the desirability or moral necessity of B_1 (e.g., driving at a certain speed) in circumstance C_1. That was something the legislators had to do—at what we might call the evaluation stage of the lawmaking process—before they could finally draft, enact, and promulgate L_1. Maybe this was something they argued about, did research on, felt unsure about, and so on. But they did not begin the process of guiding the action of those subject to their authority until they had completed all that thinking and debating at the evaluative stage. Once that was done—but only then—they were in a position to guide the action of people like P. Similarly, the pedant might say, in model (ii), a legislature that leaves it up to P (and those reviewing P's behavior) to formulate the appropriate speed for circumstance C_2 is not guiding P's action; by leaving the evaluative stage to P, it is casting him in the legislative role, leaving it up to him to guide his own action only after he has determined for himself, in his capacity as a delegated lawmaker, a speed limit for the circumstances. In other words, in model (ii), the pedant will say, step (4) is not a genuine instance of action-guidance.

I think the pedant's point is misconceived. Model (ii) as we have presented it does involve some determinate guidance offered to P by the lawmaker. True, it is not a case of the lawmaker saying, "Do precisely this." But the lawmaker identifies a salient type of circumstance or pairing of circumstances, indicates that some adjustment of behavior is appropriate when the one circumstance is overtaken by the other, attempts to focus P's practical reason on what that change of behavior should be, and indicates by whatever penal provision is attached to L_2 that P should take this whole business seriously. That is guidance. The law in model (ii) guides P's practical reasoning through certain channels and in certain directions. It evinces a certain faith in that reasoning, in the sense that it empowers P's practical reasoning rather than seeking to dominate or supersede it. But what it indicates will *not* be tolerated is a failure on P's part to orient his practical reasoning to the circumstances specified by the lawmaker.

Maybe we can quibble about words, about whether this is a case of guiding action rather than guiding the use of practical reason. For myself, I see little daylight between the two ideas. But if our pedant wants to insist on the contrast, then we should respond by revisiting the initial premise of our account—namely, that law's function is to guide action. There is, after all, nothing canonical about the phrase "guiding action," despite its repetition by Hart and his followers. If a sharp contrast between (a) "guiding action" and (b) "engaging practical reason" is causing difficulty, then we should reconsider the proposition that "guiding action" is how law characteristically proceeds. We may want to say that that is what was intended in a broad inclusive sense—a sense that might include (a) and (b)—rather than a narrow sense that focused on (a) to the exclusion of (b). We might want to say that

everything valuable and important about the premise that law characteristically proceeds by guiding action is secured by the broader sense of "guiding
action," and nothing of importance is lost by rejecting the narrow sense.

6. Raz on Authority

Our pedant might have put his point in terms of Joseph Raz's theory of authority.[12] He might say that, according to Raz, law claims authority and law
can only claim authority if particular legal directives represent somebody's
view of how somebody else should behave. This is because a claim to authority over P is always a claim that P would be better off following the guidance of the person claiming authority than trying to figure things out for
himself. So—on this interpretation of Raz's approach—nothing that does not
represent such a view can have authority attributed to it. And nothing can
plausibly count as an exercise of authority if its net effect is to leave P in the
position of having to figure out the issue for himself. Model (i) seems to satisfy this set of requirements, but—the Razian pedant will say—model (ii)
does not. In model (ii), P has to do all the figuring for himself, and the view
to which he subjects himself—the view expressed in L_2—is simply that it is
incumbent on him to do this.

   I actually believe Raz's position is (or can be made) more accommodating
than this.[13] And certainly, as I have already indicated, the guidance given in
L_2 is not quite that indeterminate. Though Raz does in some places use the
language of the law's representing the judgment of someone else on what
exactly P ought to do, in other places he phrases his position more abstractly.
One thing he says is that a law "must represent the judgment of the alleged
authority on the reasons which apply to its subjects."[14] Now, a person may
have certain reasons for action, and a person may also have certain reasons
for thinking (I mean reasons for practical thinking).[15] We sometimes say of
a person who we think has made a hasty decision, "He ought to have taken
more time and care to think this decision through," or "He had reason to
deliberate on this matter more carefully than in fact he did." Having a reason
to deliberate carefully means having a reason to pay particular attention to
the reasons that one has for acting.[16] One can be guided on the former set of
reasons (reasons to deliberate) as well as on the latter (reasons to behave in
a certain way). Often, we form our own view of how much deliberation to
expend on a given decision that we face, and sometimes we make mistakes
about this. An adviser may say to us, "I don't know what you should do about

the decision you face, but I am certain that you should take more time over it than you are proposing to take." If we accept that advice, we are in some sense accepting authority: we are submitting ourselves to the judgment of the adviser on reasons that apply to us—the set of reasons for and against taking a given amount of time to deliberate on an issue. It would be quite wrong to say that this cannot count as an exercise of authority simply because the adviser does not give us his bottom-line view on what we ought, finally, to do.

If this is correct, then Raz's conception of authority does not support the pedant's position. In model (ii), L_2 does represent the legislature's view of reasons that apply to P, but it is the legislator's view about reasons that apply to P's deliberating. The legislator has taken a view about when P's deliberating on the possibility of a change in his behavior is appropriate or requisite. The legislator says, "Such deliberating is appropriate or requisite when circumstance C_2 occurs. You had better deliberate carefully about what to do when this happens, and, since you may be second-guessed by a police officer and a court, you had better take this seriously."

So a law like the one presented in model (ii) *is* an action-guiding norm, once one recognizes the complexity and multilayered aspect of action-guidance. It mobilizes some or many of the resources of practical reason or practical intelligence possessed by the norm subject—a mobilization that might not take place if the lawmaker had not promulgated L_2—and it puts those resources to work in determining what the subject is to do. And it does so in a way that channels and directs the use of practical reason, without specifying what its outcome is to be. This is an important guidance function, and if it is our view that law aims to guide action, we should not disqualify norms like this from counting as law simply because they do not fully specify the action that is to be performed. L_2 does communicate to P what is expected of him: the difference is that what is expected of P in this case is something different in kind or level than what is expected of P in model (i).

In characterizing Raz's position, some people attribute to him the view that law, if it is to be authoritative, must be such that those subject to it can figure out what it requires without recourse to moral judgment on their own part.[17] This formulation needs to be treated very carefully. It is true that P cannot figure out what behavior to engage in, pursuant to L_2, without making a moral judgment. But what L_2 in effect says to him is something like, "Now is the time for you to engage your practical reason to figure out what difference circumstance C_2 should make to your behavior." In our driving example, Section 12603 said to Mr. Schaeffer that the dangers an automobile evidently posed to children playing in the street indicated the need for practical deliberation about his speed (either quick and implicit deliberation in the case of a skilled and responsive driver, or more sustained reflection in the case of a driver not habituated to deliberation of this kind). And *that* instruction—"Now is the time to deliberate"—can be identified without moral deliberation. True, the instruction is to deliberate, and once we have identified it, we cannot follow it without engaging in moral reasoning; but the moral reasoning is not essential to figuring out that that is what the driver is being instructed to do.

7. Minimal Guidance?

Someone might object that the guidance element in model (ii) is minimal. Simply to show that there is *some* action-guiding element in L_2 is not enough. Almost any vague provision will direct the norm subject's attention to his own behavior in some way: even "Do the right thing" can be construed as an instruction to "Watch what you are doing," so that it elicits some slight change of orientation in the practical reason of the person to whom it is addressed. But—goes the objection—this is not the same as saying that the provision succeeds in guiding action. A law must let a person know what is expected of him; it is not enough to simply alert P to the fact that something is expected of him and to gesture in a vague ballpark sort of way toward the area of action (e.g., driving or the speed at which one is driving) with which that expectation is concerned.

The objection proceeds from the fact that it is possible to guide action to a greater or lesser extent. But that is also the basis of our answer to the objection. The behavior that is elicited by a given directive can be specified in more or less detail. Section 12604 tells drivers to lower their speed from 20 mph to 15 mph when they enter a municipal area, but it does not tell them what gears to use as they lower their speed, or how sharply they should brake to bring this about. Is this an objection to Section 12604? Must every legal provision be as precise and specified as it is possible to be?[18] No—legislatures differ in what they are trying to achieve so far as the fine texture of action-guidance is concerned, and usually by their terms, they can indicate that to the citizen. So in the case of the Ohio speed limit, it is evidently no part of the legislative intention to guide the choice of transmission mode (when to downshift, etc.) at which the slowing to the lower speed is achieved. Within reason, a lowering of speed to 15 mph is acceptable by whatever means the driver chooses to use. The provision makes it clear that it is the velocity rather than the mode of achieving the velocity that it is concerned with. Something similar is true of Section 12603. A commonsense approach to the language of the provision indicates that the legislature has deliberately chosen a certain strategy of flexibility and it has communicated *that choice* to the citizen as part of the impact it expects to have on his agency. As the Ohio court observed, "It is quite obvious that in the case at bar the statute must be sufficiently elastic and adaptable to meet all the dangerous situations presented, to adequately safeguard the travelling public."[19] The statute presents itself to the citizen in that spirit.

Again, the objection we are considering (and answering) here can be restated in Razian terms. In a recent paper, Raz poses this rhetorical question: "If it is the purpose of the law to make a difference to our life, does it not follow that its realization of its purpose depends on its ability to exclude morality?"[20] He thinks the answer is yes. That does not imply that law has to require something of us that is quite different from what morality requires of us—law, he says, often "modifies rather than excludes the way moral considerations apply,"[21] Still, it seems to suggest that there is something problematic about a statute that does little more than reiterate what morality requires anyway.

So consider Section 12603. Drivers are already subject to the requirements of morality, and even before law intervenes, morality requires those who operate motor vehicles to not drive them at a speed greater than is reasonable or proper, having regard for width, traffic, use, the usual rules of such roads or highways, and so on. Even in our broader sense of action-guidance, morality requires drivers to consider how reasonable their driving is in various circumstances. All this is something that a conscientious driver would figure out without the aid of Section 12603. So what, if anything, does Section 12603 add in the way of practical guidance? What practical difference does it make?[22] With Section 12604, we know what the law adds: a determinate speed limit or set of speed limits that moral reasoning by itself would not necessarily yield. But in effect, all that Section 12603 does is to repeat the demands of morality.

I must say that I do not see this as a problem. All sorts of laws repeat the demands of morality; a law prohibiting murder does that. Laws reiterating the demands of morality serve an important function. They give public expression to important values and requirements. They help in moral education. They authorize sanctions for moral violations. And above all, they

guide the behavior of those who might not otherwise attend to moral requirements. Sure, moral requirements are incumbent on everyone; everyone
ought to be guided by them without further ado. But some are not guided
by morality because they are badly brought up or indifferent to moral considerations, and some are not guided consistently by morality in particular
situations because of weakness of will or forgetfulness or the poor quality
of their moral reasoning. So, a law like Section 12603, which merely reiter-
ates the demands of responsible driving, has an important ancillary role to
play. In playing that role, it makes two sorts of practical difference: it helps
morality to make the practical difference that morality is supposed to
make, and it makes the practical difference of forcing people to focus on
the moral demands that are incumbent on them.

8. Thick Predicates

Model (ii) concerned the legal use of all-purpose evaluative predicates—like
"reasonable" or "proper" or "appropriate." I have argued that such norms
(such standards) are action-guiding, though what they guide in the first instance is the element of practical deliberation involved in the exercise of
agency. I think the same can be said about standards that use thick moral
terms like "inattentive" and "aggressive." They, too, guide practical reasoning
(and action based on that reasoning), but they provide additional structure
and channeling for the practical deliberation that they elicit. Suppose the
Ohio General Code had complemented the provisions we have already
studied with the following further (imaginary) provision:

> Section 12605: Whoever operates a motor vehicle or motorcycle in an
> aggressive or inattentive manner on the public roads or highways shall
> be fined not more than twenty-five dollars.

Had there been cell phones and texting in 1917, the code might have included specific prohibitions on taking calls or sending text messages. Had
there been road rage back then, it might specifically have prohibited the loud
use of particular curse words. But we are imagining, instead, broader, more
abstract prohibitions.

A term like "inattentive" or "aggressive" singles out a particular kind of
evaluation that it invites us to make, relative to our conduct or (if one is a

police officer) relative to the conduct of someone else. By a *kind* of evaluation, I mean an evaluation that pays attention to a subset of all the features of a situation that might be thought relevant from the broadest evaluative point of view. A given episode of driving might be evaluated in all sorts of ways, ranging from its speed to its necessity (as in the wartime slogan, "Is your journey necessary?"), but inattentiveness focuses evaluative attention on just some of those features—namely, the driver's awareness and alertness to the surrounding circumstances, including the road, the conditions, and actions of the other road users, as well as to the information that his own automobile presents in terms of speed instruments, noise, and so on. The prohibition on inattentive driving starts us off down some paths of evaluation and not others. So, for example, a police officer given the task of pulling over inattentive drivers will be zeroing in on some particular aspects of driving, such as where the driver's gaze is directed, or on behavior (swerving, etc.) likely to result from undue distraction. And equally. the driver himself, confronted with Section 12605, will remind himself of the importance of attentiveness and include this among the dimensions on which he plans and monitors his be-havior. True, the standard does not tell him precisely what to do—where to look when, how often to glance at his dashboard or to the right and to the left at what is happening in other lanes—but it instructs him to begin thinking about what actions are required *under this heading.*

The same is true of the prohibition on aggressive driving. Before he be-came aware of this rule, it may not have occurred to the individual driver that he should develop modes of evaluation of his own conduct along this dimension of aggressiveness. He might have been thinking, "the more ag-gression the better," provided he takes sufficient care; nobody wants undue timidity on the road. Or he may not have given the matter any thought at all, routinely driving too close to cars that he wants to overtake or using his horn when someone is in his way. But now the law indicates to him that ag-gression is a bad thing and that he had better engage his practical reasoning to figure out what a prohibition on this aspect of driving behavior might rea-sonably be thought to involve in the various circumstances in which he finds himself. The law assumes that he is capable of this—that is, capable of initiating and engaging in the forms of practical reason that flow from an awareness (perhaps an awareness for the first time) that there is a problem with aggressive driving. It assumes he is capable of reflection on this matter and capable too of mapping the results of such reflection onto the monitoring and modification of his own driving habits. So this, too, is *law guiding action,* only the guidance now demands an even more complicated and constrained structuring of practical deliberation.

9. Inchoate Rules?

Henry Hart and Albert Sacks, in their book *The Legal Process,* refer to a category of norm they call "inchoate rules." An inchoate rule is a norm that has the appearance of something that seeks to manage and control all aspects of its application, but for some it reason fails to do so, leaving it, in effect, for the courts to settle the precise nature of the directive that is given. They say, "An inchoate rule is, in effect, a partial postponement of the authoritative determination of public policy as to the matters left uncertain."[23] In the account that they give, an inchoate rule does not become a complete rule until the courts have contributed significantly to our understanding of it by "reasoned elaboration." Hart and Sacks explain this process in a section of their book titled "The Process of Reasoned Elaboration of Purportedly Determinate Directions."[24]

Of the provisions we have been examining, it is arguable that Section 12604 is inchoate in this sense because it specifies speed limits but not precise delimitations of where they kick into operation. As I noted earlier, the phrase "in the business and closely built-up portions of a municipality" is not a precise specification of a zone of application for the 8 mph limit; those who know anything about urban geography know that business districts have vague edges, and the term "built-up" has its own vagueness.

Are norms like Section 12603 and Section 12605 inchoate rules? I do not think so. They are not purportedly determinate; they are, to use another phrase from Hart and Sacks, "avowedly indeterminate."[25] As I said in sections 5 and 6, and as the Ohio court noted, the legislature made clear its intention to communicate a flexible standard in Section 12603, and I am stipulating that the same sort of intention is evident from our imaginary Section 12605. The legislature does not want these norms pinned down to a precise and exact meaning that will govern all future cases; that would detract from the very elasticity that it is aiming at, and it would detract from the sort of active consideration by citizens that it is seeking authoritatively to elicit. I fear that it is harder for jurists to see this in a case like Section 12605 than it is in the case of Section 12603. If someone asks about the meaning of "reasonable" or "appropriate," all we can do is indicate that these are flexible, all-purpose predicates of evaluation that invite us to consider a number of possible factors in an open-ended way. But for terms like "aggressive" and "inattentive," it is tempting to think that the lawmakers must have had something more specific in mind, and it is tempting to try to identify what that is and call that the legislative meaning of the term. This has been the history of "originalist" approaches to the use of thick evaluative terms like "cruel" in the US Constitution (in the Eighth Amendment). Instead of reading a prohibition on "cruel punishment" as an invitation to engage in structured practical deliberation along the subset of dimensions of evaluation that the word "cruel" indicates, the temptation is to treat the word as a cipher for some particular practices that the framers of the constitutional provision must have had it in mind to condemn. Or, in the case of certain modern human rights provisions, like the prohibition on inhuman and degrading punishment in Article 3 of the European Convention on Human Rights, the temptation is to substitute an array of particular decisions by an authoritative court—shackling is degrading, corporal punishment is inhuman,and so on—for the structured deliberation that is invited by the ordinary-language meanings of these terms.[26] Both these approaches treat the norm in question as an inchoate rule, and one way or another, their strategy is to flee as soon as possible from the indeterminacy occasioned by an acknowledgment that these are evaluative terms inviting evaluative judgment. By contrast, the approach that I have taken looks for what Ronald Dworkin has called a "moral reading" of these provisions, which involves judges trying to figure out in their own voice as a matter of moral judgment what punishments are cruel (or inhuman or degrading) and what punishments are not.[27]

Maybe there are good political reasons for treating provisions like the Eighth Amendment as inchoate rules. Constitutional originalism, for example, is sometimes motivated by a distrust of judges exercising the sort of independent moral evaluation that would follow from their taking the moral reading seriously. The worry is that judges will indulge their own subjective policy preferences if they are asked to say in their own voice whether, for example, capital punishment is cruel. Maybe that fear of judicial independence or judicial subjectivity justifies the originalism approach. But what does not justify it is the proposition that the Eighth Amendment, on the moral reading, fails to give the judges any guidance. It *does* give them guidance—only, what it guides is their decision whether to engage in moral deliberation on this matter in the way that the meaning of the term "cruel" invites.

10. Chilling Behavior

I have tried to answer the objection that standards like Section 12603 and our imaginary Section 12605 fail to guide action, and that this is why their imprecision is objectionable from the point of view of the rule of law. An alternative objection is that such imprecise standards provide altogether too much in the way of action-guidance, because they chill and deter not only the behavior to which they are eventually applied, but also a lot of behavior in the vicinity, as people strive to avoid the risk of being caught out by these indeterminate provisions. A numerical speed limit deters only the behavior that exceeds 8 mph or 15 mph or whatever the limit is. But a requirement to drive at a reasonable speed or a requirement not to drive aggressively may deter much behavior that might not eventually be found by a court to be unreasonable or aggressive, simply because the agent plays it safe to avoid the risk of prosecution. This objection is very common, and it may be justified in the case of an inchoate rule—where the legislature has managed to indicate that behavior up to some specified limit is permissible but has failed to provide a determinate indication of what that limit is. However, it is not usually justified in the case of standards like the ones we are considering.

Think back to what the Ohio Supreme Court said about Section 12603 in *State v. Schaeffer*:

> The careful, conservative driver need have no fear of [the provision]. The reckless, wanton speed maniac needs to be kept in fear of it. The life of the humblest citizen must be placed above the gratification of the motor maniac, who would turn the public highways into a race course. (234)

The court's view seems to be that "chilling" the behavior of "the reckless, wanton speed maniac" may be a good thing; it may be a good thing if the formerly inattentive driver becomes hypervigilant or if the formerly aggressive driver is led by Section 12605 to become extremely, perhaps even unnecessarily, polite.

The underlying point here is that guiding action need not be conceived as an exact enterprise. Chilling action is also a way of guiding action. It brings a person's action under legal control within a broad and vaguely defined range rather than by reference to a specific act-type (such as driving at an exactly specified speed). The instruction to "Slow down," for example, guides action, and it does so even though the recipient of the instruction knows pragmatically that dropping his speed by 1 mph does not satisfy the requirement and knows too that dropping his speed *to* 1 mph may be taking things too far. Somewhere in between these extremes there is an area of behavior that the instruction guides him toward. But it is a vague area, and from the law's point of view, it probably does not matter if the desire to avoid sanctions biases things toward the lower end of the scale. Much the same, I believe, may be said of Section 12603.

If there is a serious objection to chilling action in this sort of way, it is probably better phrased in terms of a background concern for liberty rather than a background concern for guiding action as such. For example, in First Amendment doctrine, we sometimes worry that restrictions on speech in a particular area will "chill" speech in the surrounding area, and we think that this is a problem because we have a strong general commitment to freedom of speech in all but the areas where we can say with confidence that a specific restriction is needed.[28] The US Supreme Court has sometimes said that "because First Amendment freedoms need breathing space to survive, government may regulate in the area only with narrow specificity."[29] But it is not clear that any such assumption is warranted in the driving case. Do we really want to say that because the freedom to drive fast (or as one pleases) needs breathing space to survive, government may regulate in the area only with narrow specificity? I do not think so, and I think there are a great many cases like this. Often, the use of model (ii) is justified in areas where we think there is no strong background right to liberty—no background interest in freedom that requires an unchilled breathing space. We think it is justified in areas where a person's actions already warrant the watchfulness of the law and where eliciting the person's own watchfulness—even if that takes the form of general chilling caution—is by no means objectionable. Driving, at least in 1917, was just such a case.

Beyond that, the other objection that a legislature needs to confront is an apprehension of unfairness in the disparity that may sometimes occur between the citizen's idea of what is reasonable and the authorities' view of what is reasonable when the citizen's action is reviewed by the police or by the courts. We are not now concerned with the reckless, wanton speed maniac who says, "I am shocked—shocked!—to find out that I was expected to slow down in a built-up area with children playing in the street." What about the responsible driver who is just unsure about whether his good faith estimate of reasonable speed is going to coincide with that of the police? I am thinking here about the person who worries whether his own good faith calculations will be regarded by others as idiosyncratic, or the person who worries that he may be confronted with a judge or a magistrate who has an idiosyncratic view of the matter that differs from his own. Once again, this is not a concern about action-guidance, but it may be a real concern nonetheless.

I do not believe that this concern is answered, in the way philosophers are often tempted to answer it, by appealing to a notion of objectivity—that is, by saying that so long as there is an objective right answer to the question of what is a reasonable driving speed in a given set of circumstances, no one can complain about unfairness when his own subjective calculation is corrected by a court. There can be an objective right answer and still people can come up with widely disparate estimates, and so the question does have to be confronted: is it fair to subject P's estimate to review in terms of someone else's estimate, in circumstances where, with the best will in the world—objectivity or no objectivity—the two of them widely diverge?

To avoid this concern, one might want to confine the use of model (ii) as a form of action-guidance to areas of conduct where we have reason to believe there is not going to be a wide divergence in estimates of appropriate behavior. Driving, it seems to me, is such an area. In *State v. Schaeffer*, although there was a factual disagreement about how fast the defendant was driving, there seemed to be little disagreement about how fast it was appropriate to drive when large numbers of children were playing on the street. Responsible drivers and responsible law-enforcement officials were likely to converge around a fairly low number—in 1917, perhaps somewhat below the 8 mph limit laid down for built-up areas in Section 12604. In areas where there is likely to be greater divergence—whether because of different cultures in regard to the activity in question or because of different patterns of perception of what is and what is not a circumstance that promises danger— something more along the lines of model (i) may be appropriate. This might lead us to reconsider our imaginary Section 12605, or at least the part that relates to aggressive driving. Cultures of driving may have developed so disparately that we can no longer rely on a sort of background consensus to obviate the unfairness of subjecting one person's view of what is and is not aggressive to another person's view on that matter (with possible heavy penalties as a result). It is possible that an otherwise good driver might say, *not* disingenuously, "I am shocked to find that driving closely behind a vehicle that is traveling below the usual speed in the fast lane and flashing my lights to indicate that I want to overtake is treated as aggressive driving." It may be better to do what many states now do, which is to authoritatively define aggressive driving in terms of certain specific practices.[30] This represents, in effect, a shift from model (ii) to model (i).

On the other hand, cultures of driving do not come out of nowhere. They grow and develop as people begin to take less and less responsibility for the considerateness of their driving patterns. We imagined an honest driver being surprised to learn that his attitude toward overtaking was regarded by the police or the courts as aggressive. But it might be more realistic to imagine such a driver being slightly defiant about his driving and resistant to the processes of practical reasoning that the law aimed to elicit: "I don't need anyone to teach me how to drive. Those slowpokes in the fast lane need to learn to pull over and let those of us by who know how to drive at speed." The early stage of emergence of this sort of attitude represents, in effect, an assault on a certain consensus about reasonable and safe driving and an attempt to replace it with a different, perhaps more Darwinian, approach. The attitudes (and the driving) of such a person may or may not be admirable, but we may have less sympathy with his complaint about unfairness when he finds his actions authoritatively reviewed in terms of more prudent standards than those he is trying to inculcate.

Obviously, there is much more to be said on these matters of fairness and consensus, on the one hand, and stronger or weaker background commitments to liberty, on the other. I have not provided a full treatment of these points. My aim here is to illustrate simply the way in which the real concerns that they raise differ from the concerns about the action-guiding aspect of imprecise legal provisions.

11. From Traffic to Torture

Believe it or not, my main concern is not about traffic rules. I came to these issues through a different, more serious, and much darker route: the problem of legal provisions that prohibit torture.[31] The US antitorture statute (18 U.S.C. § 2340A) makes it an offense punishable by up to twenty years' imprisonment (or death, if death results) to commit, conspire, or attempt to commit torture.[32] Now, "torture" is a vivid term, and for most of us it summons up grisly and distressing images of practices that fall indisputably within its sphere of reference. But its boundaries seem contestable. Is sleep deprivation torture? What about forcing people to stand in a stress position for many hours? Is waterboarding a form of torture? All these questions have been debated. The antitorture statute actually provides a definition: "'torture' means an act committed by a person acting under the color of law specifically intended to inflict severe physical or mental pain or suffering . . . upon another person within his custody or physical control."[33] Unfortunately, this definition does not remove the indeterminacy; it just helps identify its source. Torture is vague in part because the phrase "severe physical . . . pain or suffering" is vague. Severity of pain or suffering is a continuum, but by the use of the word "torture," it seems to presuppose that we can say of a given episode of pain and suffering that either it is severe or it is not. In this respect, Section 2340A is rather like our imagined Section 12605 prohibiting aggressive driving. It invokes a standard conveyed by a thick term of evaluation, and it engages our practical reasoning in this regard on the optimistic assumption (which may or may not be justified) that—when prodded by the law—we know and agree about how to apply it.

I believe that the following points, drawn from what has been said about our paradigms of traffic law in Ohio, can help us think through the difficulties that might arise with regard to the antitorture statute.

First, the indeterminacy of Section 2340A, such as it is, does not prevent it from being action-guiding or from making a practical difference to the agency and behavior of those who are subject to it. Inasmuch as it imposes a nonnegotiable prohibition and threatens heavy penalties, it constitutes a warning to the community of people likely to be engaged in coercive interrogation that they should give the most careful thought to their choice of interrogation techniques. They are put on notice that the very thing that might attract them to a technique—its painfulness and people's inability to resist it—is itself the locus of the gravest legislative concern. So, for example, even though the law as written does not settle in a determinate way whether waterboarding is torture, it does tend to guide their agency away from such techniques.

Second, the fact that a relatively indeterminate prohibition might "chill" interrogative activity is hardly a cause for concern. For suppose it is the definition of "severe pain or suffering" that is giving pause to our imagined interrogator. He is in the business, let us say, of deliberately inflicting considerable pain on detainees already and he just want to know where exactly the severity line is so that he can push up against it but not be seen to cross it. He already has the electrodes plugged in and the dial turned up to 4 or 5; he wants to know how much higher he can go. I think we are unlikely to say of this case what we observed the Supreme Court saying about speech, that "because the practice of deliberately inflicting pain in interrogation needs breathing space to survive, government may regulate in the area only with narrow specificity." Instead, we might see the context of coercive interrogation as being a prime case for legislative watchfulness, and we may have no difficulty with the idea that the watchfulness that the law in turn elicits from interrogators may lead to an excess of caution.

Sure, opinions may differ on this. Some will say that we need to avoid chilling interrogative activity because we need the results of interrogation in our pursuit of the war against terrorism. (An analogy would be the opinion that we need fast, efficient driving, so it is important not to chill that with vague safety-oriented ordinances like Section 12603 and Section 12605.) But now, at least, we have located the nub of the dispute. It is not a general concern about vague statutes; it is a concern about the relative seriousness with which we should take the background liberty on which the statute impinges.

Third, we might conceivably identify a problem about fairness, in which an interrogator professes surprise about the way in which his estimation of which practices count as torture (or which episodes of pain count as severe) is second-guessed by a war crimes tribunal. Whether we like it or not, it is possible that under conditions of modern pluralism, different cultures have emerged that in fact treat these phenomena in quite different ways, so that someone is not just weeping crocodile tears when they say, "I am shocked— shocked!—to learn that you are going to punish me under the antitorture statute for setting dogs on prisoners or depriving them of sleep." That may be so. Alternatively, it is possible that there has been an attempt in recent years deliberately to *create* such a disparity of evaluations, to muddy the waters of human rights law and international humanitarian law so that it appears that the consensus on which Section 2340 and Section 2340A were predicated has dissolved. On this alternative account, statements of the "shocked— shocked!" variety would be part of a campaign, deliberately calibrated to foster this dissensus. If that is the case, I think we should be much less impressed by these complaints of unfairness relative to the ordinary operation of a provision like this. We should probably be less impressed by them anyway, because as the likelihood of actual prosecutions under Section 2340A is in fact vanishingly small, and the main effect of the attempt to pin down a precise meaning for "torture" or "severe" is in fact to furnish a presidential administration with a determinate envelope to push.[34]

12. The Lesbian Rule

Complaints about vagueness and imprecision are not just abstract concerns in legal philosophy. They afford us an opportunity to think more complicated thoughts in our philosophical conceptions of what it is for a legal provision to guide action, and I have tried to set out in this chapter what some of those complications might be. But we need to remember that it is vague *law* we are talking about, not just vague propositions. That we are talking about vague law means, at the end of the day, we are talking about the auspices under which punishments will be meted out and sanctions imposed; and that should alert us to the seriousness of the matter. But we should understand, too, what is at stake in the legislative or regulative enterprise. That is also a deadly serious matter—protecting people from torturers, or in our traffic case, from "the reckless, wanton speed maniac." In these and similar areas, it is good to focus on the need for legislative flexibility, or what Aristotle once called the "lesbian" rule: "For when the thing is indefinite the rule also is indefinite, like the leaden rule used in making the Lesbian molding; the rule adapts itself to the shape of the stone and is not rigid, and so too the decree is adapted to the facts."[35] The adaptability of law, secured precisely by what others would call its indeterminacy, is not incompatible with law continuing to guide the actions of its subjects. It is a valuable legislative resource and a respectful one, too, for it works in tandem with the most sophisticated understanding of people's powers of practical reasoning.

6

The Rule of Law and the Role of Courts

1. Judicial Review of Executive and Legislative Action

What role do courts play—what role should the judiciary play—in advancing or upholding the political ideal we call "the rule of law"? It is commonly said that the rule of law assigns a particular responsibility to judges to see to it that the state in all its operations conforms to the law. Certainly, the rule of law seems to require something like close judicial supervision of the executive, judicial review of executive action, and the limiting of judicial discretion. What about judicial review of legislation? Is this also required by the rule of law? Are societies that make no provision for judicial review of legislation, or which allow the practice only in a weak or limited form, deficient so far as the rule of law is concerned? Are their legislatures to that degree lawless? Should we frown on them, in the name of legality, just as much or almost as much as we would frown on an executive that escaped judicial supervision?

I am not sure how to answer these questions. One thing is clear: polities that do have strong judicial review of legislation do not envisage or practice for the legislature anything like the degree or extent of legal control that is envisaged for the executive in a rule-of-law state. The usual view about the executive is that it should act only as legally authorized and that any discretion that is vested in executive officials should be framed and guided by legal norms. In the case of the executive, the rule-of-law requirement is not just that there are certain things that the executive and its agencies may not do; anything that it does, at least so far as domestic administration is concerned, must be authorized and must take place within a constraining framework of public norms.[1]

I do not know of anyone who believes this about rule-of-law control of the legislature. Mostly, judicial review is defended on the basis that there are certain things the legislature may not do—certain rights, based on values like dignity but listed in a line-item way in a bill of rights, that it may not contravene. The constitutional function of the judiciary is to uphold these constraints. Provided these constraints are not violated, the idea is that the legislature may make laws, repeal or amend laws, or fail to make laws—as it pleases, entirely in its discretion. And defenders of strong judicial review do not envisage as a matter of principle that that discretion must be constrained or guided by judicially enforced norms.

Now what I have just said is too general; it needs to be modified in a couple of respects. First, constitutional constraints sometimes *require* the legislature to act in certain ways, as well as prohibiting it from acting in certain ways.[2] For instance, Article 26 of the Constitution of South Africa insists that "everyone has the right to have access to adequate housing," and it requires that "the state must take reasonable legislative and other measures, within its available resources, to achieve the progressive realisation of this right." So the rule of law could be violated in this context by a legislative *failure* to act. Still, once such particular constraints (positive and negative) are given their due, the legislature has uncontrolled discretion to act or not act as it pleases.

The other respect in which my formulation needs to be modified is to take account of the division of labor between legislatures that have plenary authority and legislatures that have only enumerated powers in a federal system. In the United States, the federal legislature does not have plenary legislative authority; it may legislate only on the matters laid down in Article I, Section 8 of the US Constitution. There is no legal requirement that it must address the matters listed in this provision, but it may not address areas of public policy that are not so listed, and it is the job of the federal courts to uphold this restriction. But, as the Tenth Amendment recognizes, the enumerated powers of the federal legislature are complemented by the plenary legislative authority of the states. State legislatures are bound by particular constraints laid down in their own constitutions and in the federal constitution. But subject to these constraints, they have plenary authority to pass or not pass or amend or repeal any legislation they please, without any legal constraint. As far as I know, no one thinks this is a violation of the rule of law. And in unitary states, of course—even unitary states that have strong judicial review—the national legislature almost always has straightforward plenary authority.

This is why I say the analogy with judicial control of the executive is unhelpful. There is a massive contrast between the kind of rule-of-law control envisaged for the executive and the legal control that is envisaged, even in a system of strong judicial review, for the legislature. There is no default position of plenary discretion for the executive and its agencies as there is for the legislature. Even though there are many calls today in the United Kingdom, say, for what people call the sovereignty of the British Parliament to be subjected to the rule of law, all that is envisaged under this heading is the enforcement of particular limitations on lawmaking, not an abrogation of Parliament's plenary legislative authority.[3]

2. For and against the Rule of Law

Still, I do not want to say that it is inappropriate to cite the ideal of the rule of law as a basis for insisting that there must be some legal controls on legislation, even if they are only of the modest sort that I have described, and that there must be judicial review to enforce such controls. If someone wants to say that this is what the rule of law requires, I guess we know what they mean.

I am known as an opponent of strong judicial review of legislation, even of the limited sort just described (enforcing specific constraints and the balance of plenary and enumerated powers, where appropriate).[4] I have often asked myself: What is the best way to characterize this opposition so far as the ideal of the rule of law is concerned. Does this make me an opponent of the rule of law?

Yes and no; certainly, it seems to indicate a qualification on my devotion to that ideal. But think of it this way: most of those who have faith in the rule of law see it as just one ideal for good government—one among others. As Joseph Raz has emphasized, the rule of law is not the sum of all good things. It is, Raz says, "just one of the virtues which a legal system may possess and by which it is to be judged."

> It is not to be confused with democracy, justice, equality (before the law or otherwise), human rights of any kind or respect for persons or for the dignity of man. A non-democratic legal system, based on the denial of human rights, on extensive poverty, on racial segregation, sexual inequalities, and religious persecution may, in principle, conform to the requirements of the rule of law better than any of the legal

systems of the more enlightened Western democracies. This does not mean that it will be better than those Western democracies. It will be an immeasurably worse legal system, but it will excel in one respect: in its conformity to the rule of law.[5]

Those who believe in a substantive conception of the rule of law may disagree, though even most of them will concede that the rule of law does not embrace *all* substantive political values. The implication seems to be that an evaluation of a society from the point of view of the rule of law is necessarily incomplete. We also want to evaluate it from the point of view of democracy, social justice, human rights, and so on. I would go just one step further than this. It is possible that the rule of law is not just incomplete (relative to these other ideals) as a criterion for political evaluation. It is possible that in certain circumstances, the rule of law may *compete* with these other ideals; there may be trade-offs between them. Some speculate, for example, that there may be trade-offs between the rule of law and a commitment to social justice.[6] And my position on judicial review is similar: if it is true that judicial review of legislation is required by the rule of law, then there is the prospect of a trade-off between the rule of law and democracy. For my objections to judicial review do not really deny that judicial review is required by the rule of law. (I shall record some hesitations about this, though, in the sections that follow.) My objections to judicial review are based mainly on democracy and democratic legitimacy, and so they involve a concession of the kind that Joseph Raz made: "A non-democratic legal system . . . may, in principle, conform to the requirements of the rule of law better than any of the legal systems of the more enlightened Western democracies."[7] But since the rule of law is not a complete basis for social evaluation, I am willing to infer, with Raz, that "this does not mean that [the system that respects this aspect of the rule of law] will be better than those Western democracies." And I don't mean that judicial review of legislation, as a rule-of-law requirement, fatally compromises democracy, only that it seems to involve some degree of trade-off between the rule of law and the idea that ultimately, important decisions in the polity should be made by the people or their elected representatives.

In another voice, however, we may want to question whether judicial review of legislation is in all circumstances and in all modes of its use a positive contribution to the rule of law. Quite apart from the issue of democratic legitimacy, the practice of judicial review may actually pose further problems for the rule of law. Let me explain.

Suppose we make the judiciary supreme in our constitutional scheme, by giving judges power to overrule the decisions of all other branches of government. Should we regard this as an achievement of the rule of law? Or is it just another version of the rule of men (or, as we should say, the rule of people), albeit people wearing black robes and sitting in a courtroom? Does the rule of law mean the rule of judges? Are judicial decisions at the highest level constrained by law to any greater extent than legislative decisions in a state that lacks strong judicial review? The problem becomes particularly acute once we recognize that judges cannot just enforce the law; often, they also have to make the law. So is judge-made law to be regarded as the epitome of the rule of law, or as part of the problem that the rule of law is supposed to solve?[8]

In the remainder of this chapter, I want to open up these conundrums and see if we can arrive at a nuanced set of conclusions about the relation between the rule of law and various forms of judicial power.

3. The Rule of Law and Rule by Law

Scholars sometimes distinguish between *the rule of law* and *rule by law*.[9] "Rule by law" refers to the governance strategy that a ruler (or a ruling institution) adopts in his dealings with his subjects. If he rules by law, he doesn't just manage them with particular commands and decrees and discretionary decisions. He rules using a framework of general laws, laid down in advance so that they know where they stand and so that there is a general and more or less determinate basis, available to everyone in advance, on which they can approach the disputes and controversies that break out in any complex society. Thomas Hobbes explained the importance of rule by law in these terms:

> Since it no lesse, nay it much more conduceth to Peace to prevent brawles from arising, then to appease them being risen; and that all controversies are bred from hence, that the opinions of men differ concerning Meum & Tuum, just and unjust, ... good and evill, ... and the like, which every man esteems according to his own judgement; it belongs to the same chiefe power to make some common Rules for all men, and to declare them publiquely, by which every man may know what may be called his, what anothers, what just, what unjust, what honest, what dishonest, what good, what evill, that is summarily, what

is to be done, what to be avoyded in our common course of life. But those Rules and measures are usually called the civill Lawes, or the Lawes of the City, as being the Commands of him who hath the su-preme power in the City. And the Civill Lawes (that we may define them) are nothing else but the commands of him who hath the chiefe authority in the City, for direction of the future actions of his Citizens.[10]

In the rule-of-law literature, the idea of rule *by* law is often disparaged. It is associated with a certain form of authoritarianism, whereby a strong man uses law as a means of subordinating citizens but refuses to acknowledge any legal constraints on his own actions.[11] This is fake rule of law, critics say, because it is not motivated by any real love of legality, but is "no more than what every man, who loves his own power, profit, or greatness, may, and nat-urally must do, keep those animals from hurting or destroying one another who labour and drudge only for his pleasure and advantage." That's the only reason why the authoritarian ruler allows his subjects to "have an appeal to the law, and judges to decide any controversies, and restrain any violence that may happen betwixt the subjects themselves, one amongst another."[12]

But that sells short an important part of the rule-of-law ideal. That ideal, in all its applications, always insists on rule by law *at least,* and usually this insistence in itself is regarded as a large and indispensable part of the require-ment that governments respect those who are subject to them and rule them in a way that is consistent with their freedom and their dignity.[13] More-over, rule by law is, in and of itself, a very demanding ideal, inasmuch as it requires the government in most circumstances to forego all purely discre-tionary action and to subject official decisions to covering norms of one sort or another, norms that form the basis of citizen calculability and citizen re-course to challenge governmental action.

What then does the rule *of* law envisage? What does it add to rule by law? It envisages the possibility that the *highest power* in a society is bound by law and subject to law and that governmental officials at *every* level— including the highest level—should exercise their power within a con-straining framework of public norms, rather than on the basis of their own preferences or ideology.[14] This is sometimes associated with a fantasy that law itself should be king or ultimate ruler in a political system.[15] Whether or not we can make sense of that personification, while still acknowledging that law has to be made by humans, is another matter. Realistically, this notion of the rule of law is associated with the idea that some forms of law—like common law, or customary law, or long-established constitutions—have modes of human origin that are less likely than other forms of law to make nonsense of the slogan, "The rule of laws, not men."[16] People being ruled by principles whose emergence as man-made law is in some sense immemorial is perhaps more congenial to the idea of law ultimately being in charge than people being ruled by legislation that was made by other people last week. In the latter case, the all-too-human aspect of the law that is supposed to be in charge is all too evident. In the former case, it is easier to gloss over; the constraining law is less an artifact of immediate political power.

In any case, this demanding ideal of the rule of law also has to come to terms with the fact that laws are interpreted, applied, and enforced by people, as well as being made by people. And even if the law was made or emerged eons ago, its interpretation and application has to take place in real time now. So, from the point of view of this demanding ideal of the rule of law, there are bound to be questions about the status of those who do the interpreting, the applying, and the enforcing, and where *they* fall in this normative contrast between the rule of laws and the rule of men. This is going to be a question about courts and judges, among others.

4. Hobbes's Challenge

Notoriously, Thomas Hobbes believed that a well-organized society would have at its apex a sovereign lawgiver—an uncommanded commander (maybe a monarch, maybe a sovereign parliament)—that would rule by law but would not itself be subject to legal restraint. How could it be subject to legal constraint? As the source of all legitimate coercion in the society, there would be no one to restrain it but itself. As Hobbes put it in *Leviathan* (1651):

> The Soveraign of a Common-wealth, be it an Assembly, or one Man, is not Subject to the Civil Lawes. For having power to make, and repeale Lawes, he may when he pleaseth, free himselfe from that subjection, by repealing those Lawes that trouble him, and making of new; and consequently he was free before. For he is free, that can be free when he will: Nor is it possible for any person to be bound to himselfe; because he that can bind, can release; and therefore he that is bound to himselfe onely is not bound.[17]

It sounds like a convincing argument, and its ruthless Hobbesian logic seems to indicate that it is impossible to apply the rule of law to the apex of a society's sovereign.

We think we know better. We are less accepting now of the hard logic of sovereignty that Hobbes propounded. We tend to think of sovereignty—if we think of it at all—in terms of a social and political process rather than in terms of an institution. If what we are interested in is the process of limiting government, we think it is possible to do this with a constitution and to patrol that limitation with a court or a system of courts.

But Hobbes rejected all forms of this logic of constitutionalism. It is, he said, a mistake to think that you can limit sovereignty with a constitution, because you have to do it with some other political entity—in this case, a court.

> Which errour, because it setteth the Lawes above the Soveraign, setteth also a Judge above him, and a Power to punish him; which is to make a new Soveraign; and again for the same reason a third, to punish the second; and so continually without end, to the Confusion, and Dissolution of the Common-wealth.[18]

It is an infinite regress argument. Either you have a legislative monarch or parliament which is an uncommanded commander, or you have that entity being controlled by a court, which is an uncommanded commander; and if that court is not to be an uncommanded commander, there must be some other entity that controls it, and so on. In an earlier work, *De Cive* (1642), Hobbes insisted that

> in every City there is some one man, or Councell, or Court . . . that is, supreme and absolute, to be limited onely by the strength and forces of the City it selfe, and by nothing else in the world: for if his power were limited, that limitation must necessarily proceed from some greater power; For he that prescribes limits, must have a greater power than he who is confin'd by them; now that confining power is either without limit, or is again restrained by some other greater than it selfe, and so we shall at length arrive to a power which hath no other limit, but that which is the terminus ultimus.[19]

On this logic, either you have a final human authority or you do not. If you do, then all talk of being ruled by the law is fatuous, whether or not the final authority wears a gown and sits in a court. There must always be some-body—not some scroll or text, but some *body*—who has the final word.

5. The Constitutionalist Solution

The attempt to find a way around this absolutist logic is what exercised generations of jurists after Hobbes—in James Harrington's republicanism, in the liberalism of John Locke, in the Enlightenment constitutionalism of Montesquieu and also the Federalists, all the way through to the Victorian paradoxes of Albert Venn Dicey's attempt to reconcile parliamentary sovereignty with the rule of law.[20] That disagreement remains with us today in the United States and other advanced democracies as we swing uneasily between the position that the rule of law positively requires that the Supreme Court have the final say in any constitutional crisis, and the position that judicial supremacy is as offensive to the rule of law as any other form of unreviewable hegemony in a constitutional regime.[21]

Constitutionalists—particularly in the United States—have thought it possible to break out of this rigid Hobbesian logic by empowering a court to review legislation without giving the court anything like the full power of a sovereign. The idea is that the court can do nothing except check and restrain the lawmakers on various issues; it has no real power of lawmaking itself. So it is not the super-sovereign that Hobbes describes it as. As Alexander Hamilton said in *The Federalist Papers*, "The judiciary . . . has no influence over either the sword or the purse; no direction either of the strength or of the wealth of the society; and can take no active resolution whatever."[22] True, it is like an uncommanded commander on the particular issues it addresses, but that is far from being a sovereign with plenary power. The constitutional separation of powers sees to that.

6. But Might a Supreme Court Become a Hobbesian Sovereign?

This solution to the Hobbesian problem—if it is a solution—is precarious. We can quickly be plunged back into the Hobbesian regress whenever the court that reviews legislation takes on the power of making laws or other powers associated with sovereignty. A judiciary that thinks of itself as a lawmaker is in danger of becoming a Hobbesian sovereign or super-sovereign. Its taking on these additional roles makes it harder for constitutionalists to deny that this is just the replication of human power at a higher level. The more power that courts take on, the greater the danger there is of ruining the anti-Hobbesian constitutionalist solution to the problem of applying the rule of law to the apex power in a society. For if a supreme court makes the laws to which the legislature is going to be held, then we have—here and now—a human lawmaker (a body of judges) that is not itself bound by law in its human lawmaking. (Or if it is bound, it must be bound by an entity whose own activity, in turn, raises exactly the same questions.)

This issue of whether judicial power represents the rule of law or represents a sort of judicial super-sovereign that escapes the authority of the rule of law is a perennial problem in rule-of-law studies. Should we regard strong judicial review as the epitome of the rule of law, or as yet another part of the problem that the rule of law is supposed to solve? If we believe in the rule of law, not people, does "people" include black-robed judges sitting in a courtroom? Some will say that—short of the fantasy that the laws themselves might rear up and render their own decisions—the most that the rule of law could possibly entail at this level is decisions by judges after due deliberation in a courtroom (including unreviewable decisions by judges sitting in the highest court in the land). This is, as I said, a precarious solution to the problem of the rule of law, and judges must take care that they don't begin behaving in a way that creates the impression that they are the final unreviewable sovereign power in the constitution.

7. Ways of Avoiding Judicial Sovereignty

I said before that I am an opponent of judicial review of legislation. But I am willing to make the following concession to those who defend judicial review: it is possible for a polity to embrace judicial review without necessarily giving rise to the Hobbesian problem we have just identified. The power of judicial review can be exercised more or less modestly or in a more or less aggressive or programmatic spirit. Let me identify some practices associated with judicial review that might give rise to Hobbesian apprehensions—practices that it would be advisable for the judiciary to avoid if it does not want to undermine the rule of law by taking on the mantle of judicial sovereignty.

The practice of judicial review is characteristically associated with a bill of rights, mostly listing discrete things that the branches of government must not do. Though these rights are based on deep underlying values like equality and human dignity, it is interesting that they present themselves as a list, rather than as an integrated platform or coherent policy. I think that can help us understand how things can go wrong in judicial review, how things can tilt toward judicial sovereignty.

So long as the courts confine themselves to the particular items on the list—free speech, freedom of religion, due process, privacy, nondiscrimination, reproductive rights, and so on—and deal with them one by one as they crop up in particular cases, there is no great danger of the judges' becoming Hobbesian sovereigns. But there is a danger that judicial review will tilt toward judicial sovereignty if courts begin to present themselves as pursuing a coherent *program* or *policy*, rather than just responding to particular abuses identified as such by a bill of rights—one by one, as they crop up. I know this goes against the grain of a great deal of constitutional theory. It is sometimes said that judges should have a view of the constitution as a whole, a coherent program of principle, and that they should seek in successive cases to move that program forward on a broad front. (Some call this a "living constitution" approach.) The program in question might embody a broad progressive or liberal vision, or perhaps an overall vision of a conservative free-market society. I believe that the more judges think of their work in this way, the more they are in danger of asserting themselves and their particular unreviewable power as the ascendant platform from which the overall shape of good governance is to be determined.

I think judges need to be particularly careful about this when their constitution embodies positive social and economic rights as well as civil and political rights, because it may be more difficult to hold social and economic rights apart from a programmatic vision. But it can be done. I don't want to be heard as disparaging the insertion of social and economic rights in a constitution. These rights are very important. But their presence in the constitution should not be read as empowering the judges to pursue an overall vision of social justice or anything of the sort.

So, judicial review should not be understood as an opportunity to implement a broad social program through decisions in successive cases. Equally, the judiciary should not take it upon itself to oppose the vision or overall program or policy of the elected branches. It is the responsibility of the elected branches of government to form and pursue social programs on that scale. The task of the judges is simply to spot and identify particular abuses or egregious omissions, not to oppose the program as a whole, which is none of their responsibility. Here I have in mind as an example the stance that the Supreme Court of the United States took against social and economic legislation in what we call the *Lochner* era. We define it with reference to a particular case, *Lochner v. New York* (1905).[23] But it was a long period of US constitutional history, from the 1880s to the late 1930s, in which state and federal courts struck down statute after statute, about 170 in all—statutes that together constituted a progressive program of economic and social amelioration.[24] The US courts marked out a stance of broad opposition to the program pursued by the elective branches of government, establishing in effect a "stand-off"—a tussle of power—between those branches and itself. In my view, this way of deploying the power of judicial review also gives rise to the Hobbesian problem, for now it looks like the courts have constituted themselves as a broad veto bearers with the ability to say yes or no to a whole swathe of public policy.

Another way in which the courts can present themselves, in effect, as human sovereigns in their exercise of judicial review is by making it evident that their decisions on important issues faced by the nation depend on the particular politics of the relevant judicial personnel. This point was made well by the Supreme Court of the United States in its reflections on legitimacy and constitutional stare decisis in the 1992 case of *Planned Parenthood v. Casey*.[25] Contemplating the possibility that constitutional decisions might last or be overturned simply as a function of one set of judges leaving the Court and another set of judges coming into the Court, the Court said:

> There is . . . a point beyond which frequent overruling would overtax the country's belief in the Court's good faith. Despite the variety of reasons that may inform and justify a decision to overrule, we cannot forget that such a decision is usually perceived (and perceived correctly) as, at the least, a statement that a prior decision was wrong. There is a limit to the amount of error that can plausibly be imputed to prior Courts. If that limit should be exceeded, disturbance of prior rulings would be taken as evidence that justifiable reexamination of principle had given way to drives for particular results in the short term. The legitimacy of the Court would fade with the frequency of its vacillation.[26]

The point being made here was about legitimacy—the American people's "understanding of the Court [as] invested with the authority to decide their constitutional cases and speak before all others for their constitutional ideals."[27] It was connected, the Supreme Court said, with "the character of a Nation of people who aspire to live according to the rule of law."[28] I am taking it in a slightly different direction: a court whose principles change with every alteration in the voting balance of its personnel can hardly deny that its hegemony represents the rule of men rather than the rule of law. Maybe that is impossible to deny anyway. But if it is to be denied, the court must present its members as being bound by law rather than the law being determined by the will or the vote of its members. And too-frequent "vacillation" traceable to changes in the political composition of the judiciary will inevitably undermine that presentation.

Of course, there is nothing for it but for judges to vote when there is genuine disagreement among them as to what the law is.[29] But the argument here is that if judges want to avoid the problem of judicial sovereignty as a version of rule by people, then as individuals, they may have to strain to suppress the all-too-human tendency to question past decisions when they come onto the bench, or to make their own decisions depend tendentiously on beliefs and conceptions of the law that they know are not shared by their judicial colleagues. Only by doing that will they be able to maintain the impression that it is the law that is in charge, not the competing views about the law of particular individuals who happen to be judges.[30]

8. Further Questions

The suggestions just made may seem like a tired recycling of old concerns about judicial review and judicial activism. But I am putting them to a different use here: they are presented not as condemnations of certain forms of judicial conduct but as ways of helping to preserve the integrity of the constitutionalist response to Hobbes's otherwise implacable logic of sovereignty.

The issues discussed here do not exhaust this topic of the relation between judicial review and the rule of law. If space permitted, we should also ask and answer the following questions.

First, do the procedures of judicial decision-making make a difference? I mean formal hearings, procedural due process, and the submission to the court of formal arguments and the response of the court to those arguments.[31] Does the institutional and procedural character of judicial decision-making suffice to distinguish it from other forms of political decision-making that we might be tempted to characterize in Hobbesian terms?

A second question arises from the point that neither the judges on a supreme court nor the members of an unlimited legislature are subject to review by any higher entity. Though *institutionally* unlimited, both may be bound subjectively by the constitution and by the oath they have taken to support it. Is it possible to say, nevertheless, that judges are bound by constitutional provisions in a way that legislators are not? Can this distinction be based, for example, on the professional ethos, mentality, and esprit de corps of judges? And would that be sufficient to distinguish judicial ascendancy from legislative ascendancy for the purposes of rebutting the Hobbesian challenge?

Third, quite apart from the Hobbesian issue, are there problems of legality so far as judicial decision-making is concerned? I said in section 3 that rule *by* law is an important part of the rule of law. But there are aspects of judicial decision-making that are problematic considered as a form of rule by law. For example, judicial decisions are often unpredictable and they vary from judge to judge. To the extent that judges sometimes have to make the law, their lawmaking is retroactive, at least as regards the parties in the case in which the new law is made. And the law they make, having no canonical form, is often indeterminate until it is clarified in later cases. To the extent that all this is true, we should have serious doubts as to whether rule by judges really amounts to the rule of law.[32]

I haven't been able to address these three clusters of questions. But even raising them in this abbreviated form should be enough to warn us away from any simplistic account of the relation between judicial power and the rule of law.

7

The Rule of Law and the
Importance of Procedure

1. Getting to the Rule of Law

I have said several times that the rule of law is one star in a constellation of
ideals that dominate our political morality; the others include democracy,
human rights, and economic freedom. We want societies to be democratic; we
want them to respect human rights; we want them to organize their economies around free markets and private property to the extent that this can be
done without seriously compromising social justice; and we want them to be
governed in accordance with the rule of law. We want the rule of law for new
societies—newly emerging democracies, for example—and old societies alike,
for national political communities and regional and international governance.
And we want it to extend into all aspects of governments' dealings with those
subject to them—not just in day-to-day criminal law, or commercial law, or
administrative law, but also in law administered at the margins, in antiter-
rorism law, and in the exercise of power over those who are marginalized,
those who can safely be dismissed as outsiders, and those we are tempted just
to destroy as (in John Locke's words) "wild Savage Beasts, with whom men can
have no Society or Security."[1] The rule of law does not just mean paying lip
service to the ideal in the ordinary security of a prosperous modern democracy; it means extending the rule of law into places where it is not necessarily
a familiar presence, and in societies that are familiar with the ideal, it means
extending the rule of law into some darker corners of governance as well.

When I pay attention to the calls that are made for the rule of law around
the world, I am struck by the fact that the features that people call attention

to are not necessarily the features that legal philosophers have emphasized in their academic conceptions. Legal philosophers tend to emphasize formal elements of the rule of law, such as rule by general norms rather than particular decrees; rule by laws laid down in advance rather than by retrospective enactments; rule under a system of norms that has sufficient stability (is sufficiently resistant to change) to furnish for those subject to the norms a calculable basis for running their lives or their businesses; rule by norms that are made public, not hidden away in the closets of bureaucracy; rule by clear and determinate legal norms, norms whose meaning is not so obscure or contestable as to leave those who are subject to them at the mercy of official discretion. These are formal aspects of the rule of law, because they concern the form of the norms that are applied to our conduct: generality, prospectivity, stability, publicity, clarity, and so on. And they are important, even if they are not all-important. We value them not just for formalistic reasons. In F. A. Hayek's theory of the rule of law, we value these features for the contribution they make to predictability, which Hayek thinks is indispensable for liberty.[2] In Lon Fuller's theory, we value them also for the way they respect human dignity: "To judge [people's] actions by unpublished or retrospective laws . . . is to convey to [them] your indifference to [their] powers of self-determination."[3] In Fuller's theory, too, there is a hunch that if we respect dignity in these formal ways, we will find ourselves inhibited against more substantive assaults on dignity and justice. That has proved very controversial, but it is further evidence of the point that the interests of those who adopt a formal conception of the rule of law are not just formalistic.

I have said that this formal conception is not what ordinary people have in the forefront of their minds when they clamor for the extension of the rule of law into settings or modes of governance where it has not been present before. Saying that is usually a prelude to calling for a more *substantive* vision of the rule of law. I am not as hostile as I once was to a substantive conception of this ideal.[4] I believe that there is a natural overlap between substantive and formal elements, not least because—as we have just seen—the formal elements are usually argued for on substantive grounds of dignity and liberty. I still believe it is important not to let our enthusiasm for a substantive conception—whereby the rule of law is treated as an ideal that calls directly for an end to human rights abuses, or as an ideal that calls directly for free markets and respect for private property—obscure the independent importance that the formal elements I have mentioned would have, even if these other considerations were not so directly at stake.[5] But it is probably a mistake to exaggerate the distinctiveness of our several political ideals or the clarity of the boundaries between them.

Still, it is not a substantive conception that I have in mind when I say that ordinary people are urging something other than the formal elements that I mentioned when they clamor for the rule of law. Instead, I have in mind elements of legal procedure and the institutions, such as courts, that embody them. As I said in Chapter 2, when people clamored recently in Pakistan for a restoration of the rule of law, their concern was for the independence of the judiciary and the attempt by an unelected administration to fire a whole slew of judges. When people clamor for the rule of law in China, they are demanding impartial tribunals that can adjudicate their claims. And when advocates for detainees in the US base at Guantánamo Bay clamored for the rule of law, they were demanding hearings on their clients' comprehensive loss of liberty, hearings in which they or their clients would have an opportunity to put their case, confront and examine the evidence against them, such as it was, and make arguments for their freedom in accordance with what we would say were normal legal procedures.

2. Laundry Lists

What sort of procedural principles do I have in mind? Theorists of the rule of law are fond of producing laundry lists of demands. The best known are the eight formal principles of Lon Fuller's "inner morality of law":[6]

1. Generality
2. Publicity
3. Prospectivity
4. Intelligibility
5. Consistency
6. Practicability
7. Stability
8. Congruence

I think we need to match this list with a list of procedural characteristics that are equally indispensable. As a preliminary sketch, we might say that no one should have any penalty, stigma, or serious loss imposed on him by government, except as the upshot of procedures that involve

    A. a hearing by an impartial tribunal that is required to act on the basis of evidence and argument presented formally before it in relation to legal norms that govern the imposition of penalty, stigma, loss, and so forth;

    B. a legally trained judicial officer, whose independence of other agencies of government is ensured;

    C. a right to representation by counsel and to the time and opportunity required to prepare a case;

    D. a right to be present at all critical stages of the proceeding;

    E. a right to confront witnesses against the detainee;

    F. a right to an assurance that the evidence presented by the government has been gathered in a properly supervised way;

    G. a right to present evidence in one's own behalf;

    H. a right to make legal argument about the bearing of the evidence and about the bearing of the various legal norms relevant to the case;

    I. a right to hear reasons from the tribunal when it reaches its decision that are responsive to the evidence and arguments presented before it; and

    J. some right of appeal to a higher tribunal of a similar character.[7]

These requirements are often associated with terms such as "natural justice," and as such, they are important parts of the rule of law.[8] I believe we radically sell short the idea of the rule of law if we understand it to comprise a list like Fuller's list 1 to 8 without also including something like the procedural list A to J that I have just set out. We say the rule of law is violated when due attention is not paid to these procedural matters, or when the institutions that are supposed to embody these procedures are undermined or interfered with. Equally, I think we misrepresent the debate about whether the rule of law has also a substantive dimension if we do not contrast a possible list of substantive items—such as

    (α) respect for private property;

    (β) prohibitions on torture and brutality;

    (γ) a presumption of liberty; and

    (δ) democratic enfranchisement

—with *both* of the lists I have set out (the formal list and the procedural list), not just with the formal list by itself.

3. Form and Procedure in the Work of Hayek, Fuller, and Dicey

It is remarkable how little attention is paid to demands of this *procedural* kind—demands like A to J—in the literature in academic legal and political philosophy devoted specifically to discussion of the rule of law.

The key chapter on the rule of law in Hayek's book, *The Constitution of Liberty*—the chapter titled "Laws, Commands, and Order"—makes no mention whatever of courts or legal procedures; it is wholly concerned with the relation between formal characteristics like abstraction and generality and individual freedom.[9] Later chapters in that book do talk a little about courts, but hardly ever about their procedures.[10] The same is true of Hayek's later work on the rule of law, in his trilogy *Law, Legislation and Liberty*. Hayek talks a lot about the role of judges in chapter 5 of the first volume of that work. But it is all about the role of judges in generating norms of the appropriate form, rather than about the procedures that characterize courtrooms.[11]

The case of Lon Fuller is even more instructive. Fuller calls his internal morality of law—comprising (1) generality, (2) publicity, (3) prospectivity, and so on—"procedural," but what he seems to mean is that it is not substantive. Fuller says this:

> As a convenient (though not wholly satisfactory) way of describing the distinction . . . we may speak of a procedural, as distinguished from a substantive natural law. What I have called the internal morality of law is in this sense a procedural version of natural law, though to avoid misunderstanding, the word "procedural" should be assigned a special and expanded sense so that it would include, for example, a substantive accord between official action and enacted law. The term "procedural" is, however, broadly appropriate as indicating that we are concerned, not with the substantive aims of legal rules, but with the ways in which a system of rules for governing human conduct must be constructed and administered if it is to be efficacious and at the same time remain what it purports to be.[12]

In fact, *substantive* can be contrasted either with *procedural* or with *formal*; the two contrasts are different, and patently what Fuller has in mind is what we should call a formal/substantive contrast.[13] The features of his internal morality of law all relate to the form that legal norms take, not to either the procedure of their enactment or (more important) the procedural mode of their administration. Among his eight desiderata, only one comes close to being procedural (in the sense I am distinguishing from formal)—namely, the requirement of congruence between official action and law on the books—yet that is the one for which he says (in the passage quoted) "the word 'procedural' should be assigned a special and expanded sense"!

My point is that there is very little about due process or courtroom procedure in Fuller's account of law's internal morality in chapters 2 and 3 of *The Morality of Law*.[14] Much the same is true of what Fuller says in his earlier response to H. L. A. Hart's Holmes Lecture. There, too, Fuller focuses on what we should call formal characteristics of law—generality, publicity, consistency, and so on—and his argument that they are prophylactics against injustice is based on an incompatibility between evil ends and law's forms.

> Coherence and goodness have more affinity than coherence and evil. Accepting this belief, I also believe that when men are compelled to explain and justify their decisions, the effect will generally be to pull those decisions toward goodness, by whatever standards of ultimate goodness there are. . . . Even in the most perverted regimes there is a certain hesitancy about writing cruelties, intolerances, and inhumanities into law.[15]

The whole of his discussion along these lines, and the whole of his excoriation of Nazi "legality," has to do with legislative form, not judicial procedure. That is the ground on which Fuller makes what we would call his "rule of law" argument.

I do not mean that Fuller was uninterested in procedure. Toward the end of chapter 4 of *The Morality of Law*, there is some consideration about whether the internal morality of law applies to the processes by which allocative decisions are made by government agencies in a mixed economy. Fuller says we face problems of institutional design "unprecedented in scope and importance."

> It is inevitable that the legal profession will play a large role in solving these problems. The great danger is that we will unthinkingly carry over to new conditions traditional institutions and procedures that have already demonstrated their faults of design. As lawyers we have a

natural inclination to "judicialize" every function of government. Adjudication is a process with which we are familiar and which enables us to show to advantage our special talents. Yet we must face the plain truth that adjudication is an ineffective instrument for economic management and for governmental participation in the allocation of economic resources.[16]

This indicates an interest in procedural as well as formal aspects of the rule of law (and, indeed, a skepticism about their applicability across the board of all government functions).[17] But it is remarkable that the interest in the adjudicative process shown in this passage is not matched by anything in the earlier discussion in his book of the inner morality of law.

Fuller was in fact a great proceduralist who made an immense contribution to our understanding of the judicial process.[18] Nicola Lacey has ventured the suggestion that Fuller would have been on much stronger ground in his argument with Hart had he focused on procedural and institutional as well as formal aspects of legality.[19] But he allowed Hart to set the agenda with the crucial question "What is law and what is its relation to morality?," and did not force him to open that up, in any particular way, to "What, in terms of institutional procedures, is a legal system, and what is the relation of all *that* to morality?"

Fortunately, we are not bound to follow Fuller in this. I think we can usefully pursue a procedural (and institutional) dimension of the rule of law, as well as a formal dimension, and distinguish both of them (separately as well as jointly) from a more substantive conception. There is certainly precedent for this elsewhere in the rule-of-law literature.

Albert Venn Dicey, for example, when he explained the rule of law as a distinguishing feature of the English Constitution, identified it in the first instance with the following feature:

When we say that the supremacy or the rule of law is a characteristic of the English constitution, we . . . mean, in the first place, that no man is punishable or can be lawfully made to suffer in body or goods except for a distinct breach of law *established in the ordinary legal manner before the ordinary Courts of the land.* In this sense the rule of law is contrasted with every system of government based on the exercise by persons in authority of wide, arbitrary, or discretionary powers of constraint.[20]

The passage I have emphasized is important. Without it, we tend to read the contrast between the rule of law and arbitrary government in terms of the application of a rule versus purely individualized application of punishment (without guidance by a rule). With it, however, the contrast between law and discretion has to do with institutions and procedures: a person must not be made to suffer except pursuant to a decision of a court arrived at in the ordinary manner observing ordinary legal process.

When E. P. Thompson insisted (alarming his fellow Marxists) that the rule of law was "an unqualified human good" and a "cultural achievement of universal significance," he did so by reference in large part to the importance of procedure:

> Not only were the rulers (indeed, the ruling class as a whole) inhibited by their own rules of law against the exercise of direct unmediated force (arbitrary imprisonment, the employment of troops against the crowd, torture, and those other conveniences of power with which we are all conversant), but they also believed enough in these rules, and in their accompanying ideological rhetoric, to allow, in certain limited areas, the law itself to be a genuine forum within which certain kinds of class conflict were fought out. There were even occasions . . . when the Government itself retired from the courts defeated.[21]

Procedural elements can be found also in analytic discussion. I said earlier that in recent legal philosophy the phrase "the rule of law" is often used to conjure up laundry list of features that a healthy legal system should have. These are mostly variations of the eight formal desiderata of Lon Fuller's "inner morality," but occasionally procedural and institutional considerations creep in.[22] Thus, the fourth, fifth, and seventh items on Joseph Raz's list are the following: "(4) The independence of the judiciary must be guaranteed. . . . (5) The principles of natural justice must be observed . . . open and fair hearing, absence of bias, and the like. . . . (7) The courts should be easily accessible."[23] The justifications Raz gives often go to the issue of legal determinacy (e.g., "Since the court's judgment establishes conclusively what is the law in the case before it, the litigants can be guided by law only if the judges apply the law correctly"), but at least the procedural and institutional considerations rate a mention.[24]

In many other discussions of the rule of law, however, the procedural dimension is simply ignored (or, worse, it is assumed thoughtlessly that it is taken care of by calling the formal dimension "procedural"). I do not mean that judges and courts are ignored. In the last *Nomos* volume devoted to this subject, there is extensive discussion of judicial authority and judicial discretion. Some of it is about equitable decision by judges in hard cases (together with an intriguing account of the idea of practical wisdom as applied to the judiciary), and some of it is about the interpretive techniques that judges should use in difficult cases.[25] But if one didn't know better, one would infer from these discussions that problems were just brought to wise individuals called judges for their decision (with or without the help of sources of law) and that the judges in question proceeded to deploy their interpretive strategies and practical wisdom to address those problems; there is no discussion in these papers of the highly proceduralized hearings in which problems are presented to a court, let alone the importance of the various procedural rights and powers possessed by individual litigants in relation to these hearings. Certainly, there is no indication by any of the volumes' contributors that the procedures and the rights associated with them are in and of themselves part of what we value under the heading "the rule of law."

4. Procedure and the Concept of Law

Elsewhere in this book, I have remarked on an interesting parallel between the failure of some of our leading theorists of the rule of law to highlight procedural (as opposed to formal) considerations and the failure of our leading legal philosophers to include procedural and institutional elements in their conception of law itself.[26]

For my part, I do not think we should regard something as a legal system absent the existence and characteristic operation of the sort of institutions we call courts. By "courts," I mean institutions that apply norms and directives established in the name of the whole society to individual cases and that settle disputes about the application of those norms. And I mean institutions that do this through the medium of hearings—formal events that are tightly structured procedurally in order to enable an impartial body to determine the rights and responsibilities of particular persons fairly and effectively, after hearing evidence and argument from both sides.

It is remarkable how little there is about courts in the conceptual accounts of law presented in modern positivist jurisprudence. The leading source is H. L. A. Hart's magisterial work, *The Concept of Law.* Hart conceives of law in terms of the union of primary rules of conduct and secondary rules that govern the way in which the primary rules are made, changed, applied, and enforced. He certainly seems to regard *something like* courts as essential. When he introduces the concept of secondary rules, he talks of the emergence of "rules of adjudication" in the transition from a pre-legal to a legal society. These are "secondary rules empowering individuals to make authoritative determinations of the question of whether, on a particular occasion, a primary rule has been broken."[27] Notice, however, that this account defines the relevant institutions simply in terms of their output function—the making of "authoritative determinations . . . of whether . . . a primary rule has been broken." There is almost nothing in Hart's account on the distinctive process by which this function is performed.

I think there is a considerable divergence here between what analytic philosophers say about the concept of law and how the term is ordinarily used. Most people, I think, would regard hearings and impartial proceedings and the safeguards that go with them as an essential, rather than a contingent, feature of the institutional arrangements we call legal systems.[28] For most people, their absence would be a disqualifying factor, just like the absence of free and fair elections in what was alleged to be a democracy.

Moreover, a procedural conception of the rule of law helps bring our conceptual thinking about law to life. There is a distressing tendency among academic legal philosophers to see law simply as a set of normative propositions and to pursue their task of developing an understanding of the concept of law to consist simply in understanding what sort of normative propositions these are and what relations there are between them. But law comes to life *in institutions.* An understanding of legal systems that emphasizes argument in the courtroom as much as the existence and recognition of rules provides a basis for a much richer understanding of the values that law and legality represent in modern political argument.

If it were up to me, I would bring the two concepts together—the concept of law and the concept of legality or the rule of law. (This what I argued in Chapter 2.) I would suggest that the concept of law should be understood along Fullerian lines to embrace the fundamental elements of legality, but I would argue this only if the latter were also understood to give pride of place to procedural and institutional elements. However, this is not the received position. According to Joseph Raz and others, you cannot understand what the rule of law is unless you already and independently understand what law is and the characteristic evils it is likely to give rise to.[29] I mention this further conceptual debate in order to register the point that the absence of a proper emphasis on procedural aspects on either side—in the academic account of the concept of law and in the academic account of the rule of law—may have a common source and may have something to do with our inability to see the connection between the two ideas.

5. Procedure and the Underlying Moral Concerns

The essential idea of procedure is much more than merely functional; it is more than just applying norms to individual cases. The operation of a court involves a way of proceeding that offers those immediately concerned in a dispute or in the application of a norm the opportunity to make submissions and present evidence (such evidence being presented in an orderly fashion according to strict rules of relevance oriented to the norms whose application is in question). Once presented, the evidence is made available to be examined and confronted by the other party in open court. And each party has the opportunity to present arguments and submissions at the end of this process and to answer those of the other party. In the course of all of this, both sides are treated respectfully; above all, they are *listened to* by a tribunal that is (as Fuller emphasized in "Forms and Limits of Adjudication") bound to attend to the evidence presented and respond to the submissions that have been made in the reasons that are eventually given for its decision.[30]

These requirements express an important sense, associated foundationally with the idea of a legal system, that law is a mode of governing people that treats them with respect, as though they had a view or perspective of their own to present on the application of the norm to their conduct and situation. As I said earlier, applying a norm to a human person is not like deciding what to do about a rabid animal or a dilapidated house. It involves paying attention to a point of view and respecting the personality of the entity one is dealing with. It embodies a crucial dignitarian idea—respecting the dignity of those to whom the norms are applied as *beings capable of actively explaining themselves.* This needs to be treated as an essential element in our working conception of law.

6. Apprehensions about Lawlessness

Think of the concerns expressed about the plight of detainees in Guantánamo Bay from 2003 to the present. When jurists worried that the detention facility there was a "black hole" so far as legality was concerned, it was precisely the lack of these procedural rights that they were concerned about.[31] What the detainees demanded, in the name of the rule of law, was an opportunity to appear before a proper legal tribunal, to confront and answer the evidence against them, and to be represented so that their own side of the story concerning their detention could be explained. That was the gist of their habeas corpus demands. No doubt the integrity of these proceedings would depend in part on the formal characteristics of the legal norms (whether laws and customs of armed conflict or other antiterrorist laws) that were supposed to govern their detention, whose application in their case they could call into question at the hearings that they demanded; no doubt the formal features stressed by Fuller, Hayek, and others would be important, because it is very difficult to make a case at a hearing if the laws governing detention are unacceptably vague, or indeterminate, or kept secret. Even so, we still miss out on a whole important dimension of the rule of law ideal if we do not also focus on the procedural demands themselves, which, as it were, give the formal side of the rule of law this purchase.[32]

These concerns are not just prominent in extreme cases like Guantánamo Bay. Among working lawyers, they have been at the forefront of concerns about the compatibility of the rule of law with the modern administrative state. When Dicey spoke of a "decline in reverence for the rule of law" in England at the beginning of the twentieth century, one of the things he had in mind was the transfer of authority to impose penalties or take away property or livelihood from courts to administrative entities, and the content of his concern was precisely that those entities would not act as courts acted, would not feel constrained by rules of procedure and other scruples of "natural justice" in the way that judges characteristically felt constrained.[33] True, even Dicey expressed this partly in terms of the existence of determinate rules:

> State officials must more and more undertake to manage a mass of public business. . . . But Courts are from the nature of things unsuited for the transaction of business. The primary duty of a judge is to act in accordance with the strict rules of law. He must shun, above all things, any injustice to individuals. The well-worn and often absurdly misapplied adage that "it is better that ten criminals should escape conviction than that one innocent man should without cause be found guilty

of crime" does after all remind us that the first duty of a judge is not to punish crime but to punish it without doing injustice. A man of business, whether employed by a private firm or working in a public office, must make it his main object to see that the business in which he is concerned is efficiently carried out. He could not do this if tied down by the rules which rightly check the action of a judge.[34]

I guess one *could* parse this purely in terms of judges (as opposed to managers of public business) being bound by determinate rules—and then the whole thing could be brought in under Fuller's eighth principle of congruence.[35] But, again, I think that would miss a whole dimension of the matter. It is not simply that one bunch of officials are bound to apply determinate rules while another bunch of officials are not; it is that the former operate in the context of highly proceduralized institutions in which procedural rights and duties of all sorts are oriented to allowing the application of determinate rules to be established fairly and minutely with ample opportunity for contestation. If we neglect this aspect of the rule of law, we make much of Dicey's concern about contemporary decline in regard for that ideal quite mysterious.

Something similar may be true of our concerns about the role of the rule of law in nation-building. When theorists like Robert Barro argue that it is more important to secure the rule of law in a developing society than it is to secure the institutions of democracy, what they often have in mind is the elimination of corruption and the establishment of stable legal institutions.[36] We cannot understand these concerns unless we focus on the distinctive procedural features of legal institutions and their integrity vis-à-vis the elimination of corruption, the securing of judicial independence, the guarantee of due process, and the separation of powers.

True, it has to be said also that sometimes when commentators call for the rule of law to be given priority over democracy in developing societies, what they mainly have in mind are quasi-substantive features like the protection of property, the proper enforcement of contracts, and the protection of outside investments, and the safeguarding of all this as against democratically enacted social-justice or environmental or labor-rights legislation. Sometimes this is quite cynical.[37] I have argued vehemently elsewhere against this Washington Consensus–based abuse of the idea of the rule of law, and I take it up again in Chapter Nine.

7. Law, Argumentation, and Predictability

When I set out my preliminary list of procedural characteristics of the rule of law at the beginning of this chapter, I mentioned the requirement that those facing the imposition of penalty, stigma, or serious loss at the hands of government must have the right to make legal argument about the bearing of the evidence and about the bearing of the various legal norms relevant to the case. I believe this is particularly important. It also sets up an interesting tension between the procedural requirements of the rule of law and the formal requirements that relate to the determinacy of legal norms.

In the systems with which we are familiar, law presents itself as something one can make sense of. Lawyers and judges try to see the law as a whole; they attempt to discern some sort of systematicity integrating particular items into a structure that makes intellectual sense as a whole.[38] And ordinary people and their representatives take advantage of this aspiration to systematicity and integrity in framing their own legal arguments, by inviting the tribunal hearing their case to consider how the position they are putting forward fits generally into a coherent conception of the spirit of the law. And so the determination of whether such a proposition has legal authority may often be a matter of contestation. Law becomes a matter of argument.[39]

In this regard, too, law has a dignitarian aspect: it conceives of the people who live under it as bearers of reason and intelligence. They are thinkers who can grasp the rationale of the way they are governed and relate it in an intelligible way to their own view of the relation between *their* actions and purposes and the actions and purposes of the state. Once again, I don't think we would accept that a society was governed by the rule of law if its judicial procedures did not afford parties the opportunity to make arguments of this kind in cases where the state was bearing down on them.

But this strand of the rule of law has a price, bringing with it a diminution in law's certainty. On my view, the procedural side of the rule of law requires that legal institutions accommodate reasoned argument in the affairs that concern them. But argument can be unsettling, and the procedures we cherish often have the effect of diminishing the certainty and predictability that are emphasized in the formal side of the ideal.[40] By associating the rule of law with the legal process rather than with the determinate form of the norms that are supposed to emerge from that process, the procedural aspect of the rule of law seems to place a premium on values that are somewhat different from those emphasized in the formal picture.[41] The formal picture, particularly as it is put forward by thinkers like Hayek, emphasizes clarity, determinacy, and predictability as features of governance that make private freedom possible.[42] The procedural account sponsors a certain conception of freedom also, but it is more like positive freedom: the freedom to participate argumentatively in the way that one is governed. And that positive freedom may stand in some tension with private freedom in Hayek's vision of liberty, which presupposes that law is determinate enough to allow people to know in advance where they stand and to have some advance security in their understanding of the demands that law is likely to impose on them.

The tension may also be represented as a tension between various strands of dignity associated with the rule of law. Fuller, we saw, associated his formal criteria with a dignitarian conception of the legal subject as an agent capable of monitoring and governing his own conduct. In its action-guiding aspect, law respects people as agents; the rule of law is sometimes represented as the condition of such respect.[43] But how, it may be asked, can we maintain this mode of respect if law becomes uncertain as a result of argumentation? Insisting on an opportunity for argument respects dignity, too, but perhaps at the cost of diminishing the confidence that we can have in the dignity of law's self-application at the hands of ordinary individuals. On the other hand, it is worth remembering a point made already several times in this volume—that law consists not only of determinate rules but also of standards and that law's confidence in the possibility of self-application does not necessarily presuppose that it takes the form only of determinate rules. Law's dignitarian faith in the practical reason of ordinary people may be an act of faith in their *thinking*—for example, about what is reasonable and what is not—not just in their recognition of a rule and its mechanical application. And so also it may be an act of faith not just in their ability to apply general moral predicates (such as "reasonable") to their actions but also to think about and interpret the coherent bearing of a whole array of norms and precedents to their conduct, rather than just the mechanical application of a single norm.

So we cannot just brush the argumentative aspect of law's procedures aside so far as the rule of law is concerned. As I have said now several times, this tension in the rule-of-law ideal is largely unavoidable. We should own up to the fact that the rule of law points in both directions. I think we find symptoms of this tension in the ambivalence of the rule-of-law ideal so far as the role of judges in society is concerned and in a similar ambivalence about the role of litigation.[44]

There is no denying that theories that place great stress on legal certainty, predictability, and settlement, on the determinacy and intelligibility of the norms that are upheld in society, and on the relatively straightforward character of their administration by the state are among the most influential conceptions of the rule of law.[45] According to these conceptions, the most important thing that people need from the law that governs them is certainty and predictability in the conduct of their lives and businesses. There may be no getting away from legal constraint in the circumstances of modern life, but freedom is possible nevertheless if people know in advance how the law will operate and how they have to act if they are to avoid its application. Knowing in advance how the law will operate enables one to make plans and to work around its requirements.[46] And knowing that one can count on the law's protecting certain personal property rights gives each citizen some certainty on what he can rely on in his dealings with other people and the state. Accordingly, legal theories highlight the role of rules rather than standards, literal meanings rather than systemic inferences, direct applications rather than arguments, and ex ante clarity rather than labored interpretations.[47] The rule of law is violated, on this account, when the norms that are applied by officials do not correspond to the norms that have been made public to the citizens or when officials act on the basis of their own discretion rather than according to norms laid down in advance. If action of this sort becomes endemic, then not only are people's expectations disappointed, but increasingly they will find themselves unable to *form* expectations on which they can rely, and the horizons of their planning and their economic activity will shrink accordingly. So it is natural to think that the rule of law must condemn the uncertainty that arises out of law's argumentative character.

But the contrary considerations embodied in the procedural side of the rule of law will not easily give way. As Neil MacCormick pointed out, law is an argumentative discipline, and no analytic theory of what law is and what distinguishes legal systems from other systems of governance can afford to ignore this aspect of our legal practice and the distinctive role it plays in a legal system's treating ordinary citizens with respect as active centers of intelligence.[48] A fallacy of modern positivism, it seems to me, is its exclusive emphasis on the command-and-control aspect of law, or the norm-and-guidance aspect of law, without any reference to the culture of argument that a legal system frames, sponsors, and institutionalizes. The institutionalized recognition of a distinctive set of norms may be an important feature. But at least as important is what we do in law with the norms that we identify. We don't just obey them or apply the sanctions that they ordain; we argue over them adversarially, we use our sense of what is at stake in their application to license a continual process of argument back and forth, and we engage in elaborate interpretive exercises about what it means to apply them faithfully as a system to the cases that come before us.

When positivists in the tradition of H. L. A. Hart pay attention to this aspect of interpretation and argument, they tend to treat it as an occasional and problematic sideline. The impression given is that, in most cases, the authoritative identification of legal norms using a rule of recognition is sufficient; once it is recognized, a legal norm can become a straightforward guide to official action. But, it is said, *occasionally* the language is unclear—because words have open texture or because our aims are indeterminate or because for some other reasons there is a hiccup in the interface between words and the facts that they apply to—and then, unfortunately, we have no choice but to argue the matter through.[49] And, usually, the positivist will add, the upshot is that the court just has to cut through the Gordian knot and make a new rule that can be recognized and applied more readily without controversy.[50] But this account radically underestimates the point that argumentation (about what this or that provision means or about the effect of this array of precedents) is *business as usual* in law. We would be uneasy about counting a system that did not exhibit it and make routine provision for it as a legal system.

So I don't think that a conception of law or a conception of the rule of law that sidelines the importance of argumentation can really do justice to the value we place on government treating ordinary citizens with respect as active centers of intelligence. The demand for clarity and predictability is commonly made in the name of individual freedom—the freedom of the Hayekian individual in charge of his own destiny who needs to know where he stands so far as social order is concerned.[51] But from time to time, a free Hayekian individual will find himself accused of some violation. Or his business will be subject—as he thinks, unjustly—to some detrimental regulation. Some such cases may be clear, but others may be matters of dispute. An individual who values his freedom enough to demand the sort of calculability that the Hayekian image of freedom under law is supposed to cater to is not someone whom we can imagine always tamely accepting a charge that he has done something wrong. He will have a point of view, and he will seek an opportunity to bring it to bear when it is a question of applying a rule to his case. And, when he brings his point of view to bear, we can imagine his plaintiff or his prosecutor responding with an argument of their own.[52] Courts, hearings, and arguments are not optional extras; they are integral parts of the way law works, and they are indispensable items in the package of law's respect for individual agency. To say that we should value aspects of governance that promote the clarity and determinacy of rules for the sake of freedom, but not the opportunities for argumentation that a free and self-possessed individual is likely to demand, is to sell short what the rule of law rests on: respect for the freedom and dignity of each person as an active intelligence.

8. Legal Procedures in Social and Political Decision-Making

Alexis de Tocqueville famously remarked that "scarcely any political question arises in the United States that is not resolved, sooner or later, into a judicial question."[53] Does a proceduralist account of the rule of law, with its emphasis on due process and the sort of argumentation that one finds in courtrooms, endorse this characteristic? Is a society governed by the rule of law necessarily a society in which judicial procedures loom large in the settlement of social and political questions?

I think that is, for the most part, an unwarranted extrapolation. It is one thing to say that a person threatened by the government with penalty, stigma, or serious loss must be offered an opportunity and a setting for argumentatively contesting that imposition. It is another thing to say that the courtroom setting, with its highly proceduralized modes of consideration, is an appropriate venue for settling general questions of common concern in a society. We may accept the procedural implications of the rule of law—along the lines of those set out in my list A to J in section 2—without denying that, nevertheless, in the end, the legislature, rather than the courtroom, is the appropriate place for settling such matters. Certainly, what happens in the courtroom in argument about particular applications may affect how the measures enacted in the legislature are subsequently understood. That, as I have said, may have an effect on predictability, and we should not be in the business of trying to avoid that by minimizing the impact of judicial proceedings. Such an effect can and will accrue even in a society in which courts do not have the power to override legislation, and endorsing or accepting that effect by no means amounts to an endorsement of anything like judicial review of legislation.

I do not mean that the rule of law precludes judicial review of legislation. As I implied in Chapter 6, I believe that, as a political ideal, the rule of law is neutral on the issue. In a society with a constitutional bill of rights and a practice of strong judicial review, the rule of law requires us to accept a much greater role for courts in public decision-making than I have set out here. In such a society—I am thinking particularly of the United States— arguments made in courtrooms according to the procedural principles that I say constitute the rule of law will have a greater impact on the life of a society and a greater impact probably on social predictability than they have in a society with weak or no judicial review.[54] Also, the more robust the bill of rights, the more it will seem that the upshot of taking the rule of law seriously is substantive, not just procedural and formal. This, I think, is the gist of Dworkin's position on the rule of law in *A Matter of Principle*.[55]

Some people argue that the rule of law in a society is incomplete unless legislatures as much as executive agencies are bound to act in accordance with (higher) constraining laws. I do not accept that, though I understand the position. Some even say that the crucial distinction here is between the rule of law and rule *by* law, and they say that a system of legislative supremacy is an example of the latter but not the former. A position like this is some-times associated with a general denigration of legislatures—as though, in the end, the rule of law must amount to something other than the rule of men. The position is often associated with an almost mythic reverence for common law, not conceived necessarily as deliberately crafted by judges but under-stood as welling up impersonally as a sort of resultant of the activity of courts. Hayek hints at some such nonsense when he writes in *The Constitution of Liberty* that most genuine rules of law

> have never been deliberately invented but have grown through a gradual process of trial and error in which the experience of successive generations has helped to make them what they are. In most instances, therefore, nobody knows or has ever known all the reasons and con-siderations that have led to a rule being given a particular form.[56]

In a similar way, the suggestion that legislatures need to be constrained by law rather than regarded as ultimate sources of law often involves a strange sort of constitutionalist mythology. It sees the framing of a constitution or a bill of rights as some sort of transcendent event, amounting to something other than the rule of men—perhaps it is supposed to have been a spontaneous effulgence of unprecedented superhuman virtue hovering around the activity of giants like James Madison and the Federalists. But I see no reason to associate the rule of law with any such mythology, or to embody in it any denial that law is human in origin and often the product of deliberate manufacture. Even if positivists (as I have argued) give an inadequate account of it, the rule of law is, in the end, the rule of positive law; positivity is a criterion of law; and the rule of law is a human ideal for human institutions, not a magic that somehow absolves us from human rule.

8

Stare Decisis and the Rule of Law

A Layered Approach

1. Why Rule-of-Law Justifications?

If we are going to talk about courts—especially in the common law tradition—then we have to talk about stare decisis. If we are interested in the relation between judicial decision-making and the rule of law, then we need to get a sense of the relation between the rule of law and the principle that commands respect for precedent. That's what I want to do in this chapter.

We really need a justification for stare decisis. We can't just move on past it on the ground that it's too obvious to need spelling out. Precedent may be, in the words of Justice Cardozo, "the everyday working rule of our law," but many respected jurists oppose the principle or are anxious to reduce its scope and its power.[1] The costs of stare decisis are pretty evident, in terms of the injustice or inefficiency of bad decisions. C might have won their case against D, had the court not been constrained to follow the principle set forth in *A v. B*. That would have been better for C and maybe better (in terms of justice or efficiency) for society as a whole, if we assume that the court in *C v. D*, unconstrained by stare decisis, could have improved on the law set forth in *A v. B*. There are also process costs—the immense effort that has to be invested by counsel for C and D, not to mention by the court in *C v. D*, to unearth all the relevant precedents and construct laborious arguments about what they mean, whether they can be distinguished, whether *C v. D* is a rare case in which they ought to be overridden, and so on. All this energy might have been better devoted to considering the just or efficient settlement of the dispute between C and D on its own merits. So justifying stare decisis is not just a matter of saying a few things in its favor during an after-dinner speech. It is a matter of showing why costs like the ones just mentioned are worth bearing.

Fortunately, our jurisprudence offers dozens of justifications. They include the importance of stability, respect for established expectations, decisional efficiency, the orderly development of the law, the maintenance of our traditions, Burkean deference to ancestral wisdom, formal or comparative justice, fairness, community, integrity, the moral importance of treating like cases alike, and the political desirability of disciplining our judges to reduce any opportunity for judicial activism.[2] The justification of stare decisis is a field in which many contributions have been made, but to which precious little system has been brought.

I, too, will be less than systematic in this chapter, and certainly less than comprehensive. I don't want to consider everything that can be said or has been said in favor of stare decisis. My aim is to explore a subset of justificatory considerations that fall under the heading of "the rule of law." The rule of law, we know, requires people in positions of state authority to exercise their power within a constraining framework of public norms (laws) rather than on the basis of their own preferences or ideology. It requires also that the laws be the same for all—that they be general and principled—and that they be accessible to the people in a clear, public, stable, and prospective form. It requires, finally, that penalties be imposed on people by the state only through impartial legal proceedings, and that people have access to independent courts to settle their disputes and to hold the government accountable. Is there anything in the idea of the rule of law that requires courts to follow precedent? Are there any reasons among the reasons commonly adduced for stare decisis that we can rightly regard as rule-of-law reasons? Or is the rule of law neutral on the matter, or perhaps even opposed to the rule of precedent?

Some people say that we should follow precedent because we are no wiser than our ancestors. It is a matter of epistemic humility, "the general bank and capital of nations, and of ages," and so on.[3] This may or may not be a compelling justification, but even if it is, it has little to do with the rule of law. The same can be said about justifications that point to such things as agenda limitation, decisional efficiency, and system legitimacy.[4] These are all interesting. Maybe they are important, but they are not rule-of-law justifications. So I put those arguments aside. Other justifications that are adduced for stare decisis do resonate with rule-of-law ideas: the quest for constancy and predictability in the law, and the importance of generality and treating like cases alike. Those are the justifications I shall consider. There will be some discussion of predictability in section 2, but most of my discussion (in sections 3 and following) will focus in the first instance on the rule-of-law principle of generality—especially generality understood as a constraint on the decision-making of the precedent judge (the earlier judge, who sets the precedent) and the impact of that constraint on subsequent judicial decisions. In sections 3 and 4, I argue that the rule-of-law constraint of generality is not the same principle as the one that commands us to treat like cases alike. It is not just about consistency. Instead, it is a principle that commands judges to work together to articulate, establish, and follow general legal norms. Only after developing this theme of generality do I circle back (in section 5) to the importance of constancy and calculability in the law.

Why am I interested in this subset of reasons for stare decisis? Partly, it is born of my interest in the rule of law as a political ideal. Teaching the subject year after year, I am struck by how little there is on the significance of stare decisis for the rule of law. Apart from some inconclusive discussion in the later work of F. A. Hayek, it is not addressed anywhere in the modern rule-of-law canon.[5] I would rather like to fill that gap.[6]

Partly, too, it is because the United States Supreme Court, in one of its most sustained discussions of stare decisis, cited the rule of law as a reason for not overturning precedents too often. In *Planned Parenthood v. Casey,* the justices in a plurality opinion addressed the prospect of overturning the abortion decision in *Roe v. Wade.*[7] They devoted a long section of their argument to the issue of stare decisis, insisting at the outset that "the very concept of the rule of law underlying our own Constitution requires such continuity over time that a respect for precedent is, by definition, indispensable."[8] However, the argument in *Planned Parenthood* is not quite what we are seeking, for two reasons. One is that the justices concentrate most of their attention in this passage not on the fundamental reasons for following precedent, but rather—assuming there are such reasons—on what additional considerations might be relevant to the prospect of overturning precedents in a system that already acknowledges stare decisis. Later, I argue that it is important to hold these two ideas apart: (1) the justification for following the decision in a previous case (thus making it a precedent in the first place), and (2) the justification for being cautious before one overturns an established precedent. These are separate layers in our understanding.

That they need to be separated in thought is clear from the fact that the overturning of a precedent normally *presupposes* stare decisis. At the very least, overturning a precedent supposes that the principle of the new decision, articulated in overturning the old decision, will henceforth itself be treated as a precedent. So if we really want a *foundational* account of stare decisis, we need to begin by putting the familiar reasons for and against overturning precedents to one side.

The other reason for putting the *Planned Parenthood* argument to one side is that much of it was concerned with issues of judicial legitimacy and appearances. The plurality opinion was interested in ways of creating and sustaining the impression that the Court as an institution was operating in accordance with the rule of law. It asserted that too-frequent overturning of precedent would undermine that impression:

> There is . . . a point beyond which frequent overruling would overtax the country's belief in the Court's good faith. . . . If that limit should be exceeded, disturbance of prior rulings would be taken as evidence that justifiable reexamination of principle had given way to drives for particular results in the short term. The legitimacy of the Court would fade with the frequency of its vacillation. . . . Like the character of an individual, the legitimacy of the Court must be earned over time. So, indeed, must be the character of a Nation of people who aspire to live according to the rule of law. Their belief in themselves as such a people is not readily separable from their understanding of the Court invested with the authority to decide their constitutional cases and speak before all others for their constitutional ideals.[9]

Maybe the plurality opinion is right about this. But even by its own account, preserving judicial legitimacy is not exactly a rule-of-law argument for following precedent. If there *are* rule-of-law justifications for not overturning established precedents, then overturning precedents too often may create the impression that the rule of law is not being properly attended to. And *that* would no doubt have an impact on the Court's legitimacy in the eyes of those who worry about these matters. But then we need to look at what exactly those rule-of-law justifications are supposed to be and why they are important. That's the substance of the matter; all the rest is publicity.[10]

The main reason for considering the relation between stare decisis and the rule of law proceeds in response to the possibility that these two principles sometimes pull in opposite directions. Rule of law and stare decisis: the two ideas sound congruent; they both seem to privilege what the plurality opinion in *Planned Parenthood* called "principled decision-making."[11] But it is not hard to throw them into opposition with each other.[12]

For example, it is not hard to see stare decisis as crystallizing and entrenching the rule of men (people) rather than the rule of law. Some matter arises for decision, and a political official, who happens to be a judge, settles it in a certain way in a certain case, deploying his own ideals and his own preferences. And now his decision is to be followed in all future cases in which a similar issue arises; subsequent generations of judges are to be inhibited from overturning the decision on the ground that the first judge misconstrued the law. Of course, that states it too strongly—stare decisis is not an absolute, and even in a system of precedent, earlier decisions can be revisited. But stare decisis is supposed to make a difference, and the problem for the rule of law is that the difference it makes is to give a measure of entrenched weight to an earlier decision in a way that might make it more difficult for subsequent generations of judges to apply the law as they understand it.

This difficulty is particularly apparent when stare decisis does its work alongside some source of law that is not itself based on precedent. Consider, for example, the operation of precedent in US constitutional law. The source of US constitutional law is a text framed from 1787 to 1791 and amended a few times subsequently. The text presents itself as "the supreme law of the land."[13] But its provisions are far from lucid, and in many cases their bearing is uncertain or controversial. However, if a few decisions establish a particular reading, R_1, of a constitutional clause, C, then R_1 becomes authoritative by operation of stare decisis, and it will be difficult for counsel to argue (or for a court to accept) that an alternative reading, R_2, is a more faithful understanding of C. The judge who is faced with this situation may well feel that stare decisis is thus an impediment to the rule of law. The obligation to follow precedent makes it much harder for him to decide on the basis of fidelity to the Constitution; instead, he has to submit to the continuing effect of the decisions of people in the past, even though (as he sees it) their decisions are taking us in a direction contrary to that required by the independent source of law (the text of the Constitution itself).[14]

It may be harder to see the same difficulty in those areas of law where stare decisis operates more or less alone. It is tempting to say that in common law cases, for example, all we have are precedents, so there is no legal source that can be associated with the rule of law in contradistinction to the demands of stare decisis. But the tension can arise nonetheless. In most areas of common law—such as tort, contract, and property—there are by now plenty of established doctrines that have a well-theorized life of their own, apart from the precedents that established them. These doctrines constitute a juridical background, relative to which certain problems remain unsettled here and there. If one of these problems crops up in a case, a court may purport to settle it by adopting reading R_1 of the doctrinal background; it may be said that on the basis of R_1, the legal background generates a particular solution to the hitherto unsettled problem. But as in constitutional law, various different readings of the background may be possible. Later judges may be much more impressed by a different reading, R_2, yielding the opposite solution to the problem. As before, they will think that fidelity to the law overall requires them to apply the doctrinal background in accordance with R_2 and to eschew R_1, which they regard as a distortion. If they feel strongly enough about this, they might succeed in getting the earlier precedent overturned. But to the extent that stare decisis has any influence in the matter, it will make this process more difficult. In other words, it will make it harder for them to follow their duty of fidelity to the law as they understand it, for it will press them toward (what they regard as) an erroneous reading of the doctrinal background simply because some person enshrined that reading in an earlier decision. As before, stare decisis can pull us in a direction opposite to the commands of the rule of law.

Of course, stare decisis doesn't necessarily do that in either kind of case. Just as it has the power to entrench erroneous decisions against later correction, so stare decisis also has the power to entrench correct decisions against later temptations and deviations. In both constitutional and common-law contexts, stare decisis can be the servant as well as the opponent of the rule of law. Still, the possibility of dissonance between the two principles is unsettling. That is why I think it is worth exploring the possibility that the rule-of-law ideal might command fidelity to precedent even for a person who reckons he could do better for the law by not following the principles that others have laid down.

Some might say that following precedent is so much a part of our conception of law and legal practice that any ideal plausibly denominated as "the rule of law" must necessarily involve a commitment to stare decisis.[15] In his contribution to recent debates about constitutional stare decisis, Richard

Fallon argues that establishing and following precedents can be regarded as part of the meaning of "the judicial power" that the Constitution authorizes in Article III: "Familiar sources can be adduced to suggest that 'the judicial Power' was understood historically to include a power to create precedents of some degree of binding force."[16] But this won't quite do. Some systems of law claim not to respect any principle of stare decisis.[17] Perhaps the rule of law directs us toward them or is indecisive on the matter. Also, English law, from which American legal methodology derived, knew next to nothing of constitutional review of legislation: who knows whether "the judicial power" as understood in 1787 would require stare decisis in this innovative field of constitutional law?

Anyway, even in a given legal system, law means many things. It comprises constitutions, statutes, customs, legislation, precedents, principles, doctrines, agency rules, and so on. We have known since Aristotle (and we see the point reaffirmed in Hayek's later work) that not all of these are equally privileged under the heading of "the rule of the law."[18] Maybe the authority of precedent is a marginal case of law so far as the rule of law is concerned, or maybe it is central.[19] That is what I want to find out.

2. The Right Sort of Predictability

There is one cluster of considerations commonly cited in support of the system of precedent that seems to invoke rule-of-law values. These include the importance of certainty, predictability, and respect for established expectations. By commanding that judges follow previous decisions, stare decisis is supposed to make it easier for people facing a new situation to predict how the courts will deal with it—they will deal with it in the way that they have dealt with similar situations in the past, rather than with judges striking out unpredictably with a new approach of their own. The predictability that this fosters is supposed to make it easier for people to exercise their liberty (i.e., their autonomous powers of planning and action). The connection between liberty and law's predictability is a powerful theme in the modern rule-of-law literature. Hayek put it this way in *The Constitution of Liberty*:

> In that they tell me what will happen *if* I do this or that, the laws of the state have the same significance for me as the laws of nature; and I can use my knowledge of the laws of the state to achieve my own aims as I use my knowledge of the laws of nature.[20]

Like the laws of nature, the laws of the state provide fixed features in the environment in which [one] has to move. The Supreme Court put it more succinctly in *Planned Parenthood v. Casey*: "Liberty finds no refuge in a jurisprudence of doubt."[21]

Everyone thinks that considerations of this kind are of great importance in justifying stare decisis. But they are not simple considerations. The use of stare decisis to foster predictability is a complicated idea, and it is in the complications that we find the rule of law doing its hardest work. For consider, we sometimes phrase this justification in terms of a principle about the importance of protecting expectations. But before anyone can follow this principle, there must be expectations to protect. So there seem to be two elements contained within the principle of protecting expectations:

1. Legal practice and legal decision-making should be such as to give rise to expectations.
2. These expectations should, by and large, be respected by other legal decision makers.

These two elements are inextricably bound up with each other; take either of them away and the principle collapses. Take the first element away: the precedent judge—by which I mean the judge whose decision might be supposed to lay down a precedent (as opposed to a subsequent judge, who may feel obliged to follow what the precedent judge has done)—hears a case and then just points silently to one of the parties, indicating who has won. Is it possible, on this basis, for anyone beyond the two litigants in the case to form expectations about how the courts will reach their decisions in the future? Can this decision by the precedent judge foster any expectations for a subsequent judge to respect? Subsequent parties may guess at the rationale of the decision in the precedent case by noticing some striking fact and speculating about its importance. But a guess is not an expectation. Consider a case posed by Jeremy Bentham:

> A Cadi comes by a baker's shop, and finds the bread short of weight: the baker is hanged in consequence. This, if it be part of the design that other bakers should take notice of it, is a sort of law forbidding the selling of bread short of weight under the pain of hanging.[22]

But even to know that, we have to know something of what was in the cadi's mind. As Bentham puts it, "It is evident enough that the mute sign, the act of punishment . . . can express nothing of itself to any who have not some other means of informing themselves of the occasion on which it was given."[23] Officials present at the incident who followed the cadi's gaze and watched what he mouthed as he silently strangled the baker may have formed some sort of expectation. But other expectations formed by lawyers and officials who were not present might be all over the place. One might infer, panic-stricken, that all bakers are to be hanged. Another might infer that there is something especially bad about selling bread in daylight hours during Ramadan. A third might infer that the punishment has something to do with short weight but applies only to egregious cases, and so on. Bentham says that to get anything like a legal rule, you not only have to choose among these grossly disparate speculations, but you also have to figure out

> of the boundless group of circumstances with which the act punished must necessarily have been attended . . . which of them were considered as material? what were received as inculpative? what were not suffered to operate in the way of exculpation? to what circumstances was it owing that the punishment was so great? to what others that it was no greater? These and a multitude of other circumstances which it would be needless to repeat must all be taken into the account in the description of the case.[24]

Bentham's inference from all of this was that we should abandon the idea of treating precedent decisions as sources of law and rely instead on a legislated code.[25] Others—more committed than he was to the system of precedent— might infer that expectations can never be established by single-precedent decisions. The cadi's silent decision does not make law, but someone subsequently making something of it may. Or, putting it more directly in terms that apply realistically to courts, it is not until the subsequent judge has made something of what the precedent judge did—inferring and applying a holding, a ratio decidendi—that we have anything that can form the basis of an expectation. Even so, I am inclined to say that this process cannot really get underway unless the precedent judge does something to present her decision in an articulate light that allows subsequent judges to go to work on it.

I said there were two elements: (1) legal practice and legal decision-making should be such as to give rise to expectations, and (2) these expectations should, by and large, be respected by other legal decision makers. What happens if we take the second of these elements away? The precedent judge might articulate her decision fastidiously in terms of a general principle that can be perceived as the ratio decidendi of her decision. The precedent judge makes this available for future generations of judges. But her doing so will make no sense unless she expects them to cooperate in the respecting of expectations—not necessarily by accepting and applying her formulation as canonical, but at least by participating in the creating and sustaining of expectations rooted in decisions like hers. People will not form expectations just because one judge makes an explicit attempt to create them; they will wait and see how subsequent judges respond to the precedent judge's attempt.[26]

There are two things that subsequent judges may do that undermine predictability in the legal system: (1) they may take no notice of what the precedent judge does in her case, approaching similar cases in the future with no thought about how the case that came in front of the precedent judge was decided; and (2) even after the precedent judge's decision is established as a basis for future expectations, they might decide that they can improve on it and establish their own better basis of expectations for this kind of case. What this means is that the subsequent judge becomes, as it were, his own precedent judge in respect of a new expectation, and, like the original precedent judge, he hopes that subsequent judges will pay attention to and try to follow the decision that *he* has made. This attempt to switch expectations no doubt diminishes predictability, but it need not ruin it altogether. It does not make it impossible for people to form and act on expectations about future legal decisions; it just adds an element of uncertainty to their calculations. How much uncertainty—how much damage it does to the basis of predictability— is a matter of degree and depends on all sorts of surrounding circumstances, such as the congruence of the change with existing business practices, and so on.

In most discussions of predictability, the focus is on (2). Making a case for respecting expectations involves requiring or counseling judges to limit the number of times they try to overturn established expectations and replace them with new expectations based on fresh decisions of their own. But obviously, none of this is of any importance unless we attend first to (1).

Judges who take no notice of previous decisions at all are unlikely to be impressed by attempts to establish new and better expectations. I don't mean that (2) is unimportant. Violations of (2) can become so frequent that they start to affect (1) and undermine the very possibility of establishing expectations. And even if that doesn't happen, (2) is still important in its own right. But it is secondary in the order of explanation.

My point here is about multiple layers. In addition to the ways in which the first decision maker must act to make the establishment of expectations possible, there are various ways in which subsequent decision makers must act to nourish the expectations that the first decision maker cultivated. These ways of nourishing already-planted expectations need to be considered layer by layer, as well as in relation to one another.

I said that the cluster of considerations concerned with predictability occupies a prominent place both in justifications of stare decisis and in various conceptions of the rule of law. But I doubt that they are the final word on the justification of stare decisis, even on the layered approach that I am taking in this chapter. For one thing, as I argued at the beginning of this book, the rule-of-law tradition does not treat predictability as the be-all and end-all. On the contrary, for various good reasons, it supports procedures and allows modes of argumentation that make the law much more unsettled and controversial than it would be if predictability were an overriding value. (See Chapters 1, 2, and 7.) What's more, we know that argument about precedent is one of these unsettling modes of argument. People worry, argue, and bicker about the meaning of precedents long after any predictability that the precedent might have sponsored has evaporated.[27] And they are right to worry, argue, and bicker, for the principle of stare decisis seems to introduce its own distinctive uncertainty into the law, particularly insofar as it does not operate as an absolute. Sometimes precedents will be followed; sometimes not. No one really knows when or why. Sometimes cases will be distinguished and sometimes time-honored rules will be overturned; and then just as we are getting used to that sort of flexibility, an ancient precedent will rear up all of a sudden out of its tomb, "overturning the establishments of the intervening periods, like Justinian brought to life again at Amalfi."[28]

If we really wanted predictability in law, we would be better off studying the political profiles of our judges in the legal realist manner rather than looking at precedents. Indeed, we might be better off choosing judges who could be relied on not to change their political spots. No more Justice

Kennedys. If we can make calculations based on a justice's conservatism (or others' liberalism), we will expect the justices to honor precedent when that leads to results they find congenial, and to distinguish, sideline, or overturn them when that suits their politics. Predictability in that sense is easy; what would be the point of cluttering it up with law? Everyone would know where they stood, provided they knew the name and reputation of the person who had power over them. The rule of law is not the only way of introducing calculability into human affairs; the rule of men can do it too, if the men are well enough known.[29]

It is a particular sort of predictability that the rule of law demands and that following precedent is thought to provide—namely, principled predictability, or predictability that results from mapping an official and publicly disseminated understanding of the various sources of law onto the factual situations that people confront. I don't want to dismiss the predictability approach altogether. But this discussion so far has revealed the complexity in the idea of securing predictability by protecting expectations, and I want to use that complexity to develop a different sort of rule-of-law approach to stare decisis.

3. The Rule of Law and the Precedent Judge

I indicated in the previous section that the precedent judge's work in a decision has to have a certain character before it can be used as the basis of a precedent, and certainly before it can be used as a foundation for people's expectations about future legal decisions. This sounds as though we can justify the following if-then statement as addressed to the precedent judge:

> S: If you want your decision to be the basis of a precedent, then you must work on it and present in the following way: you must issue an opinion; you must state reasons; you must try to articulate the basis of your holding as a general norm; and so on.

Fair enough. But statement S will get no grip on anyone opposed to or indifferent about precedent. It can't form part of the fundamental argument for stare decisis, for that argument has to convince even those initially opposed to or indifferent about stare decisis that the business of creating, sustaining, and following precedents is a good idea in spite of its costs and its difficulties.

What if we take out the "if" clause and just address the second part of S as an unconditional imperative to the precedent judge?

S*: You must work on your decisions and present them in the following way: you must issue an opinion; you must state reasons; you must try to articulate the basis of your holding as a general norm; and so on.

Now the precedent judge is likely to ask why, and we might set about looking for answers in the rule-of-law tradition, reasons having to do with notions of legality that require judges to act as S* commands. We need not forget the wider context of S—that is, we need not forget that this is all going to add up eventually to a case for stare decisis, but we might begin by considering reasons supporting S* that so far have nothing to do with that.

So let us consider the rule-of-law principles that bear on a judge's response to a problem that comes before her. A situation presents itself, and an official determination or resolution is needed. In a system uncontaminated by rule-of-law requirements, the judge might ask herself, "What is the best way to resolve this dispute?" But in a rule-of-law polity, she must ask, "What does the law require in this situation? Is there, for example, an established rule that bears directly and explicitly on this situation as everyone understands it?" In the situation I am imagining, the answer for the precedent judge is likely to be, "No; there is no established rule that bears directly and explicitly on this situation." So now what is to be done?

Some legal philosophers assume that when there is no law applying directly to a case, the judge should decide the case using morality. For these philosophers, the problem of precedent is this: Why should the moral solution that the precedent judge imposed on the situation (because there was no law to impose) function as law in a subsequent similar case for the subsequent judge? And for them, the most acute version of that question is this: Why should the subsequent judge be constrained by a decision on a moral issue made by the precedent judge if the precedent judge's moral opinion is (in the subsequent judge's view) morally flawed, both as it applied to the case in front of the precedent judge and as it would apply to the case that the subsequent judge has to decide?[30] I think this is an unhelpful way of presenting the issue; it makes the problem of stare decisis much more intractable than it needs to be.[31]

So let's go back to the precedent judge, faced with the initial case. Once she determines that there is no established rule that bears directly and explicitly on the situation before her, then surely the question she should ask herself is this: "What bearing, then, *does* the law have on this situation, even if it is indirect or implicit?" She must stay in touch with the law; she must try "to relate the grounds of the present determination in some reasoned fashion to previously established principles and policies and rules and standards."[32] She should not abandon the law for the siren charms of morality at the first sign of difficulty. She must ask herself something like a Dworkinian question: What does the best understanding of the law imply for a case like this, given that the existing law does not determine the matter directly or explicitly?[33]

I will say more about Dworkin in just a minute, but first let me say *why* the precedent judge must maintain a steady connection with the law, why she should try to figure out a legal answer to her problem, even when the law has no direct or explicit bearing. For one thing, this is what the rule of law requires.[34] To decide the matter morally is to submit the case to the rule of man (or in this case, woman). We might have to do this in a legal vacuum (a state of nature), but we are not in a legal vacuum simply because law does not bear directly or explicitly on the problem that we face. The rule of law is a demanding discipline, and it dictates something like a Dworkinian striving for an interpretation of such legal materials as exist in order to decide the problems that come up for official decision.[35] For another thing (though this amounts to more or less the same point), the precedent judge is to think of herself as deciding in the name of the whole society, not in her own name; not only that, but she is deciding *as a court,* as part of the judiciary.[36] The order that is issued for the case in front of her is not to be regarded as an order of this particular person; it is an order of the court. (This will be quite important when we think about the subsequent judge's relation to that order in section 4 of this chapter.)

The details of Dworkin's view of interpretive reasoning need not concern us here. He believes that there is a moral element to it, and that at various points, the precedent judge's quest for the bearing of the law on the case in front of her is likely to involve her having to make moral judgments in her own voice.[37] But these moral judgments are entangled with the legal judgments she has to make. Also—and this has proved very controversial—Dworkin believes that there is definitely a right answer to the question of the bearing of the law on the case before the precedent judge. I shall not rest anything on Dworkin's right-answer thesis, except to say that it makes sense for the precedent judge to approach the matter in that spirit. She has to figure out what bearing the law has on this case in fact; she should not think of herself as free to just *opt* for one view rather than another. By saying that the precedent judge has to "figure out" the bearing of existing law on the case in front of her in this spirit, I hope I will not be taken as subscribing to what Austin called the "childish fiction" of the declaratory approach.[38] The main point is that the precedent judge should think of herself as facing a legal problem and trying to figure out the legal solution to it. This is the attitude that she should take, even though she knows that her solution has not been directly or explicitly articulated in the law so far and that it is likely to be controversial among other jurists applying their minds to the same problem in the same spirit.[39]

So the precedent judge wrestles with the legal materials at hand, and in good Dworkinian fashion she finally figures out through interpretation what she thinks those materials require for the case in front of her. She announces her decision: "The plaintiff wins." Is that enough? We have already seen that it may not be enough to get a precedent underway. But, in my view, it is also not enough from the point of view of the rule of law. We want to know *why* the plaintiff wins, and we want that "why" to be an articulate, universalizable norm.[40] These two points are not the same. The precedent judge might just explain the process of interpretation that she has been through, connecting a decision for the plaintiff with a Herculean account of existing law. Or she might present it as an intuited (or *phronesis-based*) response to the case, based on an implicit understanding of existing law, a response that defies articulation.[41] Either way, she is failing in the duty that I am currently trying to explain.

In *Law's Empire,* Ronald Dworkin indicates that interpretation involves choosing from among a number of possible principles. He seems to assume that an interpretation is something articulable as a general principle, though he doesn't dwell on the point. I think it is important to dwell on it. The rule of law requires generality, not in the sense that all law must be general— courts can't do their job without issuing particular orders, such as "This plaintiff is to pay this defendant $100,000"—but in the sense that the making of particular legal orders is supposed to be guided by general norms.[42] One of the important tasks of the precedent judge so far as the rule of law is concerned is to leave the parties—and the public—in no doubt as to the general norm that underpinned her decision.

All sorts of reasons can be given for this requirement of generality. In the positivist tradition, the arguments for generality have been crudely pragmatic:

"No society could support the number of officials necessary to secure that every member of the society was officially and separately informed of every act which he was required to do."[43] But elsewhere, the reasons are more elevated. Decision-making according to general rules simply seems more lawlike—law in its essence is, as Edmund Burke put it, "beneficence acting by a rule."[44] And this sense of lawlikeness seems to be connected also, in Kantian fashion, with rationality.[45] Moreover, subsuming particular decisions under general rules imparts an element of impersonality to legal administration.[46] Without such a general basis, the precedent judge's decision seems to be the rule of a person over the parties appearing in front of her, not the rule of law.

Perhaps the best-known argument about the importance of judges presenting their decisions as the upshot of general rules is that of Antonin Scalia in his essay "The Rule of Law as a Law of Rules," although the interest of this article for us is compromised by the fact that some of the justifications invoked by Scalia already depend on acknowledging the importance of precedent.[47] His position is that judges deciding hard cases should lay down a rule that is to be followed in cases of that kind, rather than saying that they have personally decided the particular case simply on the "totality of circumstances" and acknowledging that other judges in future cases might well find the balance tilting slightly the other way. Scalia believes that it is especially appropriate to accept this discipline when one's decision is supposed to be rooted in some text that Congress or the Constitution provides; one should be able to state one's interpretation in a form that matches the form of the statute or the constitutional provision. Since they are (abstract) general norms, one's interpretation should be (a slightly less abstract) general norm. This, too, seems to be a matter of the rule of law, in the sense of respect for the most prominent of the materials one is interpreting.

Scalia is less sanguine about judges arriving at general norms "when one does not have a solid textual anchor or an established social norm from which to derive the general rule." Then, the pronouncement of a general rule "appears uncomfortably like legislation."[48] But those of us who are less uncomfortable with that prospect than Scalia is might still want to insist on generality. For suppose we say that the law really is indeterminate on the matter that has come before the precedent judge, and that although she must strive in Dworkinian fashion to establish the bearing of existing legal materials on the case, eventually, law is still going to have to be made rather than discovered for this case. And suppose we concede that a quasi-legislative response is necessary. Then, just as we would not want a legislature to respond with a "statute" oriented just to the particular case that posed the problem, so we would not want a court involved frankly in the task of judicial legislation to come up only with a legal position tailored for this particular case. So far as legislation is concerned, the duty of generality is familiar to us from things like the prohibition on bills of attainder. We are less familiar with the point applied to judicial legislation, but the rule-of-law arguments seem equally compelling. Even if the precedent judge thinks of herself only as deciding this particular case, we want her to think of it under the auspices of a general norm. Otherwise, as I said, her situation vis-à-vis the litigants in front of her is that of the rule of men (people) rather than the rule of law.[49]

I don't just mean that the precedent judge should have a general principle in mind, or that she should be disposed to treat like cases alike. I mean that she should cite a general norm or establish it as law (or as though it were law or as though she were making it law) and use that as the basis of her decision in the case. As I said earlier, she should leave the community in no doubt as to the general norm that was the basis of her decision. This, I believe, is a primary obligation that she has under the rule of law—to derive her particular decisions from an identified and articulated general norm. And although this is going to be crucial in my argument for stare decisis, it is actually something incumbent on her, quite apart from her establishment of a precedent.[50] Even if she knew that no one would follow her, she would have an obligation to decide on a general basis in this sense. To adapt a conceit from Kant, even if the precedent judge knew that the case in front of her was the last case her court would ever decide, she should still identify and formulate as law the general norm that, as she figures, dictates the decision in this case.[51]

To sum up then: the precedent judge, faced with a case to which existing law does not speak directly or explicitly, should attempt to figure out the bearing of the existing law on the case in front of her. Whether she understands this as *finding* the legal solution to the problem that faces her or as *creating* a legal solution for it, she should think of herself as applying a general norm to the case. And she should identify and articulate that norm. That is what the rule of law requires of her. And now I want to explain how and why that element of generality in the precedent case should be taken seriously by subsequent judges.

4. The Rule of Law and the Subsequent Judge

So let us look at the next layer. A set of facts quite similar to the one that came before the precedent judge now comes before another judge in a subsequent case. The subsequent judge may think of himself as being in the same situation the precedent judge was in: there is a body of existing law that does not directly or explicitly address cases of the kind before him. Nevertheless, he should try to figure out what bearing the body of law does have on the case in front of him, even if it is only implicit and indirect. But actually, that is not an accurate description of the situation he faces. If the precedent judge did what she was supposed to do (what the rule of law required of her), then she decided the earlier case on the basis of some general norm, R_p, the rule in the precedent case, that addressed it directly and explicitly. Arguably, R_p now exists in the law as a norm that can dispose of the case in front of the subsequent judge.

How should the subsequent judge think about this? A first point is that, like the precedent judge, he should think of himself not as an individual charged with deciding cases but as a member of a court. Any decision he reaches so far as the case before him is concerned is going to have to stand not as his decision but as a decision of the court to which he belongs. Not only that, but it will have to stand in the name of the very court to which the precedent judge belonged and to which her decision must be attributed.[52] The subsequent judge shares with his fellow judges, including the precedent judge, the responsibility of seeing that cases that come before the court are decided on the basis of the rule of law. They exercise that responsibility together, albeit in sequence.[53]

One thing that the subsequent judge might infer from all this is that he must adopt a Dworkinian attitude toward the case in front of him. Like the precedent judge, he must consider the indirect and implicit bearing of existing legal materials on the case, even while he acknowledges that they have no direct or explicit bearing. He must try to interpret the law to figure out what to do about his case. The body of law he interprets may include the fact of the precedent judge's decision in the precedent case. But this does not mean that he treats the precedent judge's decision as a precedent. It's just one particular outcome attributable to the law, along with all the other materials, particular and general, whose overall bearing he must consider.

Is this enough? Is this the only obligation that the subsequent judge has to the precedent judge's decision? No. It's no doubt better than ignoring the precedent judge's decision altogether (though aware that he is facing a similar case). But I think that if this is all the attention that the subsequent judge pays to the precedent judge's decision, then he is failing in his duty (in his part of their shared duty) to the rule of law. For if he did that, he would be selling short the general norm on which the precedent judge predicated her decision. He—and through him, the court to which he and the precedent judge belonged—would be giving the lie to the notion that the precedent judge decided her case on the basis of a general norm, R_p. Perhaps the subsequent judge will deny this. He might say, "Everyone knows that the precedent judge decided her case on the basis of a general norm, R_p. We can't take that away from her, even though I intend to decide the similar case that has come before me on a different basis." But in saying this, he has made the general aspect of the precedent judge's decision into something purely notional. The generality of her decision now has no real presence in the legal environment. At best, the rule in the earlier case, R_p, exists simply as a public account of why the precedent judge reached the particular decision she did. Or it is just an assurance of what we earlier called the "universalizability" of her decision, as a feature of her subjective decision-making. Worse still, it takes on the character of something just rigged up by the precedent judge to get the decision she wanted.[54] One way or another, if the subsequent judge takes this approach, then R_p does not exist now as law; it does not stand in a rule-of-law relation to the precedent judge's decision. It is rather as though the precedent judge, the person, decided a particular case that came before her on the basis of a set of good reasons that happened to appeal to her, and the most that R_p does is sum up those reasons. As the precedent judge presented her decision—indeed, as the court in whose name she spoke presented the decision—the general norm she articulated promised to be much more than that. But the subsequent judge's approach to a subsequent similar case has sold short that promise.

The precedent judge played her part. She figured out the bearing of existing law on the case in front of her, summed that up in a general norm, and presented that norm as the basis of her decision for one or the other party. She didn't merely have universalizable reasons in mind. She did all she could, all that was legitimately in her power, to identify or establish a general norm, R_p, as the upshot of those reasons and to show how a particular decision could be derived from that. But, as a judge, there was only so much she could do in this regard. If no one else picked up R_p and carried it forward as a general norm of this legal system, then her part—the work she did for the rule-of-law principle of generality—was in vain.

Affirmatively, then, what is the subsequent judge's responsibility? The subsequent judge's responsibility is to treat R_p as a genuine legal norm to which the court that he belongs to has already committed itself. He is to act as though it was a general norm with a positive legal presence, and not just a notional presence in the world. It is there now, because of what the precedent judge did, as part of the repertoire of legal resources available for dealing with the cases that come before him. And since the case now before him is similar to the case that the precedent judge addressed using R_p, then R_p should be used by him as a basis for dealing with that case. That is what is required of him now by the rule of law. If other judges behave in this way, then the court to which they all belong will be (and will be seen as) an institution that decides cases on a general basis, rather than just as an institutional environment in which individuals make particularized case-by-case determinations.

That is the core of my position. But here's an objection: Hasn't all of this been just a long-winded way of saying that the precedent judge legislates and the subsequent judge is bound (to a certain extent) by her legislating? For some legal theorists, like Hans Kelsen and Joseph Raz, the best way to understand the system of precedent is to say frankly that it is a form of judicial legislation, which differs in some respects (mostly in its ready revisability) from other forms of legislation.[55] Why not just say that and be done with it? I am convinced that there is a difference between my rule-of-law approach and a quasi-legislative approach. The precedent judge has the same rule-of-law obligation in *all* cases to identify and articulate the general norm from which her particular decision is derived, regardless of whether these are cases involving what positivists would describe as judicial legislation.[56] Legal realists may not see any difference; it is all judicial legislation so far as they are concerned. Jurists of a nonrealist stripe will not accept that account. But even they should acknowledge that the precedent judge has a duty to articulate her decision in the form of a general norm, even when she is (as they think) discovering the law rather than making it. The fact that she has to firm up the existing law and figure out its implications to fulfill the duty of generality makes it look as though she is legislating. And as I said in section 3, I don't want to say that her action is purely declaratory or that there is no creative element. But the duty to come up with a general norm is, as I have stressed, incumbent on her just in virtue of the fact that she is deciding a case. Because of the way in which the precedent judge's discharge of her rule-of-law duty implicates the subsequent judge's discharge of his, her discharge of her duty seems as though it has a legislative effect. But it is not in any sense a matter of the subsequent judge submitting to her authority (which is what legislation usually involves).

Also, even if we were to describe all this as judicial legislation, there would be a further question about where it comes from and what authorizes it. Modern positivists might be content to say that judges have just developed the custom of deferring to general pronouncements of law by other judges in certain circumstances, and that's all that is needed to make it part of a rule of recognition. But we might want to probe deeper and more dynamically than that. There has been certainly no explicit delegation of legislative authority in the constitutional system of those societies that recognize stare decisis. Instead, it has developed or evolved out of other practices. Joseph Raz suggests that it has developed out of the practice of taking judicial decisions as final and dispositive, even when they are mistaken.[57] I am sure that is part of it, though it leaves unbridged the gap from finality in one case to authority over other cases. I suggest that what looks like judicial legislation has developed out of this prior commitment to generality: (1) legislation or no legislation, the precedent judge has an obligation to articulate the legal premise of her decision as a general norm, R_p; and (2) the subsequent judge has an obligation as part of the same court to keep faith with the generality of R_p. Out of all that, something that looks like judicial lawmaking emerges.

I have labored these points enough. Now I want to acknowledge and address three complications in the subsequent judge's position. The first is about the subsequent judge's articulation of R_p; the second is about distinguishing; and the third is about the prospect of overruling.

First: the formulation of R_p. In the model we have been using, R_p is formulated clearly by the precedent judge in her opinion. She explains the Dworkinian reasoning that led to R_p from the existing legal materials, and then she articulates R_p and applies it to the case in front of her. In the real world that we know, however, judges do this more or less well, more or less clearly, and (if several judges are involved on an appellate court) in a more or less coordinated fashion.[58] The precedent judge may leave the basis of her decision half-articulated or clumsily articulated. When that happens, the subsequent judge has additional work to do. As part of the responsibility outlined in the previous paragraphs, he has to identify the general rule that the precedent judge should have articulated. He has to bring it to the light of day, show it to the world, and apply it to the similar case in front of him.[59] Even if the precedent judge has had a stab at formulating the basis of her decision, her exact formulation is not canonical. There is no particular reason to be textualist about the general rules figured out or crafted by judges in the course of reaching their decisions; the reasons that justify textualism in the case of legislation don't really apply here.[60] Nor is there any reason to pay attention to the precedent judge's original intent; her authority in this matter is not that sort of authority. The important thing is for the subsequent judge to figure out in broad terms the rule that was reached by the court as the upshot of the precedent judge's interpretation of the existing legal materials on the case in front of her, the rule that justi-fied her decision in that case, and to apply that rule, however formulated, to the similar case that he (the subsequent judge) has to address. The spirit of this exercise is that the subsequent judge must think of himself as acting in the name of the selfsame entity that decided the case that came before the precedent judge. Depending on the circumstances and the felicities of the precedent judge's formulation, this may or may not involve verbal fi-delity on the part of the subsequent judge to what the precedent judge actually said.

Second: distinguishing subsequent cases from precedent cases. One case may seem superficially similar to another, but the judge may be convinced that there are differences that preclude simply subjecting a subsequent case to the same rule that decided the precedent case. In principle, this is no dif-ferent than recognizing that an existing and acknowledged rule does not apply to a case that does not exactly fit the rule's norm conditions. For example, a given statutory provision may apply properly to one case but not another, even though the second is superficially similar to the first; therefore, we "distinguish" the second case. And similarly, the rule that the precedent judge figured out as a basis for her decision in the precedent case may not apply to a subsequent case, despite superficial similarities. There may be things about the second case that pose a distinct legal problem, which requires a new and distinct lawlike solution to be figured out by the subse-quent judge in the form of a rule—a solution that represents the Dworki-nian bearing of the existing legal materials (including the gravitational force of the precedent judge's rule) on the case in front of the subsequent judge. To distinguish a case, then, is not just to "come up with" some difference. It is to show that the logic of what the precedent judge figured out does not, despite appearances, apply. It means pointing to some additional problematic feature of the subsequent case that requires additional figuring.

My point is that both these ways of orienting oneself to a rule laid down in an earlier case—reformulating and distinguishing—can be approached in a spirit more or less consonant with the rule of law. Legal realists are fond of pointing out that the subsequent judge can formulate the rule that he is supposed to be following any way that he likes in order to suit his own view about how the case in front of him should be decided. They say that he can distinguish any given factual situation from any other. And so he can, but the rule of law commands him to approach these delicate judgments in a responsible spirit of deference. He should try to arrive at the formulation that best approaches a norm that solves the problem that confronted the precedent judge (in the way that she solved it), and then he should consider whether the acceptance of that solution as a general norm also settles the case that he confronts. If an honest reckoning shows that it doesn't, then the responsible thing to do is to distinguish the case and identify and solve the distinct issue that *it* poses. But if the precedent judge's solution considered as a general norm does have the capacity to solve what is essentially the same legal problem posed by the second case, then the subsequent judge should apply it. That is what keeping faith with the generality of law requires so far as he is concerned.

5. Overruling and Stability

I want to devote a separate section to the third of the complications I mentioned: the possibility that the subsequent judge might overturn the rule laid down by the precedent judge in the precedent case. I do so because I want to emphasize as strongly as I can that the issue of constancy, of not lightly overturning the rule laid down in an earlier case, is an *additional* layer in our understanding of precedent. It is an *additional* way in which the rule of law bears on stare decisis. The argument from generality—and the duty of a subsequent judge to keep faith with the generality of an earlier judge's decision—is what gets precedent going, so far as the rule of law is concerned. But all law is changeable: in no context does the rule of law dictate immutability. But the rule of law does counsel against too-frequent changes in the law, and this applies as much to precedent as to other sources of law.

So the subsequent judge may become convinced that the rule laid down by the precedent judge is misconceived or harmful. This conviction may be

rooted in a number of considerations. The subsequent judge may have
come to believe that the rule, R_p laid down by the earlier judge did not
really reflect the background legal materials that were in existence at the
time; in a strongly felt case of this kind, he may claim that the precedent
judge's decision was an error *per incuriam*. Or the background legal materials might have changed, leaving R_p stranded, as it were.[61] Or it might
just be that R_p has worked out badly, leading to considerable injustice,
inefficiency, and difficulty in the law. These are all cases for countenancing
the prospect of overturning R_p and setting about figuring a new legal solution for cases of this kind. Most systems of precedent permit this, at least
where the precedent judge and the subsequent judge are judges on the
same bench.

One may ask, "Well, why bother formally overturning R_p? Why not just
distinguish it for all future cases? There is enough flexibility, not to say indeterminacy, in the system of precedent as it is to allow future judges to get
out from under misconceived precedents." But frankly acknowledging the
possibility of formally overturning a precedent has its advantages. The British
House of Lords drew attention to these advantages when it issued its famous
Practice Statement of 1966:

> Their lordships regard the use of precedent as an indispensable foun-
> dation upon which to decide what is the law and its application to in-
> dividual cases. It provides at least some degree of certainty upon which
> individuals can rely in the conduct of their affairs, as well as a basis for
> orderly development of legal rules. Their lordships nevertheless rec-
> ognise that too rigid adherence to precedent may lead to injustice in
> a particular case and also unduly restrict the proper development of
> the law. They propose therefore to modify their present practice and,
> while treating formal decisions of this House as normally binding, to
> depart from a previous decision when it appears right to do so.[62]

The official acknowledgment that precedents could be overturned made it
possible for lawyers in Britain to advance explicit arguments that a precedent should be overturned, and it allowed such arguments to be candidly
considered by the court so that it could give public reasons for and against
a change. No doubt judges continued the practice of sometimes distinguishing cases disingenuously or in bad faith. But there was a considerable
advantage in terms of transparency with the new approach.

In some cases, it may be a matter of judgment as to whether full-scale overturning is appropriate. R_p may need tweaking or amending rather than repudiation. Something akin to distinguishing may be proper in a case of this kind.[63] Analogies to legislation are not always appropriate, but in that domain, one sees a variety of possible measures taken with regard to statutes that have come to seem unsatisfactory. Some, like enacting a new statute to supersede an old, are analogous to full-scale overturning. Others, like small-scale amendment, are more like this latter kind of distinguishing.

So far as full-scale overturning is concerned, the 1966 Practice Statement is quite clear about the need for caution. The House of Lords' decisions are to be treated as normally binding, and the power to overturn is not to be used lightly, and it is to be used more cautiously in some areas than others.[64] This, again, is what the rule of law requires: the laws should be relatively stable. If they are changed too often, "people will find it difficult to find out what the law is at any given moment and will be constantly in fear that the law has been changed since they last learnt what it was."[65] The need for constancy is perhaps particularly important in regard to judge-made law. So far as legislation is concerned, the processes are cumbersome and hard to mobilize (though this is more true in the United States than in parliamentary systems). But judicial decisions are made every day, each one with the potential to change the law. In the case of legislation, one usually has notice that change is in the offing. This is apparent from the beginning of a bill's passage until the end. But in judicial decision-making, one might not know that the law has changed until one scrutinizes a myriad of opinions.

Many of the rule-of-law arguments for constancy involve the values of certainty, predictability, and respecting established expectations that I mentioned in section 2. But it is not just about calculability. It is about people having time to take a norm on board and internalize it as a basis for their decision-making. Aristotle argued that "the habit of lightly changing the laws is an evil" and based this claim on the proposition that "the law has no power to command obedience except that of habit, which can only be given by time."[66] The vastly increased coercive apparatus of the modern state means that this is less the case now than it was in Athens 2,300 years ago. If we want to, we *can* enforce laws that the citizenry have not yet gotten used to. But in doing so, we show contempt for the dignity of ordinary agency and the ability of people to be guided by the law, to internalize it, and to self-apply it to their conduct. Upholding dignity in this sense is one of the things that the rule of law requires.

I have emphasized that refraining from overruling is not the same as basic respect for the principle of a previous decision, which is the essence of following a precedent. It is an additional layer, with its own distinctive rule-of-law rationale. It is possible, however, for the two layers to collapse into each other. A court whose members overturn a precedent almost as soon as it is recognized not only fails in the rule-of-law discipline of constancy, but comes close to making it impossible for there to be anything to be constant to. The subsequent judge may say that he respects the idea of precedent and that he is just trying to get the right principle established. But if every subsequent judge responds as he does—overturning the principle that a precedent judge has acted on and purporting to replace it even before it has gotten established—then there will be no precedents whatsoever. And the rule-of-law defect here will switch from inconstancy to a failure to establish and act on general principles at all. However, the possibility of this sort of collapse should not lead us to ignore the distinction between the two layers and the distinct ways in which rule-of-law principles are engaged.

6. Against Particularism and Analogy

I am conscious that the approach I have taken is different from that favored by a number of writers. Here is what Neil Duxbury says about precedent:

> A precedent is a past event—in law the event is nearly always a decision—which serves as a guide for present action. . . . Understanding precedent therefore requires an explanation of how past events and present actions come to be seen as connected. . . . To follow a precedent is to draw an analogy between one instance and another; indeed, legal reasoning is often described—by common lawyers at least—as analogical or case-by-case reasoning.[67]

If the rule of law supports stare decisis, on Duxbury's account, it must be because the rule of law commands something like analogical reasoning. Perhaps the rule of law requires like cases to be treated alike, and we engage in analogical reasoning and subject the relation between any two given cases to analogical scrutiny in order to ensure that like cases *are* being treated alike, or that when cases are treated differently, that there is some significant difference between them. An account along these lines would not require us to focus specifically on the general norm from which the precedent judge drew her decision, nor would it require us to focus on the obligation of a subsequent judge to keep faith with the fact of the precedent judge having worked with that general norm. That there should be such a norm and that the two judges should work together to give it positive presence in the law would not be the key to the matter. Instead, the key would be the relation between the two decisions—the precedent judge's decision and the subsequent judge's decision—considered as particulars. We might identify a principle as summing up the relation of normative similarity between the two decisions: the features in respect of which they were alike and the appropriate response to those features. But the establishment of such a principle would matter less than the discernment of relevant similarities and differences between particular cases and the appropriate responses to them.

I don't want to disparage the principle of treating like cases alike.[68] Nor do I deny that it is has a role to play in the processes that I have been outlining. I think it is particularly important in the kind of Dworkinian figuring out of the bearing through integrity of existing law on a new case that we discussed in section 3. Nor do I deny that a lot of what I have said in this chapter could be recast using the language of analogical reasoning, though it would be a bit of a strain.[69]

Maybe treating like cases alike has a role to play in the justification of something like stare decisis in a subset of cases—cases in which a more or less arbitrary drawing of lines or setting of numbers is involved. The precedent judge has to decide the appropriate sentence for an offense (and there are no guidelines of any sort in place); she decides that the appropriate sentence is x years of imprisonment. The subsequent judge, in a similar case some months later with an equally deserving offender, might feel bound to sentence him to x years as well, even though with a free hand the subsequent judge might have chosen a higher number y. The idea of treating the two like cases alike on the basis of comparative justice is what seems to do the work here, particularly in cases where everyone knows that the precedent judge was not really arriving at a substantive norm when she chose x as the appropriate number.[70] The subsequent judge may have more confidence in his duty (based on fairness) to treat the defendant in front of him exactly how the defendant in front of the precedent judge was treated than he has in any content-laden principle that is supposed to apply to both judges.

Duxbury will say that his particularist account keeps faith with the fact that the job of a court is to settle a particular case, not to legislate: "The primary objective of the court which produced the precedent was to decide a dispute, not issue an edict which later courts can readily identify and accept."[71] Therefore, he might say, a respectable account of stare decisis must be formulated as an account of the relation between dispute-settling in one particular case and dispute-settling in another. But actually, Duxbury is not quite right in his account of the basic judicial function. The primary objective of the court that produced the precedent was to decide a dispute *according to law*, and it is the "according to law" that is and ought to be the focus of subsequent judges' decision-making. Subsequent judges, too, have to decide disputes according to law, and the argument I have made in this chapter is that the general norm articulated as the basis of the decision in the first case is necessarily part of *the law* with which the second case is properly addressed. Whether the precedent judge thinks of herself as declaring the law, figuring the law out, or making the law, she must be credited—or, rather, the court to which she belongs must be credited—with deciding the matter on the basis of a general norm. And subsequent judges must play their part in crediting her decision in these terms, showing in their own decision-making that there was a general norm in play.

7. Conclusion

Even if I have not convinced you in this chapter about the importance of generality in the case for stare decisis (and about the distinction between generality and the principle of treating like cases alike), I hope I have convinced you of two other things. First, the rule of law generates a distinctive perspective on stare decisis. It is possible to exaggerate; I do not endorse the position of the Supreme Court in a 1987 case where it said that "the rule of law depends in large part on adherence to the doctrine of *stare decisis*."[72] That's too strong. But it might be true the other way around: the justification of stare decisis might depend to a large extent on the rule of law.

And second, if the justification of stare decisis does depend on the rule of law, it is best to understand the impact of rule-of-law principles on stare decisis in layers. One principle, the principle of constancy, counsels against lightly overturning such precedents as we have. Another principle, the principle of generality, requires all judges to base their decisions on general norms and not just leave them as freestanding particulars. Another principle, the principle of institutional responsibility, requires subsequent judges not to give the lie to the use by precedent judges of certain general norms to make their decisions. And, finally, a fundamental principle of fidelity to law requires the precedent judge to approach her decision as far as she can by trying to figure out the implicit bearing of such existing law as there is on the case in front of her. She figures out the bearing of the law, she formulates it into a general norm, a subsequent judge takes note of the general norm that she has used, he plays his part in establishing this norm as something whose generality is more than merely notional, and succeeding generations of judges try to maintain the constancy and stability of the body of law that emerges from all this by not overturning precedents lightly or too often. That is the layered way in which the rule of law bears on the question of stare decisis.

9

Legislation and the Rule of Law

1. The View under Consideration

In this chapter, I would like to explore the relation between legislation and the political ideal we call "the rule of law." I want to consider a view that is implicit in some recent writing about the rule of law and about what law can contribute to a society's economic development: it is the suggestion that the rule of law involves keeping legislation and the propensity to legislate under very strict legal control.

I get the impression from this literature that the extent of a society's adherence to the rule of law is not determined (or is determined only in very small part) by the effectiveness of its enforcement of existing legislation or by its capacity to enforce future legislation; on the contrary, there is often a sense that a society's score on the rule-of-law index may be diminished by the effective enforcement of legislation if the tendency of such legislation is to interfere with market processes, limit property rights, or make investment in the society more precarious or in other ways less remunerative to outsiders. The rule of law, in this view, requires a government to offer assurances that it will not legislate in this way or that it will keep such legislation to a minimum. Indeed, the rule of law may call for legal and constitutional guarantees for property rights (and perhaps also for other rights) against legislative encroachment, and it may require provision for judicial review— that is, for offending legislation to be struck down by courts. That is the view I want to consider in this chapter, and for convenience, I shall refer to it as "the view under consideration."

I said at the beginning that the view under consideration is implicit in some recent rule-of-law literature. Actually, it is quite difficult to find books or articles arguing explicitly for it at any length. The view under consideration lurks around the edges of recent rule-of-law discussions, but it seems to be assumed rather than spelled out in what is said about the contribution law can make to economic liberalization or about the tensions between the rule of law and democracy. I have decided not to worry too much about this. If anyone can show that I am attacking a straw man—that is, that no trace of this view infects any serious recent discussion of the rule of law—no one will be happier than me. I fear that the view under consideration is capable of doing a lot of damage to one of our most important political ideals; it converts the rule of law into an ideological tool and discredits it in the eyes of many people. So it would be good if the currency of this view turned out to be a figment of my anxious imagination. But I am afraid it is not, and I think it is worth bringing the view out into the open and discussing it, even if it cannot be attributed canonically to anyone. It would be an unhappy result if such a view were current in rule-of-law conversations but could not be criticized for lack of a citation.

The view under consideration is one element in a more general approach to the rule of law that associates the rule of law in a given country with the promotion of market institutions and with an atmosphere conducive to profitable investment and the protection of property rights (both those of the country's inhabitants and those of outsiders who participate for the time being in its economy).[1]

Indeed, the view under consideration is one element of an approach that associates the rule of law with what is sometimes called the Washington Consensus.[2] This chapter identifies, highlights, and perhaps exaggerates the particular issue of legislation in these approaches. My aim in doing so is to contribute to some broader critical literature on these matters.[3] In particular, I wish to vindicate what I have called elsewhere "the dignity of legislation"; to dispute the implied antipathy between the rule of law and legislative governance; and to defend traditional formal and procedural accounts of the rule of law against the radical reconceptions that seem to be involved in the view under consideration.[4]

2. Stronger and Weaker Versions

The view under consideration comes in various shapes and sizes, and, as I said, it is not always explicit. Sometimes the antipathy to legislation is apparent only by what is emphasized and what is omitted in a stated conception of the rule of law. Below, I give some examples.

Frank Upham (who, I think, is as critical of the view under consideration as I am) cites a paper by a former president of the World Bank that says that, according to the rule of law: "A government must ensure that it has an effective system of property, contracts, labor, bankruptcy, commercial codes, personal rights law and other elements of a comprehensive legal system that are effectively, impartially, and cleanly administered by a well-functioning, impartial and honest judicial and legal system."[5] What is missing here? Well, there is no reference to enforcement of legal regulation of the marketplace and limitations placed on the use of property (e.g., for ecological reasons) or compliance by business, industry, and commerce.[6]

In their well-known study, "Governance Matters," Kaufmann, Kraay, and Mastruzzi use as the basis of a rule-of-law index "several indicators which measure the extent to which agents have confidence in and abide by the rules of society. These include perceptions of the incidence of crime, the effectiveness and predictability of the judiciary, and the enforceability of contracts."[7] By its terms, this is a measure of the rule of law that could have been used in the time of Adam Smith, without regard to the rise of the modern legislative and regulatory state.

Robert Barro argues for the use of a rule-of-law index in development studies that will focus on a subset of the factors that we would normally associate with law. And he is quite frank about the purpose of this order of priorities:

> The general idea of these indexes is to gauge the attractiveness of a country's investment climate by considering the effectiveness of law enforcement, the sanctity of contracts, and the state of other influences on the security of property rights. . . . The willingness of customers to pay substantial amounts for this information is perhaps some testament to their validity.[8]

Thomas Carothers believes that aid agencies need to focus on rule-of-law priorities that have everything to do with markets and property and little to do with regulation: "Aid officials assert that the rule of law is necessary for a full transition to a market economy—foreign investors must believe that they can get justice in local courts, contracts must be taken seriously, property laws must be enforceable, and so on."[9] Compliance with legislation, the enforcement of regulation—these aspects of the rule of law are deafening in their silence here.

So what is being implied about legislation in this silence, in this refusal to give it any share of the attention that is given to the rule of law? I think we can distinguish three versions of the view under consideration, three separate claims that might be made about the antipathy between the rule of law and legislation.

At its most extreme, the view under consideration involves a fairly thoroughgoing antipathy between the rule of law and legislation as such. For example, F. A. Hayek in his later work contrasts law with legislation and suggests that the rule of law comes close to meaning the opposite of the rule of legislation.[10] The legislative mentality is inherently managerial, according to Hayek; it is oriented in the first instance to the organization of the state's administrative apparatus; and its extension into the realm of public policy generally means an outward projection of that sort of managerial mentality, and that, he says, is the very thing the rule of law is supposed to oppose. The rule of law, says Hayek, refers to an order of norms that is emergent rather than manufactured and that exists and develops more like common law than like legislation.[11] Legislation may occasionally be necessary if law's implicit development has led us into a some sort of cul-de-sac, but this acknowledgement by Hayek is grudging; it is a reluctant recognition that it may sometimes be necessary to compromise the rule-of-law ideal, rather than a recognition of legislation's inherent place in that ideal.[12]

A more moderate position recognizes the positive importance of certain kinds of legislation so far as the rule of law is concerned. It is important, for example, that there be a clearly articulated criminal code. (Even those rule-of-law theorists who seek to model their ideal on unlegislated private law are not comfortable with the idea of common law offences.) And often, in a developing society, legislation is necessary in order to establish the institutions and procedural frameworks through which law operates, and by which legal rights are protected, and maybe also to establish clear procedures and expectations in the area of corporate law, bankruptcy, and so on.[13] Still, these moderate versions distinguish between legislation as a framing and facilitating device for the autonomous operation of a well-functioning market system, and legislation as a medium through which regulatory, distributive, or other public policy goals are pursued. Legislation of the latter sort is inherently subject to suspicion from the point of view of the rule of law, according to moderate versions of the view under consideration, for it threatens to radically limit or undermine the property rights, market arrangements, and investment opportunities that law is supposed to frame and guarantee.[14] So this antipathy focuses on things like environmental legislation, certain legislation favorable to labor, minimum wage legislation, health-and-safety legislation, restrictions on freedom of contract, restrictions on investment or on profit taking, legislation nationalizing assets or industries, price restrictions, and so on. Legislation of these kinds is seen as essentially a device of political control of the economy, and so it is thought to be incompatible with the idea that law, rather than politicians, should ultimately be in control.

A weaker version of the view under consideration can be imagined. This would involve not much more than an insistence that legislation can sometimes undermine the rule of law, but it would acknowledge that legislation as such does not necessarily do this, and nor for that matter does the sort of social legislation that the moderate view frowns on. The legislation that is suspect on this weakest version of the view under consideration would be legislation that removes legal remedies, or obstructs the operation of the courts, or precludes judicial review of executive action, and so on. This version of the view under consideration comes close to being something that almost any defender of the rule of law can accept, though some will want to add that threats to the rule of law can come from other sources of law as well. For example, courts can behave in ways that undermine legal protections. Law, we know, can be turned on itself; law of any provenance is capable of undermining the rule of law.

In what follows, I will seek to discredit the view under consideration in its extreme version and in the moderate version. The weakest version can be conceded, with the notation that this concession is much less than defenders of the view under consideration normally have in mind.

3. The Rule of Law and Democracy

Those who espouse the view under consideration do not necessarily deny that societies have a legitimate aspiration to govern themselves through legislation. They may accept that a modern society needs an elected legislature, and they will recognize this as part of the normal aspiration to democracy. But democracy and the rule of law are separable political ideals, and sometimes they pull in different directions.[15] So the view under consideration may be thought of as a way of highlighting a possible tension between these ideals.

We should not quarrel with this. It is true that one cannot have democracy without the rule of law—at least to the extent necessary to maintain a legal framework for elections and elective institutions, to guarantee protection for free political speech and loyal opposition, and to ensure that the executive complies with measures enacted by the elected representatives of the people. But these are rudimentary conceptions of the rule of law (matching a thin or procedural notion of democracy). Procedural democracy, even procedural democracy secured by law, is compatible with violations of the rule of law in other ways, just as it is compatible with violations of individual or minority rights.[16]

More importantly, one can establish the rule of law even in the absence of democracy (thick or thin). This may not be considered satisfactory as a static outcome, but it may be important as an order of developmental priorities. Scholars like Robert Barro have suggested that democratization should take second place to legalization in nation-building.[17] Indeed, this is supposed to be one of the most important implications of the view under consideration. We should strive to establish legal institutions and legal protections for property rights and markets first, before establishing the institutions of democracy. On this view, the establishment of the rule of law is given priority over the effective operation of elective institutions. But, of course, this order of priorities is likely to be upset if we treat the operation of and deference to a legislature as in any way key to the establishment of the rule of law.

But how far should we take this point that democracy and the rule of law are separable political ideals? We know that the constellation of our political values comprises a number of separate ideals: it includes respect for human rights and the principle of free markets as well as democracy and the rule of law, and none of these four values should be identified with any of the others. No doubt there are myriad connections among them, and there are possibly some tensions as well—some of which are highlighted in the view under consideration. However, I do not think it is appropriate to construe any of these values as being inherently opposed to any of the others, as though we necessarily had to choose or trade off democracy against the rule of law, or democracy against human rights, or human rights against free-market economy, and so on. But even in its moderate form, the view under consideration comes close to this "necessary incompatibility" thesis, so far as democracy and the rule of law are concerned. Its denigration of legislation, particularly social and economic legislation, is associated with a sense of its being undesirable for the people of a country to act collectively, even through the medium of (what we would ordinarily call) law, to pursue social justice, heal social antagonisms, diminish inequality, or take control of the conditions of their social and economic life.[18] That, I think, is not a healthy proposition to associate with the rule of law.

4. Legislation as the Epitome of Lawmaking

From one point of view, it is quite odd that the effective operation of a legislature should be separated in this way from the rule of law. After all, legislation is law on most accounts, and the legislature is one of the main sources of law in any well-functioning legal system.[19]

Of course, it is not the only source of law and legal change. Law also comes into existence and changes through the decisions of courts. But the legislature occupies a preeminent role, largely due to the fact that it is an institution set up explicitly to make and change the law.[20] Although the lawmaking role of the courts is well known to legal professionals, judicial decision-making does not present itself in public as a process for changing or creating law. Judges constantly assure the public—disingenuously, we (insiders) know, but constantly—that their role is to find the law, not make it. Lawmaking by courts is not a transparent process; lawmaking in a legislature, by contrast, is lawmaking through a procedure dedicated publicly and transparently to that task. Now, this ought to matter. One of the most important things about the rule-of-law ideal is its emphasis on transparency in governance, and one would think that that would be important in the present context as well.

Not only this, but if the rule of law requires that law be taken seriously and held in high regard in a society, one would think that particular emphasis should be given to the legitimacy of the processes by which legislatures enact statutes. Again, think of the contrast with courts. Not only do judges pretend diffidently that they are finding, not making the law, but we know also that any widespread impression among members of the public that judges were acting as lawmakers would seriously detract from the legitimacy of their decisions. And this popular perception is not groundless. Courts are not set up in a way that is calculated to make lawmaking legitimate. Legislatures, by contrast, are organized—and occasionally reformed and rehabilitated—explicitly to make their lawmaking legitimate. If we think that the operation of the electoral system has led to some section of the community being wrongly disenfranchised so far as legislative representation is concerned, that will be widely regarded as a reason for reforming a legislature. We want our laws to be made in an institution that properly represents us all. In this and other ways, we pay constant attention to the issue of the legitimacy of the legislature as a lawmaker. We pay attention to the legitimacy of courts, too, but not to their legitimacy as lawmakers; instead, we look at issues like fairness inter partes, and issues about procedure and delay, judicial independence, and perhaps also the substantive rationality of decisions. We strive to maintain their legitimacy as forums for dispute resolution, but for anyone who understands that the lawmaking of courts can end up binding the whole community, this is a very curious way to go about securing legitimacy for legal change.

In general, legislation has the characteristic that it gives ordinary people a stake in the rule of law, by involving them directly or indirectly in its enactment, and by doing so on terms of fair political equality. Tocqueville remarked on this in his early observation of the United States: if you want to instill respect for law, he said, making law through elective processes is one of the best ways to do it.[21] Of course, every law will have its opponents, those whose representatives were outvoted in the relevant session of the legislature. Still,

> in the United States everyone is personally interested in enforcing the obedience of the whole community to the law; for as the minority may shortly rally the majority to its principles, it is interested in professing that respect for the decrees of the legislator which it may soon have occasion to claim for its own.[22]

If, on the other hand, legislation is denigrated as a source of law for the purposes of the rule-of-law ideal, then it is not at all clear where the respect for law, which the rule of law requires, is supposed to come from.

I shall return to the themes of this section throughout this chapter, and particularly at the end. It does seem to me that if the view under consideration is to be answered, it has to be answered on this ground. The rule of law should not be wedded to a superstitious view of law or to a view that makes the processes of legal change obscure or illegitimate. Also, the rule of law should not be divorced from the idea that legislation is a means by which the members of the society can take control of the basic structure of their society, publicly and transparently. The rule of law may not be the same as democracy, but still we should not commit ourselves to any conception of the rule of law that regards this aspiration to democratic control as inherently suspicious.

5. The Rule of Laws, Not Men (and Legislators Are Mostly Men)

On the other hand, it has to be said that there are good reasons for people devoted to of the rule-of-law tradition to feel uneasy about legislation.

The rule-of-law tradition involves an aspiration to be ruled by law rather than men. But it is hard not to see this as a false contrast; after all, laws are made by men, interpreted by men, and enacted by men. The rule of law, it would seem, is not an alternative to rule by men, but at most, a particular mode of human rule. This point—as old as Hobbes, maybe even as old as Aristotle—may be concealed by various forms of mystification.[23] We may pretend that the common law grows and develops under its own steam, and that it is not a device by which some humans rule others. Or we may say that being ruled by an old constitution (like the US Constitution) is not really being ruled by its framers, because they are dead and gone for a century or two, and we are ruled only by what they made, not by the framers themselves. But we really cannot say anything like that about legislation. Legislation, I said earlier, is a process for lawmaking dedicated publicly and explicitly to that task, and just because of that transparency, its human face is unavoidable. Our legislators are known to us, and their assemblies are all too human in their antics and machinations. Legislators are people like us, or if they are not people like us, they are distinguished as politicians (with whom familiarity breeds contempt) rather than as mythic lawgivers like Solon, Moses, or Madison. Their rule over us certainly seems to be a very clear instance of rule by men. And so, one understands the impulse to distance legislation from the rule of law, for fear of the giving the whole game away.

Another way of expressing the same point is to say that there is an uncomfortable relation between the rule of law and legal positivism.[24] Legal positivism emphasizes the provenance of law in human actions and practices and ultimately in the exercise of power.[25] Since law is understood by positivists as a human artifact, there is going to be some difficulty building anything on a sharp contrast between the rule of law and the rule of men. To the extent that they emphasize the distinctiveness of law as a mode of exercise of human power, legal positivists may be able to develop an account of rule by law as a valuable ideal. But it is commonly said that rule by law is not as important an ideal as the rule of law, and the trouble with positivism is that it does not seem to leave much room for the latter. Of course, if the positivists are right about the nature of law, then rule-of-law theorists just have to get used to it. And—it is worth adding—if positivists are right about the nature of law, they are right about all sources of law, not just legislation in particular. Positivism gives the same rule-of-men account of common law and adjudication.

Here's a third way of expressing the same anxiety about legislation. Legislation seems so much a matter of will, or of processes (like election and majority decision) that combine wills to produce a contingent and sometimes even mechanical result, that it seems ill-suited for celebration under the auspices of a political ideal whose purpose many understand to be the taming of will in politics. The legislative process produces law simply by virtue of a bunch of politicians deciding—just *willing*—that law is to be produced. As I said in *The Dignity of Legislation*, there does seem to be something brazen and impudently decisionist about this: "You want the rule of law? You want our wills to be controlled by law? Well, we'll show you: we will use our wills to make whatever laws we like, and turn your so-called rule-of-law controls in our favor."[26] And this, as I indicated, is said by the very men—powerful politicians—to whose rule the rule of law was supposed to be an alternative.

Admittedly, this apprehension about sheer decisionism under the cloak of law can be applied to other legal sources as well. There are similar apprehensions about activist judges or about courts that understand their own power in purely decisionist terms.[27] Rule by judges is sometimes seen as the very sort of rule by men that the rule of law is supposed to supersede.[28] When Justice Stevens of the US Supreme Court wrote in his dissent in *Bush v. Gore* (2000) that the true loser in that case was the rule of law, he meant precisely to contrast that ideal with a decision of a willful and politically motivated (or at best, lawlessly and pragmatically motivated) majority of his brethren on the bench.[29] But although this cynicism about the law can be turned in this way against judicial lawmaking, it is more common (and more easily available to lazy minds) as turned against legislation.

Yet another way of capturing the same uneasiness, underlying the view under consideration, is to think about the relation between legislation and the state. The rule of law is commonly seen as a way of limiting the power of the state, keeping the power of the state under control. But legislation is normally understood as one of the most important aspects of the power of the modern state. It is not the sole mode of state action, but with regard to the more important policies of the state, it is often an indispensable step in policy implementation. As Edward Rubin puts it, legislation is the mobilization of governmental resources: when the state needs something done, legislation is often the way it does it, or the first step in its doing it.[30] From this point of view, the sanctification of legislation as "law" (with the normative significance usually associated with the rule of law) seems quaint and outdated. At best, if legislation is law, it is state law—law that the state has control of and manipulates as a tool for its own purposes. But, it is said—and this is a common theme of the view under consideration—that the value we place in the rule of law is not in the rule of state law. What we want is a rule-of-law state, and that is something quite different.[31]

So if legislation is viewed just as a governmental directive, then obviously it is a mistake to regard enforcement of and compliance with such directives as signifying anything very important in relation to the rule of law. Enforcement of and compliance with legislation would be a measure of how powerful and effective the state is, and how well organized its apparatus is. But it would not tell us much about controls on that apparatus, and that is mostly what we want to know under the heading of "the rule of law." (This is not quite the case. Sometimes we concern ourselves under the heading of "the rule of law" with a government's ability to raise taxes and maintain and use a police force and an organized array of other officials to enforce its basic rules of social order. An impoverished, powerless government is not an example of the rule of law on any account. But this is usually thought to be important for the rule of law only at a very elementary level. Once the basic social and fiscal power of state is established, rule-of-law attention turns largely to its control and limitation. At least that is the perspective of the view under consideration.)

6. The Who and the How

This section commences my main attack on the view under consideration. The view under consideration looks at legislation purely in terms of who (or what) initiates and controls it—powerful men (or the state). It looks at legislation as a matter of power and asks who or what wields this power. But other aspects of legislation are important also for the rule of law. In section 7, I shall talk about the formal characteristics of legislation. In this section, I shall talk about procedural and institutional aspects. Historically, both have been important in the rule-of-law heritage. In both cases, the importance of these features of the rule-of-law tradition belies any claim that legislation is incompatible with or repugnant to the rule of law. And in both cases, the view under consideration can be seen as corrosively reductive: it makes a case against legislation as though the procedural and formal disciplines imposed on legislation were unimportant, as though all that mattered were that legislation is an instrument of state power.

The claim that we can reconcile the rule of law with the prominent position of legislation as an exercise of political power was put forward in its best-known form by the Victorian jurist A. V. Dicey. In a section of his treatise titled "Relation between Parliamentary Sovereignty and the Rule of Law," Dicey argued that the appearance of opposition between these two principles is a delusion.[32] The ascendancy of legislation in a parliamentary system, he argued, means that executive authority is mostly restricted to the forms laid down in statute law:

> The rigidity of the law constantly hampers (and sometimes with great injury to the public) the action of the executive. . . . The fact that the most arbitrary powers of the English executive must always be exercised under Act of Parliament places the government, even when armed with the widest authority, under the supervision, so to speak, of the Courts. Powers, however extraordinary, which are conferred or sanctioned by statute, are never really unlimited, for they are confined by the words of the Act itself, and, what is more, by the interpretation put upon the statute by the judges. Parliament is supreme legislator, but from the moment Parliament has uttered its will as lawgiver, that will becomes subject to the interpretation put upon it by the judges of the land, and the judges, who are influenced . . . by the general spirit of the common law, are disposed to construe statutory exceptions to common law principles in a mode which would not commend itself either to a body of officials, or to the Houses of Parliament, if the Houses were called upon to interpret their own enactments.[33]

Legislation, Dicey was saying, operates in the context of separation of powers. It establishes a framework of legality for executive action and it is enforced by judges who—if things are working well—are insulated not just from executive interference, but from legislative interference as well. The legislature in England may be subject to a large degree of executive control, but once a bill is enacted and leaves the legislature, it passes out of the control of either of those agencies and into the hands of the courts. So even if the initiation of legislation is a governmental measure, it is a measure that subsequently becomes subject to the institutional controls of an articulated system, with important points of decision clearly separated from the initiation of a bill.[34]

Of course, Dicey's England is not the same as, say, the modern United States, and Dicey acknowledged that what he said was not true of some European systems either. As to the United States, the contrasts work in two directions. On the one hand, there is a much greater formal separation of power between executive and legislature, so that the US legislatures may act more independently. Also, legislation is subject to judicial control in an additional sense in the United States: judges can review legislation and strike it down for incompatibility with constitutional standards, as well as control the basis of its interpretation. In the other direction, judicial interpretation of statutes is less susceptible to legislative influence in England than in the United States. Dicey's claim that the English Bench have always refused, in principle at least, to interpret an act of Parliament "otherwise than by reference to the words of the enactment" and that "an English judge will take no notice . . . of anything which may have passed in debate," is perhaps less true than it was, but it is much more true of an English judge than an American one.[35]

Anyway, the detail of these comparisons matters less than the general point. Legislation is not just the exercise of state power; it is the exercise of state power in the context of articulate institutional relations, a context that has been structured with a view to rule-of-law considerations.[36] For example, the rule of law accords great significance to the generality of legislation and to the distinction between a statute and a bill of attainder; this is important because if legislation is general in character, then legislators and their dependents will be subject to the rules they enact, along with everyone else, and there is thus less potential for oppression.[37] But the general form of law secures this only if there is a prophylactic against cahoots between legislators and prosecutors or between legislators and judges; the separation of powers that Dicey emphasizes provides that prophylactic, and that's one of the reasons why these procedural and institutional features have traditionally been thought so important.

So far, I have considered procedure in the sense of principles separating the process of lawmaking from processes of interpretation and application. But we should also consider the procedural aspects of legislating itself, for those, too, are important for the rule of law. Dicey thought it important to stress that "the commands of Parliament (consisting as it does of the Crown, the House of Lords, and the House of Commons) can be uttered only through the combined action of its three constituent parts, and must, therefore, al-

ways take the shape of formal and deliberate legislation."[38] Legislating is not
the same as passing a resolution or issuing a decree; it is a formally defined
act consisting of a laborious process. In a well-structured legislature, that
process involves successive stages of deliberation and voting in each of three
institutions, in two of which the legislative proposal is subject to scrutiny at
the hands of myriad representatives of various social interests. When Aristotle gave his defense of general laws (as opposed to rule by the ad hoc discretion of magistrates), he emphasized the laboriousness of this process:

> It is highly appropriate for well-enacted laws to define everything as
> exactly as possible and for as little as possible to be left to the judges: . . .
> legislation results from consideration over much time, while judg-
> ments are made at a moment, so it is difficult for the judges to deter-
> mine justice and benefits fairly.[39]

And the theme has been prominent in the rule-of-law tradition ever since.

These procedural virtues—legislative due process, if you like—are of the
utmost importance for the rule of law. Bicameralism, checks and balances
(such as executive veto), the production of a text as the focus of deliberation, clause-by-clause consideration, the formality and solemnity of the treatment of bills in the chamber, the publicity of legislative debates, successive
layers of deliberation, and the sheer time for consideration (formal and in-
formal, internal and external to the legislature) that is allowed to pass between the initiation and the final enactment of a bill—these are all features
of legislative due process that are salient to an enactment's eventual status
as law (for the purposes of our thinking about the rule of law). To wish to
be subject to the rule of law is to wish to be subject to processes like these,
and to enactments that have been through processes like these. When we
say, for example, that the rule of law requires that no one should be punished except in accordance with the violation of some rule that was laid down
before he offended—*nulla poena sine lege*—we do not just have in mind an
edict or a decree issued in advance. We have in mind that the prohibition
that he is accused of violating must be one that was enacted in advance
through the laborious solemnity of the legislative process—enacted as law,
not just given out as notice.

Once again, the danger of the view under consideration is that it radically underestimates the importance of legislative due process. Claiming a
general incompatibility between legislation and the rule of law or (in the

more moderate version) saying that incompatibility between the rule of law has to do with the subject matter of legislation, not with the procedures and forms involved in its enactment, treats these aspects of the rule-of-law heritage as though they did not matter.

Cynics will respond that much of what we call legislation is not in fact enacted scrupulously according to these forms and procedures; much legislation is enacted in a way that makes a mockery of the procedural principles I have been emphasizing. This is certainly true of some legislation, and it is deplorably true as a matter of the general practice of some legislatures. I once argued that the unicameral legislature of New Zealand is in danger of falling into this category.[40] Legislation in that system is commonly enacted in a rush, in a mostly empty chamber, without any proper provision for careful deliberation and debate; the legislative process is wholly dominated by the executive and subject only to norms of efficiency and executive convenience; and it is often enacted under conditions of urgency, with a parliamentary majority controlled by the executive used to force closure motions in debate after debate. The result is exactly the sort of thing that critics of legislation complain about: ill-considered measures being put into effect simply because the executive wants them "on the books," and parliamentary process being used or abused simply as an instrument of political power. This is legislation in opposition to the rule of law: it flouts the notion of legislative due process; it sits unsatisfactorily with the separation of powers (though mercifully, the judiciary remains active and independent in New Zealand); and it really does elide the idea of the rule of law and rule by the state.

But the proper response to that sort of case is retail criticism of the particular legislative process in rule-of-law terms, not jumping to the conclusion that there is some sort of wholesale antipathy between legislation and the rule of law. The trouble with extreme versions of the view under consideration is that they act as though the rule-of-law criteria applicable to legislation did not matter; they say that legislation as such is problematic, whether it is disciplined by these procedural criteria or not. And the trouble with the more moderate version of the view under consideration is that it also sidelines considerations of legislative due process. On the moderate view, once we establish that legislation affecting markets or legislation limiting property rights has been enacted, it does not matter whether it was enacted essentially by state decree or whether it went scrupulously through the processes ordained for legislation's status as law.

7. Lon Fuller's Inner Morality of Law

Much the same is true of rule-of-law criteria traditionally applied to the *form* of legislation. We recognize that sometimes it is important for the law to be deliberately changed, but from the perspective of the rule of law, we think it important that these changes be prospective, that they be general in character, not ad hoc, and that they generate a coherent, intelligible, and relatively stable body of regulation. The view under consideration tends to be corrosively cynical of this, too, when it argues that it is legislation as such or the content of particular legislation, not its form, that matters for the rule of law.

I find such cynicism quite disconcerting, for I was brought up on discussions of the rule of law that apply particularly to the formal attributes of legislation. Here, what I have in mind is Lon Fuller's jurisprudence. Fuller does not use the phrase "the rule of law" in regard to the principles he sets out in chapter 2 of his book, *The Morality of Law;* he calls his eight principles (of generality, publicity, prospectivity, intelligibility, consistency, practicability, constancy, and congruence) "the inner morality of law."[41] But they have been adopted by the jurisprudence community as a fair statement of central elements of the rule-of-law ideal, and a rule-of-law theorist would puzzle his readers if he did not refer to them. Fuller's principles are introduced with a little fable about a hapless legislator, Rex, who did not understand these principles and imposed, to his subjects' consternation, decrees which were ad hoc, secret, retroactive, unintelligible, contradictory, impossible, etc. Rex was a bad legislator and we are supposed to infer from Fuller's presentation that a good legislator would follow these eight principles.

I suppose one could adapt Fuller's requirements to apply to other modes of lawmaking—for example, lawmaking by courts. Certainly, there have been times when the common law failed most of Fuller's tests; Jeremy Bentham spilt gallons of ink arguing that it was impossible to infer any clear general rules, let alone public or consistent rules, from the activity of English judges. Bentham's "Judge & Co." fare no better than Fuller's "King Rex" by the standards of the internal morality of law. Not only that, but lawmaking by judges has a sort of retroactivity built in (and heroic efforts have to be made, as they are sometimes made by the US courts, to limit the retroactive effect of judge-made law).[42] It is actually quite strange that Fuller said so little about courts in *The Morality of Law.* As I said in Chapter 7, he was one of the foremost theorists of the legal process and wrote deeply and powerfully about the distinctiveness of adjudication.[43] Yet, in the writing for which he is most celebrated so far as the rule of law is concerned, there is next to nothing on procedural issues and very little in the way of rule-of-law principles focusing on courts.[44] The independence of the judiciary, for example, or the importance of fair and timely access to justice, rates no mention in *The Morality of Law*.[45]

Anyway, the fact is that Fuller's work in *The Morality of Law* illustrates a strong (and in my view, a healthy) tendency to associate the rule of law with formal virtues of legislation, as opposed to other modes of law and law-making. The rule of law—he seems to say—is not satisfied unless legislation takes a certain form. And so there is a puzzle in regard to the view under consideration. It is rather odd to highlight the Fullerian requirements as the essence of the rule of law if there is something about legislation as such that offends that ideal.

Now, whether a given piece of legislation satisfies Fuller's eight principles is of course an open question. To the extent that it does not—to the extent that it is retrospective or ad hoc or unintelligible or one of a series of bewilderingly frequent changes—then to that extent we should say the rule of law is compromised.[46] And it may happen that a lot of the legislation that is of concern in moderate versions of the view under consideration does violate the rule of law in this way. Hayek thought this was likely to be true of legislation seeking to implement social justice: it would require constant (and, he thought, futile) adjustments of statutory rights and responsibilities on a more or less day-to-day basis.[47] However, he did not think this was true of basic welfare legislation; if he opposed that on rule-of-law grounds, it would have to be on the basis of an extreme version of the view under consideration.[48] Others may disagree with that concession. Guido Pincione, for example, has argued that welfare rights are necessarily vague and indeterminate, and that for this reason, legislation installing them probably falls foul of the rule of law as Fuller conceives it.[49] Todd Zywicki suggests that "heavy regulation of the economy is inconsistent with compliance with the rule of law" because it makes obedience to law "practically impossible" for any business that wants to make money, thus failing Fuller's criterion of practicability.[50] And Hayek believes that the micromanagement of a mixed or socialist economy inevitably requires administrative means that go beyond and probably violate the rule of law.[51]

(Interestingly, Fuller seems prepared to actually concede this last point, though he draws from it conclusions that are opposite to Hayek's. Hayek seems to argue that if a mode of governance cannot be conducted within the rule of law, then it should not be undertaken. Fuller, however, thinks that this possibility may lead us to rethink the significance of the rule of law—maybe it is important in some areas and not in others; in some areas of governance maybe we have to learn to do without it.)[52]

It seems to me that issues like these are worth arguing about. The argument has content: it has empirical as well as conceptual elements; it is complicated in an interesting way; it raises well-defined normative questions that people can argue about (Are the Fullerian criteria actually as important as traditional rule-of-law theorists say they are? Are they necessarily more important than the policy goals that cannot effectively be pursued without violating them?); and it does not just announce as a matter of definition that legislated rules that regulate markets or limit property rights are for that reason alone contrary to the rule of law. But the view under consideration is much more peremptory. It says, never mind the formal or procedural criteria; social and economic regulation is by definition inconsistent with the rule of law.

I guess sooner or later we are going to have to confront the contrast between substantive and nonsubstantive conceptions of the rule of law, because in the end, that is what really seems to be at stake in this controversy. The view under consideration—at least in its moderate version—is committed to a substantive conception of the rule of law. We will deal with this head-on in section 9. Up to now, I have emphasized the procedural and formal aspects of traditional approaches to the rule of law mainly to set the stage for an appreciation of how much we would be in danger of jettisoning if we were to adopt the view under consideration.

8. Rule by Law and Legal Instrumentalism

What usually happens when people adopt some version of the view under consideration is that they draw a distinction between the rule *of* law and rule *by* law, and they say that Fuller's eight principles (inasmuch as they apply to legislation) are best regarded as constitutive of the latter. (This issue we will discuss in more detail in Chapter 10.) Sometimes this move is accompanied by an acknowledgement that rule by law is an important ideal (certainly compared to rule by decree or rule by managerial discretion). But its importance is usually held to fade into insignificance compared to the rule of law—that is, to a mode of legal rule in which the activity of legislators as well as all other officials is severely restricted.[53]

According to the view under consideration, the idea of rule by law is associated with legal instrumentalism—a jurisprudential approach that treats
law just as a tool of policy, a means to an end for those in power.[54] That last
phrase makes it sound disreputable, but legal instrumentalism is as much
the view that law helps us promote the common good as the view that law
helps a particular ruler pursue his own political objectives; it is a very general characterization. Still, general or not, it seems to be suspect from the
perspective of the view under consideration. So, for example, Brian Tamanaha argues that legal instrumentalism is in tension with the rule of law
because by treating law as a means, it places no limits on law's content; anything can be a means, depending on circumstances.[55] Full discussion of this
must await our consideration of substantive conceptions of the rule of law
in section 9. For now, it is enough to say (in response to Tamanaha) that
even if certain means are or ought to be ruled out, it does not follow that
legal instrumentalism is false; law can be a means to an end even if the
means are selected from a constrained or limited range.

This is not the place to try and figure out what a noninstrumentalist
theory of law might involve. Possibilities include expressivist accounts of law,
formalist accounts, and (more ambiguously) accounts of the point of a law
that identify its aim in terms that are so close to the terms of the law's requirements or prohibitions that they make it difficult to talk about means
and ends. (So, for example, one might say that the aim of a law punishing
murder with death is just that murder be punished with death, whether or
not that contributes to a further aim like reducing crime.) One interesting
idea that Hayek emphasizes is that the task of law is to facilitate the purposes
of individuals rather than to pursue any purposes of its own.[56]

Another possible version of noninstrumentalism is the suggestion by Jeffrey Kahn, following Robert Bolt's Sir Thomas More, that law is to be understood not as a tool but as a sort of guarantee of safe passage: "The law is not an
instrument of any kind. The law is a causeway upon which, so long as he keeps
to it, a citizen may walk safely."[57] Kahn thinks that this image of the law as a
safe causeway is undermined if law is used as an instrument.[58] It is a little unclear what this means. The image of law as a causeway conveys for Kahn the
idea that the published laws are a reliable guide to what is prohibited and what
is permitted; so long as one pays attention to them and observes them, one
may proceed unmolested by the state. But this presupposes that there are laws
prohibiting some conduct—out there in the marshes, on either side of the
causeway—and the image does not seem to exclude the possibility that most

such laws have a (respectable) instrumental justification. What protects us is not the rejection of instrumentalism but the guarantee that even if law is being used as an instrument, it will not be extended beyond the reach of its explicit terms. This operates as a rule-of-law constraint on law's instrumentality, but it certainly does not require a noninstrumental view of law. Moreover, the causeway idea actually works best with law understood as legislation. When offenses and penalties are legislated, people know where they stand. It is legislation, together with the formal and procedural principle *nulla poena sine lege*, that gives us the guarantee of safe passage.

It is a mistake, then, for opponents of legal instrumentalism to denigrate the formal and procedural guarantees usually associated with rule by law. The importance of such guarantees stands unabated, even while jurists flounder about trying to come up with some sort of noninstrumentalist jurisprudence.

Here's another example. Brian Tamanaha argues that legal instrumentalism is antithetical to the rule of law because it tends to subvert even the formal and procedural principles associated with that ideal:

> In relation to the conduct of lawyers and judges, an instrumental understanding of law suggests that legal rules and processes are tools to be manipulated to achieve desired objectives, rather than as binding dictates. Lawyers stretch and twist legal rules that stand in their way; judges reason toward ends or goals, setting aside or creatively interpreting legal rules if need be. In both situations an instrumental view of law detracts from the essential characteristic that defines rules: their binding quality. Legal instrumentalism at this level operates against the formal rule of law requirements that the legal rules be certain and stable, and be applied equally to all according to their terms.[59]

Tamanaha may be right that there is an instrumentalist approach to interpretation that undermines rule of law safeguards—I mean an approach that licenses judges effectively to rewrite laws when they seem under- or overinclusive relative to their purpose or to purposes that the judge thinks ought to be pursued. And he is right that this is a prevalent vice in modern US jurisprudence.[60] But we should be less cavalier than Tamanaha in how we pursue this point. Criticizing instrumentalism in interpretation is not the same as criticizing instrumental conceptions of law. In fact, Tamanaha's critique presupposes that formal and procedural standards of the rule of law are important, even though they do not amount to a noninstrumental jurisprudence.

So here is where we stand. Traditional rule-of-law theorists have emphasized procedural requirements like due process in litigation and in legislation, along with the separation of powers and formal requirements like generality, publicity, prospectivity, constancy, and clarity. Their critics are alarmed because these standards implicitly acknowledge that law is an instrument wielded by men. The traditional view concedes that men rule; it just insists that their rule be subject to the formal and procedural constraints of legality. In their rush to discredit that view—and to argue in favor of a substantive conception—critics play down the importance of the procedural and formal constraints. But there is no reason why we should follow them in this—that is, we should not pretend that there is no important content to the requirement of rule by law, just because our understanding of it does not match the constitutional fantasies of those who talk of the rule of laws, not men.

9. Substantive Conceptions of the Rule of Law

It is time now to say something about substantive conceptions of the rule of law. The most popular versions of the view under consideration purport to favor what is called a substantive rather than a merely procedural or formal conception of the rule of law.[61] How should we think about this?

The contrast between substantive and formal / procedural conceptions is a hardy perennial in the rule-of-law literature.[62] A substantive conception of the rule of law associates the rule of law with the promotion of some value such as economic freedom or individual liberty or human rights. The thought is that the rule-of-law ideal aims directly at these substantive values (or some subset of them), and that legislation or other governmental measures that tend to oppose or undermine such values are eo ipso violations of the rule of law, irrespective of their formal and procedural attributes.

The distinction, though, is not as clear as defenders of the view under consideration sometimes suggest. It is necessary to distinguish two propositions:

(α) The rule of law requires the protection or promotion of certain substantive values.

(β) The point of the rule of law is the protection or promotion of certain substantive values.

A great many traditional rule-of-law theorists with whose work I am familiar hold a version of (β). Very few of them hold (α). Lon Fuller, for example, believes that the point of his inner morality of law—which, as we said, is mostly formal—is to respect human dignity and secure a certain equality or reciprocity between ruler and ruled.[63] Those values are the raison d'être of the eight principles he lays down, but the principles themselves are not to be reduced to the values that give them their point. Similarly, F. A. Hayek in his early writings maintains that the point of the rule of law is individual liberty, but on his account, the rule of law is not reducible to the promotion of individual liberty, nor does every measure for the protection of liberty qualify as the rule of law. These are both examples of views that hold (β) but not (α).

So, when we distinguish between formal / procedural and substantive conceptions of the rule of law, it is not necessarily a distinction between conceptions that take certain values seriously and those that do not. It is usually a distinction between those that use the term "rule of law" simply as a slogan for the pursuit of certain other values and those that adopt formal and / or procedural principles of legality for the sake of the promotion of certain other values. Maybe there are some conceptions of the rule of law that reject both (α) and (β). An example might be

(γ) The point of the rule of law is to enable rulers to efficiently pursue whatever aims they want to pursue.

This would be a purely strategic conception of the rule of law; its strictures would be comparable in their moral force to telling the ruler to keep his bayonets sharp.[64] Some of the things that Fuller says in *The Morality of Law* give the impression that his account is of this kind, but he later devotes several pages to denying this, and I think we have to accept that his view is of type (β), not type (γ).[65] Some might call (γ) an instrumental view of the rule of law, and if they did, we would know what they meant. But then we would have to be extra careful to avoid equating the sort of view discussed in section 8 with this sense of instrumentalism. In that section, we noted that a distinction is sometimes made between the rule of law and rule by law. The latter concedes that law is an instrument of power and that it may be used as a means to an end, but insists nevertheless that it must be disciplined by various formal and procedural principles of legality (that Fuller, Dicey, and others have expounded). This insistence is most likely to be motivated by a view of type (β), not by a view of type (γ). The idea is that even if power is being exercised over us, we are better off—in regard to values like dignity or liberty or equality—when it is exercised through the medium of measures that have the formal and procedural attributes associated with legality than when power is exercised by decree, by managerial discretion, or by terror. What I am saying, then, is that we should not use an equivocation on "instrumental" as a way of correlating the distinction between (α) and (β) with the distinction between the rule of law and rule by law. Any such correlation is bogus.

All that apart, what can be said for or against a view of type (α)? The case that is made is sometimes quite cynical. It is said that we should use any means necessary to persuade governments to respect substantive values such as property rights and the principle of free markets. Since everyone happens to be in favor of the rule of law at the moment, we might as well use the good vibrations associated with that phrase to support the Washington Consensus and drive home its points about markets and property. It is said that if we were to confine ourselves to the more traditional formal / procedural implications of the rule of law, we would be in danger of associating a very popular slogan with principles whose enforcement may not necessarily inure to the benefit of market values.[66] And that would be a waste. So, on this account, it is better to forget the traditional rule-of-law baggage (which has the additional drawback of endorsing a dangerously pro-legislation mentality) and substitute in the substantive values of the Washington Consensus. That seems to be the argument.

I guess we should be grateful that the view under consideration acknowledges the manipulative aspect of this preference for a substantive conception of the rule of law. But frankness in this context is not necessarily disarming. For consider, first, how we are to decide which values should be incorporated into a substantive conception. Those who favor property rights and market economy will no doubt scramble to privilege their favorite values in this regard. But so too will those who favor human rights, or those who favor political participation, or those who favor civil liberties or social justice. The result, in my view, will be a general decline in political articulacy, as people struggle to use the same term to express disparate ideals.[67]

If the first of these groups—the group that favors markets and the protection of property rights—wins out in its struggle for possession of the phrase, then the others will probably not be fooled for long. They will just abandon "the rule of law" (even with the slogan's heritage of good vibrations) and find some other way of expressing what matters to them. Some of them may have had suspicions about "the rule of law" all along, and critical legal studies (CLS) scholars have often regarded it very warily. There was a great deal of excitement in the 1970s when the Marxist historian E. P. Thompson acknowledged the rule of law as an unqualified human good, and that sparked an interesting debate.[68] But I suppose we have to excuse the substantivists for not being interested in that; after all, for them, "the rule of law" is acknowledged to be just a slogan that we manipulate to promote market development and the protection of investor portfolios.

In the end, if there is an argument for a substantive conception, it is an argument that moves from (β) to (α): if you are going to pursue certain values, maybe it is sensible to pursue them directly rather than through formalist or proceduralist strategies that might have only a contingent relation to the values in question. This is a fair point, but it is not really an argument in favor of associating "the rule of law" with the direct pursuit of these values. There is a constant temptation to read too much into the rule of law, as though it were supposed to be the sum total of our political philosophy, or as though failure to acknowledge that it is the sum of all good things might drive us to the position that it is no good at all.[69] But I insisted at the very beginning of this book that the rule of law is not the sum of all good things; it is properly regarded as one star among others in the constellation of modern political values (the others include democracy, human rights, and economic freedom). And the fact is, we already have terminology for the direct pursuit of economic freedom; we don't need to use the phrase "the rule of law" for that.

10. The Importance of Social and Economic Legislation

The general impression created by the view under consideration is that there is something dodgy about legislation from the perspective of the rule of law, something inherently unhealthy about it, especially when it goes beyond the institution of property rights and the establishment and liberalization of markets. The idea seems to be that if we accord any legitimacy at all to such legislation, it is only as an indulgence to majoritarian democracy, for it has no credentials at all from a rule-of-law perspective.[70]

I want to end this chapter by arguing that there is something deeply troubling about this view, and that we need to understand that the sort of tasks undertaken by legislatures so far as the limitation of property and regulation of the marketplace are concerned in fact represent a central and important function of law—a function that it is important for the rule of law to come to terms with.

The argument begins with a concession. A case can perhaps be made that the establishment and protection of property rights is one of the paradigmatic functions of law. This assignment responds to some of the most elementary circumstances of the human condition, such as our need for resources, our limited altruism, and what David Hume called "the easy transition from one person to another . . . of the enjoyment of such possessions as we have acquir'd by our industry and good fortune."[71] It is part of what H. L. A. Hart called "the minimum content of natural law."[72] And maybe one can extend the assignment to include the setting up of markets, though as many have noted, the establishment of private property is often sufficient (as well as necessary) for that.[73] All this we can grant to the view under consideration.

But it is inevitable in the world we live in that the legitimacy of property rights will be affected over time by changes in circumstances, both in their character and in their distribution. Extreme and growing inequalities are not always tolerable, and the consequences of privatization in various areas are not always easy to foresee. We cannot foresee what the consequences will be of people's exercise of the freedoms that property rights confer. If liberty is not to become license, these effects need to be reviewed from time to time in light of changing circumstances or advances in our knowledge of social cause and effect. Moreover, what markets can and cannot produce, and how efficient they are (or what social goals they promote or retard in various circumstances) are not always calculable a priori. New public goods are conceivable, new externalities come to light, and new modes of provision are imagined. This, too, varies over time and with circumstances, in the face of social, economic, ecological, and demographic change. The law needs to come to terms with such changes. That matters like these may need collective attention from time to time is not a cranky or anomalous position; it is not Bolshevik or socially destructive. It is the ordinary wisdom of human affairs. No conception of governance, no conception of law that fails to leave room for changes and adjustments of this sort can possibly be tolerable. And it seems to me that any conception of the rule of law that denigrates the very idea of such changes and that treats their enforcement as an inherent derogation from that ideal has to be wrong.

Any particular proposal for change will no doubt have its opponents, and sometimes, or often, the opponents will be right. But again, the criticism needs to be retail, not wholesale. If someone claims that once markets and property rights have been established, any change or any regulation is out of the question, it seems to me that their perspective is necessarily that of an outsider, interested only (like Robert Barro's investors) in what can be extracted from a given society, rather than the perspective of someone who lives in the society and who cares about changes in the quality of life (and changes in the distribution of the quality of life among his or her fellow inhabitants) that markets and property rights are supposed to contribute to. Responsiveness to these changes and willingness to pursue concerns about them is the hallmark of the responsible citizen, and we should be wary of adopting any conception of the rule of law that is designed to sideline or discredit that. We should be especially wary when such a conception is advocated from an external or predatory point of view.

So changes in the regulation of property and market structures are not necessarily out of order. Of course, everything depends on the mode of such changes. Constant day-to-day managerial meddling or changes imposed by decree are rightly regarded as incompatible with the rule of law. But legislated changes are not necessarily incompatible with the rule of law. On the contrary, not only does an adequate conception of the rule of law have to leave room for them but an adequate conception of the rule of law will discipline these changes, subjecting them to formal and procedural criteria of legality. The rule of law will insist on changes to markets and property rights enacted openly through procedures that are transparent and clear, changes proposed in a form that can be debated, changes that are formulated prospectively in general terms, changes that take the form of established schemes that people can expect to see upheld and enforced in the medium and long term, changes set out publicly in intelligible legal texts and then given to independent judicial tribunals for interpretation, administration, and enforcement.

It is possible, I suppose, that this task of the review and modification of market structures and property rights—indispensable, as I have said, for a responsible and well-governed society—could be assigned to courts rather than legislatures. No doubt some last-ditch defenders of what I have called "the view under consideration" will want to insist on this. But that would be a strange and misbegotten position—as though the sensible thing for a society to do would be to remove this process of change from institutions dedicated to the conscious and transparent consideration of social arrangements and to vest it in institutions whose role is mysterious and obfuscated.

No doubt there are all sorts of good arguments based on democracy against entrusting this to courts. But my argument in this chapter is mainly a rule-of-law argument, not a democratic one. The rule of law counsels openness and transparency in governance and the enactment of measures that are clear and general, public and prospective. As I said in section 4, legislation and the legislative process is the place where we bring together a sense of society's occasional need for change with the most scrupulous requirements of openness, inclusiveness, deliberation, and due process. The tendency of the view under consideration, the view that I have been attacking, is to subvert these requirements, to smuggle in tendentious ideological positions and to do everything possible to close down any sense that people are collectively in control of their destiny. This may be done in the service of a particular economic theory, or a theory of limited government, or a hypothesis about nation-building, or as part of a frankly extractive or predatory enterprise. But it is not a respectable position, and respectable defenders of the rule of law should have nothing to do with it.

10

Rule *by* Law

A Much-Maligned Preposition

1. The Rule of Law: Its Status and Formulation

I have taught a class called "The Rule of Law" for many years, and one of the things I tell my students early on is that they should not get hung up on that four-word phrase. The same meaning can be conveyed by a single noun—"legality"—or by a whole paragraph.

Some say it was Albert Venn Dicey who first used the phrase "the rule of law."[1] But if Dicey gets the accolade, it is only because we don't count slight variations on the phrase, like John Adams's "the government of laws and not of men" or the Greek phrase νόμον ἄρχειν in book III of Aristotle's *Politics*.[2] We also have to consider Lon Fuller's term, "the inner morality of law"—which is taken as canonical in some modern philosophical debates about the rule of law, even though Fuller hardly ever used the latter phrase.[3]

We worry also about the normative status of *the rule of law*. I see it as a compelling political ideal for a liberal democracy; however, I also think it's just one among many—one star in a constellation of ideals that also includes human rights, democratic government, individual freedom, national security, and social justice. Dicey called the rule of law a feature characterizing the political institutions of England—one of two such features, along with the sovereignty of Parliament.[4]

Its exact legal status is unclear. In Britain, the statute that established the Supreme Court of the United Kingdom stated in its first section that nothing in the act is intended to adversely affect "the existing constitutional principle

of the rule of law."[5] That sounds as though the principle of the rule of law
has legal work to do, which the legislative draftsman does not want inad-
vertently to upset. In some jurisdictions, notably New Zealand, "the rule of
law" is presented as part of the content of lawyers' ethical obligations: "Every
lawyer who provides regulated services must, in the course of his or her practice, comply with the following fundamental obligations: . . . the obligation
to uphold the rule of law and to facilitate the administration of justice."[6] But
what does this obligation involve, and how is it enforced?

There is an issue, too, about whether the rule of law is supposed to operate as a "principle" in Ronald Dworkin's sense—that is, as an undercur-
rent of integrity in the law that helps us with the interpretive and doctrinal
work we have to do in hard cases.[7] Remember Dworkin's example: the
principle that says "No one should profit from his own wrong-doing," which
was famously decisive in the 1889 New York case of *Riggs v. Palmer* (the
young man who murdered his grandfather and then sought to take a bequest
under the old man's will).[8] I think it is an interesting question whether our
judges should use the rule of law as a background normative principle to
help in the decision of cases in constitutional and administrative law, or
whether it just operates decorously as part of the legal system's public relations. I don't mean that as cynically as it sounds. Something might be a
principle of our constitution—something that captures its spirit and that
might be highlighted in a comparative analysis—but still it may not really
be of much normative use within the legal system (e.g., in settling cases).
So, there are lots of tough questions surrounding this one little phrase, "the
rule of law."

2. The Pronoun

For those who are hung up on exact formulations, there is a particular issue,
which I have indicated in the title of this chapter. I mean the contrast between "the rule of law" and the idea of "rule *by* law." One little preposition—
"of" rather than "by," or "by" rather than "of"—but a lot of meaning packed
into the difference. This difference plays out in our use of "the rule of law"
to characterize a legal system mostly from the outside. It is not a difference
that does any internal doctrinal work.

Still, it is supposed to be important in classifying legal and political systems. And the beginning of wisdom is to note that the contrast is *always* intended to the detriment of "rule by law."[9] Rule by law is seen as a debased

version of the rule of law. That's what I mean by a much-maligned preposition. A 2008 book published by Cambridge University Press called *Rule by Law* has as its subtitle *The Politics of Courts in Authoritarian Regimes.*[10] Rule by law is almost always associated in the literature with the use of law as a tool or instrument to serve the ends of power in an authoritarian regime. It is the bad brother in the relationship. "Rule by law" means the state uses law to control its citizens but never allows law to be used by the people to control the state. Its connection to the rule *of* law—that noble ideal on which we rightly pride ourselves—is by way of caricature, perversion, or at best, imperfect approximation. What I would like to do in this chapter is ask whether this denigration of rule *by* law is warranted.

3. Hobbing and Locking

Something like this contrast between *the rule of law* and *rule by law* has been present in our juridical tradition at least since Thomas Hobbes, though it hasn't always been characterized using those phrases. Hobbes thought that since people disagree about *mine* and *thine,* it would conduce to peace "to make some common Rules for all men, and to declare them publiquely, by which every man may know what may be called his, what anothers."[11] So legal rules (e.g., about property) were important. But Hobbes also thought that it would undermine peace—indeed, it would undermine the very logic of sovereignty—for the ultimate lawmaker to be bound by the laws he applied to his subjects.[12] So Hobbes's position adds up to rule *by* law as that is usually understood: the sovereign uses laws as a way of keeping peace among his subjects, but he is himself free from the laws he lays down. He has control over the subjects' legal property, if he wants it. His authority is absolute, in the technical sense of *ab legibus solutus*.

Now John Locke denounced this conception in an anticipation of Orwellian imagery. Without referring explicitly to Hobbes, Locke said that an absolute sovereign's concern for his subjects is like the concern of a farmer for the animals "who labour and drudge . . . for his pleasure and advantage." If the farmer wants profitably to exploit the animals, then he has to keep peace in the farmyard, "keep those animals from hurting or destroying one another." But "if it be asked what security . . . [there is] in such a state against the . . . oppression of [the] absolute ruler"—that is, what security do the animals have against the farmer—"the very question can scarce be borne. . . . Betwixt subject and subject, [the absolutists] will grant, there must be . . .

laws, and judges for their mutual peace and security. But as for the ruler, he . . . is above all such circumstances."[13] That's rule by law: law for the subject but not for the ruler. The rule of law, by contrast, would place emphatic legal limits on what the government could do.

Locke was never clear about how the rule *of* law in this specific sense was supposed to work. If Thomas Hobbes had heard Locke's critique, he would have said (as indeed he did say, though not to Locke):

> For to be subject to laws is to be to be subject to the Commonwealth, that is, to the sovereign representative, that is, to himself which is not subjection, but freedom from the laws. Which error, because it setteth the laws above the sovereign, setteth also a judge above him, and a power to punish him; which is to make a new sovereign; and again for the same reason a third to punish the second; and so continually without end, to the confusion and dissolution of the Commonwealth.[14]

On this account, anything beyond rule by law was an impossibility. For all his enthusiasm for legal restraints, Locke offered no constitutional mechanism to answer this point, save a vague threat of revolution against any ruler who threw off the yoke of the laws. It never occurred to him to experiment with the idea that a court could control the sovereign without becoming a (super-)sovereign itself. (This is the possibility we discussed in Chapter 6.)

4. Analytic Legal Philosophy

Before going any further, I want to say something about the *rule of law* and *rule by law* in jurisprudence. There is a large literature on the rule of law in analytic legal philosophy, but you could spend weeks ransacking it before you came across any mention of the contrast between rule of law and rule by law. Raz didn't mention it, Dworkin didn't mention it, Lord Bingham didn't mention it, Lon Fuller didn't mention it, Matt Kramer doesn't mention it, Andrei Marmor doesn't mention it, and nor do I (or nor *did* I until relatively recently).[15] David Dyzenhaus and Brian Tamanaha have been honorable exceptions.[16]

Most of us were bogged down trying to figure out what "the rule of law" meant, why it was important, and whether it posed a threat to legal positivism. We paid no attention to its bad brother; we didn't even know it had a bad brother. It is a remarkable example of how analytic discussion can seal itself off from the wider context in which its concepts flourish. For in political science and in the literature on law and development, people like Thomas Carothers talk about little else.[17]

It may also be ideological. I remember being quite taken aback on one of my earliest visits to the United States (to a Liberty Fund conference at Snowbird, Utah) to hear conservative/libertarian scholars saying that the sort of rule-of-law principles that analytic philosophers debated in the wake of Raz's famous article or the Hart/Fuller confrontation were not really what the rule of law meant at all.[18] At best, it was rule *by* law. They said I needed to read Hayek and Oakeshott, not Raz or Fuller, to find out what the rule of law really meant.[19] Maybe they were right. It is certainly true that there was a whole challenging world of rule-of-law ideas out there that didn't really fit into my cramped analytic understanding. One of the things I will try to do in this chapter is bring a number of these strands into relation with one another, to promote, I hope, a broader understanding.

5. Other Ways of Understanding Rule by Law

So far, we have considered the most common way of distinguishing the rule of law from rule by law: under the rule of law, the state or government itself is constrained by law; under rule by law, there is law in the system but it does not constrain the government. However, this is not the only way of distinguishing the two.

Sometimes rule *by* law is associated with lack of procedural values: the laws are there, but they are not enforced with norms of procedural due process.[20] Or it is associated with defects in institutional values: there are compromises on the independence of the judiciary—telephone justice, for example, where the judges (e.g., Soviet judges) wait for a phone call from their superiors to tell them how to decide a case.[21] Or, the contrast between rule *by* law and the rule *of* law is sometimes correlated with the difference between formal (thin) and substantive (thick) understandings of legality.[22] Is a society's commitment to law associated with a commitment to justice and to human rights? Or is the allegiance to legality narrower than that? This is a distinction the analytic philosophers do understand. Joseph Raz is famous for insisting on a *thin* sense of the rule of law. The rule of law, he says, is just one of the virtues a society may have. And it may have it while lacking the others:

> A non-democratic legal system, based on the denial of human rights . . . [or] on racial segregation . . . may, in principle, conform to the

requirements of the rule of law better than any of the legal systems of the more enlightened Western democracies. This does not mean that it will be better than those Western democracies. It will be an immeasurably worse legal system, but it will excel in one respect: in its conformity to the rule of law.[23]

Raz thought it was necessary to separate these issues to keep them clear. Tom Bingham in his book *The Rule of Law* did not agree. In an exasperating exhibition of the English attitude to intellectual authority, Lord Bingham wrote: "While . . . one can recognize the logical force of Professor Raz's contention, I would roundly reject it in favor of a 'thick' definition [of the rule of law], embracing the protection of human rights within its scope."[24] Well, sometimes people try to capture this difference by saying that Raz's jurisprudence comprises a theory of rule *by* law, as opposed to Lord Bingham's richer or thicker notion of the rule *of* law. Charles Lugosi defines "rule by law" as a mode of rule "where the government may exercise arbitrary executive powers and may abridge at will constitutional civil liberties." He contrasts this with "rule of law," in which "justice is the defining characteristic."[25] Elsewhere, he ventures into the realm of hyperbole, maintaining that there can be no rule of law "without a moral component that squares with the eternal and natural law of God . . . [as] a standard of righteousness"; without that, says Lugosi, "there can be no rule of law, but [only] the tyrannical imposition of rule by law."[26]

Still, as I said before, in the main, most jurists are content to define "rule by law" as a failure to use law to limit the state. Randall Peerenboom's formulation is typical: "In a rule by law regime, law is merely a tool to serve the interests of the State, and there are no meaningful legal limits on the rulers."[27] Or, as Arthur Garrison puts it, "Rule by law requires the people to be subservient to the law, but it makes no such demand of the sovereign."[28] As such, rule by law is treated as an icon of despotism, not freedom.

6. China

China is often cited as Exhibit A in this parade of horrors. If you use Westlaw to look up US articles contrasting "rule of law" and "rule by law" in the same paragraph, about half of them—half of the almost 300 articles you'll find—are about China.

Some years ago, we all celebrated the 800th anniversary of Magna Carta (1215), and in October 2015 the *Financial Times* reported a story about Beijing's insistence that a Magna Carta exhibition be shifted from Renmin University to the relative seclusion of the British ambassador's residence. The *FT* observed that

> China's view of the rule of law chafes somewhat with that espoused by the Magna Carta. . . . China is promoting its own rule of law while in the throes of a political consolidation under Mr. Xi that has led to tighter controls over civil society, the media and academics. Observers quip that China's vision is closer to "rule by law," where an authoritarian state exerts its power through laws and courts rather than itself being subject to those laws, as enshrined in Magna Carta.[29]

The term the Chinese use for "the rule of law"—法治 or *fazhi*—involves very little more than the idea that citizens and firms will be expected to abide by the laws laid down for their behavior.[30] Unencumbered as it is by prepositions, the Chinese term could as easily be translated as "law rule." And though it has that in common with Aristotle's phrase νόμον ἄρχειν, it lacks anything like the Aristotelian connotation that law itself might be in charge, quite apart from the politicians who make it. In the 1970s and 1980s, Chinese scholars debated whether *fazhi* might represent a combination of rule by men and rule of law: "Those who supported the combination theory argued that law was meaningless without men because law was made and applied by men. They believed that rule by men and rule by law should be combined and that emphasis on either model would be one-sided."[31] But the combination theory in the end represented an abandonment rather than a compromise of any real rule of law: "The apparently popular combination view actually rejected the idea of the supremacy of law, viewing law simply as an official tool for ruling."[32]

In fact, complaints about legality in China are many and varied. I don't just mean China's lack of democracy or its failure to respect fundamental political rights. Even if we follow Raz and adopt a thin theory of the rule of law, still there is an awful lot in Chinese arrangements to give us pause. There is the "demonizing [of] constitutionalism"; the cracking down on lawyers doing what we regard as lawyers' work (that is, providing a voice and some modicum of due process for opponents of the regime in the proceedings that are taken against them).[33] There is the routine deprivation of dissidents' rights to a fair trial.[34] These are violations closely tied to the core values of legality.

7. Transition from Rule by Law toward the Rule of Law

Is the difference between rule *by* law and the rule *of* law a difference of kind or a difference of degree? China, we know, is a society in transition, and we watch it to see whether rule by law can transform itself over time into the rule of law.

Some commentators have doubts about the prospect of such a transition. They see the trajectory as heading almost inevitably in the other direction, along lines indicated by Hayek in *The Road to Serfdom* or by Dicey in some of the gloomier prefaces he wrote to later editions of his *Introduction to the Study of the Law of the Constitution*.[35] Arthur Garrison tells us that "history has no example of a democracy, republic, or society long enduring without falling into tyranny when rule by law is employed over the rule of law."[36] Charles Lugosi maintains that the difference between the two ideas is a difference of kind, admitting of no degrees along which a transition might proceed: "The United States was founded upon the rule of law. Rule by law is its antithesis. There is no middle ground."[37] Others are less dogmatic. Randall Peerenboom, for example, says that

> the establishment of rule of law is a long-term process. No legal system can transform itself from rule by law into a fully implemented rule of law overnight. All countries now known for rule of law initially went through a period in which legal institutions were weak and rule of law was imperfectly implemented.[38]

If this is true, then it may be hard to tell, at any given moment, whether we have in front of us a system of rule by law that is improving or a system of rule of law that is not developing as well as it might do.[39]

8. Rule of Law as Neoliberal Ideology

The contrast between rule *by* law and the rule *of* law is also pursued from another, more ideological direction.[40]

There are various indexes of the rule of law that you can get on the internet, set up by various organizations like Freedom House, Political Risk Services, and the World Justice Project. They use various measures, various criteria such as judicial independence, lack of corruption, the enforceability of contracts, and so on to determine which countries are better than others so far as the rule of law is concerned. (In 2022 the United States ranked twenty-sixth on the most prestigious such index, that of the World Justice Project. Top of the list was Denmark. My home country, New Zealand, came in at number 7.)[41]

Some of these indexes use as one of their criteria *the cost of doing business* in a country. This means mostly the cost of complying with regulations, and for that appraisal, it measures the overall extent of regulation in an economy. For instance, an organization called the Center for Financial Stability offers a reading of the rule of law that takes as one key factor the "Burden of Government Regulation," a measure obtained by asking businesses, "How burdensome is it for businesses in your country to comply with governmental administrative requirements (e.g., permits, regulations, reporting)?"[42] Other indexes measure similar factors, but indirectly. They ask how easy it is to mount legal challenges to regulations—the easier they are to challenge, the more we have of the rule of law. Or they ask whether the state imposes "arbitrary" pressures on private property.[43]

Now, if we take this seriously, it would seem to follow that a society's score on a rule-of-law index should be diminished by the existence and proper enforcement of legislative and regulatory requirements.[44] For neoliberal ideologists, regulation is inherently subject to suspicion; and the rule of law requires that legislative and regulatory burdens be kept to a minimum. This is under the heading of the rule of law, mind you—not a separate measure of economic freedom or efficiency. It is as though the more rules there are, the less rule of law there can be. Other things equal, a marginal increase in regulation counts against a country's score for the rule of law.[45] The rule of law state, we are told, is not the same as the rule of state law.[46]

Regulation is condemned on this approach, not just for the costs it imposes on business and investment, but also for what it represents jurisprudentially. As we saw in Chapter 9, it represents the power of political majorities in legislatures and the power of human rulemakers in administrative agencies. How, it is asked, can these all-too-human sources of constraint count as anything other than the rule of men?[47]

Affirmatively, this neoliberal jurisprudence seeks to privilege forms of law that represent something other than the ascendancy of the current generation of lawmaking politicians. Law has many different meanings, and I guess every conception of the rule of law emphasizes some forms of law rather than others. I am talking now about conceptions that highlight forms of law that stand at the greatest distance from the legislative mentality.

Let me explain. Since ancient Athens, the rule-of-law tradition has involved an aspiration to be ruled by laws rather than men. Now it is hard not to see this as a false contrast; after all, laws are made by men, interpreted by men, and enacted by men. Law is something that humans must take agency in and responsibility for.[48] As Hobbes once pointed out, law can no more rule us by itself, without human agency, than a cannon can dominate a city without an ironmonger to cast it and an artilleryman to load, point, and fire it.[49]

Well, those who pursue the neoliberal version of the contrast think they can square this circle by focusing on laws whose human origins are in some sense diffuse or immemorial. Immemorial like the laws of burial that Antigone appealed to: "They are not of today and yesterday; they live forever; no one knows from whence they came."[50] We're not talking necessarily about natural law, but perhaps something like customary law or common law—law that is not so evidently a top-down product of powerful human lawmakers, but instead something that bubbles up from below, like a Dworkinian principle. Richard Epstein talks of bottom-up versus top-down law.[51] Common law grows and develops under its own steam, and need not be seen as a device by which some identifiable humans rule over others. No doubt there is a lot of mythology in this. A more realistic view of common law identifies it with the rule of what Bentham called "Judge & Co."[52] But the human element is diffuse, and at any given time, the law that emerges is a resultant of the work of many people, rather than the intentional product of a domineering majority ruling us from Capitol Hill or some other legislature.

Or, if we *are* ruled by top-down law, maybe we can put some salutary distance, historically, between us as the subjects of rule and the human authors of the law that is supposed to be our ruler. Perhaps being ruled by a 235-year-old constitution (like the US Constitution) is not really being ruled by its framers, because they are dead and gone, and we are ruled only by what they made, not by James Madison and Alexander Hamilton themselves. (This explains some of the appeal of constitutional originalism to neoliberal ideologists, and the otherwise bewildering absence of constitutional originalism elsewhere in the world, where most constitutions are more recent creations.)

These are all versions of what we might call "autonomous law"—law that operates in relative independence of the power of the current generation of human politicians.

And so we have this second account of the contrast between the rule of law and rule by law. The ascendancy of autonomous law, like common law or an immemorial constitution, counts as the rule of law. But if we emphasize instead legislation and the administrative apparatus of the regulatory state—law that is made by current power holders rather than law that emerges or law that has been there, for all practical purposes, since the beginning—then we are talking not about the rule of law, but about rule *by* law or (even worse) the rule of men. I will return in the last few sections of this chapter to the unnecessary difficulties that the ideological approach entails.

9. The Pincer Movement

The two contrasts I have mentioned have developed more or less independently. One associates rule by law with legal authoritarianism and rule of law with the subjection of the state to legal control. The other associates the rule of law with forms of law that are not themselves subject to government control, and rule by law with enacted legislation and state regulation.

Together, they work in a sort of pincer movement to suggest that anyone who (like me) respects the dignity of legislation as a mode of lawmaking is implicitly a defender of legal authoritarianism, and that the only real alternative to legal authoritarianism is the ascendancy of autonomous law like common law. Those who want anything substantial in the way of regulation are assimilated to Chinese-style authoritarians. And those who want a government subject to law are deemed to be opposed to a greater role for regulation in our society. There is a tendency to crowd out all the space in between. But I think the space in between is crucial, and it deserves more exploration.

And maybe some of the defenders of the ideological understanding of the rule *of* law / rule *by* law contrast can concede this. Despite their antipathy to enacted "law," some of them acknowledge that free societies may from time to time be unable to get by without some legislative enactments. F. A. Hayek acknowledged this in *Law, Legislation and Liberty*. He said that the desirability of autonomous law did not mean that it might not sometimes

> develop in very undesirable directions, and that when this happens correction by deliberate legislation may not be the only practicable way out. For a variety of reasons the spontaneous process of growth may lead into an impasse from which it cannot extricate itself by its own

forces or which it will at least not correct quickly enough. . . . The fact that law that has evolved in this way has certain desirable properties does not prove that it will always be good law or even that some of its rules may not be very bad. It therefore does not mean that we can altogether dispense with legislation.[53]

Most of us would call this is the voice of sanity. But Hayek and his friends treat it as a grudging and dangerous, albeit necessary concession.

At any rate, Hayek seems to be saying that when autonomous law gets stuck in this sort of path-determined way, or when it is appropriated by one class to the detriment of another, or when in some other way it becomes manifestly unjust, the ideologist's rule-of-law ban on enacted law has to be rescinded. And then what is important is that the resulting legislation be subject to the discipline of legality, which is what the other rule of law theorists in the thin Fuller tradition were insisting on all along. "In such situations," says Hayek,

it is desirable that the new rule should become known before it is enforced; and this can be effected only by promulgating a new rule which is to be applied only in the future. Where a real change in the law is required, the new law can properly fulfil the proper function of all law, namely that of guiding expectations, only if it becomes known before it is applied.[54]

It is unclear whether this represents, in Hayek's eyes, a sort of "Plan B" version of the rule *of* law or an acknowledgement that the idea of rule *by* law does have legitimate work to do.

10. Putting a Good Face on Rule by Law

In any case, other jurists have already begun to explore the region in between the rule *of* law and rule *by* law, starting from a sense that what we define as rule *by* law should not actually be dismissed. They say that if it is taken at face value, rule *by* law is actually a quite demanding ideal and quite important.

For, first of all, rule *by* law, disreputable though it may be, can be contrasted with forms of authoritarian and arbitrary government that really don't use law at all. Now, you read some weird overheated stuff in this literature.

I've seen respectable scholars claim that Hitler ruled by law. That, of course, is dangerous nonsense; the invocation of the Nazis should remind us that there are many forms of rule by evil men that barely involve law at all. Societies can be ruled by terror (say, in Lon Fuller's account, or Hannah Arendt's account, or Tim Snyder's recent account of the lawless realities of the so-called Nazi state).[55] Compared to this mode of "governance," rule *by* law is positively benign.

Second, we should value rule *by* law to the extent it implies that rulers do accept something like the formal discipline of legality (at least so far as laws applying to or between their subjects are concerned). I mean the insistence that laws be general, clear, prospective, public, and relatively stable. Such discipline may not incorporate any substantive elements of justice or rights, but this thin version of legality does still have moral significance, in the respect it pays to human agency and to the need for clarity and predictability. Rule by law "can be a way a government . . . stabilizes and secures expectations."[56] Even if it remains instrumental to the purposes of the lawmaker, it involves also what Lon Fuller called a bond of reciprocity with the purposes of those who are governed, who are assured thereby that the standards that are promulgated *are* those that will be used to evaluate their actions. As Fuller scholar Ken Winston puts it, under rule by law, "the commitment to rules—[that is, to] fixed standards of general applicability[—] . . . [is] the ruler's chosen mechanism of governance. . . . The commitment to rules is deliberate and firm, and the instrumentalism is consistent and principled."[57]

A similar theme is pursued in the work of Martin Krygier. Though Krygier reserves his ultimate allegiance for a conception of the rule of law that involves legal control of arbitrary power, he acknowledges the political and intellectual credentials of rule *by* law. Rule by law is not just a bogus caricature of the rule-of-law ideal. It has its own dignity, and he associates it not just with tricks of authoritarian pretensions to legality, but with the *Rechtsstaat* conception of governance:

> What was distinctive of a *Rechtsstaat* was not that the state was subject to law that had other sources and independent guardians, but that it acts in a *rechtlich* (lawful, legal) way; "according to some nineteenth-century (and early twentieth-century) constructions, there is a relation of near-identity between the state and its law . . . within the system of rule the law is the state's standard mode of expression, its very language, the essential medium of its activity."[58]

If Krygier or Winston are right, then two consequences follow. First, as I said, rule *by* law now comes to seem more demanding. And actually, it may be unclear whether Chinese-style legal authoritarianism really satisfies the demands of rule by law at all. The Chinese regime instead represents law and legal procedures being used selectively, in an authoritarian and often inconsistent way, to make political suppression and social control more politically effective.

In any case, the more all this is emphasized, the less sharp a contrast there is with the rule of law. For both formulations now hold that government is constrained by its use of legal method, constrained at least to keep faith with the formal and perhaps the procedural consequences of its choosing to use law rather than arbitrary decrees or the terrorizing scream of command as its mode of rule. Generality has to be taken seriously; so do publicity and prospectivity, and so—very important—does procedure. I emphasize that last point: procedure follows form. I don't think a regime can be said to be using law as an instrument of administration (and therefore ruling *by* law) if that law is not administered in a lawlike way with lawlike processes. But if due process is part of what we mean when we talk about "rule by law," then the space in between these two ideals is becoming crowded and indeed, the distance between them is narrowed.

I said that a government that pledges itself to rule by law is *constrained* by its pledge. A word now about "constraint." A government can be constrained in at least two ways. (1) It may be constrained by the substantive provisions of, say, a bill of rights, because these provisions may be enforced by courts against it, perhaps at the suit of non-state actors. When that works, we have *the rule of law* in the sense that has dominated this essay. (2) But if a government commits to ruling by law, it is in a sense constrained by its commitment, even though there may be no legal provision that can be enforced to that effect.[59] This is what we should say about Dicey's understanding of the rule of law. It is also, for example, what we would have had to have said about the principle condemning retroactive legislation in common law countries that had no written constitutional prohibition to that effect—for example, New Zealand, before the passage of the New Zealand Bill of Rights Act 1990. Section 26(1) of that statute says that "no one shall be liable to conviction of any offence on account of any act or omission which did not constitute an offence by such person under the law of New Zealand at the time it occurred." But it wasn't the case that retroactivity was perfectly OK before 1990.[60] It happened occasionally, but it was almost always treated as disreputable and as a derogation from standards of legality. Governments would be embarrassed by having to legislate retroactively, because they were committed to ruling by law, and law is something laid down in advance. The constraint here, however, was self-constraint—wanting to live up to one's commitment to rule in this way.[61]

I guess one could say that one of the key differences then between the rule of law and rule by law is that any constraint a government is under, in respect of the latter, is really just a matter of self-constraint, which may be uneven and fragile, as compared with real and enforceable constitutional requirements.

11. How Demanding Is Rule by Law?

In its most favorable sense, the idea that a government will rule by law is associated with something like Lon Fuller's inner morality of law: laws will be general, clear, stable, prospective, and enforced scrupulously according to their terms. That, as I have said, is quite a demanding agenda. Even so, it can be construed in a more or less demanding way.

In the less demanding way, it requires that governments ensure that any laws they enact or enforce be subject to this discipline; the use of retrospective legislation or the use of statute or case law that is unduly vague or not properly publicized detracts from the claim that the society is being ruled by law.

But what about measures or government interventions that don't present themselves as law at all? Governments do all sorts of things: they enter into contracts, they schedule police patrols, they promote some officials and fire others. Are these, too, to be subject to the Lon Fuller–type discipline? A more demanding version of rule by law would say yes. It would require that all government measures be subject to this discipline— that is, that government rule only through or under the auspices of measures that are lawlike in this sense.[62] Or if that is impractical, we might be driven to a more permissive version, which is that there should be some laws, administered as such, in the government's mode of ruling, but who knows how many and what they will be, or how great a proportion of administrative measures they will cover?

Or we might adopt an intermediate position: that rule by law requires that any measure that impacts on people or businesses, on their lives, liberty, and property—that is, any measure that purports to *rule* them—must be subject to this discipline. If we take the syntax and vocabulary of the phrase "rule by law" seriously, that seems to be what it requires: we are not to be *ruled* except by law. I think this is what Dicey meant when he said in his first rule-of-law principle that "no man is punishable or can be lawfully made to suffer in body or goods except for a distinct breach of law established in the ordinary legal manner before the ordinary Courts of the land."[63] It can still be expanded or contracted, depending on whether "made to suffer in body and goods" is confined to penalties only or extends to all the costs and disadvantages imposed by the administrative state.

Anyway, the point of this section has been that rule *by* law can mean various different things, and some of them tend to lean over in the direction of what we sometimes call the rule *of* law. The "contrast" between them is now quite subtle.

12. Government under Law

Equally, we can explore the space between rule *by* law and the rule *of* law from the other direction. As we have seen, on the traditional contrast, rule *by* law is contrasted with a situation in which the government is subject to legal limitation and constraint (the rule *of* law). But this latter, too, is something that can be made more or less demanding. There are weak versions and strong versions.

A weak version requires only that the government be subject to proper constraint by whatever there happens to be in the way of laws to limit its conduct. Such constraints may be many or few. Maybe there are only a handful of laws that purport to restrain the government—an antitorture principle, for example, and a procedure of habeas corpus. Provided nobody is actually waterboarded, and provided detentions are legally justified, then the government has a free hand. It observes the principle of legality simply by complying with the handful of rules that actually exist to limit its conduct. Could that be all there is to the rule of law?

Some will say no. They will say we only really have a ruler subject to law when all the major modalities of government action are pursued and exercised within a constraining legal framework. We only really have a government subject to law when most everything the government does is authorized by law and undertaken within a framework of legal supervision. In a way, it's a difference of logic. On the weaker version of government's subjection to law, the government's freedom begins where legal restraint comes to an end. A more demanding version rejects that logic. It says that under the rule of law, it is important that the government should in all things act under legal authorization.

The difference surfaces in controversies in English-style legal systems over what is known as "the third source" of governmental authority, and in US jurisprudence in controversies over the scope of presidential prerogative. In the debate within English-style polities, the question is, may the government act freely in the absence of legal constraint, even when it is not

(1) enforcing or implementing legislation,

and even when it is not

(2) exercising what is traditionally regarded as the royal prerogative.

The "third source" of authority for executive action would be

(3) a reservoir of undefined executive authority for executive officials to simply act for the public good in areas where there is no controlling law.

The United States approaches essentially the same question with three slightly different categories of presidential power:

(1*) the president exercises the authority of the executive in enforcing and implementing acts of Congress;

(2*) he also exercises the other powers enumerated in Article II of the Constitution—for example, the power of commander in chief of the armed forces.

And then there is the question of whether, in addition to (1*) and (2*),

(3*) the president has a reservoir of prerogative power to act for the general good, and if he does, how far that prerogative power extends and what sort of re-view (if any) it is subject to. I will not venture here into the substantive literature on presidential prerogative.[64] It has all sorts of assumptions and ramifications. (I have seen debates about the US position conducted in terms that appeal to John Locke's late seventeenth-century notion of the prerogative.)[65]

In British-style systems, the "third source" is sometimes debated in terms of whether we want to uphold the traditional contrast between the freedom of the citizen and the freedom of the official. So, for example, in New Zea-land, the chief justice once insisted that "public officials do not have freedom to act in any way they choose unless prohibited by law, as individual citi-zens do," but later cases have made it clear that the Court of Appeal at least does not adopt her position.[66] Possibly, though, this is a red herring. The third source is not supposed to be a power for the government to do just anything it likes—which would be the analogue of individual freedom in the absence of legal constraint. In the hand of government, it is still supposed to be a source of authority to act for the public good, and it takes its rise not from a theory of freedom, but from an understanding that law can't always lay down in advance what the public good might require.

The debate over the third source or over the extent of presidential pre-rogative can also be seen as a debate about how demanding the distinctive ideal of the rule *of* law is, as opposed to rule *by* law. If the rule *of* law is a matter of a government's observance of legal constraints, then it may be posed, philosophically, as a question about the nature of constraint. Is con-straint necessarily an affirmative existence—something one can point to in this or that statutory or constitutional prohibition or requirement? Or does the "constraint" that the rule of law involves mean submission to a general spirit of limitation, which can sometimes be inferred from the silence of the constitution and which means never acting without specific authorization? I can imagine a stickler for the rule of law insisting on the latter under-standing and being happy to relegate the former position to *somewhere in between* the rule of law and rule by law, especially because the "third source" is often defended in exactly the sort of pragmatic spirit that has led to a gen-eral decline in respect for the rule of law.[67]

But equally, one might say that *both* these positions are associated with rule by law. After all, a demand that the government should rule *by* law can easily be read as a demand that it should use only legally defined powers. If this makes sense, then we have to concede that the little preposition "by" in "rule by law" by no means elicits pure submission to government authority. It makes a strong demand on the state to say that it must actually use *law* to implement its will. If, on the other hand, we are sometimes happy as a matter of convenience to allow government to act without explicit legal authorization, then it is not altogether clear which of the two positions we began with we are compromising—rule *of* law or rule *by* law. If each of our two positions can be understood in weaker or stronger ways, and if either version of the two of them can be parsed as a version of the other, then the usefulness of the distinction between them is beginning to evaporate.

13. Too Literal?

We have ended up in this situation by taking the phrase "rule by law" literally. It requires, as we said, that any *ruling* that is going on must be conducted according to *the discipline of legality*. And that, we have seen, is both a demanding ideal and a quite problematic one—not at all the easy lark that authoritarians are supposed to be comfortable with. Indeed, it is not clear whether *the rule of law,* also taken literally, adds anything to this conception.

But maybe these phrases should not be understood literally. Literalism, we might say, is the mark of an analyst's naivety. (I write as an analytic legal philosopher.) Perhaps "rule by law" should be treated as a term of art in political science, whose meaning cannot be parsed by analyzing the meaning of its component parts. We need to look at how it is used by Tom Carothers and others. For them, it just means something like the bad-faith, haphazard, and purely instrumental use of law and courts for political advantage by a regime that does not intend to be bound by law when it finds that inconvenient and does not intend ever to provide its subjects with any hope of enforcing legal constraints against it. That's clear enough, and we might say that the contrast between that conception and the mode of government we call the rule *of* law is politically quite useful, notwithstanding the conundrums we have been exploring in these last two or three sections.

Fair enough. But still, the variety of possibilities we have been exploring do not evaporate with this move away from literalism. They just become analytic possibilities under the single heading of the rule of law, and they remind us of the various ways in which that ideal is a contestable matter of degree. Apart from anything else, this means that a regime transitioning out of rule *by* law (understood now in the nonliteral sense) has a number of different weak rule-*of*-law positions to reach for—stepping stones, as it were, to a more full-blooded commitment to legality.

14. A Mess?

What should we conclude from all this? The ideal of the rule of law operates in a messy terrain. Law can mean different things: different kinds of rules, different sources of rules, different ways of elaborating and administering rules, even different senses of discretion. And in keeping with the practice of drawing up laundry lists for what *the rule of law* requires, it presents us with layer after layer of demands, from Dicey's three principles to the eight principles embodied in Fuller's "inner morality." There are multiple formal requirements, multiple procedural and institutional requirements, and, if one sides with Lord Bingham against Professor Raz, multiple substantive principles as well. As I have pointed out elsewhere, and as should be perfectly clear from this chapter, the rule of law is an essentially contested concept.[68] This is not intended at all as a skeptical point, but rather as an indication of how we make progress in our understanding of the rule of law: we make progress by arguing about it, rather than by reading off its requirements from some canonical definition.

If it were up to me, we would downplay the contrast between the rule *of* law and rule *by* law. It is more trouble than it is worth. One little preposition seems to have begotten a whole labyrinth of largely verbal issues concerning the way in which law is put to work in the modern state. I know there is something a little pathetic in a philosopher trying to reform ordinary usage, especially a usage as well entrenched in the blogosphere as this one. But the idea of rule *by* law—and the possibilities and discipline that it entails—is both too close to the rule *of* law and too important to abandon to the authoritarians.

Of course, we should acknowledge that legal means can sometimes be used to undermine the rule of law, and that that ideal is not satisfied simply by enforcing commands that have the word "law" pasted onto them. But equally, not every instrumental use of law is disqualified under this acknowledgment. Law can be an instrument for the public good; legality is not just political cover for the lawmakers. Moreover, the use of law as an instrument of rule already involves submission to a demanding discipline—formally, procedurally, and in the acceptance of a need for legal authorization for government action. "Instrumental" does not just mean authoritarian. It already implicates government in a compact of legality where citizens' subjection to law is matched with an assurance that the rules laid down in advance are the ones that will be applied to her conduct and applied as law, with legal procedures and legal safeguards.[69] This is not a minimal assurance. Though you can array it under the heading "rule by law" if you like, it already captures a considerable element of what the rule of law is supposed to involve. And I think it would be best if we didn't allow this one little preposition—in "rule *by* law"—to sell short the challenge of that commitment.

11

The Rule of Law in Public Law

Is the political ideal we call "the rule of law" biased toward private law? There are definite tendencies in that direction, and these tendencies make it difficult to develop an understanding of how the rule of law applies in the realm of public administration. The tendency toward private law also introduces an unwelcome ideological element, inasmuch as the rule of law can all too easily become associated with special respect for the rights of property owners, employers, and investors in cases of conflict between these rights and the business of public administration.

Of course, the business of public administration is not self-justifying. And the rule of law is not doing its proper normative work unless it disciplines and constrains the way that business is carried out. Still, we should consider the prospects for a normatively robust conception of the rule of law that does not minimize or deprecate the mission of public administration. That is what I shall undertake in this chapter.

1. A Unified Ideal?

The task of developing a conception of the rule of law that applies to public law in particular faces an immediate challenge from those who deny the importance of the traditional distinction between public and private law. Maybe there is no distinction. Maybe we should say that in the last analysis, all law involves the operation of the state on society; all law is public law in some ultimate sense.[1] If so, then perhaps the rule of law should be conceived as an entirely general idea, prescribing the uniform application of a discipline of legality to state action across the board. After all, whether the state is operating in the field of public administration or whether it is resolving private disputes, we have to face the possibility that it might be acting ex-tralegally, without reference to legal rules, principles, and procedures. We might say, normatively, that the point of the rule of law is to foreclose that possibility—again, across the whole field. We might say that, but should we? When we subject the state's operation in the field of public administra-tion to the discipline of the rule of law, should we use exactly the principles we use when we apply the discipline of legality to the resolution of private disputes?

Philosophers of law have usually assumed that the rule of law is a unified ideal, albeit one that consists of a list of items (Lon Fuller's eight principles of "the inner morality of law," for example).[2] On the unified approach, one would begin an essay of this kind with a very general definition of the rule of law and then try to derive various aspects of its application to the spe-cific case of the activity of the state and its agencies. So we might say something like the following. The rule of law comprises a requirement that people in positions of authority should exercise their power within a con-straining framework of public norms. It also includes a requirement that there be general rules laid down to govern the conduct of ordinary people, rules whose public presence enables people to figure out what is required of them and what the legal consequences of their actions will be. And the rule of law insists on the role of courts, operating according to recognized stan-dards of due process and offering an impartial forum in which disputes can be resolved in an evenhanded way.

So far as private law is concerned, these principles generate a demand for clearly defined rights of property and contract that can form a basis for stable expectations upheld and enforced by the courts. And so far as public administration is concerned, these same principles are supposed to generate limits on official discretion, a requirement of fair and consistent adminis-tration of existing rules by officials dealing with individual cases, and the establishment of procedures that allow people to challenge the legality of of-ficial action when it impacts adversely on their interests.

All this seems fine as a preliminary understanding. But how far can we take these abstractions? A more elaborate understanding of the rule of law will inevitably reflect the jurist's path to that abstraction. For example, the array of principles cited by Fuller seems to betray a preoccupation with the direct application of rules to the conduct of individuals, a preoccupa-tion that is perhaps most at home in criminal law. It may be less obviously applicable to the constitutional or legislative regulation of administrative agencies.[3] By contrast, an emphasis on legal certainty is likely to betray its private law origins: predictability matters most in areas of contract and property, where businessmen crave security of expectations and financiers need to be able to calculate what they can count on in the enterprises into which they have invested their funds.

In addition, we must bear in mind that the rule of law is a contested concept.[4] It is likely that the direction from which one tries to reach a neutral conception of legality—neutral as between public and private law—will be reflected in the way one deals with some of the contested issues. These include debates about the distinction between the rule of law and the rule of men; the distinction between the rule of law and rule *by* law; instrumental versus noninstrumental understandings of legality; and debates about the inclusion of substantive as well as formal and procedural elements in the rule of law. This is not just academic contestation: the way one approaches these debates affects one's view of judicial lawmaking, official discretion, and the deference due to administrative regulations. It is likely to make some considerable difference to how one approaches these issues, whether one begins from a public law or a private law standpoint.

2. Is the Rule of Law Essentially a Private Law Idea?

The quest for abstraction is one thing. It is another thing to associate the rule of law with private law and to say frankly that in public law, the rule of law represents the normative dominance of private law considerations when public and private come into conflict.

I have heard civil law formalists say that private law is the epitome of law and that what the rest of us call public law is a relatively marginal phenomenon.[5] On this view, *law as such* takes the security of private rights very seriously: it consists of a formal structure in which disputes are resolved and in which private interests of various sorts are adjusted to one another while still preserving their fundamental character as rights. And the rule of law, on this account, represents a determination to uphold these private rights in *every* area of governance. Now, there is no reason to suppose that public administration in and of itself will be sensitive to private law concerns; indeed, there is a standing danger that private law concerns will be sidelined. So—according to this view—the point of the rule of law as a normative ideal is to bring these concerns insistently to the attention of officials and to demand that everything they do should be constrained by law in this sense.

Should we accept this? Public lawyers do have to come to terms with the interpenetration of private and public concerns. Much of the regulatory activity of the administrative state affects the content and exercise of private rights, in the public regulation of property, for example, or in the governance of employment relations. And the rule of law must have something to say about this. Still, although public administration needs to take proper account of private law rights, it is not necessarily the job of the rule of law in public law to make our administrators back down whenever a preexisting private law right rears up in their path. The role of the rule of law is not just to be representative of private rights or to stand sentinel for the protection of private property rights in the face of public law regulation. Certainly, it is the job of the rule of law to be *alert* to the way in which individual rights, including property and contractual rights, may be affected by public regulation. Its job is to stand against any arbitrariness. But this not a way of protecting private law rights from the impact of public law as such; it is a way of protecting them from the *arbitrariness* of public law. So we need to develop a sense of the distinction between arbitrary and nonarbitrary state action that can be applied in this domain.

3. Ideological Manipulation of the Rule-of-Law Ideal

What I am criticizing here is quite a common view. Societies in which the rule of law is thought to flourish are supposed to be societies where rights of ownership are protected, contracts enforced, and a predictable environment established for enterprise and investment. And the idea that the rule of law must make sure that private rights are not sidelined helps explain the curious imbalance of some of the conceptions of the rule of law that we find in political economy. Consider, for example, the following account, which we considered also in Chapter 9. According to James Wolfensohn, former President of the World Bank, the rule of law means that a "government must ensure . . . it has an effective system of property, contracts, labor, bankruptcy, commercial codes, personal rights law and other elements of a comprehensive legal system that are effectively, impartially, and cleanly administered by a well-functioning, impartial and honest judicial and legal system."[6] What is missing from Wolfensohn's definition is any reference to public law— where law's effectiveness includes compliance with legal regulations by business, industry, and commerce and the application and enforcement of such regulations by the agencies of the state. These regulations include health and safety requirements, limits on contracts (for example, in labor markets), and environmental legislation affecting use of property. Respect for legislation and the enforcement of regulations—these aspects are deafening by their silence in Wolfensohn's definition. Yet they are surely exactly the issues we need to address if we are to understand the relevance of the rule of law for public law.

Sometimes it is not just silence. Some ways of conceiving and measuring the rule of law are actively hostile to any sort of respect for regulation. An organization called the Center for Financial Stability offers a reading of the rule of law that measures as one key factor the "Burden of Government Regulation," a measure obtained by asking businesses, "How burdensome is it for businesses in your country to comply with governmental administrative requirements (e.g., permits, regulations, reporting)?"[7] If we take this seriously, it seems to follow that a society's score on a rule-of-law index should be diminished by the effective enforcement or self-application of these public law requirements. On this approach, regulation of this kind is inherently subject to suspicion, and the rule of law seems to require that such requirements be kept to a minimum.

The case that is made for this conception is sometimes quite cynical. The real aim, we are told, is to persuade governments to uphold substantive values such as property rights, investment values, and the principle of free markets. And since everyone happens to be in favor of "the rule of law" at the moment, we might as well use the good vibrations associated with that phrase to drive home these points about markets and property.[8] Indeed, on this account, it might be better to forget the traditional rule-of-law principles (which in the hands of someone like Fuller seem to presuppose a pro-legislation mentality) and just link the phrase "the rule of law" with market values. That seems to be the strategy. Economists are ingenuous about the advantages of this approach. Defending the use of rule-of-law indices like those of the Center for Financial Stability, Harvard economics professor Robert Barro observes that "the general idea of these indexes is to gauge the attractiveness of a country's investment climate by considering the effectiveness of law enforcement, the sanctity of contracts, and the state of other influences on the security of property rights."[9] "The attractiveness of a country's investment climate"—Barro means its attractiveness to foreign investors. And he believes "the willingness of [such] customers to pay substantial amounts for this information is perhaps some testament to their validity."[10]

Is this an inappropriate perspective from which to develop an account of the rule of law to apply to public administration? The Barro perspective is that of an extractive and predatory investor, looking to the society and the interests of its members for what it can get out of them.[11] As such, it is quite different from the perspective of someone who lives in the society and who cares about the quality of life among their fellow inhabitants. We should be wary of adopting any conception of the rule of law that is designed to push this latter perspective to one side.

4. A Fresh Start

What is needed is an understanding of the rule of law that is not opposed in principle to the mission of public administration and is not just the shadow of private or external concerns.

Some elements in a public law conception of the rule of law will be familiar. It will involve, in the first instance, an emphasis on rules and standards in the governance of conduct. The familiar principles of Fuller's "inner morality of law" specify that laws must be general, prospective, public, clear, consistent, practicable, and stable.[12] These principles have obvious application in any domain where conduct is being legally regulated. A public law conception of the rule of law will also involve an emphasis on judicial procedures. The importance of such procedures has always been a key concern about public administration in the rule-of-law tradition. At the end of the nineteenth century, jurists like A. V. Dicey watched with dismay the replacement of what were previously judicial or quasi-judicial tribunals with more managerial boards and inspectorates.[13] It is a fault of Fuller's analysis in *The Morality of Law* that the chapter in which he presents his "inner morality" says so little about procedures. Analytic legal philosophers have tended to follow him in this (whether they are supporting or criticizing his account).[14] Elsewhere in his work, however, Fuller has placed more emphasis on the procedural aspect. And it is plain that both the formal and procedural sides will need to be emphasized in a conception of the rule of law that is fit for public law.

Notice, however, that Fuller's account so far presupposes that one is already in the business of making law and ruling through law and legal tribunals. But as Fuller himself concedes, it may not be appropriate to use law or legal methods for every task of public administration.

As lawyers we have a natural inclination to "judicialize" every function of government. Adjudication is a process with which we are familiar and which enables us to show to advantage our special talents.
Yet we must face the plain truth that adjudication is an ineffective
instrument for economic management and for governmental participation in the allocation of economic resources.[15]

Something could be said along the same lines about the issuance and enforcement of rules. Officials may find they can they can be more effective
using well-informed discretion rather than the mechanical application of
rules. Rules may be too simple to take into account all the circumstances
that ought to make a difference to the way particular situations are resolved.
Laying down rules in advance, without knowing what kinds or combinations
of circumstances will have to be faced, and applying those rules through rigid
judicial procedures may not be what fair and effective administration
requires.

Now, it is possible to interpret these possibilities as simple opposition to
the rule of law. The rule of law, after all, is a controversial ideal, and there is
controversy not only as to what it involves, but also as to whether we ought
to be following any version of it at all. Some are happy to dismiss it altogether
as archaic legalism in favor of a more frankly managerial approach.

However, instead of abandoning the idea of law altogether, we might re-
conceive the rule of law so that it is more sensitive to the needs of administration. So, for example, we might insist on the use of promulgated rules and
legalized due process in some areas but not others—in areas where something like a penalty is in the offing, but not in areas where interventions of
a non-punitive kind are involved. Or one might imagine an array of cases,
ranging from purely administrative decisions at one end, through cases that
require a modicum of due process, all the way up to cases that represent in
effect the full application of criminal law standards.

Something similar may be said about tribunals. In the view of A. V. Dicey,
the rule of law required that "no man is punishable or can be lawfully made
to suffer in body or goods except for a distinct breach of law established in
the ordinary legal manner *before the ordinary Courts of the land.*"[16] The
phrase I have emphasized seems to preclude specialist administrative tribunals. But other apostles of the rule of law have been more accommodating
in this regard. F. A. Hayek regarded Dicey's condemnation of dedicated
administrative tribunals as unfortunate. That dispute may seem obsolete

today, but only because Anglo-American jurists have now been able to reconcile the two positions that Dicey thought incompatible: tribunals embodying dedicated specialist familiarity with some field of public administration, along with the judicialized operation of such tribunals and a
reasonably clear set of standards for them to apply.[17]

In this connection, we may also want to say that the norms deployed in
public administration can range from highly operationalized rules to general norms that have more the character of standards and require argument
and judgment in their application. The kind of individual thoughtfulness
sponsored by norms of this latter kind need not be regarded as incompatible in principle with the rule of law, provided one is alert to the kinds
of cases in which their application might prove arbitrary.[18] (Cases in which
there is reasonable congruence between the judgments of citizens and the
judgments of officials are cases in which the use of standards is consistent
with nonarbitrary administration; but if, on account of animus or asym-
metries of expertise, there is no expectation of congruence, then rules are
preferable.)[19]

So, too, with administrative discretion. It is natural to contrast official
discretion with the application of rules, but there is a range of possibilities
in between and some of the intermediate possibilities seem compatible with
a moderate conception of the rule of law. Discretion need not be free
standing. It can be guided by standards or left unguided. It can be framed,
authorized, and constrained by legislation. Earlier exercises of it can inform
subsequent exercises. It can be subject or not subject to review. In each of
these dimensions, the element of sheer human willfulness can loom larger
or smaller compared to the considerations of legality.

5. The Role of Legislation

Inevitably, if law is to play any significant role at all, the landscape of public
administration will be dominated by legislation and by rules made by agencies under the auspices of legislation, both of which will frame, authorize,
guide, and constrain the official discretion that is needed for intelligent and
effective governance.

We noted earlier that some conceptions count the burden of state regulation as something that tends to diminish the rule of law. But it is not the
function of the rule of law to assess the substantive justifiability of particular measures, to say whether their benefits are worth the burdens they

impose or whether the burdens and benefits are distributed equitably. The rule of law deals with the way we are governed, not with the justification of governmental measures.

Nevertheless, it is worth saying something general about this form of governance, if only because certain rule-of-law theorists have condemned most forms of legislation as incompatible in principle with the rule of law.[20] They condemn it for its complicity with state power and its voluntarism: something becomes law on the basis of nothing but a political determination that the law should be thus and so. But these characterizations are tendentious. We might say—more favorably—that legislation involves the representatives of the community taking responsibility for the conditions under which members of the community live their lives and conduct their business. In most countries, legislation is organized democratically, and it is no accident that theorists of the rule of law who deprecate legislation also regard democracy and democratization as low priorities in nation-building. Economists like Robert Barro have suggested that we should strive to establish legal protections for property rights and markets first, before establishing democracy institutions. On this account, the function of the rule of law is to protect property, contracts, and markets from the depredations of democracy.[21]

Now it is true that the rule of law does not necessarily entail democracy. The two are distinguishable stars in the constellation of our political ideals. But this does not mean the rule of law should be understood as inherently hostile to democratic governance. The view that I am criticizing seems to regard it as undesirable for the people of a country to act collectively through the medium of (what we would ordinarily call) law to pursue social justice, diminish inequality, or take control of the conditions of their social and economic life. That, I think, is not a healthy proposition to associate with the rule of law.

6. Stability in Public Law

If the role of law in public administration means a legal environment dominated by legislation and if rule-of-law complaints about the voluntaristic and political character of these legal arrangements are rejected, then what becomes of the rule of law's investment in stability and the security of expectations?

The rule of law has always been associated with the value of predictability in human affairs. The most important thing that people need from the law that governs them, we are told, is predictability in the conduct of their lives and businesses. Tom Bingham observed that "no one would choose to do business, perhaps involving large sums of money, in a country where parties' rights and obligations were undecided." That sounds like a private law concern, but a similar point is made insistently in the area of public law as well. It is, according to F. A. Hayek, a matter of freedom: "Government in all its actions [must be] bound by rules fixed and announced beforehand, rules which make it possible to foresee with fair certainty how the authority will use its coercive powers in given circumstances and to plan one's individual affairs on the basis of this knowledge."[22] One is free so far as the impact of government action is concerned not because one's choices are completely untrammeled by regulation, but because one can predict when and how the state will intervene and work around, just as one works around the laws of nature.[23]

The demand for stability is important, but it cannot be absolute.

The rule of law seeks as stable a set of legal arrangements as it is reasonable to expect in the circumstances. Law must not change so often that people lose the opportunity to come to terms with it and organize their lives around it. But "reasonableness" here cannot be divorced from an awareness of the tasks of legislation and rulemaking in a changing world. What counts as arbitrary or unreasonable must be predicated on an understanding of the inevitable rhythms of changing circumstances and political possibilities.

At any given time, a society faces its problems with a given heritage of customs, statutes, case law, and regulative arrangements. Now, however serviceable this array may have been in previous times, there is no guarantee it will continue to work in the future. New problems may emerge or be identified. As the society develops socially and economically, new frameworks and institutions may be necessary. Old ways of dealing with existing problems may prove limited or counterproductive in new circumstances. New ways may emerge for evaluating both problems and solutions, and old ways may be contested. The balance of concern for different sections of the community may shift, posing difficult questions of equity. None of this is straightforward; much of it is contested; and all of it is important.

No society capable of self-government can remain passive or inert in face of these changes. And legislation—the deliberate alteration of a society's rules and structures—is the proper way of responding to these developments. To its detractors, legislation may seem too much a matter of will, or of processes (like election and majority-decision) that combine wills to produce a politically contingent result, to deserve celebration under the auspices of a political ideal—the rule of law—whose purpose many understand to be the taming of will in politics.

But law *is* changeable. That is one of the ways we contrast law with morality, even positive morality.[24] Morality changes over time, but it cannot be the subject of deliberate or intentional change. Setting up a legal system, however, establishes the possibility that changes may be made intentionally in the way that a society is ordered. It involves the union of primary rules of conduct, which may once have been immemorial, with secondary rules that empower a society to take responsibility for the primary order, adapting it flexibly to changing social conditions and keeping track of the changes that stand in the name of us all. That is what law essentially is, and the principle we call the rule of law cannot in its essence be antagonistic to that.

This helps us understand why private law rights cannot be insulated from the impact of these changes. It is not reasonable to demand an extent of legal stability that precludes such impact. Some of the changes that a society has to face up to legislatively will involve reconsideration of the overall effect on the environment of the private use of resources. From time to time this will involve some alteration in the content of property rights. Also, societies may have inherited distributions of land and other resources that are massively inequitable and represent a residue of injustice that in other regards has been repudiated. The rule of law cannot impose obstacles to the responsible remediation of this.[25] Similarly, contractual rights will accumulate in a way that defines the structure of markets, and these, too, may need to be limited or regulated when a society confronts market failure, market crisis, or market inequity.

How one evaluates all this in regard to the rule of law will depend on one's perspective. Considered purely as an investor, unconcerned with the conditions of human life in a given society, a person might be impervious to concerns of this kind, expecting that his private rights will be secure and available for exploitation by him at any time on the same basis as they were when he acquired them. And from this point of view, it might seem that the function of the rule of law is to underpin such expectations with legal certainty. The point of view of a member of the society in question may be quite different. The responsible citizen knows that there is such a thing as a public agenda confronting a changing world with evolving ideas about what is need for the fair pursuit of the public good. He knows that these changes and the legislation they elicit are bound to affect the environment in which property rights are held and exercised, contracts enforced, and investments secured. The responsible citizen understands all that.

As I said in Chapter 9, the proposition that matters like these may need collective attention from time to time is not an anomalous or socially destructive position; it is the ordinary wisdom of human affairs. No conception of governance, no conception of law or the rule of law that fails to leave room for changes and adjustments of this sort can possibly be tolerable. And it seems to me that any conception of the rule of law that denigrates the very idea of such changes and treats their enactment and application as an inherent derogation from the rule of law has to be wrong.

True—any particular proposal for change will have its opponents, and sometimes the opponents will be right. They may be right because a proposed environmental regulation proves unnecessary or because a given piece of social legislation represents nothing more than cynical rent seeking by one faction exploiting another. But the opponents are not necessarily right, and certainly not right simply on the ground that once property rights have been established, any change or regulation is out of the question.

7. No More than Rule *by* Law?

Does all this amount to anything more than rule by law? I mentioned earlier that some commentators draw a distinction between the rule of law and rule *by* law.[26] The one is supposed to lift law above politics. The other—rule by law—involves the instrumental use of legal forms and procedures as tools of political power. On this account, rule by law is a version of rule by men since it is comfortable with the highest authority being wholly unconstrained in the measures it lays down.

My own view is that this distinction between rule of law and rule by law is overblown, involving as it does a mythic quest for forms of law that come into existence and operate without any human agency.

But perhaps the more demanding idea of the rule of law is not altogether inapplicable. Perhaps, in certain pockets of public law, it can be used to consecrate a form of constitutionalism—the idea that the legislature as well as the state is subject to substantive constraints (constraints based on individual rights, for example) in its lawmaking.[27] That is a possibility, and the further the framers of the Constitution are from us in time, the more this might seem like law itself ruling us. In fact, constitutional constraints are usually few and negative, and mostly they leave legislative and regulatory discretion untouched. And anyway, even if we forget about the human framers, there is no getting away from the role of human judges in interpreting and applying these constraints. Does the empowerment of the judiciary represent the rule of law or the rule of men? Some think that a ruling counts as the rule of law, provided it is done through the hierarchy and procedures of courts; short of the fantasy that the laws could speak for themselves and render their own objective decision, this is the most the rule of law could possibly entail. Others say that there is always a danger that activist judges will take advantage of the authority given to them to make themselves into the very despots whose rule the rule of law is supposed to supersede. The issue remains bitterly unsettled.[28]

Beyond the rather meagre and contested constraints of the Constitution, the rule of law in the public realm certainly places limits on prerogative power and it supports the practice of judicial review of executive action. This represents the subordination of the powerful to the rule of law: "Be you never so high, the law is above you."[29] Still, this is almost always review on the basis of legislation, and it cannot be denied that the statutes appealed to in these reviews are themselves laid down in the first instance under the model of rule by law.

In any case, we should not accept the disparagement of rule by law that the contrast with the rule of law is supposed to suggest. Sometimes the phrase "rule by law" is used as though it were just a fig leaf for authoritarian rulers.[30] And the impression is given that rule by law serves only the instrumental purposes of the regime and that it cannot be understood as a political ideal inuring to the benefit of those being governed. In fact, an insistence on being ruled by properly structured norms and by institutionalized legal procedures serves the interests of citizens at least as much as their rulers. By imposing a reasonable amount of stability, it lets people know where they stand, and as a mode of rule it treats them with the dignity of responsible agents capable of self-applying the norms that are made for the community. There is always the possibility that these values might be neglected in public administration, and it is the function of the rule of law in public law to see that they are taken seriously.

8. Constructing a Conception

A final word about the methodology that has been used here. One has to feel a little self-conscious about constructing an understanding of the rule of law that is dedicated to governance in the public realm and that is intended to see off some dominant ideological conceptions that apparently have a problem with the very idea of public administration. Defenders of those conceptions will denounce what I have set out in this chapter as incompatible with what the rule of law really requires.

But there is no "really" here: there is no commanding exemplar, no canonical authority for conceiving of the rule of law one way rather than another. There is a heritage dating back to Aristotle of concern for legality and enthusiasm for the possibility that legal modes of rule may take the edge off human power. And there are various ways of interpreting that heritage in regard to the challenges of governance faced by every generation.[31] I have argued that it is possible to construct a moderate understanding of the rule of law that takes seriously the mission of the modern administrative state. That understanding is built up out of the heritage of the rule-of-law tradition, but it reserves the right to think anew about what the rule of law requires in this particular environment. The grounds for criticizing other understandings as inadequate or ideological is not that they fail to embody what the rule of law objectively entails, but that they are predicated on perspectives and concerns that are quite inappropriate for good-faith elaboration of this ideal—an ideal that is, after all, supposed to serve the needs and promote the freedom and dignity of those who live in a given society and are engaged in the responsible endeavor of self-government.

Notes

Introduction

1. For the idea of an essentially contested concept, see W. B. Gallie, "Essentially Contested Concepts," *Proceedings of the Aristotelian Society* 56 (1955–1956): 167. For its application to the rule of law, see Richard Fallon, "The Rule of Law as a Concept in Constitutional Discourse," *Columbia Law Review* 97 (1997): 6; Jeremy Waldron, "The Rule of Law as an Essentially Contested Concept," in *Cambridge Companion to the Rule of Law,* ed. Jens Meierhenrich and Martin Loughlin (Cambridge: Cambridge University Press, 2021); and Jeremy Waldron, "Is the Rule of Law an Essentially Contested Concept (in Florida)?," *Law and Philosophy* 21 (2002): 137–64.

2. See, e.g., Jeremy Waldron, "Participation: The Right of Rights," *Aristotelian Society Proceedings* 98 (1998): 307; Waldron, "Is Dignity the Foundation of Human Rights?," in *The Philosophical Foundations of Human Rights,* ed. S. Matthew Liao, Massimo Renzo, and Rowan Cruft (Oxford: Oxford University Press, 2015); and Waldron, "Democracy and Human Rights: Good Companions," in *Human Rights: Old Problems, New Possibilities,* ed. David Kinley, Wojciech Sadurski, and Kevin Walton (Oxford: Edward Elgar, 2014), 145.

3. F. A. Hayek, *The Road to Serfdom* (London: Routledge Classics, 2001), 81.

4. Lon Fuller, *The Morality of Law* (New Haven, CT: Yale University Press, 1964).

5. Fuller, 162.

6. Henry Hart and Albert Sacks, *The Legal Process: Basic Problems in the Making and Application of Law,* ed. William Eskridge and Philip Frickey (Westbury, NY: Foundation Press, 1994), 120–21.

7. State v. Schaeffer, 96 Ohio St. 215, 117 N.E. 220 (1917).

8. My own views about judicial review of legislation suggest that we may have here a trade-off between two of the stars in our constellation of political values: democracy (in

the respect that legislation commands) and the rule of law (if indeed it is the case that it requires judicial review). See Jeremy Waldron, "The Core of the Case against Judicial Review," *Yale Law Journal* 115 (2006): 1346.

9. Jeremy Waldron, *The Dignity of Legislation* (Cambridge: Cambridge University Press, 1999).

1. Thoughtfulness and the Rule of Law

1. Plato, *The Statesman,* ed. Julia Annas and Robin Waterfield (Cambridge: Cambridge University Press, 1995), 59.

2. Jeremy Waldron, *The Dignity of Legislation* (Cambridge: Cambridge University Press, 1999); and Waldron, "Principles of Legislation," in *The Least Examined Branch: The Role of Legislatures in the Constitutional State,* ed. Richard Bauman and Tsvi Kahana (Cambridge: Cambridge University Press, 2006).

3. Thomas Hobbes, *De Cive,* ed. Howard Warrender (Oxford: Clarendon Press, 1983), 137–38.

4. Planned Parenthood of Southeastern Pennsylvania v. Casey, 505 U.S. 833 (1992).

5. Roe v. Wade, 410 U.S. 113 (1973). Roe was in fact overthrown as a precedent in Dobbs v. Jackson Women's Health Organization, 597 U.S. ___ (2022).

6. Planned Parenthood v. Casey, 866.

7. Planned Parenthood v. Casey, 868.

8. See Jeremy Waldron, "Lucky in Your Judge," *Theoretical Inquiries in Law* 9 (2008): 185.

9. Thomas Carothers, "The Rule of Law Revival," *Foreign Affairs*77 (1998): 96 (my emphasis).

10. A. V. Dicey, *Introduction to the Study of the Law of the Constitution,* 8th ed. of 1915 (Indianapolis: Liberty Classics, 1982), 120–21; John Rawls, *A Theory of Justice,* rev. ed. (Cambridge, MA: Harvard University Press, 1999), 206–13; Richard Fallon, "The Rule of Law as a Concept in Constitutional Discourse," *Columbia Law Review* 97 (1997): 1; Cass Sunstein, "Rules and Rulelessness" (John M. Olin Law & Economics Working Paper No. 27, University of Chicago Law School, 1994); Lon L. Fuller, *The Morality of Law,* rev. ed. (New Haven, CT: Yale University Press, 1969), 38–39; Joseph Raz, "The Rule of Law and Its Virtue," in *The Authority of Law: Essays on Law and Morality* (Oxford: Clarendon Press, 1979), 214–19; John Finnis, *Natural Law and Natural Rights* (Oxford: Clarendon Press, 1980), 270–73; and Tom Bingham, *The Rule of Law* (London: Allen Lane, 2010), passim.

11. Robert S. Summers, "Principles of the Rule of Law," *Notre Dame Law Review* 74 (1999): 1691.

12. Vallejo v. Wheeler (1774), 1 Cowp. 143, 153, cited by Bingham, *Rule of Law,* 38.

13. Bingham, *Rule of Law,* 38.

14. F. A. Hayek, *The Road to Serfdom* (London: Routledge Classics, 2001), 75.

15. Raz, "Rule of Law and Its Virtue," 210.

16. Hayek, *Road to Serfdom,* 78. For the World Bank view, see, for example, the following essays by Ibrahim Shihata: "The World Bank and 'Governance' Issues in Its Borrowing Members," in *The World Bank in a Changing World: Selected Essays,* ed. Antonio

Parra, Barber Conable, Franziska Tschofen, and Ibrahim Shihata, vol.1 (The Hague: Martinus Nijhoff, 1991), 53, and "Legal Framework for Development" and "Relevant Issues in the Establishment of a Sound Legal Framework for a Market Economy," both in *The World Bank in a Changing World: Selected Essays and Lectures,* ed. Antonio Parra, Barber Conable, Franziska Tschofen, and Ibrahim Shihata, vol. 2 (The Hague: Martinus Nijhoff, 1995).

17. See F. A. Hayek, *The Constitution of Liberty* (London: Routledge & Kegan Paul, 1960), 153, 156–57.

18. Antonin Scalia, "The Rule of Law as a Law of Rules," *University of Chicago Law Review* 56 (1989): 1175.

19. Bingham, *Rule of Law,* 44–46.

20. Kenneth Culp Davis, *Discretionary Justice: A Preliminary Inquiry,* new ed. (Westport, CT: Greenwood Press, 1980).

21. Laurence Tribe of Harvard Law School is on record as saying that he rejects Justice Scalia's exaltation of an ideal of legal formalism under which regularity and predictability and closure count for more than substantive justice. "That," says Tribe, "is not my notion of the Rule of Law at all." See Lawrence Tribe, "Revisiting the Rule of Law," *New York University Law Review* 64 (1989): 728.

22. See Simon Chesterman, "The UN Security Council and the Rule of Law: The Role of the Security Council in Strengthening a Rules-Based International System" Final Report and Recommendations from the Austrian Initiative, 2004–2008 (Federal Ministry for European and International Affairs, and Institute for International Law and Justice, New York University, 2008), https://www.iilj.org/wp-content/uploads/2017/08/unsc_and_the_rule_of_law.pdf.

23. See Chapter 7 below.

24. Fuller, *Morality of Law,* 38–39.

25. Sunstein, "Rules and Rulelessness," 3.

26. For the idea of self-application as a most important moment in the legal process, see Henry Hart and Albert Sacks, *The Legal Process: Basic Problems in the Making and Application of Law,* ed. William Eskridge and Philip Frickey (Westbury, NY: Foundation Press, 1994), 120.

27. State v. Stanko, 974 P2d 1132 (1998).

28. See State v. Schaeffer, 96 Ohio St. 215, 117 N.E. 220 (1917) and the discussion of the general problem of vagueness and standards in relation to that case in Chapter 5, below.

29. Fuller, *Morality of Law,* 68.

30. Hayek, *Road to Serfdom,* 81.

31. This is based on some discussion in Jeremy Waldron, "Inhuman and Degrading Treatment: The Words Themselves," *Canadian Journal of Law and Jurisprudence* 23 (2010): 269, reprinted in Waldron, *Torture, Terror, and Trade-Offs: Philosophy for the White House* (New York: Oxford University Press, 2010), 276.

32. See Ronald Dworkin, "The Model of Rules," in *Taking Rights Seriously* (Cambridge, MA: Harvard University Press, 1977), 32 ff.; and Dworkin, *Freedom's Law: The Moral Reading of the American Constitution* (Cambridge, MA: Harvard University Press, 1996).

33. See also Chapter 7 below.

34. Nicola Lacey, "Out of the 'Witches' Cauldron?—Reinterpreting the Context and Re-assessing the Significance of the Hart-Fuller Debate," in *The Hart-Fuller Debate in the Twenty-First Century*, ed. Peter Cane (Oxford: Hart Publishing, 2010), 1.

35. Lon Fuller, "The Forms and Limits of Adjudication," *Harvard Law Review* 92 (1978): 364.

36. Fuller, 365.

37. Fuller, 366.

38. Fuller, 388.

39. Fuller, *Morality of Law,* 176.

40. See also the discussion of courtroom civility in Jeremy Waldron, "Civility and Formality," in *Civility, Legality, and Justice in America,* ed. Austin Sarat (Cambridge: Cambridge University Press 2014), 46.

41. See David Luban, *Legal Ethics and Human Dignity* (Cambridge: Cambridge University Press, 2007); David Luban, "Lawyers as Upholders of Human Dignity (When They Aren't Busy Assaulting It)," *University of Illinois Law Review* 3 (2005): 815–45; Frank Michelman, "The Supreme Court and Litigation Access Fees: The Right to Protect One's Own Rights," *Duke Law Journal* (January 1974): 1153; and Jeremy Waldron, *Dignity, Rank, and Rights* (New York: Oxford University Press, 2012) 61–62.

42. Neil MacCormick, *Rhetoric and the Rule of Law: A Theory of Legal Reasoning* (Oxford: Oxford University Press, 2005), 14–15, 26–28.

43. John Rawls, *Political Liberalism,* new ed. (New York: Columbia University Press, 1996), 212 ff.

44. Ronald Dworkin, *Law's Empire* (Cambridge, MA: Harvard University Press, 1986), 157–58.

45. Dworkin, 130, 159.

46. Richard Fallon, "Stare Decisis and the Constitution," *NYU Law Review* 76 (2001): 570; and Henry Monaghan, "Stare Decisis and Constitutional Adjudication," *Columbia Law Review* 88 (1988): 723.

47. Roe v. Wade, 410 U.S. 113 (1973).

48. H. L. A. Hart, *The Concept of Law,* 2nd ed. (Oxford: Clarendon Press, 1994), 124 ff.

49. See Davis, *Discretionary Justice,* 27 ff.

50. Dworkin, *Freedom's Law,* 345.

51. Alexis de Tocqueville, *Democracy in America* (London: Penguin Books, 2003), 315.

52. See discussion in Jeremy Waldron, *Law and Disagreement* (Oxford: Oxford University Press, 1999), 289–91.

53. F. A. Hayek, *Rules and Order,* vol. 1 of *Law, Legislation and Liberty* (Chicago: University of Chicago Press, 1973), 116.

54. Raz, "Rule of Law and Its Virtue," 210–11.

55. See Jeremy Waldron, "Is the Rule of Law an Essentially Contested Concept (in Florida)?," *Law and Philosophy* 21 (2002): 137.

56. Aristotle, *Politics,* trans. Benjamin Jowett (New York: Cosimo, 2008), 140 (III.16, 1287a).

57. Ernest Weinrib, "The Intelligibility of the Rule of Law," in *The Rule of Law: Ideal or Ideology,* ed. Allan Hutchinson and Patrick Monahan (Toronto: Carswell, 1987).

2. The Concept and the Rule of Law

1. See "Gathering Storm," editorial, *New York Times,* November 8, 2007, A32: "The American Bar Association, its members horrified by events in Pakistan, has written to General Musharraf and condemned his 'profound breach of the rule of law.'"

2. "Exile in Siberia: Absence of the Rule of Law Undermines Russia's Economy," *Financial Times,* February 7, 2008, 10. See also "Russia Must Abjure Political Violence: To Win Respect, Moscow Must Itself Respect Rule of Law," *Financial Times,* July 20, 2007, 10.

3. "Exile in Siberia," 10.

4. See also Arkady Ostrovsky, "Investment Dries Up as Rule of Law Seeps Away in Russia," *Financial Times,* March 1, 2005, 20.

5. "Military Tribunals Are Not the Way: Guantanamo Is beyond the Rule of Law and Should Be Shut," *Financial Times,* February 12, 2008, 8.

6. Bush v. Gore, 531 U.S. 98, 128–29 (2000) (Stevens, J., dissenting).

7. The term "law" is used in two ways. Sometimes it is used in the sense of a legal system: "The United States has a system of law." Other times, it is used in the sense of legal propositions: "It is the law that you have to file a tax return by April 15." The two senses are clearly connected. A considerable amount of what I am going to say in this chapter will focus on the first sense. This is the sense in which I will argue that the rule of law and the concept of law need to be brought closer together. In section 9, I will address the connection between the rule of law and the concept of law in the second sense.

8. See F. A. Hayek, *The Constitution of Liberty* (London: Routledge & Kegan Paul, 1960), 156–57: "The rationale of securing to each individual a known range within which he can decide on his actions is to enable him to make the fullest use of his knowledge. . . . The law tells him what facts he may count on and thereby extends the range within which he can predict the consequences of his actions."

9. See Lon Fuller, *The Morality of Law* (New Haven, CT: Yale University Press, 1969), 39.

10. See A. V. Dicey, *Introduction to the Study of the Law of the Constitution,* 8th ed. of 1915 (Indianapolis: Liberty Press, 1961), 103 ff.

11. See Jeremy Waldron, "The Rule of Law as a Theater of Debate," in *Dworkin and His Critics,* ed. Justine Burley (Oxford: Blackwell, 2004), 319

12. See, e.g., H. L. A. Hart, "Problems of Philosophy of Law," in *The Encyclopedia of Philosophy,* ed. Paul Edwards (New York: Macmillan, 1967), 6:273–74: "The requirements that the law . . . should be general . . . ; should be free from contradictions, ambiguities, and obscurities; should be publicly promulgated and easily accessible; and should not be retrospective in operation are usually referred to as the principles of legality."

13. See Joseph Raz, "The Rule of Law and Its Virtue," in *The Authority of Law: Essays on Law and Morality* (Oxford: Clarendon Press, 1979), 224.

14. See Jeremy Bentham, *An Introduction to the Principles of Morals and Legislation,* ed. J. H. Burns and H. L. A. Hart (London: Athlone Press 1970), 293–94.

15. See H. L. A. Hart, *The Concept of Law,* 2nd ed. (Oxford: Clarendon Press, 1994), 210: "This sense, that there is something outside the official system . . . is surely more likely to be kept alive among those who are accustomed to think that rules of law may be iniquitous, than among those who think that nothing iniquitous can anywhere have the status of law."

16. Besides Hart, *Concept of Law,* see Jules Coleman, *The Practice of Principle* (Oxford: Clarendon Press, 2001).

17. See John Austin, *The Province of Jurisprudence Determined,* ed. Wilfrid E. Rumble (Cambridge: Cambridge University Press 1832); Jeremy Bentham, *Of Laws in General,* ed. H. L. A. Hart (London: Athlone Press, 1970); and Thomas Hobbes, *Leviathan,* ed. Richard Tuck (Cambridge: Cambridge University Press, 1988).

18. See Thomas Aquinas, "The Summa of Theology," in *St. Thomas Aquinas on Politics and Ethics,* ed. Paul E. Sigmund (New York: W. W. Norton, 1988): "A tyrannical law, since it is not in accordance with reason, is not a law in the strict sense, but rather a perversion of law."

19. See John Fortescue, "In Praise of the Laws of England," in *On the Laws and Governance of England,* ed. Shelley Lockwood (Cambridge: Cambridge University Press 1997); John Locke, *Two Treatises of Government,* ed. Peter Laslett (Cambridge: Cambridge University Press 1967).

20. See, generally, Evgeny Pashukanis, *Law and Marxism: A General Theory* (London: Ink Links 1978), 47–64. See also Lon Fuller, "Pashukanis and Vyshinsky: A Study in the Development of Marxian Legal Theory," *Michigan Law Review* 47 (1949): 1159.

21. Pashukanis, *Law and Marxism,* 101.

22. Pashukanis, 133.

23. See Lon Fuller, "Positivism and Fidelity to Law—a Reply to Professor Hart," *Harvard Law Review* 71 (1958): 660:

> To me there is nothing shocking in saying that a dictatorship which clothes itself with a tinsel of legal form can so far depart from the morality of order, from the inner morality of law itself, that it ceases to be a legal system. When a system calling itself law is predicated upon a general disregard by judges of the terms of the laws they purport to enforce, when this system habitually cures its legal irregularities, even the grossest, by retroactive statutes, when it has only to resort to forays of terror in the streets, which no one dares challenge, in order to escape even those scant restraints imposed by the pretence of legality—when all these things have become true of a dictatorship, it is not hard for me, at least, to deny to it the name of law.

See also Fuller, *Morality of Law,* 170–81.

24. Fuller, *Morality of Law,* 38.

25. Fuller, 165–66.

26. See Fuller, "Positivism and Fidelity to Law," 650, criticizing the assumption that "the only difference between Nazi law and . . . English law is that the Nazis used their laws to achieve ends that are odious to an Englishman."

27. Fuller, 650–52.

28. Cf. Fuller, "166: "There is much reason to believe that our approach to the problem of drug addiction is wrong, and that more would be achieved through medical and rehabilitative measures than through the criminal law."

29. See, generally, Martin Shapiro, *Courts: A Comparative and Political Analysis* (Chicago: University of Chicago Press, 1981), 1–64; and Lon Fuller, "The Forms and Limits of Adjudication," *Harvard Law Review* 92 (1978): 363–81.

30. Hart, *Concept of Law,* 96–97.

31. Hart, 97.

32. Hart acknowledges that secondary rules will define processes for these institutions. But he seems to think that this can vary from society to society and that nothing in the concept of law constrains that definition.

33. See Joseph Raz, *Practical Reason and Norms* (Princeton, NJ: Princeton University Press, 1990), 136: "Primary norm-applying organ[s] . . . are institutions with power to determine the normative situation of specified individuals, which are required to exercise these powers by applying existing norms, but whose decisions are binding even when wrong."

34. See Raz, 134.

35. Raz, 136.

36. Raz, 217.

37. See Shapiro, *Courts,* 1: "Whenever two persons come into a conflict that they cannot themselves solve, one solution appealing to common sense is to call on a third for assistance in achieving a resolution."

38. See Fuller, "Forms and Limits," 387–88.

39. Austin, *Province of Jurisprudence,* 28–29.

40. Hart, *Concept of Law,* 21.

41. Hart, 114. See also Jeremy Waldron, "All We Like Sheep," *Canadian Journal of Law & Jurisprudence* 12 (1999): 169.

42. See Henry Hart and Albert Sacks, *The Legal Process: Basic Problems in the Making and Application of Law,* ed. William Eskridge and Philip Frickey (Westbury, NY: Foundation Press, 1994), 120–21: "Every directive arrangement which is susceptible of correct and dispositive application by a person to whom it is initially addressed is self-applying. . . . Overwhelmingly, the greater part of the general body of the law is self-applying, including almost the whole of the law of contracts, torts, property, crimes, and the like."

43. Joseph Raz has pursued the idea of law's action-guiding character in this connection most thoroughly. See Raz, "Rule of Law and Its Virtue," 214: "If the law is to be obeyed it must be capable of guiding the behavior of its subjects. It must be such that they can find out what it is and act on it. This is the basic intuition from which the doctrine of the rule of law derives: the law must be capable of guiding the behavior of its subjects."

44. Fuller, *Morality of Law,* 162.

45. Coleman, *Practice of Principle,* 203–4, insists that we can talk about the connection between the concept of law and the guidance of action and what action-guidance involves without pursuing or invoking these moral ideals.

46. See Chapter 3 below.

47. See Jeremy Waldron, "Principles of Legislation," in *The Least Examined Branch: The Role of Legislatures in the Constitutional State,* ed. Richard W. Bauman and Tsvi Kahana (Cambridge: Cambridge University Press, 2006), 22.

48. Raz, *Practical Reason and Norms,* 129–31.

49. Raz, 158–61.

50. Just to complicate matters, we sometimes distinguish between divine positive law and other parts of God's law that are supposed to be discernible by reason. Positive can sometimes just mean *made* (even made by God) rather than specifically man-made. See Austin, *Province of Jurisprudence,* 38–39.

51. See Saint Augustine, *City of God,* ed. Marcus Dodds (Peabody, MA: Hendrickson, 2009), 101 (IV, 4).

52. Cf. Hans Kelsen, *Pure Theory of Law* (Berkeley: University of California Press, 1967), 47: "Why is the coercive order that constitutes the community of the robber gang . . . not interpreted as a legal order? . . . Because no basic norm is presupposed according to which one ought to behave in conformity with this order. But why is no such basic norm presupposed? Because this order does not have the lasting effectiveness without which no basic norm is presupposed."

53. Cf. Jeremy Waldron, "Does Law Promise Justice?," *Georgia State University Law Review* 17 (2001): 761, exploring similar suggestion about relation between law and justice.

54. See Jeremy Waldron, "Transcendental Nonsense and System in the Law," *Columbia Law Review* 100 (2000): 31–32.

55. See Raz, *Practical Reason and Norms,* 123–48.

56. See Ronald Dworkin, *Law's Empire* (Cambridge, MA: Harvard University Press, 1986), 165–66.

57. See Fuller, *Morality of Law,* 65–70.

58. On the other hand, some positivist theories present the descriptive characteristics that they regard as definitive of law in a way that is quite explicit about the values that motivate the choice of these characteristics. See Jeremy Waldron, "Normative (or Ethical) Positivism," in *Hart's Postscript: Essays on the Postscript to the Concept of Law,* ed. Jules Coleman (Oxford: Oxford University Press, 2001), 411.

59. See Hart, *Concept of Law,* 91–94.

60. See, generally, John Finnis, *Natural Law and Natural Rights* (Oxford: Clarendon Press, 1980), 9–18, explaining distinction between focal and peripheral or deviant cases of concepts like "law."

61. Hart, *Concept of Law,* 209.

62. Hart, 207–9.

63. Hart, 210.

64. Modern positivist theories include a condition of efficacy. See, e.g., Hart, 116–17, describing minimum conditions necessary for the existence of a legal system as (1) effective acceptance of rules as common public standards of official behavior; and (2) general obedience of rules by private citizens; and Kelsen, *Pure Theory,* 11–12, 47–48, 211–14, arguing that validity of legal norms requires a minimum of effectiveness.

65. See Fuller, *Morality of Law,* 81–91.

66. See Jeremy Waldron, "Retroactive Law: How Dodgy Was Duynhoven?," *Otago Law Review* 10 (2004): 653, arguing that importance of the rule of law requirement of prospectivity is connected to importance of systematicity in law.

67. See Fuller, *Morality of Law,* 40, describing Hitler's Germany as "a general and drastic deterioration in legality."

68. Finnis, *Natural Law,* 270.

69. See Dworkin, *Law's Empire,* 176–86.

70. See Bentham, *Of Laws in General,* 193. See also Gerald Postema, *Bentham and the Common Law Tradition* (Oxford: Clarendon Press, 1986), 328–36.

71. Cf. Dworkin, *Law's Empire,* 104–8, taking a similarly open approach to the question of whether Nazi Germany had a legal system..

72. See Dworkin, 3–43.

73. Cf. Neil MacCormick, *Rhetoric and the Rule of Law* (Oxford: Oxford University Press, 2005) 27: "These contests are not some kind of a pathological excrescence on a system that would otherwise run smoothly. They are an integral element in a legal order that is working according to the ideal of the rule of law."

74. Dworkin, *Law's Empire,* 20–23, discussing Tennessee Valley Authority v. Hill, 437 U.S. 153 (1978).

75. Endangered Species Act, 16 U.S.C. § 1536(a)(2) (2000).

76. Sindell v. Abbott Laboratories, 607 P.2d 924 (1980). See Ronald Dworkin, "Hart's Postscript and the Character of Political Philosophy," *Oxford Journal of Legal Studies* 24 (2004): 3.

77. Tennessee Valley Authority v. Hill, 194.

78. See Dworkin, *Law's Empire,* 24–25.

79. Dworkin, 25.

80. See MacCormick, *Rhetoric and the Rule of Law,* 14–15, 26–28.

81. See Hart, *Concept of Law,* 135–36, arguing that courts perform a rule-producing function at margins where there is uncertainty about applicability of rules.

82. Finnis, *Natural Law,* 270.

83. For a fine account of this, see MacCormick, *Rhetoric and the Rule of Law,* 12–31, which describes the tension between the rule of law—which is supposed to provide certainty and predictability—and the argumentative character of law, and argues that reconciliation is possible if the rule of law is viewed as dynamic rather than static, allowing new certainties to emerge from old certainties through rational argument.

3. How Law Protects Dignity

1. See Jeremy Waldron, "Cruel, Inhuman, and Degrading Treatment: The Words Themselves," *Canadian Journal of Law and Jurisprudence* 23 (2010): 269, reprinted in Jeremy Waldron, *Torture, Terror, and Trade-Offs* (New York: Oxford University Press, 2010).

2. See Trop v. Dulles, 356 U.S. 86, 100 (1958), on the role of dignity in the Eighth Amendment, and Furman v. Georgia, 408 U.S. 238 (1972), on the role of dignity in death penalty jurisprudence.

3. See Jacques Maritain, *The Rights of Man and Natural Law* (New York: Publisher, 1955), 65; and James Griffin, *On Human Rights* (Oxford: Oxford University Press, 2008), 5–6, 21–22.

4. Christopher McCrudden, "Human Dignity in Human Rights Interpretation," *European Journal of International Law* 19 (2008): 655.

5. For the idea of status, see R. H. Graveson, *Status in the Common Law* (London: Athlone Press, 1953). See also the discussion in Jeremy Waldron, *Dignity, Rank, and Rights* (New York: Oxford University Press, 2012), 57–61, 137–43.

6. Immanuel Kant, *Groundwork of the Metaphysics of Morals,* in *Practical Philosophy,* ed. Mary Gregor (Cambridge: Cambridge University Press, 1996), 84–85.

7. Immanuel Kant, *The Metaphysics of Morals,* in *Practical Philosophy,* 579; and Kant, *Critique of Practical Reason,* in *Practical Philosophy,* 269.

8. Cf. Tekin v. Turkey (2001) 31 E.H.R.R. 4.

9. See, e.g., Patrick Lee and Robert George, "The Nature and Basis of Human Dignity," *Ratio Juris* 21 (2008): 173.

10. For some connections, see also the discussion in Jeremy Waldron, "The Image of God: Rights, Reason, and Order," in *Christianity and Human Rights: An Introduction,* ed. John Witte and Frank Alexander (Cambridge: Cambridge University Press, 2010).

11. See H. L. A. Hart, "Are There Any Natural Rights?," *Philosophical Review* 64 (1955): 175, reprinted in Jeremy Waldron, ed., *Theories of Rights* (Oxford: Oxford University Press, 1984), 180.

12. But see H. L. A. Hart, "Bentham on Legal Rights," in *Oxford Essays in Jurisprudence,* ed. A. W. B. Simpson (Oxford: Oxford University Press, 1973), for the beginnings of a retreat from this position.

13. Joel Feinberg, "The Nature and Value of Rights," *Journal of Value Inquiry* 4 (1970): 243.

14. Ronald Dworkin, *Taking Rights Seriously* (Cambridge, MA: Harvard University Press, 1977).

15. Lon Fuller, *The Morality of Law* (New Haven, CT: Yale University Press, 1964).

16. See, e.g., H. L. A. Hart, review of *The Morality of Law,* by Lon Fuller, *Harvard Law Review* 78 (1965): 1284.

17. Jeremy Waldron, "Positivism and Legality: Hart's Equivocal Response to Fuller," *New York University Law Review* 83 (2008): 1135, esp. 1154–56.

18. Lon L. Fuller, "Positivism and Fidelity to Law—a Reply to Professor Hart," *Harvard Law Review* 71 (1958): 636–37, 644–45.

19. Lon Fuller, *Morality of Law,* 162.

20. For the idea of self-application, see Henry M. Hart and Albert Sacks, *The Legal Process: Basic Problems in the Making and Application of Law* (Westbury, NY: Foundation Press, 1994), 120–21. See also Chapter 4 below.

21. Joseph Raz, "The Rule of Law and Its Virtue," in *The Authority of Law: Essays on Law and Morality* (Oxford: Clarendon Press, 1979), 221.

22. Jules Coleman, *The Practice of Principle* (Oxford: Clarendon Press, 2001), 194–95, 205–6.

23. Joseph Schumpeter, *Capitalism, Socialism and Democracy* (New York: Harper, 2008), ch. 22.

24. See, e.g., Hart and Sacks, *Legal Process,* 150–52.

25. See Chapter 5 below.

26. H. L. A. Hart, *The Concept of Law,* 2nd ed. (Oxford: Clarendon Press, 1994), 96.

27. For more elaboration of this argument, see Chapter 7 below.

28. Lon Fuller, "The Forms and Limits of Adjudication," *Harvard Law Review* 92 (1978): 358.

29. Jeremy Waldron, "Dignity and Rank," *European Journal of Sociology* 48 (2007): 201.

30. 1399 Rolls Parl. III. 424 / 1, as cited in *Oxford English Dictionary,* s.v. "dignity."

31. See, e.g., Teresa Iglesias, "Bedrock Truths and the Dignity of the Individual," *Logos: A Journal of Catholic Thought and Culture* 4 (2001): 111.

32. See Waldron, "Dignity and Rank," 215 ff.

33. James Whitman, "Human Dignity in Europe and the United States," in *European and US Constitutionalism,* ed. G. Nolte (Cambridge: Cambridge University Press, 2005), 97. See also Gregory Vlastos, "Justice and Equality," in Waldron, *Theories of Rights,* 41.

34. Isabel, Countess of Rutland's Case (1606) 6 Co. Rep. 52 b, 77 E.R. 332, 336.

35. Countess of Rutland's Case, 333.

36. Max Weber, *Economy and Society* (Berkeley: University of California Press, 1978), 894–95.

37. David Luban, *Legal Ethics and Human Dignity* (Cambridge: Cambridge University Press, 2007); Luban, "Lawyers as Upholders of Human Dignity (When They Aren't Busy Assaulting It)," *University of Illinois Law Review* 3 (2005): 815.

38. Luban, "Lawyers as Upholders of Human Dignity," 819, quoting Alan Donagan, "Justifying Legal Practice in the Adversary System," in *The Good Lawyer: Lawyers' Roles and Lawyers' Ethics,* ed. David Luban (Lanham, MD: Rowman & Littlefield, 1983), 130.

39. See, e.g., Austin Sarat and Thomas Kearns, "A Journey through Forgetting: Toward a Jurisprudence of Violence," in *The Fate of Law,* ed. Austin Sarat and Thomas Kearns (Ann Arbor: University of Michigan Press, 1993). The suggestion there is that law is always violent and that the most important feature about it is that it works its will, in Cover's phrase, "in a field of pain and death." Robert Cover, "Violence and the Word," *Yale Law Journal* 95 (1986): 1601.

40. Fuller, *Morality of Law,* 108–9.

41. Cf. E. P. Thompson, *Whigs and Hunters: The Origin of the Black Act* (Harmondsworth, UK: Penguin Books, 1976), 265.

42. Weber, *Economy and Society,* 54.

43. This formulation is adapted from Jeremy Waldron, "Torture and Positive Law: Jurisprudence for the White House," *Columbia Law Review* 105 (2005): 1726, reprinted in Waldron, *Torture, Terror and Trade-Offs.*

44. Hannah Arendt, *The Origins of Totalitarianism* (New York: Harcourt, Brace, Jovanovich, 1973), 441.

45. By the "moral orthopedics" of human dignity, I have in mind what some Marxists, following Ernst Bloch, used to call "walking upright." See Jan Robert Bloch and

Caspers Rubin, "How Can We Understand the Bends in the Upright Gait?," *New German Critique* 45 (1988): 9–10. See also the account in Aurel Kolnai, "Dignity," *Philosophy* 51 (1976): 253–54.

46. US Constitution, Thirteenth Amendment: "Neither slavery nor involuntary servitude, *except as a punishment for crime* . . . shall exist within the United States, or any place subject to their jurisdiction" (my emphasis).

47. James Whitman has argued that US history tells quite a different story from the development of dignitarian jurisprudence in Europe. See Whitman, "Human Dignity in Europe and the United States"; and Whitman, *Harsh Justice: Criminal Punishment and the Widening Divide between America and Europe* (Oxford: Oxford University Press, 2005). See also Nicola Lacey, *The Prisoners' Dilemma: Political Economy and Punishment in Contemporary Democracies* (Cambridge: Cambridge University Press, 2008), 30–40.

48. See, e.g., Harriet Chiang, "Justices Limit Stun Belts in Court," *San Francisco Chronicle,* August 23, 2002; and William Glaberson, "Electric Restraint's Use Stirs Charges of Cruelty to Inmates," *New York Times,* June 8, 1999.

49. See, e.g., "37 Prisoners Sent to Texas Sue Missouri," *St. Louis Post-Dispatch,* September 18, 1997 ("Missouri prisoners alleging abuse in a jail in Texas have sued their home state and officials responsible for running the jail where a videotape showed inmates apparently being beaten and shocked with stun guns"); and Mike Bucsko and Robert Dvorchak, "Lawsuits Describe Racist Prison Rife with Brutality," *Pittsburgh Post-Gazette,* April 26, 1998.

50. See Jeremy Waldron, "Does Law Promise Justice?," *Georgia State University Law Review* 17 (2001): 760–61. For analogous arguments about justice, see Philip Selznick, *The Moral Commonwealth: Social Theory and the Promise of Community* (Berkeley: University of California Press, 1992), 443; and John Gardner, "The Virtue of Justice and the Character of Law," *Current Legal Problems* 53 (2000): 1.

4. Self-Application

1. Henry Hart and Albert Sacks, *The Legal Process: Basic Problems in the Making and Application of Law,* ed. William Eskridge and Philip Frickey (Westbury, NY: Foundation Press, 1994), 120. Numbers in parentheses in the text are page references to this book.

2. Margaret Jane Radin, "Reconsidering the Rule of Law," *Boston University Law Review* 69 (1989): 795.

3. Radin, 795.

4. Kenneth Karst, "Judging and Belonging," *Southern California Law Review* 61 (1988): 1966.

5. See Myres McDougal and Michael Reisman, *International Law in Contemporary Perspective: The Public Order of the World Community* (Westbury, NY: Foundation Press, 1981), 5; Conor Clarke, "Is the Foreign Intelligence Surveillance Court Really a Rubber Stamp? Ex Parte Proceedings and the Fisc Win Rate," *Stanford Law Review* 66 (2014): 129; Gary Lawson, "Legal Indeterminacy: Its Cause and Cure," *Harvard Journal of Law and Public Policy* 19 (1996): 428; and Lawrence Solum, "Originalism as Transformative Politics," *Tulane Law Review* 63 (1989): 1608.

6. On second thought, maybe there is a connection in cases where the application of a given norm does not seem to involve any change (or much of a change) from the natural course of events. Consider norms of accession in property: the ewes in my flock bear lambs; the lambs naturally stay in the flock (with their mothers); so the rule that the off-spring of my sheep become my property is easy to apply (by me and by neighboring farmers) because it more or less applies itself. Tom Merrill, "Accession and Original Ownership," *Journal of Legal Analysis* 1 (2009): 479, remarks on such cases as follows:

> Whatever the ultimate explanation for perceptions of prominent connection, it seems clear that prominent connection allows us to assign ownership in a way that is easy to understand, is self-applying, and generates very little conflict. Accession thus functions in a manner analogous to other bright line rules of property law, such as the rules against unlicensed boundary crossings of land or asportations of chattels. These rules establish principles of resource management that are simple, intuitive, and self-applying and hence operate with very low information costs.

"Self-applying" here could mean either of the things distinguished in the text.

7. Also, the Hart and Sacks idea of self-application should not be confused with "au-tonomous law," which is law created and administered by no one in some libertarian fantasies about the difference between the rule of law and rule by law. See Chapter 10 below.

8. Neil Duxbury, "Faith in Reason: The Process Tradition in American Jurisprudence," *Cardozo Law Review* 15 (1993): 658–59.

9. L. Gillarde Co. v. Joseph Martinelli & Co., USCA, 2nd Circuit, 1948, 168 F2d 276.

10. The same is true in many other areas of family law: adoption is another example of individually administered law; so is legal "emancipation" of minors; so, in a way, is marriage itself (through licensing and the authorization of celebrants). Question: Is this true of all changes of legal status?

11. Cf. Hart and Sacks, *Legal Process,* 121: "Case by case application by officials is charac-teristically resorted to when accuracy of application is highly valued. But the consequences in restricting the freedom of private action and burdening public administration are drastic."

12. For the distinction, see Meir Dan-Cohen, "Decision Rules and Conduct Rules: On Acoustic Separation in Criminal Law," *Harvard Law Review* 97 (1983): 625.

13. According to Hart and Sacks's account of "reasoned elaboration," a key duty of the court is to interpret the provision in dispute "so as to facilitate accurate self-application" in the future *Legal Process,* 145.

14. But we should not neglect the role of legal professionals in helping individuals with the self-application of norms. Charles Lewis and Michael Morkin, "Restrictions on Attorney Contacts with Adversaries' Former Employees," *Illinois Bar Journal* 83 (1995): 246, make this point, though they confuse things a little by using the separate meaning of "self-application" that we distinguished in Section 3(a) above:

> Our system of justice is not self-applying; it takes individuals specially skilled and trained in fashioning and presenting legal arguments. Since the average person is

incapable of knowing the principles of law and the rules of legal procedure, society has entrusted the legal profession with the unique privilege of representing the rights of others and in applying the judicial machinery to individual cases.

15. And sometimes institutionalized provision is made for this. Section 7 of the New Zealand Bill of Rights Act provides that

where any Bill is introduced into the House of Representatives, the Attorney-General shall, (a) in the case of a Government Bill, on the introduction of that Bill; or (b) in any other case, as soon as practicable after the introduction of the Bill, bring to the attention of the House of Representatives any provision in the Bill that appears to be inconsistent with any of the rights and freedoms contained in this Bill of Rights.

16. Henry Monaghan, "Foreword: Constitutional Common Law," *Harvard Law Review* 89 (1975): 20–21. For other discussions of the Miranda rule as self-applying, see Susan Klein, "Miranda Deconstitutionalized: When the Self-Incrimination Clause and the Civil Rights Act Collide," *University of Pennsylvania Law Review* 143 (1994): 425; Mitchell Berman, "Constitutional Decision Rules," *Virginia Law Review* 90 (2004): 1; and Anjana Malhotra, "The Immigrant and Miranda," *Southern Methodist University Law Review* 66 (2013): 323.

17. Monaghan, "Foreword," 20n.

18. I owe the distinction between arterial and capillary jurisprudence to Ronald Dworkin (in conversation).

19. Jeremy Bentham, *Of Laws in General,* ed. H. L. A. Hart and J. H. Burns (London: Athlone Press, 1970); Oliver Wendell Holmes, "The Path of the Law," *Harvard Law Review* 10 (1897): 457; H. L. A. Hart, *The Concept of Law,* 2nd ed. (Oxford: Clarendon Press, 1994); Joseph Raz, *Practical Reason and Norms,* 2nd ed. (Princeton, NJ: Princeton University Press, 1990); and Scott Shapiro, *Legality* (Cambridge, MA: Harvard University Press, 2011).

20. For example, Shlomo Pill, "Recovering Judicial Integrity: Toward a Duty-Focused Disqualification Jurisprudence Based on Jewish Law," *Fordham Urban Law Journal* 39 (2011): 533: "Jews study the halacha, transcend their base instincts by self-applying the Torah's . . . laws to their lives, and consult their rabbis when they are unsure about what the law requires."

21. For the absence of any role for officials and official determinations in natural law theory, see Jeremy Waldron, "What Is Natural Law Like?," in *Reason, Morality, and Law: The Philosophy of John Finnis,* ed. John Keown and Robert George (Oxford: Oxford University Press, 2013), 73.

22. Victor Mather, "Tough Call in a Sport: To Referee or Not," *New York Times,* June 19, 2016, reports a debate taking place within the community of those who play Ultimate Frisbee: "Traditionally that sport takes place without an umpire or referee; the players simply apply the rules to themselves and call fouls on themselves (or each other) when appropriate. But lately that process has been leading to sustained altercations."

23. Bill Pennington, "After Unseen Violation, a Striking Act," *New York Times,* June 19, 2016.

24. Joseph Raz, "The Rule of Law and Its Virtue," in *The Authority of Law* (Oxford: Clarendon Press, 1979), 210.

25. Section 375(2)(a) of the New York State Vehicle and Traffic Law.

26. Cf. Hart, *Concept of Law,* 140: "Very often when a person accepts a rule as binding . . . he may see what it requires in a given situation quite intuitively, and do that without first thinking of the rule and what it requires."

27. Hart, *Concept of Law,* 56–57, 85–90.

28. Stephen Perry, "Hart's Methodological Positivism," in *Hart's Postscript: Essays on the Postscript to "The Concept of Law,"* ed. Jules Coleman (Oxford: Oxford University Press, 2012), 327.

29. It is a bit like Max Weber offering a modal rather than a functional definition of the state in "Politics as a Vocation," in *From Max Weber: Essays in Sociology,* ed. W. W. Gerth and C. Wright Mills (London: Routledge & Kegan Paul, 1970), 77–78.

30. Raz, "Rule of Law and Its Virtue," 214.

31. Raz, 214:

The law must be open and adequately publicized. If it is to guide people they must be able to find out what it is. For the same reason its meaning must be clear. An ambiguous, vague, obscure, or imprecise law is likely to mislead or confuse at least some of those who desire to be guided by it.

Raz, 217:

Since the court's judgment establishes conclusively what is the law in the case before it, the litigants can be guided by law only if the judges apply the law correctly. Otherwise people will only be able to be guided by their guesses as to what the courts are likely to do—but these guesses will not be based on the law but on other considerations.

32. Hart, *Concept of Law,* 40.

33. Hart, 128.

34. Hart, 136.

35. Hart, 128.

36. Hart, 130.

37. The two are beginning to be brought together with the publication of Hart's essay (or notes) on "Discretion," *Harvard Law Review* 127 (2013): 652. This piece dates from 1956 and Hart's participation in a legal philosophy discussion group at Harvard. See also Geoffrey Shaw, "H. L. A. Hart's Lost Essay: Discretion and the Legal Process School," *Harvard Law Review* 127 (2013): 666.

38. H. L. A. Hart, "Positivism and the Separation of Law and Morals," *Harvard Law Review* 71 (1958): 593; and Lon Fuller, "Positivism and Fidelity to Law: A Reply to Hart," *Harvard Law Review* 71 (1958): 630.

39. John Gardner, "The Many Faces of the Reasonable Person," *Law Quarterly Review* 131 (2015): 563.

40. Gardner, 14.

41. Joseph Raz, "Incorporation by Law," *Legal Theory* 10 (2004): 1.

42. Raz, "Rule of Law and Its Virtue," 214.

43. Cf. Gardner, "Many Faces," 14: "It is, if you like, a legally deregulatory legal effect."

44. Cf. Jeremy Waldron, "Inhuman and Degrading Treatment: The Words Themselves," *Canadian Journal of Law and Jurisprudence* 23 (2010): 269; reprinted in Waldron, *Torture, Terror, and Trade-Offs: Philosophy for the White House* (New York: Oxford University Press, 2010).

45. See Chapter 5 below.

46. See also Edna Ullman-Margalit, *The Emergence of Norms* (Oxford: Clarendon Press, 1977).

47. Fuller, *Morality of Law,* 162.

48. See the discussion of choice and coercion in Jeremy Waldron, "Terrorism and the Uses of Terror," *Journal of Ethics* 8 (2004): 5, reprinted in Waldron, *Torture, Terror, and Trade-Offs.*

49. Hart, *Concept of Law,* 8, 21–23.

50. Bruce Ackerman, *Social Justice in the Liberal State* (New Haven, CT: Yale University Press, 1980), 19 ff.

51. Ackerman, 31.

52. Ackerman, 21.

53. Ackerman, 34.

54. Bruce Ackerman, "What Is Neutral about Neutrality?," *Ethics* 93 (1983): 377.

55. Ackerman, 377.

56. Ackerman, *Social Justice,* 23, 235.

57. See David Hume, *A Treatise of Human Nature,* ed. L. A. Selby-Bigge (Oxford: Oxford University Press, 1888), 487–88; and Hart, *Concept of Law,* 194–95.

58. Quite apart from anything else, Ackerman's concept leaves no room for Rawls's important idea of "the strains of commitment" as a way of testing conceptions of justice. See John Rawls, *A Theory of Justice,* rev. ed. (Cambridge, MA: Harvard University Press, 1999), 125–26, 153–54. If everything were done by force fields, we would no longer have to ask whether the self-restraint required by putative principles of justice was tolerable. This idea was key to Rawls's argument against utilitarianism—that it might require of us sacrifices we couldn't sincerely undertake to make.

5. Vagueness and the Guidance of Action

1. Lon Fuller, *The Morality of Law* (New Haven, CT: Yale University Press, 1964), 68.

2. Joseph Raz, "The Rule of Law and Its Virtue," in *The Authority of Law* (Oxford: Clarendon Press, 1979), 214.

3. Raz, 214.

4. H. L. A. Hart, *The Concept of Law,* 2nd ed. (Oxford: Clarendon Press, 1994), 206–7.

5. Fuller, *Morality of Law,* 162.

6. Raz, "Rule of Law and Its Virtue," 222.

7. State v. Schaeffer, 117 N.E. 220 (1917). Numbers in parentheses in the text are references to pages of this case report.

8. In this chapter I shall not pursue the distinctions that are sometimes needed as between different kinds of indeterminacy such as ambiguity, vagueness, and contestability. I set these out in Jeremy Waldron, "Vagueness in Law and Language: Some Philosophical Perspectives," *California Law Review* 82 (1994): 509.

9. I mean "internalize" in the straightforward sense given by condition (2); I do not mean anything more deeply psychological than that, nor do I mean, necessarily, that the person comes to endorse the norm in question.

10. Fuller, *Morality of Law,* 162; and Raz, "Rule of Law and Its Virtue," 221. See also Chapter 4 above.

11. See Hart, *Concept of Law,* 40, on "the 'puzzled man' . . . who is willing to do what is required if only he can be told what it is"; and John Finnis, *Natural Law and Natural Rights* (Oxford: Clarendon Press, 1980), 11–18, on the idea of "the law-abiding citizen" as the central perspective from which to understand law.

12. Joseph Raz, *The Morality of Freedom* (Oxford: Clarendon Press, 1986), chs. 2–3.

13. I see no point in getting into a debate about what precisely Raz meant. He has used a number of formulations in different books and essays, and it is his general position in this matter, not any particular formulation, that is useful for jurisprudence.

14. Joseph Raz, *Practical Reason and Norms,* 2nd ed. (Princeton, NJ: Princeton University Press, 1990), 219.

15. I am not drawing the familiar distinction here between practical and epistemic authority; instead, I am distinguishing between practical reasons for acting in some matter and practical reasons for deliberating (in a certain way or in a certain set of circumstances or for a certain time) over how to act in that matter.

16. I could use the language of "second-order" reasons here, but I think that would be a mistake, at least as an interpretation of Raz's view. According to Raz, a second-order reason is a reason to act (or not act) on a reason (*Practical Reason and Norms,* 39). That is not what I am talking about. I am talking about reasons to pay attention to reasons— reasons to think or deliberate about reasons. This, too, is a second-order idea, but it is a different sort of second-order idea.

17. E.g., Ronald Dworkin, "Thirty Years On," *Harvard Law Review* 115 (2002): 1671–75.

18. Cf. the discussion of detail and abstractness in F. A. Hayek, *The Constitution of Liberty* (London: Macmillan, 1960), 150–53. Hayek believes that specifying action in fine detail is typical of the rule of custom, whereas abstract, coarse-grained guidance is typical of the rule of law.

19. State v. Schaeffer, 117 N.E. 220 (1917), at 236.

20. Joseph Raz, "Incorporation by Law," *Legal Theory* 10 (2004): 8.

21. Raz, 9.

22. Jules Coleman, *The Practice of Principle* (Oxford: Clarendon Press, 2001), 137–48.

23. Hart and Sacks, *The Legal Process,* ed. William Eskridge and Philip Frickey (Westbury, NY: Foundation Press, 1994), 139.

24. Hart and Sacks, 145–50.

25. Hart and Sacks, 150.

26. See Jeremy Waldron, "Inhuman and Degrading Treatment: The Words Themselves," *Canadian Journal of Law and Jurisprudence* 23 (2010): 269.

27. Ronald Dworkin, *Freedom's Law: The Moral Reading of the American Constitution* (Cambridge, MA: Harvard University Press, 1996).

28. E.g., Citizens United v. Federal Election Commission, 558 U.S. 310 (2010) at 329: "Applying this standard would thus require case-by-case determinations. But archetypical political speech would be chilled in the meantime."

29. National Association for the Advancement of Colored People v. Button, 371 U.S. 415 (1963), at 433, quoted in Citizens United v. FEC, at 892.

30. Florida's definition is typical: "aggressive driving" means "at least two of the following: speeding, unsafe or improper lane change, following too closely, failure to yield right of way, improper passing, failure to obey traffic control devices." See https://www.fdot.gov/Safety/programs/aggressive-driving.shtm.

31. Jeremy Waldron, "Torture and Positive Law," *Columbia Law Review* 105 (2005): 1681, reprinted in Jeremy Waldron, *Torture, Terror, and Trade-Offs: Philosophy for the White House* (New York: Oxford University Press, 2010).

32. 18 U.S.C. § 2340A.

33. 18 U.S.C. § 2340(1).

34. More extensive discussion can be found in Waldron, "Torture and Positive Law," 1695–703.

35. Aristotle, *Nichomachean Ethics,* ed. W. D. Ross (Oxford: Oxford University Press, 1980), 133 (bk. V, ch. 10).

6. The Rule of Law and the Role of Courts

1. See the discussion of judicial review in Tom Bingham, *The Rule of Law* (London: Allen Lane, 2010), 60–62.

2. See the discussion in Jeremy Waldron, "Constitutionalism: A Skeptical View," in *Contemporary Debates in Political Philosophy,* ed. Thomas Christiano and John Christman (Chichester, UK: Wiley-Blackwell, 2009), 267.

3. See Bingham, *Rule of Law,* 160–70.

4. Jeremy Waldron, "The Core of the Case against Judicial Review," *Yale Law Journal* 115 (2006): 1346; and Waldron, *Law and Disagreement* (Oxford: Oxford University Press, 1999).

5. Joseph Raz, "The Rule of Law and Its Virtue," in *The Authority of Law: Essays on Law and Morality* (Oxford: Clarendon Press, 2009), 211.

6. See, e.g., Morton Horwitz, "The Rule of Law: An Unqualified Human Good?," *Yale Law Journal,* 86 (1977): 566.

7. Raz, "Rule of Law and Its Virtue," 211.

8. I first raised these questions in Jeremy Waldron, "Is the Rule of Law an Essentially Contested Concept (in Florida)?," *Law and Philosophy* 21 (2002): 142–43, 147–48.

9. I talk about this distinction in detail in Chapter 10, below. For another discussion, see also Brian Tamanaha, *On the Rule of Law: History, Politics, Theory* (Cambridge: Cambridge University Press, 2004), 92–93.

10. Thomas Hobbes, *De Cive: The English Version,* ed. Howard Warrender (Oxford: Oxford University Press, 1983), 94–95 (VI, 9).

11. See the discussion in Tom Ginsburg and Tamir Moustafa, eds., *Rule by Law: The Politics of Courts in Authoritarian Regimes* (Cambridge: Cambridge University Press, 2008).

12. John Locke, *Two Treatises of Government,* ed. Peter Laslett (Cambridge: Cambridge University Press, 1988), 328 (II, § 93).

13. See, e.g., F. A. Hayek, *The Constitution of Liberty* (London: Macmillan, 1960), 148–61; Raz, "Rule of Law and Its Virtue"; and Lon Fuller, *The Morality of Law* (New Haven, CT: Yale University Press, 1969), 33–94.

14. Tamanaha, *On the Rule of Law,* 92.

15. Plato, *Laws* (Mineola, NY: Dover, 2016), 81 (716): "For that state in which the law is subject and has no authority, I perceive to be on the highway to ruin; but I see that the state in which the law is above the rulers, and the rulers are the inferiors of the law, has salvation, and every blessing which the Gods can confer."

16. See Richard Epstein, *Design for Liberty: Private Property, Public Administration, and the Rule of Law* (Cambridge, MA: Harvard University Press, 2011), 63, for the view that the ascendancy of law that arises "from the bottom up" (like common law property rights) is a better candidate for the rule of law than law that is understood as a top-down artifact of human power (legislation).

17. Thomas Hobbes, *Leviathan,* ed. Richard Tuck (Cambridge: Cambridge University Press, 1988), 184 (ch. 16).

18. Hobbes, 224 (ch. 29).

19. Hobbes, *De Cive,* 103 (VI, 18).

20. James Harrington, *The Commonwealth of Oceana,* ed. J. G. A. Pocock (Cambridge: Cambridge University Press, 1992), 8 ff.; Locke, *Two Treatises,* 326–30 (II, §§ 89–94); Montesquieu, *The Spirit of the Laws,* ed. Ann Cohler et al. (Cambridge: Cambridge University Press, 1989), 154 ff. (bk. 11, chs. 2–6); James Madison, Alexander Hamilton, and John Jay, *The Federalist Papers,* ed. Lawrence Goldman (Oxford: Oxford University Press, 2008), 256ff., 379ff. (no. 51 by Madison and no. 78 by Hamilton); Albert Venn Dicey, *Introduction to the Study of the Law of the Constitution* (Indianapolis: Liberty Classics, 1982), 268–73.

21. See Waldron, "Is the Rule of Law Essentially Contested?," 147–48.

22. Madison, Hamilton, and Jay, *Federalist Papers,* 380 (no. 78 by Hamilton).

23. Lochner v. New York, 198 U.S. 45 (1905).

24. See the discussion in William Forbath, *Law and the Shaping of the American Labor Movement* (Cambridge, MA: Harvard University Press, 1989), 170 ff.

25. Planned Parenthood v. Casey, 505 U.S. 833 (1992).

26. Planned Parenthood v. Casey, at 866. The Court cited an observation from Justice Stewart's dissent in *Mitchell v. Grant,* 416 U.S. 600, 636 (1974): "A basic change in the law

upon a ground no firmer than a change in our membership invites the popular misconception that this institution is little different from the two political branches of the Government." These fears were realized in the recent decision of the Supreme Court in Dobbs v Jackson Women's Health, 597 U.S. ___ (2022), striking down the abortion case of Roe v. Wade, 410 U.S. 113 (1973).

27. Planned Parenthood v. Casey, at 868.

28. Planned Parenthood v. Casey at 868.

29. See Jeremy Waldron, "Five to Four: Why Do Majorities Rule on Courts?," *Yale Law Journal* 123 (2014): 1692.

30. See also Gerald Postema, "Protestant Interpretation and Social Practices," *Law and Philosophy* 6 (1987): 283.

31. See Lon Fuller, "Forms and Limits of Adjudication," *Harvard Law Review* 92 (1978): 353.

32. See the arguments by Jeremy Bentham cited in Gerald Postema, *Bentham and the Common Law Tradition* (Oxford: Clarendon Press, 1986), 233 ff.

7. The Rule of Law and the Importance of Procedure

1. John Locke, *Two Treatises of Government,* ed. Peter Laslett (Cambridge: Cambridge University Press, 1967), 274 (II, § 11).

2. F. A. Hayek, *The Constitution of Liberty* (Chicago: University of Chicago Press, 1960), esp. chs. 9–10.

3. Lon Fuller, *The Morality of Law* (New Haven, CT: Yale University Press, 1969), 162.

4. See Jeremy Waldron, "The Rule of Law in Contemporary Liberal Theory," *Ratio Juris* 2 (1989): 79. For a discussion of substantive rule-of-law ideas, see Paul Craig, "Formal and Substantive Conceptions of the Rule of Law: An Analytical Framework," *Public Law,* Autumn 1997, 467.

5. See Chapter 9 below.

6. See also the lists in John Finnis, *Natural Law and Natural Rights* (Oxford: Clarendon Press, 1980), 270; John Rawls, *A Theory of Justice,* rev. ed. (Cambridge, MA: Harvard University Press, 1999), 206–13; and Joseph Raz, "The Rule of Law and Its Virtue," in *The Authority of Law: Essays on Law and Morality* (Oxford: Clarendon Press, 1979), 214–19.

7. I have adapted this list from A. Wallace Tashima, "The War on Terror and the Rule of Law," *Asian American Law Journal* 15 (2008): 264.

8. In the United Kingdom and elsewhere, the term "natural justice" is used to refer to the most elementary aspects of what Americans would call procedural due process. See, for example, Paul Jackson, *Natural Justice* (London: Sweet and Maxwell, 1979).

9. Hayek, *Constitution of Liberty,* 148–61.

10. See Hayek, 218–19, for the suggestion that, apart from the formal characteristics of the rule of law, its procedural aspects are unimportant: "They presuppose for their effectiveness the acceptance of the rule of law as here defined and . . . , without it, all procedural safeguards would be valueless."

11. F. A. Hayek, *Rules and Order,* vol. 1 of *Law, Legislation and Liberty* (Chicago: University of Chicago Press, 1973), 94–123.

12. Fuller, *Morality of Law*, 96–97.

13. Brian Tamanaha, *On the Rule of Law: History, Politics, Theory* (New York: Cambridge University Press, 2004), gets this right by locating his discussion of Fuller in a chapter called "Formal Theories." That is then contrasted with a chapter called "Substantive Theories." Procedural theories don't rate a mention, but at least it is not assumed by Tamanaha that everything nonsubstantive is procedural.

14. There is a reference to "due process" in Fuller, *Morality of Law*, 105–6, but that is in the technical sense of the term, and it addresses whether ex post facto laws violate due process (in that sense).

15. Lon L. Fuller, "Positivism and Fidelity to Law: A Reply to Hart," *Harvard Law Review* 71 (1958): 636–37.

16. Fuller, *Morality of Law*, 176.

17. For the implications of this for Fuller's theory, see Jeremy Waldron, "The Appeal of Law: Efficacy, Freedom, or Fidelity," *Law and Philosophy* 13 (1994): 272–75.

18. See Lon Fuller, "The Forms and Limits of Adjudication," *Harvard Law Review* 92 (1978): 353.

19. See Nicola Lacey, "Out of the 'Witches' Cauldron'? Reinterpreting the Context and Reassessing the Significance of the Hart-Fuller Debate," in *The Hart-Fuller Debate in the Twenty-First Century*, ed. Peter Cane (Oxford: Hart, 2010), 1.

20. A. V. Dicey, *Introduction to the Study of the Law of the Constitution*, 8th ed. of 1915 (Indianapolis: Liberty Classics, 1982), 110 (my emphasis).

21. E. P. Thompson, *Whigs and Hunters: The Origin of the Black Act* (Harmondsworth, UK: Penguin Books, 1977), 265–66.

22. See, e.g., Finnis, *Natural Law and Natural Rights*, 270.

23. Raz, "Rule of Law and Its Virtue," 216–17.

24. Raz, 217.

25. See the essays on equitable judgment and practical reason by Lawrence Solum, "Equity and the Rule of Law" and Stephen Burton, "Particularism, Discretion, and the Rule of Law," both in *Nomos XXXVI: The Rule of Law*, ed. Ian Shapiro (New York: New York University Press, 1994).

26. See Chapter 2 above.

27. H. L. A. Hart, *The Concept of Law*, 2nd ed. (Oxford: Clarendon Press, 1994), 96.

28. See, e.g., Jamil Anderlini, "Rewards and Risks of Chinese Legal Career," *Financial Times*, July 24, 2008, where a dissident Chinese lawyer, commenting on abuses of the "court" system in China, observes: "Actually, there is no real legal system in the western sense in China."

29. Raz, "Rule of Law and Its Virtue," 224.

30. Fuller, "Forms and Limits," 366–67.

31. See, e.g., Johan Steyn, "Guantanamo Bay: The Legal Black Hole," Twenty-Seventh F. A. Mann Lecture, November 25, 2003, http://www.statewatch.org/news/2003/nov/guantanamo.pdf.

32. It is also worth noting that the demand for a clear rule to apply to and to regulate the detention is not only a demand for something that the potential detainees can use ex ante to guide their conduct—as though terrorists most needed to know what they were

forbidden to do! The demand for the formal aspects of the rule of law is often just a way of getting to the procedural aspects of the rule of law, which is what the detainees really care about.

33. See Dicey's introduction to *Introduction to the Study of the Law,* lv–lvii.

34. Dicey, lvii.

35. Fuller, *Morality of Law,* 39, 81–91.

36. Robert Barro, "Democracy and the Rule of Law," in *Governing for Prosperity,* ed. B. Bueno de Mesquita and H. Root (New Haven, CT: Yale University Press, 2000). See also Robert Cooter, "The Rule of State Law versus the Rule of Law State: Economic Analysis of the Legal Foundations of Development," in *The Law and Economics of Development,* ed. Edgardo Buscaglia, William Ratliff, and Robert Cooter (Greenwich, CT: JAI Press, 1997), 101.

37. For examples, see the World Bank ideal of rule of law as described by Frank Upham, "Mythmaking in the Rule of Law Orthodoxy" (working paper no. 30, Democracy and Rule of Law Project, Carnegie Endowment for International Peace, Washington, DC, September 2002), http://www.carnegieendowment.org/files/wp30.pdf.

38. See also the discussion in Jeremy Waldron, "Transcendental Nonsense and System in the Law," *Columbia Law Review* 100 (2000): 30–40.

39. The legal philosopher who has done the most to develop this theme is Ronald Dworkin, particularly in *Law's Empire* (Cambridge, MA: Harvard University Press, 1986).

40. See the discussion of the relation between civil disobedience and disputes about which laws are valid in Ronald Dworkin, *Taking Rights Seriously* (Cambridge, MA: Harvard University Press, 1977), 184–205. I have discussed this argumentative aspect of Dworkin's conception of the rule of law in Jeremy Waldron, "The Rule of Law as a Theater of Debate," in *Dworkin and His Critics,* ed. Justine Burley (Oxford: Blackwell, 2004), 319.

41. See Richard Fallon, "The Rule of Law as a Concept in Constitutional Discourse," *Columbia Law Review* 97 (1997): 6.

42. See, e.g., Hayek, *Constitution of Liberty,* 152–57.

43. Raz, "Rule of Law and Its Virtue," 214

44. See the discussion in Jeremy Waldron, "Is the Rule of Law an Essentially Contested Concept (in Florida)?," *Law and Philosophy* 21 (2002): 137.

45. See also Thomas Carothers, "The Rule of Law Revival," *Foreign Affairs* 77 (1998): 95; and Jeffrey Kahn, "The Search for the Rule of Law in Russia," *Georgetown Journal of International Law* 37 (2006): 359–61.

46. See, especially, Hayek, *Constitution of Liberty,* 153, 156–57.

47. See also James R. Maxeiner, "Legal Indeterminacy Made in America: U.S. Legal Methods and the Rule of Law," *Valparaiso University Law Review* 41 (2006): 517; and Antonin Scalia, "The Rule of Law as a Law of Rules," *University of Chicago Law Review* 56 (1989): 1175.

48. Neil MacCormick, *Rhetoric and the Rule of Law: A Theory of Legal Reasoning* (Oxford: Oxford University Press, 2005), 14–15, 26–28.

49. Hart, *Concept of Law,* 124–36.

50. Hart, 135–36.

51. See, e.g., Hayek, *Constitution of Liberty,* 148–61.

52. There is a fine account of this in MacCormick, *Rhetoric and the Rule of Law,* 12–31.

53. Alexis de Tocqueville, *Democracy in America* (London: Penguin Books, 1984), 315.

54. For the contrast between strong and weak judicial review, see Stephen Gardbaum, *The New Commonwealth Model of Constitutionalism: Theory and Practice* (Cambridge: Cambridge University Press, 2013). See also Jeremy Waldron, "The Core of the Case against Judicial Review," *Yale Law Journal* 115 (2006): 1346.

55. Ronald Dworkin, "Political Judges and the Rule of Law," in his collection *A Matter of Principle* (Cambridge, MA: Harvard University Press, 1985), 9.

56. Hayek, *Constitution of Liberty,* 157. This line of thought is even more pronounced in Hayek's later work; see Hayek, *Rules and Order,* 72 ff.

8. Stare Decisis and the Rule of Law

1. Benjamin Cardozo, *The Nature of the Judicial Process* (New Haven, CT: Yale University Press, 1921), 20. For opposition to stare decisis especially in constitutional law, see, e.g., Gary Lawson, "The Constitutional Case against Precedent," *Harvard Journal of Law and Public Policy* 17 (1994): 23.

2. For good general surveys, see Neil Duxbury, *The Nature and Authority of Precedent* (Cambridge: Cambridge University Press, 2008); and Michael Gerhardt, *The Power of Precedent* (New York: Oxford University Press, 2008).

3. Edmund Burke, *Reflections on the Revolution in France,* ed. L. G. Mitchell (Oxford: Oxford University Press, 1993), 87. The same can be said about arguments that stare decisis helps preserve our traditions and the character of our community. See, e.g., Anthony Kronman, "Precedent and Tradition," *Yale Law Journal* 99 (1990): 1029.

4. See, e.g., Henry Paul Monaghan, "Stare Decisis and Constitutional Adjudication," *Columbia Law Review* 88 (1988): 744–52 (system legitimacy and agenda limitation); and Frederick Schauer, "Precedent," *Stanford Law Review* 39 (1987): 599–600 (decisional efficiency).

5. See F. A. Hayek, *Rules and Order,* vol. 1 of *Law, Legislation and Liberty* (London: Routledge & Kegan Paul, 1973), 94–123.

6. There is quite a good discussion in Neil MacCormick, *Rhetoric and the Rule of Law* (Oxford: Oxford University Press, 2005) 143, where MacCormick says that "faithfulness to the rule of law calls for avoiding any frivolous variation in the pattern of decision-making from one judge or court to another." There is also a chapter titled "Towards a Rule of Law Ideology for Precedents" in Raimo Siltala, *A Theory of Precedent* (London: Hart, 2000), 151–79. Unfortunately, Siltala's book is not an easy read, but it does offer a good account in Fullerian terms of the rule-of-law difficulties with the system of precedent.

7. Planned Parenthood of South East Pennsylvania v. Casey, 505 U.S. 833 (1992); Roe v. Wade, 410 U.S. 113 (1973). Roe has been sustained at least once before on the ground of stare decisis in a way that made a connection with the rule of law. See City of Akron v. Akron Center for Reproductive Health, 462 U.S. 416, 419–20 (1983): "Arguments

continue to be made, in these cases as well, that we erred in interpreting the Constitution. Nonetheless, the doctrine of stare decisis, while perhaps never entirely persuasive on a constitutional question, is a doctrine that demands respect in a society governed by the rule of law. We respect it today, and reaffirm *Roe v. Wade*." Roe v. Wade was finally overturned by the Supreme Court in Dobbs v. Jackson Women's Health, 597 U.S. __ (2022).

8. Planned Parenthood v. Casey, at 854.

9. Planned Parenthood v. Casey, at 866 and 868. We discussed this at some length in Chapter 6.

10. I am also not going to consider the justification set out in 1787 by Alexander Hamilton, *The Federalist*, ed. Lawrence Goldman (Oxford: Oxford University Press, 2008), 379 ff.: "To avoid an arbitrary discretion in the courts, it is indispensable that they should be bound by strict rules and precedents, which serve to define and point out their duty in every particular case that comes before them." This, too, sounds as though it presupposes stare decisis. Or, if not, it sounds as though we have had to invent stare decisis in order to furnish judges with more law to be faithful to.

11. See Planned Parenthood v. Casey, at 866.

12. See Lawson, "Constitutional Case against Precedent," 23; and Michael Stokes Paulsen, "Abrogating Stare Decisis by Statute: May Congress Remove the Precedential Effect of Roe and Casey?," *Yale Law Journal* 109 (2000): 1535.

13. U.S. Constitution, Art. VI, cl. 2.

14. This argument is particularly powerful if the justification for following precedent is mainly pragmatic (i.e., decisional efficiency or the commercial advantages of predictability).

15. Cf. Monaghan, "Stare Decisis and Constitutional Adjudication," 748: "Precedent is, of course, part of our understanding of what law is."

16. Richard Fallon, "Stare Decisis and the Constitution: An Essay on Constitutional Methodology," *New York University Law Review* 76 (2001): 579–81. Fallon goes on to say:

It is settled that the judicial power to resolve cases encompasses a power to invest judgments with "finality." . . . And there can be little doubt that the Constitution makes Supreme Court precedents binding on lower courts. If higher court precedents bind lower courts, there is no structural anomaly in the view that judicial precedents also enjoy limited constitutional authority in the courts that rendered them.

17. See John Henry Merryman, *The Civil Law Tradition: An Introduction to the Legal Systems of Western Europe and Latin America*, 2nd ed. (Stanford, CA: Stanford University Press, 1985), 22: "Stare decisis . . . [is] rejected by the civil law tradition." See also Michael P. Van Alstine, "Stare Decisis and Foreign Affairs," *Duke Law Journal* 61 (2012): 989: "The vast majority of states that compose the international system do not follow stare decisis."

18. See Aristotle, *The Politics*, ed. Stephen Everson (Cambridge: Cambridge University Press, 1988), 88–89 (bk. III, ch. 16): "A man may be a safer ruler than the written law, but not safer than the customary law." See also Hayek, *Rules and Order*, 72–73 (denigrating legislation as a marginal and problematic kind of law).

19. For the distinction between central and marginal cases of law and its significance in jurisprudence, see John Finnis, *Natural Law and Natural Rights* (Oxford: Clarendon Press, 1980), 9–16.

20. F. A. Hayek, *The Constitution of Liberty* (London: Macmillan, 1960), 142, 153.

21. Planned Parenthood v. Casey, at 844.

22. Jeremy Bentham, *Of Laws in General,* ed. H. L. A. Hart (London: Athlone Press 1970), 153.

23. Bentham, 184.

24. Bentham, 184.

25. See Gerald Postema, *Bentham and the Common Law Tradition* (Oxford: Clarendon Press, 1986), 192–97, 275–78.

26. I don't mean that there is no point to a judge articulating reasons for her decisions unless she expects others to follow her ratio decidendi. There are other reasons why we value judicial reason-giving. Lon Fuller, in "The Forms and Limits of Adjudication," *Harvard Law Review* 92 (1978): 388, says that the requirement that a judge give reasons is not just to encourage the judge to be thoughtful, but because without such a requirement, the parties would have to

> take it on faith that their [reasoned] participation in the decision[-making] has been real, [and] that the [court] has in fact understood and taken into account their . . . arguments. It is also a matter of accountability: we want the judge to explain the grounds of her decision to the public, who might otherwise have doubts about the legitimacy of what she has done.

27. See Ronald Dworkin, *Law's Empire* (Cambridge, MA: Harvard University Press, 1986), 130, 157–58.

28. Bentham, *Of Laws in General,* 187. For this indeterminacy in constitutional law, see Monaghan, "Stare Decisis and Constitutional Adjudication," 743:

> Because a coherent rationale for the intermittent invocation of stare decisis has not been forthcoming, the impression is created that the doctrine is invoked only as a mask hiding other considerations. As a result, stare decisis seemingly operates with the randomness of a lightning bolt: on occasion it may strike, but when and where can be known only after the fact.

29. Scholars in the critical legal studies (CLS) movement have always acknowledged this, even in the midst of their arguments about indeterminacy. See, e.g., Joseph Singer, "The Player and the Cards: Nihilism and Legal Theory," *Yale Law Journal* 94 (1984): 20:

> It is perfectly possible for there to be predictable patterns of behavior and decisionmaking even though the arguments advanced to justify the choices do not determine the outcomes. Saying that decisionmaking is both indeterminate and nonarbitrary simply means that we can explain judicial decisions only by reference to criteria outside the scope of the judge's formal justifications.

30. E.g., Larry Alexander, "Constrained by Precedent," *Southern California Law Review* 63 (1989): 4.

31. For insistence on the same point, see MacCormick, *Rhetoric and the Rule of Law,* 144:

It must seem doubtful whether any adequate understanding of precedent . . . could proceed in the absence of an adequate theory of legal justification. Only by knowing the kinds of justifying reasons which are proper to judicial decisions can we know the possible elements of judicial precedents. Surprisingly, a great deal of writing about precedent has proceeded without full regard to the prerequisites of an articulate theory of legal justification.

32. Henry Hart and Albert Sacks, *The Legal Process: Basic Problems in the Making and Application of Law,* ed. William Eskridge and Philip Frickey (Westbury, NY: Foundation Press, 1994), 569. For this citation I am obliged to Larry Alexander and Emily Sherwin, "Judges as Rule Makers," in *Common Law Theory,* ed. Douglas Edlin (Cambridge: Cambridge University Press, 2010), 41.

33. See Dworkin, *Law's Empire,* 225–75.

34. Cf. John Gardner, "Some Types of Law," in Edlin, *Common Law Theory,* 66–67:

Typically judges set about adding to case law by applying existing law. . . . They argue that a certain ruling, even if not required by existing law, would be consistent with existing law and a sound development of existing law. They proceed in this way because they have a professional moral duty (usually crystallized in their oath of office) to keep faith with whatever existing law there is on any subject on which they may make a ruling.

35. I think this is the position defended in Ronald Dworkin, "Hart's Postscript and the Character of Political Philosophy," *Oxford Journal of Legal Studies* 24 (2004), especially in the long section titled "Legality" (23–37).

36. Joseph Raz insists that even judges are humans and that moral decision-making is the default mode of decision-making for them as it is for all of us. Joseph Raz, "Incorporation by Law," *Legal Theory* 10 (2004): 14. But for the difference between moral decision-making in one's own name and various forms of moral decision-making in the name of a whole society, see Jeremy Waldron, "Judges as Moral Reasoners," *International Journal of Constitutional Law* 7 (2009): 2.

37. Dworkin, *Law's Empire,* 256.

38. John Austin, *Lectures on Jurisprudence,* ed. Robert Campbell (London: Lawbook Exchange, 2004), 654, refers to "the childish fiction employed by our judges, that judiciary or common law is not made by them, but is a miraculous something made by nobody, existing, I suppose, from eternity, and merely declared from time to time by the judges."

39. One other rather technical point about Dworkin's work: I am assuming that his account of law as interpretation is not itself a theory of stare decisis (so that I am not smuggling in such a theory at this stage). His account of law as interpretation is a general theory about how to solve legal problems, how to interrogate legal materials, and

how to determine what the law says on some topic even when it does not speak clearly. I am bolstered in this assumption by the fact that at various points in *Law's Empire*, Dworkin seems to treat stare decisis as a separate issue that he has mostly not discussed. See, e.g., Dworkin, *Law's Empire*, 337,401–2. Law as interpretation is a way of dealing with precedents (as well as statutes and constitutional provisions). In its application to common law systems, it assumes that we are already committed to stare decisis. But it is somewhat complicated by Dworkin's suggestion that precedents have "gravitational force" as well as what he has called "enactment force." See Ronald Dworkin, *Taking Rights Seriously* (Cambridge, MA: Harvard University Press, 1977), 111. I think the interpretive method is supposed to be (among other things) a way of accounting for the former. And it is complicated, too, by his suggestion that what stare decisis amounts to as a principle in a given legal system will itself be a matter of interpretation. See Dworkin, *Law's Empire*, 24–26.

40. A norm is "universalizable" if its application is dictated by general terms and not restricted to particular cases by the use of a proper name or any particular reference. See R. M. Hare, *Freedom and Reason* (Oxford: Clarendon Press, 1963), 12. An example of a nonuniversalizable norm might be a bill of attainder or a norm specifying that the interest of some particular person is to be given priority.

Also, please note that I use the term "norm" advisedly to include rules, standards, and principles. This raises some difficult issues. Part of me believes that it is a matter of judgment whether the general norm presented by the precedent judge as the basis of her decision in a case is more like a standard than a rule; it depends on the circumstances of the case and their relation to background doctrine. After all, some explicit doctrinal norms have a rule-like form while others have a standard-like form; why shouldn't that be true of the norms embodied in precedents also? Stephen Perry, "Judicial Obligation, Precedent and the Common Law," *Oxford Journal of Legal Studies* 7 (1987): 235–36, has argued that the norm embodied in a precedent should always be understood as a principle. I don't think Perry's view necessarily conflicts with the first point I make in this endnote. Under the heading of "principle," Perry wants to pick up on the Dworkinian attribute of "weight" and the fact that the relevant norm does not have a canonical formulation. On the former point, see Dworkin, *Taking Rights Seriously*, 26–28. In my view, those two points could be granted and still there would be a matter of judgment whether the relevant "principle" was to be rulelike or standard-like. However, I suspect Perry disagrees; he thinks that the norms embodied in precedents (and principles generally) present their reasons transparently, whereas it is part of the idea of a rule that those reasons are opaque.

41. For more on this approach to the law, see Lawrence Solum, "Equity and the Rule of Law," in *The Rule of Law*, ed. Ian Shapiro (New York: New York University Press, 1994).

42. Joseph Raz, "The Rule of Law and Its Virtue," in *The Authority of Law: Essays on Law and Morality*, 2nd. ed. (Oxford: Clarendon Press, 2009), 213.

43. Hart, *Concept of Law*, 21; and John Austin, *The Province of Jurisprudence Determined*, ed. Wilfrid Rumble (Cambridge: Cambridge University Press, 1995), 28–29: "To frame a system of duties for every individual of the community, were simply impossible: and if it were possible, it were utterly useless."

44. Burke, *Reflections*, 59.

45. Neil MacCormick insists that even the most particularistic decision-making always has a universalistic dimension: "The 'because' of justification is a universal nexus, in this sense: for a given act to be right because of a given feature, or set of features, of a situation, materially the same act must be right in all situations in which materially the same feature or features are present." MacCormick, *Rhetoric and the Rule of Law*, 91.

46. Hayek, *Constitution of Liberty*, 152–53. Hayek defines law as "a 'once-and-for-all'" command that is directed to unknown people and that is abstracted from all particular circumstances of time and place and refers only to such conditions as may occur anywhere and at any time.

47. Antonin Scalia, "The Rule of Law as a Law of Rules," *University of Chicago Law Review* 56 (1989): 1175.

48. Scalia, 1185.

49. There has always been a problem about prospectivity so far as creative judicial decision-making is concerned. Fresh judicial decisions in areas of law previously indeterminate are always somewhat retroactive so far as the particular litigants are concerned. But notice that the precedent judge would not avoid this by eschewing the formulation of a general rule, for a particularized decision would be in effect retroactively too, or it would suffer from some exactly similar vice. And remember, too, that if there is a problem of retroactivity in judicial lawmaking, it is only a problem for the first pair of litigants; after that, the judge-made rule operates prospectively.

50. See MacCormick, *Rhetoric and the Rule of Law*, 91, for a similar view about generality: "This does not depend on any doctrine or practice of following precedents. On the contrary, the rationality of a system of precedents depends upon this fundamental property of normative justification." However, I am not sure whether this prior insistence on generality in MacCormick's work is anything much more than what I have called mere notional universalizability. What MacCormick says is,

> A justifiable decision of the legal dispute has to make a ruling on the issues in contention between the parties as to the relevancy of any proposition adduced as a proposition of law by either party or as to the interpretation of such a proposition. . . . A ruling of this kind must be logically universal or at least must be in terms which are reasonably universalizable. (152–53)

I maintain that the precedent judge (and her court) has to also establish and give actual positive presence to the principle of her decision as a legal norm.

51. Cf. Immanuel Kant, *The Metaphysics of Morals*, ed. Mary Gregor (Cambridge: Cambridge University Press 1996), 106: "Even if a civil society were to be dissolved . . . (e.g., if a people inhabiting an island decided to separate and disperse throughout the world), the last murderer remaining in prison would first have to be executed, so that each has done to him what his deeds deserve."

52. At this stage, I assume for simplicity that the precedent judge and the subsequent judge are on the same bench of the same court.

53. See Gerald Postema, "Protestant Interpretation and Social Practices," *Law and Philosophy* 6 (1987): 283.

54. In this respect, it is rather like the rigged generality that one finds in legislation that talks in "general" terms about any city "in the state which according to the last census had a population of more than 165,000 and less than 166,000." See Lon Fuller, *The Morality of Law* (New Haven, CT: Yale University Press, 1964), 47.

55. See Hans Kelsen, *General Theory of Law and State* (Cambridge, MA: Harvard University Press, 1945) 144; Joseph Raz, "Law and Value in Adjudication," in *Authority of Law*, 180.

56. Kelsen, *General Theory*, 144, acknowledges this, writing that "from the dynamic point of view, the decision of the court represents an individual norm, which is created on the basis of a general norm."

57. Joseph Raz, "Interpretation: Pluralism and Innovation," in *Between Authority and Interpretation* (Oxford: Oxford University Press, 2009), 320: "The power of courts to set binding precedents . . . [is] no more than an extension of the power to settle authoritatively the litigation before the court." But Raz goes on to indicate something that is quite like the position I am defending. The power of the courts to set precedents, he says, is "an extension of the power of the courts from authoritatively settling a particular cause of action to settling through their interpretive reasoning what is the law which will bind not only the litigants before them, but lower courts in the future, and through them bind all of us" (320).

58. See Neil MacCormick, "Why Cases Have Rationes and What These Are," in *Precedent in Law*, ed. Laurence Goldstein (Oxford: Oxford University Press, 1987), 171.

59. How he does this—the techniques he uses—is something we will not go into here. There is a massive literature on this. Melvin Eisenberg, for example, explains the difference between "minimalist," "result-centered," and "announcement" approaches and argues (persuasively, in my view) against any approach that confines itself to the first two. See Eisenberg, *The Nature of the Common Law* (Cambridge, MA: Harvard University Press, 1988), 52; Eisenberg, "Principles of Reasoning in the Common Law," in Edlin, *Common Law Theory*, 87–93. I really don't want to go into this here, not because I think it unimportant (it is hugely important), but because one can't do everything, and I don't think that these matters can be resolved without a clear sense of why stare decisis matters, which is what I am trying to establish in this chapter.

60. These reasons include plurality and diversity in the legislature, and the politics and compromise that particular formulations involve. See Jeremy Waldron, *Law and Disagreement* (Oxford: Oxford University Press, 1999), 77–87; and John Manning, "The Absurdity Doctrine," *Harvard Law Review* 116 (2003): 2409–19. For a discussion of why courts have no reason to treat common law formulations in a textualist spirit, see Perry, "Judicial Obligation," 235–36.

61. Cf. Planned Parenthood v. Casey, at 855, discussing the possibility that the law has moved on, leaving a given precedent as a doctrinal "remnant."

62. Practice Statement [1966] 3 All E.R. 77 (U.K., House of Lords).

63. See Eisenberg, *Nature of the Common Law*, 93:

> In the mode of legal reasoning known as distinguishing, the court begins with a rule that was explicitly adopted in a precedent and is literally applicable to the case at hand. The court does not reject the rule, but neither does it apply the rule. Instead the court determines that the adopted rule should be reformulated by carving out an exception that covers the case at hand.

64. The Practice Statement concluded as follows: "In this connexion [their lordships] will bear in mind the danger of disturbing retrospectively the basis on which contracts, settlement of property and fiscal arrangements have been entered into and also the especial need for certainty as to the criminal law." Practice Statement [1966], at 77.

65. Raz, "Rule of Law and Its Virtue," 214.

66. Aristotle, *Politics,* ed. Stephen Everson (Cambridge: Cambridge University Press, 1988), 49 (bk. II, ch. 8).

67. Duxbury, *Nature and Authority of Precedent,* 1–2.

68. I make a great deal of it in Jeremy Waldron, *Partly Laws Common to All Mankind: Foreign Law in American Courts* (New Haven, CT: Yale University Press, 2012), 109–41. See also Jeremy Waldron, "Treating Like Cases Alike in the World: The Theoretical Basis of the Demand for Legal Unity," in *Highest Courts and Globalisation,* ed. Sam Muller and Sidney Richards (The Hague: Hague Academic Press, 2010), 99.

69. Eisenberg, *Nature of the Common Law,* 83, denies that reasoning by analogy is "qualitatively different from reasoning from precedent . . . which . . . turn[s] on reasoning from standards." He says it differs from reasoning from precedent "only in form."

70. Cf. David Lyons, "Formal Justice, Moral Commitment, and Judicial Precedent," *Journal of Philosophy,* 81 (1984): 585, quoted in Theodore Benditt, "The Rule of Precedent," in Goldstein, *Precedent in Law,* 92. For the idea of comparative justice, see Joel Feinberg, "Noncomparative Justice," in *Rights, Justice, and the Bounds of Liberty* (Princeton, NJ: Princeton University Press, 1980), 265.

71. Duxbury, *Nature and Authority of Precedent,* 150.

72. Welch v. Texas Department of Highways and Public Transportation, 483 U.S. 468, 478–79 (1987). I am obliged to Jane Pek, "Things Better Left Unwritten: Constitutional Text and the Rule of Law," *New York University Law Review* 83 (2008): 1998, for this reference.

9. Legislation and the Rule of Law

1. The literature is very extensive. For examples, see Thomas Carothers, "The Rule of Law Revival," *Foreign Affairs* 77 (1998): 95; Carothers, *Aiding Democracy Abroad: The Learning Curve* (Washington, DC: Carnegie Endowment for International Peace, 1999); Robert Barro, "Determinants of Democracy," *Journal of Political Economy* 107 (1999): 158–83; Ibrahim Shihata, "The World Bank and 'Governance' Issues in Its Borrowing Members," in *The World Bank in a Changing World: Selected Essays,* ed. Antonio Parra, Barber Conable, Franziska Tschofen, and Ibrahim Shihata, vol. 1 (Boston: Martinus Nijhoff, 1991), 53; Shihata, "Legal Framework for Development," in Parra et al., *World Bank in a Changing World,* vol. 2 (Boston: Martinus Nijhoff, 1995), 127; and Shihata, "Relevant Issues in the Establishment of a Sound Legal Framework for a Market Economy," in Parra et al., *World Bank in a Changing World,* 2:187.

2. See, for example, John Williamson, "Democracy and the 'Washington Consensus,'" *World Development* 21 (1993): 1329. I am obliged to J. M. Ngugi, "Policing Neo-liberal Reforms: The Rule of Law as an Enabling and Restrictive Discourse," *University of Pennsylvania Journal of International Economic Law* 26 (2005): 599, for this reference.

3. For other critiques, see Ngugi, "Policing Neo-liberal Reforms"; K. E. Davis, "What Can the Rule of Law Variable Tell Us about Rule of Law Reforms?," *Michigan Journal of International Law* 26 (2004): 141; and Frank Upham, "Mythmaking in the Rule of Law Orthodoxy" (working paper no. 30, Democracy and Rule of Law Project, Carnegie Endowment for International Peace, Washington, DC, September 2002), http://www .carnegieendowment.org/files/wp30.pdf.

4. See Jeremy Waldron, *The Dignity of Legislation* (Cambridge: Cambridge University Press, 1999).

5. J. Wolfensohn quoted in Upham, "Mythmaking," 10.

6. Compare Davis, "What Can the Rule of Law Tell Us," 151: "The selection of illegal strikes as opposed to violations of health and safety legislation to illustrate the concept of routine non-compliance with law is telling."

7. Daniel Kaufmann, Aart Kraay, and Massimo Mastruzzi, "Governance Matters IV: Governance Indicators for 1996–2004" (World Bank Policy Research Working Paper Series No. 3630, May 2005), 130–31, http://papers.ssrn.com/sol3/papers.cfm?abstract_id =718081.

8. Barro, "Determinants of Democracy," 173.

9. Carothers, *Aiding Democracy Abroad*, 164.

10. F. A. Hayek, *Rules and Order*, vol. 1 of *Law, Legislation and Liberty* (Chicago: University of Chicago Press, 1973), 72–73, 124–44. In his earlier discussions of the rule of law, e.g., in F. A. Hayek, *The Constitution of Liberty* (London: Macmillan, 1960), 157, the strong form of the view under consideration is discernible (just), but it is very muted. Mostly, the conception of the rule of law presented in the earlier book could be applied naturally to legislation, as when Hayek says,

> It is because the lawgiver does not know the particular cases to which his rules will apply, and it is because the judge who applies them has no choice in drawing the conclusions that follow from the existing body of rules and the particular facts of the case, that it can be said that laws and not men rule. (*Constitution of Liberty,* 153)

11. The view under consideration is associated affirmatively, with a celebration of something like the common law. Needless to say, in this celebration, the rule-of-law difficulties of the common law—its opacity, the ad hoc character of its development, its unpredictability, its inherent retroactivity—are conveniently forgotten. For good accounts, see Jeremy Bentham, *Of Laws in General,* ed. H. L. A. Hart (London: Athlone Press, 1970), 184–95; and Gerald Postema, *Bentham and the Common Law Tradition* (Oxford: Clarendon Press, 1986), 267–301.

12. Hayek, *Rules and Order,* 88–89.

13. See, e.g., Katharina Pistor, "Company Law and Corporate Governance in Russia," in *The Rule of Law and Economic Reform in Russia,* ed. Jeffrey Sachs and Katharina Pistor (Boulder, CO: Westview Press, 1997), 165. See also the section titled "Legislation to Encourage Foreign Investment" in Shihata, "Relevant Issues," 138.

14. For example, see Shihata, "Relevant Issues," 205: "An over-regulated economy undermines new investment, increases the costs of existing ones and leads to the spread of

corruption. Multiplication of laws and regulations often reduces their quality and the chances of their enforcement. The absence of judicial review, or its high cost . . . add to the negative impact."

15. See Joseph Raz, "The Rule of Law and Its Virtue," in *The Authority of Law* (Oxford: Clarendon Press, 1979), 210–11.

16. See, e.g., Fareed Zakaria, *The Future of Freedom: Illiberal Democracy at Home and Abroad* (New York: Norton, 2003).

17. Barro, "Determinants of Democracy," 11: "The advanced Western countries would contribute more to the welfare of poor nations by exporting their economic systems, notably property rights and free markets, rather than their political systems, which typically developed after reasonable standards of living had been attained."

18. See also Robert Barro, *Getting It Right: Markets and Choices in a Free Society* (Cambridge, MA: MIT Press, 1996), 7: "Although tests of this hypothesis are hampered by the limited availability of data on the rule-of-law concept, the information available suggests that, if anything, democracy is a moderate deterrent to the maintenance of the rule of law. This result is not surprising because more democracy means that the political process allows the majority to extract resources legally from minorities (or powerful interest groups to extract resources legally from the disorganized majority)."

19. However, as I noted in Waldron, *Dignity of Legislation,* 15–16, and in Waldron, *Law and Disagreement* (Oxford: Oxford University Press, 1999), 33–48, there is a troubling tendency in modern positivist jurisprudence to play down the centrality of legislation, particularly democratic legislation, in our philosophical understanding of law.

20. See also Jeremy Waldron, "Principles of Legislation," in *The Least Examined Branch: The Role of Legislatures in the Constitutional State,* ed. Richard Bauman and Tsvi Kahana (Cambridge: Cambridge University Press, 2006), 22–23.

21. Alexis de Tocqueville, *Democracy in America* (London: Penguin Books, 1994), 244–48.

22. Tocqueville, 247.

23. Thomas Hobbes, *Leviathan,* ed. Richard Tuck (Cambridge: Cambridge University Press, 1996), 471, attributes the contrary view (that rule by law is a genuine alternative to rule by men) to Aristotle:

> And therefore this is another error of Aristotle's politics, that in a well-ordered Commonwealth, not men should govern, but the laws. What man that has his natural senses, though he can neither write nor read, does not find himself governed by them he fears, and believes can kill or hurt him when he obeyeth not? Or that believes the law can hurt him; that is, words and paper, without hands and swords of men?

But actually, Aristotle, *The Politics,* ed. Stephen Everson (Cambridge: Cambridge University Press, 1988), 66 (bk. III, ch. 10), was well aware of the point, and took the provenance of laws in different regimes of rule by men as an important variable in his rule-of-law account:

> Someone may say that it is bad in any case for a man, subject as he is to all the accidents of human passion, to have the supreme power, rather than the law. But

what if the law itself be democratical or oligarchical, how will that help us out of our difficulties? Not at all; the same consequences will follow.

24. See, e.g., Jeffrey Kahn, "The Search for the Rule of Law in Russia," *Georgetown Journal of International Law* 37 (2006): 359–61. See, generally, S. Coyle, "Positivism, Idealism and the Rule of Law" *Oxford Journal of Legal Studies* 26 (2006): 257; and John Gardner, "Legal Positivism: 5 1/2 Myths," *American Journal of Jurisprudence* 46 (2001): 207–11.

25. Notice, though, that this impression is clearest when we focus on traditional "sovereign / command" versions of legal positivism, like those of Bentham and Austin. The tension between positivism and the rule of law is less palpable in versions that eschew the command theory—e.g., in Kelsen's or in Hart's theory. Law on these accounts is presented not as top-down command but as a system of rules nested within rules.

26. See Waldron, *Dignity of Legislation,* 12, 24.

27. See, e.g., Herbert Wechsler, "Toward Neutral Principles of Constitutional Law," *Harvard Law Review* 73 (1959): 11–12.

28. See the discussion in Jeremy Waldron, "Is the Rule of Law an Essentially Contested Concept (in Florida)?," *Law and Philosophy* 21 (2002): 142–43, 147–48.

29. Bush v. Gore, 531 US 98, 128–29 (Stevens J., dissenting):

> It is confidence in the men and women who administer the judicial system that is the true backbone of the rule of law. Time will one day heal the wound to that confidence that will be inflicted by today's decision. One thing, however, is certain. Although we may never know with complete certainty the identity of the winner of this year's Presidential election, the identity of the loser is perfectly clear. It is the Nation's confidence in the judge as an impartial guardian of the rule of law.

30. Edward Rubin, "Law and Legislation in the Administrative State," *Columbia Law Review* 89 (1989): 372–73.

31. Robert Cooter, "The Rule of State Law versus the Rule-of-Law State: Economic Analysis of the Legal Foundations of Development," in *The Law and Economics of Development,* ed. Edgardo Buscaglia, William Ratliff, and Robert Cooter (Greenwich, CT: JAI Press, 1997), 101.

32. Albert Venn Dicey, *Introduction to the Study of the Law of the Constitution* (Indianapolis: Liberty Classics, 1982), 268.

33. Dicey, 271, 273.

34. Dicey, 269.

35. English courts have been permitted to consult legislative history only since *Pepper (Inspector of Taxes) v. Hart* [1993] AC 593, and only in very constrained circumstances. For discussion of the present position, see Lord Steyn, "*Pepper v. Hart*: A Re-examination," *Oxford Journal of Legal Studies* 21 (2001): 59.

36. Consider, for example, the argument in 1656 of James Harrington, *The Commonwealth of Oceana,* ed. J. G. A. Pocock (Cambridge: Cambridge University Press, 1992), 22–25, discussing the articulate relation between senate and assembly in the proposing of laws and voting on laws.

37. Cf. John Locke, *Two Treatises of Government,* ed. Peter Laslett (Cambridge: Cambridge University Press, 1988), 330 (II, § 94): "By which means every single person became subject, equally with other the meanest men, to those laws, which he himself, as part of the legislative, had established; nor could any one, by his own authority; avoid the force of the law, when once made; nor by any pretence of superiority plead exemption, thereby to license his own, or the miscarriages of any of his dependents."

38. Dicey, *Introduction to the Study,* 268.

39. Aristotle, *The Rhetoric,* ed. G. A. Kennedy (New York: Oxford University Press, 1991), 32 (1354b). This passage is cited repeatedly by Antonin Scalia, "The Rule of Law as a Law of Rules," *University of Chicago Law Review* 56 (1989): 1176, 1182.

40. Jeremy Waldron, "Compared to What? Judicial Activism and the New Zealand Parliament," *New Zealand Law Journal* 441 (2005): 144.

41. Lon Fuller, *The Morality of Law* (New Haven, CT: Yale University Press, 1964), 95.

42. See, e.g., Teague v. Lane, 489 U.S. 288 (1989).

43. Lon Fuller, "The Forms and Limits of Adjudication," *Harvard Law Review* 92 (1978): 353. See the discussion in Chapter 7 above.

44. We sometimes say, lazily, that Fuller's eight principles are procedural rather than substantive ideals. And Fuller says this too, in *Morality of Law,* 96. But that is not the case: with the possible exception of congruence, Fuller's eight principles have nothing to do with the procedures by which law is made or applied; they have to do with the formal characteristics of enactments. (The laziness here is due to a widespread but false assumption that everything that is not substantive is procedural.)

45. Compare Raz, "Rule of Law and Its Virture," 216–17.

46. Note the acknowledgement in Fuller, *Morality of Law,* 39, that the rule-of-law criteria are multiple, and in each case, a matter of degree.

47. See F. A. Hayek, *The Mirage of Social Justice,* vol. 2 of *Law, Legislation and Liberty* (London: Routledge & Kegan Paul, 1976), 85–88.

48. Hayek, *Mirage of Social Justice,* 87: "There is no reason why in a free society government should not assure to all protection against severe deprivation in the form of an assured minimum income, or a floor below which nobody need descend. . . . So long as such a uniform minimum income is provided outside the market to all those who, for any reason, are unable to earn in the market an adequate maintenance, this need not lead to a restriction of freedom, or conflict with the rule of law."

49. Guido Pincione, "Market Rights and the Rule of Law: A Case for Procedural Constitutionalism," *Harvard Journal of Law and Public Policy* 26 (2003): 413–14.

50. Todd Zywicki, "The Rule of Law, Freedom, and Prosperity," *Supreme Court Economic Review* 10 (2003): 8.

51. F. A. Hayek, *The Road to Serfdom* (Chicago: University of Chicago Press, 1972), 72–87.

52. Thus, consider Fuller, *Morality of Law,* 173, 176:

Tasks of economic allocation cannot be effectively performed within the limits set by the internal morality of law. The attempt to accomplish such tasks through adjudicative forms is certain to result in inefficiency, hypocrisy, moral confusion, and frustration. . . . If these portents of what lies ahead can be trusted, then it is plain that we shall be faced with problems of institutional design unprecedented in scope and importance. It is inevitable that the legal profession will play a large role in solving these problems. The great danger is that we will unthinkingly carry over to new conditions traditional institutions and procedures that have already demonstrated their faults of design. As lawyers we have a natural inclination to "judicialize" every function of government. Adjudication is a process with which we are familiar and which enables us to show to advantage our special talents. Yet we must face the plain truth that adjudication is an ineffective instrument for economic management and for governmental participation in the allocation of economic resources.

53. See, e.g., Kahn, "Search for the Rule of Law," 363–64.

54. Kahn, 356 ff.

55. Brian Tamanaha, "The Tension between Legal Instrumentalism and the Rule of Law," *Syracuse Journal of International Law and Commerce* 33 (2005): 132.

56. Hayek, *Rules and Order*, 112–13.

57. Robert Bolt, *A Man for All Seasons* (New York: Random House, 1962), 152–53, quoted in Kahn, "Search for the Rule of Law," 354.

58. Kahn, 372.

59. Tamanaha, "Tension," 133.

60. For a useful discussion, see J. F. Manning, "Textualism and the Equity of the Statute," *Columbia Law Review* 101 (2001): 1.

61. See, e.g., Matthew Stephenson, "The Rule of Law as a Goal of Development Policy" (brief prepared for the World Bank, 2001), cited in Ngugi, "Policing Neo-liberal Reforms," 534.

62. See, e.g., Paul Craig, "Formal and Substantive Conceptions of the Rule of Law: An Analytical Framework," *Public Law* (Autumn 1997): 467.

63. Fuller, *Morality of Law*, 39–40, 162–63. This must be distinguished from a further, better-known and much more controversial thesis of Fuller's which is that following the rule of law is incompatible with wickedness or at the very least that it makes substantive injustice much less likely. This latter thesis of Fuller's may be connected with the one in the text in the way suggested by John Finnis, *Natural Law and Natural Rights* (Clarendon Press, 1980) 273.

A tyranny devoted to pernicious ends has no self-sufficient reason to submit itself to the discipline of operating consistently through the demanding processes of law, granted that the rational point of such self-discipline is the very value of reciprocity, fairness, and respect for persons which the tyrant, ex hypothesi, holds in contempt.

Or it may be defended on the basis that evil aims are in their nature less amenable to the sort of formal discipline imposed by Fuller's inner morality of law. Lon Fuller, "Positivism and Fidelity to Law: A Reply to Hart," *Harvard Law Review* 71 (1959): 636–37,

645–48, 650–52. In any case, the Fullerian version of (β) may be true even if the further thesis considered in this footnote is not.

64. Raz, "Rule of Law and Its Virtue," 225–26, suggests that the rule of law is of this character:

> Of course, conformity to the rule of law also enables the law to serve bad purposes. That does not show that it is not a virtue, just as the fact that a sharp knife can be used to harm does not show that being sharp is not a good-making characteristic for knives. . . . Being sharp is an inherent good-making characteristic of knives. A good knife is, among other things, a sharp knife. Similarly, conformity to the rule of law is an inherent value of laws, indeed it is their most important inherent value. . . . Conformity to the rule of law is . . . a moral requirement when necessary to enable the law to perform useful social functions; just as it may be of moral importance to produce a sharp knife when it is required for a moral purpose.

But mostly Raz adopts a version of (β), albeit a negative version: "The rule of law is a negative virtue in two senses: conformity to it does not cause good except through avoiding evil and the evil which is avoided is evil which could only have been caused by the law itself." Raz, "Rule of Law and Its Virtue," 224.

65. See Fuller, *Morality of Law,* 96–97, 200–201.

66. See Stephenson (as quoted in Ngugi, p. 536): "What we really should be interested in—that is, the essence of the rule of law—is the substantive or functional outcome. Whether or not the formal characteristics contribute to that outcome ought to be a matter for research, not presumption."

67. For concerns about the way in which the use of a substantive conception of the rule of law forecloses political debate, see Ngugi, "Policing Neo-liberal Reforms," 515, 554–66.

68. E. P. Thompson, *Whigs and Hunters: The Origin of the Black Act* (Harmondsworth, UK: Penguin Books, 1977), 266:

> I am insisting only upon the obvious point, which some modern Marxists have overlooked, that there is a difference between arbitrary power and the rule of law. We ought to expose the shams and inequities which may be concealed beneath this law. But the rule of law itself, the imposing of effective inhibitions upon power and the defence of the citizen from power's all-intrusive claims, seems to me to be an unqualified human good. To deny or belittle this good is, in this dangerous century when the resources and pretensions of power continue to enlarge, a desperate error of intellectual abstraction.

For subsequent discussion, see Morton Horwitz, "The Rule of Law: An Unqualified Human Good?," *Yale Law Journal* 86 (1977): 566; Lynn Henderson, "Authoritarianism and the Rule of Law," *Indiana Law Journal* 66 (1991): 399.

69. Cf. Raz, "Rule of Law and Its Virtue," 211: "If the rule of law is the rule of good law, then to explain its nature is to propound a complete social philosophy. But if so, the term lacks any useful function."

70. See, e.g., Williamson, "Democracy and the 'Washington Consensus,'" 1330.

71. David Hume, *A Treatise of Human Nature,* ed. L. A. Selby-Bigge and P. H. Nidditch (Oxford: Clarendon Press, 1978), 487–89. (I have reversed the order of two quotations here, without altering the sense.)

72. H. L. A. Hart, *The Concept of Law,* 2nd ed. (Oxford: Clarendon Press, 1994), 193–200.

73. See James Buchanan, *The Limits of Liberty: Between Anarchy and Leviathan* (Chicago: University of Chicago Press, 1975), 17–34.

10. Rule *by* Law

1. Albert Venn Dicey, *Introduction to the Study of the Law of the Constitution,* 8th ed. of 1915 (Indianapolis: Liberty Classics, 1982), 107.

2. John Adams, in his *Constitution for the Commonwealth of Massachusetts* (1780), justified the separation of powers by reference to the aspiration that "the government of this commonwealth" might be "a government of laws and not of men." Aristotle, *Politics,* ed. Stephen Everson (Cambridge: Cambridge University Press, 1988), 88–89 (bk. III, ch. 16). The Greek phrase is translated by Jowett as "the rule of the law": "The rule of law, it is argued, is preferable to that of any individual (τὸν ἄρα νόμον ἄρχειν αἱρετώτερον μᾶλλον ἢ τῶν πολιτῶν ἕνα). On the same principle, even if it be better for certain individuals to govern, they should be made only guardians and ministers of the law."

3. Lon Fuller, *The Morality of Law* (New Haven, CT: Yale University Press, 1964), ch. 2. Fuller doesn't use the term "the rule of law" in the book, except for a few pages (209–11) in the final chapter, "Reply to Critics."

4. Dicey, *Introduction to the Study,* 107.

5. Constitutional Reform Act 2005 (UK), § 1(a).

6. Section 4 of the Lawyers and Conveyancers Act (NZ) 2006.

7. Ronald Dworkin, "The Model of Rules," in *Taking Rights Seriously* (Cambridge, MA: Harvard University Press, 1977). See also Dworkin's discussion of "legality" in "Hart's Postscript and the Character of Political Philosophy," *Oxford Journal of Legal Studies* 24 (2004): 1.

8. Riggs v. Palmer, 115 N.Y. 506 (1889).

9. Occasionally, however, "rule by law" is used just in its ordinary idiomatic sense (in connection with the rule of law), not charged with the special meaning we are considering here. See, for example, Richard Fallon, "The Rule of Law as a Concept in Constitutional Discourse," *Columbia Law Review* 97 (1997): 23.

10. Tom Ginsberg and Tamir Moustafa, eds., *Rule by Law: The Politics of Courts in Authoritarian Regimes* (Cambridge: Cambridge University Press, 2008).

11. Thomas Hobbes, *De Cive: The English Version,* ed. Howard Warrender (Oxford: Oxford University Press, 1983) 74–75 (VI, 9).

12. Thomas Hobbes, *Leviathan,* ed. Richard Tuck (Cambridge: Cambridge University Press, 1988), chs. 26 and 29.

13. John Locke, *Two Treatises of Government,* ed. Peter Laslett (Cambridge: Cambridge University Press, 1988), 346 (II, § 93).

14. Hobbes, *Leviathan,* ch. 29.

15. See Joseph Raz, "The Rule of Law and Its Virtue," in *The Authority of Law: Essays on Law and Morality* (Oxford: Clarendon Press, 1979); Ronald Dworkin, "Political Judges and the Rule of Law," in *A Matter of Principle* (Cambridge, MA: Harvard University Press, 1985); Tom Bingham, *The Rule of Law* (London: Allen Lane, 2010); Fuller, *Morality of Law;* Matthew Kramer, "On the Moral Status of the Rule of Law," *Cambridge Law Journal* 63 (2004): 65; Andrei Marmor, "The Rule of Law and Its Limits," *Law and Philosophy* 23 (2004): 1; and Jeremy Waldron, "Is the Rule of Law an Essentially Contested Concept (in Florida)?," *Law and Philosophy* 21 (2002): 137.

16. See, e.g., David Dyzenhaus, *The Constitution of Law: Legality in a Time of Emergency* (Cambridge: Cambridge University Press, 2006), 18ff.; and Brian Tamanaha, *On the Rule of Law: History, Politics, Theory* (Cambridge: Cambridge University Press, 2004), 92–93.

17. Thomas Carothers, "The Rule-of-Law Revival," *Foreign Affairs* 77 (1998); and Carothers, "Rule of Law Temptations," *Fletcher Forum of World Affairs* 33 (2009).

18. H. L. A. Hart, "Positivism and the Separation of Law and Morals," *Harvard Law Review* 71 (1958): 593; Lon Fuller, "Positivism and Fidelity to Law: A Reply to Hart," *Harvard Law Review* 71 (1958): 630; H. L. A. Hart, *The Concept of Law*, 2nd ed. (Oxford: Clarendon Press, 1994), 206–7; Fuller, *Morality of Law;* H. L. A. Hart, review of *The Morality of Law,* by Lon Fuller, *Harvard Law Review* 78 (1965): 1281. The paper I presented at the conference was Jeremy Waldron, "The Rule of Law in Contemporary Liberal Theory," *Ratio Juris* 2 (1989): 79.

19. F. A. Hayek, *Rules and Order,* vol. 1 of *Law, Legislation and Liberty* (London: Routledge & Kegan Paul, 1973); and Michael Oakeshott, "The Rule of Law," in *On History and Other Essays* (Indianapolis: Liberty Fund, 1999).

20. E.g., Adrian Vermeule, "Our Schmittian Administrative Law," *Harvard Law Review* 122 (2009): 1101–2: "Rule by law lacks content, whereas the rule of law adds a broad set of procedural and substantive norms associated with liberal legalism and, in America and the Commonwealth countries, the common law."

21. For "telephone justice," see Jeffrey Kahn, "The Search for the Rule of Law in Russia," *Georgetown Journal of International Law* 37 (2006): 379.

22. See, e.g., David S. Rubenstein, "Taking Care of the Rule of Law," *George Washington Law Review* 86 (2018): 182: "Substantive (or thick) rule of law conceptions . . . demand more than rule by law; they require rule by good law." See also Vermeule, "Our Schmittian Administrative Law," 1101, which says that the distinction between the rule of law and rule by law "is roughly equivalent to the jurisprudential distinction between the 'thick' and 'thin' versions of the rule of law." Vermeule confuses this, however, by saying that Fuller's principles of legality are characteristic of a thick conception (1101). That is not so; they are almost always understood in the literature—and will be here—as characteristic of a thin conception.

23. Raz, "Rule of Law and Its Virtue," 211.

24. Bingham, *Rule of Law,* 67.

25. Charles Lugosi, "Rule of Law or Rule by Law: The Detention of Yaser Hamdi," *American Journal of Criminal Law* 30 (2003): 278.

26. Charles Lugosi, "How Secular Ideology Is Marginalizing the Rule of Law and Catholic Contributions to Law and Society," *Journal of Catholic Legal Studies* 47 (2008): 152.

27. Randall Peerenboom, "Let One Hundred Flowers Bloom, One Hundred Schools Contend: Debating Rule of Law in China," *Michigan Journal of International Law* 23 (2002): 500.

28. Arthur Garrison, "The Traditions and History of the Meaning of the Rule of Law," *Georgetown Journal of Law and Public Policy* 12 (2014): 581.

29. Lucy Hornby, "Freedom Charter: Magna Carta Non Grata as Beijing Blocks Exhibition," *Financial Times*, October 15, 2015.

30. "China with Legal Characteristics," *The Economist*, November 1, 2014.

31. Yuanyuan Shen, "Conceptions and Receptions of Legality: Understanding the Complexity of Law Reform in Modern China," in *The Limits of the Rule of Law in China*, ed. Karen Turner, James Feinerman, and R. Kent Guy (Seattle: University of Washington Press, 2015), 26.

32. Shen, 27.

33. Paul Gewirtz, "What China Means by 'Rule of Law,'" *New York Times*, October 19, 2014; and Nancy Tang et al., "China's 'Rule by Law' Takes an Ugly Turn: A Recent Spate of Arrests and Detentions Is Another Sign of the Communist Party's Intolerance for Dissent," *Foreign Policy*, July 14, 2015.

34. Peerenboom, "Let One Hundred Flowers Bloom," 512.

35. F. A. Hayek, *The Road to Serfdom* (Chicago: University of Chicago Press, 1976); cf. Dicey, *Introduction to the Study*, lv: "The ancient veneration for the rule of law has in England suffered during the last thirty years a marked decline."

36. Arthur Garrison, "Hamiltonian and Madisonian Democracy, the Rule of Law and Why the Courts have a Role in the War on Terrorism," *Journal of the Institute of Justice and International Studies* 8 (2008): 132.

37. Lugosi, "Rule of Law or Rule by Law," 278.

38. Peerenboom, "Let One Hundred Flowers Bloom," 523–24.

39. Peerenboom, 524:

> The distinction between rule by law and rule of law seems to be a conceptual one rather than an empirical one. A system in which law is only meant to serve as a tool of the ruling regime without binding government officials is rule by law. It seems counter-intuitive to argue that a system in which law is meant to be supreme but which falls short of that ideal in practice is for that reason rule by law.

40. What follows summarizes work I have done in chapter 3 of my book *The Rule of Law and the Measure of Property* (Cambridge: Cambridge University Press, 2012), and in "The Rule of Law in Public Law," in *Cambridge Companion to Public Law*, ed. Mark Elliott (Cambridge: Cambridge University Press, 2015). See also Chapter 9 above.

41. See WJP Rule of Law Index, World Justice Project, https://worldjusticeproject.org /rule-of-law-index/global/2022 (last visited December 13, 2022).

42. See "CFS 2012–2013 Rule of Law Index (RLI)," Center for Financial Stability, http://www.centerforfinancialstability.org/rli.php (last visited December 13, 2022). In the 2012–2013 CFS report, New Zealand ranks number 2 overall for rule of law in this index,

but number 14 for "Burden of Government Regulation." The United States ranked number 34 for rule of law overall and number 76 for burden of government regulation.

43. Economists are ingenuous about the advantages of this approach. Defending the use of rule-of-law indices like those of the Center for Financial Stability, Harvard economics professor Robert Barro observes that "the general idea of these indexes is to gauge the attractiveness of a country's investment climate by considering the effectiveness of law enforcement, the sanctity of contracts, and the state of other influences on the security of property rights." When he says "the attractiveness of a country's investment climate," Barro means its attractiveness to foreign investors. He believes "the willingness of [such] customers to pay substantial amounts for this information is perhaps some testament to their validity." See Robert Barro, "Determinants of Democracy," *Journal of Political Economy* 107 (1999): 173.

44. I discuss this in Chapter 11.

45. In this regard, the rule of law is sometimes set against democracy. In the order of developmental priorities, it is sometimes said that we need secure rule of law first, by establishing a strong culture of opposition to overregulation, before we set up democratic assemblies with popular majorities that may tend to abuse their legislative powers in this way. I have spent some of the best years of my life arguing for the dignity of legislation and against this antilegislative view of the rule of law—in my Hamlyn Lectures, for example, on *Rule of Law and The Measure of Property,* as well as in Chapter 9 above.

46. Cf. Robert Cooter, "The Rule of State Law and the Rule-of-Law State: Economic Analysis of the Legal Foundations of Development," bePress (Berkeley Law), January 31, 1997, https://works.bepress.com/robert_cooter/48/.

47. For an extreme version of this, distinguishing sharply between law and legislation, see Hayek, *Rules and Order,* 72–93.

48. See Gianluigi Palombella, "The Measure of Law: The Non-instrumental Legal Side from the State to the Global Setting (and from Hamdan to al Jedda)," *Ius Gentium* 38 (2014): 129.

49. Thomas Hobbes, as cited by James Harrington, *The Commonwealth of Oceana,* ed. J. A. G. Pocock (Cambridge: Cambridge University Press, 1992).

50. Sophocles, *Antigone,* lines 496–503.

51. See Richard Epstein, *Design for Liberty: Private Property, Public Administration, and the Rule of Law* (Cambridge, MA: Harvard University Press, 2011).

52. See Gerald Postema, *Bentham and the Common Law Tradition* (Oxford: Clarendon Press, 1989), 273–75.

53. Hayek, *Rules and Order,* 88.

54. Hayek, 89. And indeed, this is what Hayek himself had insisted on in his earlier work on the rule of law in *The Constitution of Liberty* (London: Macmillan, 1960).

55. Fuller, "Positivism and Fidelity to Law," 648–57, 658–60; Hannah Arendt, *The Origins of Totalitarianism* (New York: Harcourt, Brace, Jovanovich, 1951), 378 ff.; and Timothy Snyder, *Black Earth: The Holocaust as History and Warning* (New York: Crown 2015).

56. Gary Goodpaster, "Law Reform in Developing Countries," *Transnational Law and Contemporary Problems* 13 (2003): 686.

57. Kenneth Winston, "The Internal Morality of Chinese Legalism," *Singapore Journal of Legal Studies* (December 2005): 316.

58. Martin Krygier, "Rule of Law (and *Rechtsstaat*)" (UNSW Law Research Paper No. 2013-52, University of New Soutch Wales, August 15, 2013), https://papers.ssrn.com /sol3/papers.cfm?abstract_id=2311874, quoting Gianfranco Poggi.

59. The situation is complicated by the fact that some of the norms associated with ruling by law can be found also in constitutions and bills of rights and enforced as such under the rule of law. The prohibitions on ex post facto legislation and bills of attainder in Article I of the US Constitution are good examples. Other such norms have no constitutional presence, or their constitutional presence is more indirect and a matter of inference and controversy; the requirement that laws must be brought to the attention of those whom they obligate is an example.

60. For one thing, the NZ Parliament was in a sense constrained after 1978 by its ratification of the International Covenant on Civil and Political Rights, whose Article 15(1) also prohibits the retroactive imposition of criminal liability. But that constraint could not be enforced domestically. For the use of international or regional rights conventions to convey some of the requirements of rule by law, see Jeremy Waldron, "Rule-of-Law-Rights and Populist Impatience," in *Human Rights in a Time of Populism,* ed. Gerald Neuman (Cambridge: Cambridge University Press, 2020).

61. Cf. Jon Elster, *Ulysses and the Sirens* (Cambridge: Cambridge University Press, 1984).

62. For the significance of the phrase "under the auspices of," see Raz, "Rule of Law and Its Virtue," 213:

> The doctrine of the rule of law does not deny that every legal system should consist of both general, open, and stable rules (the popular conception of law) and particular laws (legal orders), an essential tool in the hands of the executive and the judiciary alike. . . . What the doctrine requires is the subjection of particular laws to general, open, and stable ones. It is one of the important principles of the doctrine that the making of particular laws should be guided by open and relatively stable general rules.

63. Dicey, *Introduction to the Study,* 110.

64. See, for example, the discussion in Benjamin Kleinerman, *The Discretionary President: The Promise and Peril of Executive Power* (Lawrence: University Press of Kansas, 2009). See also Richard Pious, "Public Law and the 'Executive' Constitution," in *Executing the Constitution: Putting the President Back into the Constitution,* ed. C.S. Kelly (New York: SUNY Press, 2007).

65. See Thomas Langston and Michael Lind, "John Locke and the Limits of Presidential Prerogative," *Polity* 24 (1991): 49.

66. Elias CJ in Hamed v. R [2011] NZSC 101, [2012] 2 NZLR 305, § 24. She quoted a British case, R v. Somerset County Council, ex parte Fewings [1995] 1 All ER 513 (QB) at 524, per Laws J.:

> For private persons, the rule is that you may do anything you choose which the law does not prohibit. It means that the freedoms of the private citizen are not

conditional upon some distinct and affirmative justification for which he must burrow in the law books. Such a notion would be anathema to our English legal traditions. But for public bodies the rule is opposite, and so of another character altogether. It is that action to be taken must be justified by positive law.

See Minister for Canterbury Earthquake Recovery v. Fowler Developments Ltd. [2013] NZCA 588.

67. For a pragmatic defense of the third source, see Bruce Harris's comment on Chief Justice Elias's position in Hamed, at B. V. Harris, "Recent Judicial Recognition of the Third Source of Authority for Government Action," New Zealand Universities Law Review 26 (2014): 60:

In an ideal world the Chief Justice's point of view in expecting democratic pre-action approval for all executive action should prevail. However, in the real world there are good practical reasons for recognizing that the government should be free to do that which is not prohibited by positive law. It is not possible for Parliament to anticipate all needed government authority, or for it to provide for all needed government authority with appropriate prescription.

It is exactly this sort of casual approach that drove rule-of-law sticklers like Albert Venn Dicey to despair!

68. Waldron, "Is the Rule of Law Essentially Contested?" See also Fallon, "The Rule of Law as a Concept in Constitutional Discourse," Columbia Law Review 97 (1997): 7.

69. See Fuller, Morality of Law, 39, and the interpretation of Fuller's account in Jeremy Waldron, "Why Law—Efficacy, Freedom, or Fidelity?," Law and Philosophy 13 (1994): 259.

11. The Rule of Law in Public Law

1. Cf. Hans Kelsen, Pure Theory of Law, trans. Max Knight (Berkeley: University of California Press, 1967), 282: "The Pure Theory of Law . . . sees in the private legal transaction just as much as in an administrative order an act of the state."

2. See Lon Fuller, The Morality of Law, rev. ed. (New Haven, CT: Yale University Press, 1969), 33–94 (listing generality, prospectivity, publicity, consistency, practicability, clarity, stability, and congruence with official action as the eight principles of the inner morality of law). See also the eight principles identified by Joseph Raz in "The Rule of Law and Its Virtue," in The Authority of Law, 2nd ed. (Oxford: Clarendon Press, 2009), 210.

3. See Edward Rubin, "Law and Legislation in the Administrative State," Columbia Law Review 89 (1989): 369.

4. See the discussion in Jeremy Waldron, "Is the Rule of Law an Essentially Contested Concept (in Florida)?," Law and Philosophy 21 (2002): 137–64.

5. For example, Boudewijn Sirks, "Civil Law and Common Law," his valedictory lecture on July 14, 2014, as Regius Professor of Civil Law at University of Oxford.

6. James D. Wolfensohn, "A Proposal for a Comprehensive Development Framework," CDF proposal, World Bank, January 21, 1999), 10–11, http://web.worldbank.org/archive /website01013/WEB/0__CO-87.HTM. I have discussed views of this kind extensively in

Jeremy Waldron, *The Rule of Law and the Measure of Property* (Cambridge: Cambridge University Press, 2012), 76–111.

7. See "CFS 2012–2013 Rule of Law Index (RLI)," Center for Financial Stability, 2021, http://www.centerforfinancialstability.org/rli.php.

8. See, e.g., Matthew Stephenson, "The Rule of Law as a Goal of Development Policy" (brief prepared for the World Bank, 2001), cited in Joel Ngugi, "Policing Neo-liberal Reforms: The Rule of Law as an Enabling and Restrictive Discourse," *University of Pennsylvania Journal of International Economics and Law*, 26 (2005): 534.

9. Robert Barro, "Determinants of Democracy," *Journal of Political Economy* 107 (1999): 173.

10. Barro, 173.

11. For example, see Ibrahim Shihata, "Relevant Issues in the Establishment of a Sound Legal Framework for a Market Economy," in *The World Bank in a Changing World: Selected Essays*, ed. Antonio Parra, Barber Conable, Franziska Tschofen, and Ibrahim Shihata, vol. 2, (Dordrecht: Martinus Nijhoff, 2000), 205: "An over-regulated economy undermines new investment, increases the costs of existing ones and leads to the spread of corruption."

12. Fuller, *Morality of Law,* 33–94.

13. See A. V. Dicey, *Introduction to the Study of the Law of the Constitution,* 8th ed. of 1915 (Indianapolis: Liberty Fund, 1982), lv–lxi.

14. For a general discussion, see Chapter 7 above.

15. Fuller, *Morality of Law,* 176.

16. Dicey, *Introduction to the Study,* 110.

17. F. A. Hayek, *The Constitution of Liberty* (University of Chicago Press, 1978), 200–204.

18. See the discussion in Cass Sunstein, "Rules and Rulelessness" (Coase-Sandor Working Paper Series in Law and Economics No. 27, Coase-Sandor Institute for Law and Economics at Chicago Unbound, University of Chicago, 1994), http://chicagounbound .uchicago.edu/cgi/viewcontent.cgi?article=1434&context=law_and_economics; Jeremy Waldron, "Thoughtfulness and the Rule of Law," *British Academy Review,* 18 (2011): 1–11, https://www.thebritishacademy.ac.uk/publishing/review/18/thoughtfulness-and -rule-law/.

19. There is a useful discussion in Robert Post, "Reconceptualizing Vagueness: Legal Rules and Social Orders," *California Law Review* 82 (1994): 491–507.

20. In his later work, Friedrich Hayek contrasted law with legislation. He said that the legislative mentality is inherently managerial; it is oriented in the first instance to the organization of the state's own administrative apparatus; and its extension into the realm of public policy means an outward projection of that sort of managerial mentality into society at large. See F. A. Hayek, *Rules and Order,* vol. 1 of *Law, Legislation and Liberty* (Chicago: University of Chicago Press, 1973), 72–73, 124–44.

21. Robert Barro, "Democracy and the Rule of Law," in *Governing for Prosperity,* ed. Bruce Bueno de Mesquita and Hilton L. Root (New Haven, CT: Yale University Press, 2000), 209–31.

22. F. A. Hayek, *The Road to Serfdom* (London: Routledge Classics, 2001), 75.

23. Hayek, *Constitution of Liberty,* 153.

24. See H. L. A. Hart, *The Concept of Law,* 2nd ed. (Oxford: Clarendon Press, 1994), 92–96, 175–78.

25. See the helpful discussion in Ronald Cass, "Property Rights Systems and the Rule of Law," in *The Elgar Companion to Property Right Economics,* ed. Enrico Colombatto (London: Edward Elgar, 2003), 222–48.

26. See, e.g., Brian Tamanaha, *On the Rule of Law: History, Politics, Theory* (Cambridge: Cambridge University Press, 2004), 3.

27. See, e.g., Francis Fukuyama, *The Origins of Political Order: From Prehuman Times to the French Revolution* (New York: Profile Books, 2011), 246: "The rule of law can be said to exist only where the preexisting body of law is sovereign over legislation."

28. See Waldron, "Is the Rule of Law an Essentially Contested Concept?," 137–38, 142–44, 147–48.

29. Thomas Fuller in 1733, as quoted by Lord Denning in Gouriet v. Union of Post Office Workers [1977] Q.B. 729, at 762.

30. Tom Ginsburg and Tamir Moustafa, eds., *Rule by Law: The Politics of Courts in Authoritarian Regimes* (Cambridge: Cambridge University Press, 2008). See also Jothie Rajah, *Authoritarian Rule of Law: Legislation, Discourse and Legitimacy in Singapore* (Cambridge: Cambridge University Press, 2012).

31. There is a useful discussion of interpretive methodology in relation to the rule-of-law heritage in Ronald Dworkin, "Hart's Postscript and the Character of Political Philosophy," *Oxford Journal of Legal Studies* 24 (2004): 23–26.

Acknowledgments

I have been teaching classes on the rule of law at Columbia Law School and New York University Law School for more than twenty-five years, and I owe a considerable debt to the students who took these classes and to the deans, colleagues, and faculty committees who have made it possible for this to be the center of my teaching for so long. I would also like to thank my editors at Harvard University Press, Ian Malcolm and then Sam Stark, along with their referees and their editorial staff, for all their help and patience with this collection.

As one gets older, a list of acknowledgments begins to read like an obituary. I want to put on record my thanks to the following teachers and friends who have passed from this life but to whom I owe great debts of gratitude: Chief Justice Arthur Chaskalson of the South African Constitutional Court, Justice Antonin Scalia of the United States Supreme Court, and Professors Malcolm Anderson, Curtis Berger, Ronald Dworkin, John Gardiner, David Goldey, Kent Greenawalt, Sanford Kadish, David Lieberman, Neil Mac-Cormick, and Joseph Raz.

Jurists to whom I am still able to convey thanks include Hon. Harry Edwards (DC Circuit Court of Appeals, retired), Hon. Richard Posner (Seventh Circuit Court of Appeals, retired), Aharon Barak and Dorit Beinisch (both former presidents of the Supreme Court of Israel), Sir Stephen Sedley (formerly of the UK Court of Appeal), Dame Sian Elias (former chief justice of New Zealand), Sir Kenneth Keith (formerly of the International Court of Justice), and Sir Bruce Robertson and Sir Edmund Thomas (both formerly of the New Zealand Court of Appeal).

Other friends and colleagues to whom thanks are due include: Larry Alexander, José Alvarez, Richard Bellamy, Seyla Benhabib, Mark Bennet, Jules Coleman, Robert Cooter, Meir Dan-Cohen, Kevin Davis, David Dyzenhaus, Timothy Endicott, Richard Epstein, Richard Fallon, John Finnis, Barry Friedman, Roberto Gargarella, Tom Ginsburg, Leslie Green, Douglas Hay, Kirstin Howard, Samuel Issacharoff, John Ferejohn, Moshe Halbertal, Mark Henaghan, George Kateb, Tómas Kennedy-Grant, Jeff King, Martin Krygier, Mattias Kumm, Nicola Lacey, Daryl Levinson, John Manning, Andrei Marmor, Campbell McLachlan, Frank Michelman, Henry Monaghan, Michael Moore, Liam Murphy, Thomas Nagel, Matthew Palmer, Stephen Perry, Gerald Postema, Noel Reynolds, Michael Robertson, Edward Rubin, Kristen Rundle, Wojciech Sadurski, Frederick Schauer, Sam Scheffler, John Smillie, Richard Stewart, Peter Strauss, Cass Sunstein, John Tasioulas, Roberto Mangabeira Unger, Nadia Urbinati, Adrian Vermeule, and Kenji Yoshino.

As always, Carol Sanger of Columbia Law School has given me her love and support together with the benefit of her good advice. For that, my greatest thanks are due.

With the exception of the Introduction, the essays in this collection have already been published in various journals and collections of essays. The details of the earlier publications are as follows:

Chapter 1: "Thoughtfulness and the Rule of Law," *British Academy Review* 18 (2011).

Chapter 2: "The Concept and the Rule of Law," *Georgia Law Review* 43, no. 1 (2008): 1–61.

Chapter 3: "How Law Protects Dignity," *Cambridge Law Journal* 71, no. 1 (2012): 200–222.

Chapter 4: "Self-Application" (Public Law and Legal Theory Research Paper Series no. 16–4, New York University School of Law, 2016).

Chapter 5: "Vagueness and the Guidance of Action," in *Philosophical Foundations of Language in the Law,* ed. Andrei Marmor and Scot Soames (Oxford: Oxford University Press, 2011), 58–82.

Chapter 6: "The Rule of Law and the Role of Courts," *Global Constitutionalism* 10, no. 1 (2021): 91–105.

Chapter 7: "The Rule of Law and the Importance of Procedure," in *Getting to the Rule of Law,* ed. James Fleming (New York: New York University Press, 2011).

Chapter 8: "Stare Decisis and the Rule of Law: A Layered Approach," *Michigan Law Review* 111, no. 1 (2012): 1–31.

Chapter 9: "Legislation and the Rule of Law," *Legisprudence* 1, no. 1 (2007): 91–123.

Chapter 10: "Rule *by* Law: A Much-Maligned Preposition" (Public Law and Legal Theory Research Paper Series no. 19–19, New York University School of Law, 2019).

Chapter 11: "The Rule of Law in Public Law," in *The Cambridge Companion to Public Law,* ed. Mark Elliott and David Feldman (Cambridge: Cambridge University Press, 2015), 56–72.

Index

absolutism, 237
accession (in property law), 283
Ackerman, Bruce, 117–119, 286n58
acoustic separation, 104
actuarial techniques, 44
Adams, John, 235, 307n2
adjudication, 23; and procedures, 157
administrative state, 210, 259, 269
adoption, 283
agency, 6, 50–51, 107, 125
aggressive driving, 140–142, 134–137, 288n30
aim, indeterminacy of, 71, 111, 175
analogy, 55, 204–206
analytic argument, 1
animals, 77
Antigone, 244
Aquinas, Thomas, 43
arbitrariness, 20, 36, 243, 246, 259; Dicey on, 165, 219; Hayek on, 3; Raz on, 40
Arendt, Hannah, 247
argumentation, 18, 25–27, 36, 56, 70–74, 84–86, 279n83; Fuller on, 23–24; in politics, 30–31; uncertainty due to, 38–39, 66–67, 85, 172–173
Aristotle, 33–34, 185, 216, 235, 241; on constancy, 203; on different kinds of law, 294n18; image of the lesbian rule, 144; on law-making, 221; on rule of laws, not men, 302–303n23, 307n2
arrest, 87–88

aspirational character of rule of law, 5, 63, 93–95
Athens, ancient, 88, 244
attainder, bill of, 95, 220
Augustine, 43, 53
Austin, John, 42, 48; on declaratory theory, 193, 296n38; on generality of law, 297n43
authoritarianism, 9, 150, 245, 268
authority, 130–132, 287n15
autonomous law, 9, 244
autonomy, 81, 117

bandits, 117
bankruptcy, 102, 211
Barro, Robert, 171, 260–261; on investors' perspective, 210, 233, 260, 310n43; on sequentialism, 213, 264, 302n17
Bentham, Jeremy, 18, 41, 42, 106; on unpredictability of common law, 64, 186–187, 223, 244, 295n, 301n11
bicameralism, 220–221
Bill of Rights, 28, 154–155
Bingham, Tom, 14–16, 238, 240, 254, 265
bioethics, 78
black hole, 170
Bolt, Robert, 226
brutality, 91–92
bureaucracy, 64
Burke, Edmund, 180, 194
Bush v. Gore, 36, 217, 303n29

Carothers, Thomas, 14, 210, 239, 253
Cass, Ronald, 314n25
causeway, as image of legal safety, 226–227
Center for Financial Stability, 243, 260,
     309–310n42
certainty, 14–16, 37, 69–70, 123; unsettled by
     argumentation, 25, 38–39, 66–67, 85
change, legal, 9; necessity of, 265–266
checks and balances, 221
Chesterman, Simon, 17
chilling behavior, 138, 142, 288; effect on
     liberty, 139
China, 161, 240–241; authoritarianism of, 248;
     complaints about legality in, 241; rule by law
     in, 241, 309nn27–34
choice theory of rights, 79
Cicero, 43
City of Akron v. Akron Center for Reproduc-
     tive Health, 293–294n7
civil disobedience, 292
civility, 274
civil society, 32
clarity, 6, 14, 20, 26, 120, 125, 175
closure, 16
codes, legal, 211
codification, 55
coercion, 5, 50, 87, 117; brutality of, 282n49;
     dignified, 90–93
coherence, 25, 55, 66, 70, 85, 172–173
Cold War, 42
Coleman, Jules, 51, 81–82, 277
commands, 42, 93, 117
common good, 53–54, 226
common law, 9, 64, 151, 183–184, 216,
     244–255; unpredictability and opacity of,
     301n11
community, 53
comparative justice, 300
compliance, 61, 107, 109
concentration camps, 44
conduct rules, versus decision rules, 112
Congress of the United States, 146
congruence, 62
consistency, 55, 62, 181
constancy, 8, 12, 17, 203, 206, 233
constitution, 7; as "living" framework, 155;
     rule-of-law provisions in, 311n59
constitutional constraints, 7, 146, 154–155
constitutionalism, 153, 267
Constitution of the United States, 19, 95, 183,
     216, 244–245, 251; Eighth Amendment, 19,
     75, 114, 137; First Amendment, 139

constraints, 250–251
contestation about law, 66–67, 85–86
contract, 100, 184, 257
Cooter, Robert, 292n36, 303n31
corporate law, 211
courts, 2, 7, 45–48, 83, 167; as law-making
     institutions, 55–56, 214
Cover, Robert, 106, 281
critical legal studies, 99, 231, 295
cruelty, 137
customary law, 151, 244

Davis, Kenneth Culp, 16, 30
death penalty, 94
debt, imprisonment for, 87–88
decisionism, 217
degradation, 77, 93
deliberation, 11; political, 31–32, 176–177, 221
democracy, 2–3, 31, 51–52, 148; as analogy
     with legal system, 42, 45, 58, 60, 168;
     definition of, 82; imperfect, 64, 88; and
     legislatures, 51–52; ranking below rule of
     law in development priorities, 171, 213; rule
     of law's hostility towards, 8–9, 264; as threat
     to rule of law, 212–213, 310n45
Denmark, 243
determinacy, 6, 69, 174, 295n29
development, 213; aid, 210; law and, 9
Dicey, A.V., 14, 16, 153, 229, 235, 250, 254,
     261; on administrative tribunals, 262–263;
     on the ascendancy of legislation, 219; on
     consulting legislative history, 303nn32–35;
     on decline of rule of law, 242, 309n35; on
     parliamentary sovereignty, 219; on
     procedure, 165–166, 170–171
dignity, 3–4, 60, 75–78, 150, 279n2; and
     agency, 50–51, 86, 116; and coercion, 90–92;
     meaning of, 76–77; normative character of,
     77; place-holder theory of, 76; and point of
     view, 25, 84, 169, 172; and rank, 86–89; and
     reasoning, 56, 85–86, 128; and self-
     application, 80, 82; underpinning rule of
     law, 5–6, 229
disagreement, 9
discretion, 1, 15–16, 20, 30, 115, 257;
     framing of, 262; H.L.A. Hart's essay on,
     285; weak, 22
distributive policy, 211
divine law, 52, 278n50
divorce, 6, 102
Dobbs v. Jackson Women's Health, 28,
     293–294n7

Donagan, Alan, 89–90
due process, procedural, 4, 22–23, 38, 70, 82–84, 215; in China, 241; different versions of, 47–48, 83
Duxbury, Neil, 100–101, 204–206
Dworkin, Ronald, 22, 27, 31, 66–69, 177, 238; on argumentation, 292n39; on disagreement, 66–9; on integrity, 54, 64, 205; on interpretation of existing law, 192–194, 196, 199–200, 205, 296–297n39; on legality, 296n35, 307n7, 314n31; moral reading of the Constitution, 137; on predictability, 28; on principles, 236, 244; right answer thesis, 192–193; rights thesis, 79–80
Dyzenhaus, David, 238

efficacy, as condition for law, 278
efficiency, 82, 180, 229
Eisenberg, Melvin, 299n59, 299n63, 300n69
elections, 45, 58, 61, 64, 70, 214
Elias, Sian, 311–312
emergent law, 9, 151, 177, 244
empirical method, 41
enacted law, 9
Endangered Species Act, 67
enforcement, 127
environmental law, 212, 260
Epstein, Richard, 244, 289n16
equality, basic, 77
equality, legal, 2, 49
equity, 167, 291
essentially contested concepts, 2, 271n, 288n8
European Convention on Human Rights, 21, 75, 95, 137
execution, 87
executive branch, 145
expectations, 7, 16, 27, 37; formation of, 174, 186; respect for, 188, 258
expressivist accounts of law, 226

factors, 114
fairness, 205
Fallon, Richard, 14, 28, 185, 294n16, 307n9
Federalists, 153, 178, 294n10
Feinberg, Joel, 79, 300
Finnis, John, 14, 63, 71; on focal and peripheral cases of law, 278, 295n19; on Fuller's hypothesis about moral significance of rule of law, 305–306n63; on the law-abiding citizen, 287n11

formal aspects of rule of law, 4–5, 7, 16, 17, 22, 37–38, 160
formalism, 34, 226, 273n21
formality, 31
Fortescue, John, 43
framers (of US Constitution), 13, 216
freedom: economic, 2–3, 209
Freedom House, 242
Fukuyama, Francis, 314
Fuller, Lon, 4, 14, 37, 39, 43–44, 62–63, 80–81, 238, 260, 307; on adjudication, 23–24, 169, 223–224, 295, 305; on clarity, 20, 120; on coercion, 90–91; on concept of law, 276; on consistency, 55; on dignity of human agency, 5, 50, 80–81, 116, 125, 160, 229; on economic allocation, 164–165, 225, 304–305; on inner morality of law, 17, 37, 161, 163–165, 222–225, 235, 247, 249, 254, 257, 261, 304; on legislation, 246; on Nazi Germany, 62–63, 247, 276n23; on procedure, 23, 165, 261–262; on rule of law as precluding certain forms of iniquity, 305–306n63; on values underlying rule of law, 229–231

Gardbaum, Stephen, 293n54
Gardner, John, 113–114, 296n34
Garrison, Arthur, 240
generality, 8, 17, 37, 48–49, 60, 62; fake, 299n54; justification of, 194–195; and stare decisis, 180–181, 196–197, 204, 206
Geneva Conventions, 75, 78, 95
genocide, 44
German Democratic Republic, 42
Ginsberg, Tom, 237, 314n30
God, 52, 240
government under law, 250–253
Guantánamo Bay, 18, 35, 39, 93–94, 161; concerns about procedure at, 169–170
guidance, of action, 6, 20–21, 109–110, 124–130; formulaic character, 129; Raz on, 277n43, 285n31

habeas corpus, 170
Hamed v. Regina, 311n66
Hamilton, Alexander, 13, 153, 244, 294n10
Hare, R.M., 297n40
Harrington, James, 153, 303n36
Harris, Bruce, 312n67
Hart, Henry, 6, 50, 80, 96, 105, 110, 114–115, 136

Hart, H.L.A., 30, 48–49, 60–61, 175; on adjudication, 168; debate with Fuller, 23, 80, 164–165, 239; on guidance of action, 109–110, 117; on internal aspect of rules, 106, 109; on minimum content of natural law, 118, 232; as positivist, 42, 59, 71; on prelegal societies, 57; on primary and secondary rules, 46, 83, 168; on the puzzled man, 287; on rights, 79; on self-application, 110–112, 120

Hayek, F.A., 3, 20, 26, 163, 239, 287n; on decline of rule of law, 242; on Dicey, 262–263; on emergent law, 177; on generality and impersonality, 298; later work of, 32, 163, 181, 185; on legislation, 211, 245–246, 294, 301, 313; on liberty, as value underlying rule of law, 229; on predictability, 14–15, 26, 73, 160, 173, 185, 265; on procedural aspects of rule of law, 290n10; on purpose of law, 226; on social justice, 224; on the use of knowledge, 275n8; on welfare provision, 304

hearings, 5, 18, 23, 46–47, 167

Henderson, Lynn, 306n68

heteronomy, 29

Hitler, Adolf, 247

Hobbes, Thomas, 12, 42, 216, 244; on absolutism, 237–238; regress argument of, 152–153; on rule of laws, not men, 302n23; on sovereignty, 149–152

Holmes, Oliver Wendell, 106

Horwitz, Morton, 306

House of Lords, 15–16; Practice Statement of 1966, 202–203, 299, 300n64

human life, 78

human rights, 2–4, 16, 20, 75–76

Hume, David, 118, 232

humiliation, 77

humility, 180

Hussein, Saddam, 43

ideals, constellation of, 2–3, 33, 159, 213–214, 231, 235, 264

impartiality, 83

impersonality, 49

indeterminacy, different forms of, 287. See also determinacy

inequality, 232, 264

inflexibility, 11

inhuman and degrading treatment, 4, 20–22, 92–93, 114, 137

inner morality of law, 80

institutional aspects of rule of law, 4, 7, 17–18

instrumentalism, legal, 226–229, 254–255, 268

integrity, 25, 54, 62, 64, 205

interest theory of rights, 79

internalization of norms, 108–109, 125, 127, 203, 287

international arena, 17

International Covenant on Civil and Political Rights, 75, 95

interpretation, 15, 71

interrogation, 93, 142–143

intuitive decision-making, 193

investment, 15, 211, 233, 258–260, 266

Iraq, 43, 58

Judeo-Christian doctrine, 86

judges, 13, 55–56, 214; absence of constraints upon, 149; activism of, 268; enacting own preferences, 137; as members of a court, 196; as moral agents, 296; voting among, 157

judgment, 128–130; as involving guidance, 129

judicial review of executive action, 7, 268

judicial review of legislation, 7, 145–147, 177, 271–272, 288n4; more or less aggressive, 154; as rule of laws or rule of men, 154

judicial supremacy, 7, 153

judiciary, 145; independence of, 4, 17, 38, 222, 239; as lawmakers, 149, 153, 198; powerlessness of, 153; as rule by men, 268, 289–290n26

jurisprudence, general, 5, 36, 70, 83; capillary, 106, 284n18; censorial versus expository, 42; descriptive, 41

justice, 53

Kahn, Jeffrey, 226–227

kangaroo courts, 46

Kant, Immanuel, 29, 49, 77, 194–195, 298

Karst, Kenneth, 99

Kaufmann, Daniel, 210

Kelsen, Hans, 198, 278n52; on unity of private and public law, 312n1

Kim Jong-Il, 43

knowledge, public, 49–50

Kraay, Art, 210

Kramer, Matthew, 238

Kremlinology, 59

Kronman, Anthony, 293n3

Krygier, Martin, 247–248, 311n58

labor law, 212

Lacey, Nicola, 23, 165, 274n34

law, concept of, 5, 35–74; changeability as a
    feature of, 266; connection to rule of law,
    36–37, 39–41, 62–65, 167–168; evaluative
    content of, 59–60; narrow understandings
    of, 56–62; technicality of, 89
law-applier, 19
law-making, 12, 19, 55; by courts, 51, 55, 203,
    214; by legislature, 214; popular role in, 215
law schools, 13
Lawson, Gary, 293n1, 294n12
lawyers, 49, 281, 283–284; ethical obligations
    of, 236
legality, 9, 40, 68–69, 253; principles of, 275
legal process materials, 96, 100, 106
legal realism, 198, 201
legal system, 42, 59, 65, 88–9, 165, 275;
    aspirational character of, 94–95
legislation, 8–9, 51–52, 55, 263–264;
    democratic character of, 264; denigration of,
    8, 177; dignity of, 10, 12, 209, 302n19;
    formal and procedural constraints on, 219;
    intent of, 220; limited by rule of law, 208,
    211, 220; site of legal change, 214, 234;
    social and economic, 213, 231–234; under
    urgency, 222
legislative due process, 220–222
legislature, 214; relation to other institutions,
    220
legitimacy, 156, 180, 182, 214–215
liberty, 4, 5, 15, 37; made possible by predict-
    ability, 265; as value underlying rule of law,
    228–229
Liberty Fund, 239
licenses, 103
limited speed zones, 19
literalism, 15, 69
litigation, 23
Lochner v. New York, 156
Locke, John, 43, 150, 153, 159; on individual
    legislators' subjection to law, 304; opponent
    of absolutism, 237–238; on prerogative, 252
Luban, David, 25, 89–90, 281
Lugosi, Charles, 240, 242

MacCormick, Neil, 25–26, 70–71, 174–175; on
    generality, 298n; on precedent, 293n6,
    296n31
Madison, James, 13, 178, 216, 244
Magna Carta, 240–241
majoritarianism, 8, 10, 231
managerialism, 10, 43, 211, 230, 262
manipulation, psychological, 44

Manning, John, 299n, 305n60
Mansfield, William Murray, 14
market economy, 208–209, 232; legal
    framework for, 211; regulation of, 210,
    231–232
market share liability, 67
Marmor, Andrei, 238
Mastruzzi, Massimo, 210
McCrudden, Christopher, 76
mechanical jurisprudence, 16
Merrill, Tom, 283n
Merryman, John Henry, 294n17
methodology (in jurisprudence), 59
Michelman, Frank, 25
Monaghan, Henry, 28, 105, 295n28
Montana, 19
Montesquieu, Baron de, 153
moral evaluation of law, 60
morality, 106, 113; as basis for legal decision in
    hard cases, 191; demands of repeated in the
    law, 133; positive, 266; as separated from
    law, 276n15
moral reading of the Constitution, 22
More, Thomas, 226
Moses, 216
Moustafa, Tamir, 237, 314n30

narcotics, 44, 277
nation-building, 171, 213
natural justice, 7, 38, 70, 162, 170
natural law, 34, 42, 44, 52, 59, 284n21; in
    definition of rule of law, 240
natural rights, 79
Nazi Germany, 43–45, 63; so-called legal
    system of, 44, 164, 247
neo-liberal ideology, 243–244
New Zealand, 13, 222, 236, 243, 252; and
    human rights, 311; New Zealand Bill of
    Rights Act, 248–249, 284n15
Ngugi, Joel, 301n3, 306n67, 313n8
Nicene Creed, 29
nobility, 87
normative thinking, 72, 89, 93–95
norms, legal, 4, 48–49
North Korea, 43

Oakeshott, Michael, 239
oath, to uphold Constitution, 158
obedience, 61
objectivity, 140
officials, 6
Ohio, 6–7, 121

open texture, of language, 71, 111–112, 175
operationalization, 15
originalism, 137, 244
orthopedics, moral, 93
Orwell, George, 237
overruling, 12–13

Pakistan, 17, 35, 39, 161, 275n1
Parliament of the United Kingdom, 147, 219
Pashukanis, Evgeny, 43, 45
Peerenboom, Randall, 240, 242, 309
Pepper (Inspector of Taxes) v. Hart, 303
Perry, Stephen, 109, 297, 299
personhood, 48, 60
phronesis, 193
Pincione, Guido, 224
Pistor, Katharina, 301n13
Planned Parenthood of SE Pennsylvania v. Casey, 12–13, 156–157, 181, 186
planning, 15
Plato, 11, 289n15
plenary authority, 146–147
Political Risk Services, 242
political science, 59
politics, 63
populism, 311
positivism, legal, 25–26, 30, 33, 49, 53, 83,
    216–217; casual positivism, 5, 42–45, 57–59,
    70–71; descriptive character of, 41;
    normative, 278n58; old fashioned
    sovereignty-based versions of, 303n25
positivity, 5, 51–53, 178
Postema, Gerald, 279n70, 290n30, 295n25,
    301n11
practical reason, 21, 114, 129, 131, 135
pragmatism, 68
precedents, 8, 12–13, 27–29; arguments
    concerning, 189; distinguishing, 200–201;
    gravitational force of, 200; as judicial
    legislation, 198–199; overturning, 181–182,
    189, 201–204
predatory point of view, 233
predictability, 4, 8, 28, 158, 264–265; effect of
    argumentation upon, 25–26, 173–174;
    judicial reputation as the basis of, 189–190;
    and individual planning, 174; not the be-all
    and end-all, 189; in private law, 258; as
    required by rule of law, 14, 72; and stare
    decisis, 185–190, 294n14
pre-legal societies, 57, 59
Prerogative, 251–252
president (of the United States), 251–252

price restrictions, 212
primary norm-applying institutions, 46–47,
    277
principled decision-making, 183
principles, 8, 55, 65, 193, 236; in relation to
    precedents, 297n40
private law, 4, 9–10, 256–259; and demand for
    immunity from change, 266; and demand
    for predictability, 258
private ordering, 100–102
privatization, 232
procedural aspects of rule of law, 7–8, 17,
    22–27, 38, 47; listed, 162; popular interest
    in, 17; relation to formal aspects, 170,
    291–292n32
procedure, 4, 83, 257
property rights, 160, 174, 184, 208–209, 222,
    230, 243; necessity of, 232, 237; regulation
    of, 259; rule of law as favoring, 257
prospectivity, 17, 298n49. *See also* retroactivity
psychiatry, 44
public administration, 256–257, 263
public good, 53–54, 226
public goods, 232
publicity, 37, 49, 56, 226
public law, 9–10, 256; as possibly covering all
    law, 256–257
punishment, 91; constraints on, 92–93

racism, 44, 94
Radin, Margaret, 98–99
rank, equalization of, 86–87
ratio decidendi, 188
Rawls, John, 14, 286n58
Raz, Joseph, 14, 15, 32–33, 54, 113–114, 239,
    296n36; on action guiding, 81, 106, 110,
    120–121; on authority, 130–132, 287; on
    dignity and the rule of law, 81, 125; on
    generality, 107–108, 311; on instrumental
    understanding of the rule of law, 306n; on
    legislatures, 52; on the meaning of the rule
    of law, 40, 148–149, 166, 168, 254; on
    precedent, 198, 299n57; on primary organs,
    46–47
reason, 4, 33, 55, 60, 66; rule of, 123
reasonable care, 4, 20, 123
reasonableness, 3, 6, 18, 20, 113, 122, 265
reasoned elaboration, 21–22, 82, 114–115,
    136–137, 283n13
reason-giving in law, 295n26
reasons, 130; second-order, 287n16
Rechtsstaat, 247

reciprocity, 247

recognition, rules of, 26, 49, 72

regulation, 243, 259–260; burden of, 243, 260, 263; impact on private law rights, 259

representation, legal, 25, 89–90

representation, political, 51–52, 214, 264

respect, 48, 50, 73–74, 77, 116, 150; in administration of sanctions, 92; for law, 215; for point of view, 84, 169, 173

retroactivity, 44, 63, 158, 279; in common law, 298

Riggs v. Palmer, 236

rights, legal, 78–79; in private law, 258; social and economic, 155. *See also* human rights

rights thesis, 79–80

Roe v. Wade, 12, 28, 181, 293–294n7

Roman Catholic doctrine, 78

Rubin, Edward, 217–218

rule by law, 9, 149–151, 177, 216, 225–226, 239–240, 267–268; and acceptance of discipline of legality, 228; different from rule of law, 236–237, 267, 308n22; and lack of procedural values, 239; literal understanding of, 253–254; as thin rule of law, 239; transition to rule of law, 242; valuable aspects of, 246

rule of law, 9; academic understandings of, 17, 39, 160; in constitutional adjudication, 157; as a constitutional principle, 235–236; contested character of, 33, 68, 258; definition, 1–2, 257, 269; distinctive contribution of, 3; heritage of, 269; indexes of, 208, 210, 242–243, 260; lay understandings of, 17–18, 22–23, 39, 168; rule of laws, not men, 1, 8, 11–12, 149, 178, 216–217; thick and thin conceptions of, 240; upholding rights in private law, 258; use as an ideological tool, 209, 260; value-laden character of, 3

ruler, law as, 150–151

rules, 4, 6, 15, 17, 19–22, 114, 124–125, 194–195, 262; inchoate, 114–115, 136–137

Russia, 35, 239, 275

Sacks, Albert, 6, 50, 80, 90, 105, 114

Scalia, Antonin, 15, 194–195; on Aristotle, 304; on the importance of rules, 194, 273, 292

Schumpeter, Joseph, 82

secondary rules, 46, 83

secret decrees, 44

security, of expectations, 15. *See also* expectations

self-application, 6, 19, 50, 91, 96–97, 107–110, 260, 277; in constitutional law, 104; courts as second-guessing, 96, 105; justification of, 103; and liberty, 116; patterns of, 115; of standards, 97, 108, 112–115; versus individually administered regulations, 102

self-control, 5, 77–78

Selznick, Philip, 282

separation of powers, 38, 219

sequentialism, 264

settlement, 37, 69

Shapiro, Martin, 47

Shapiro, Scott, 106

Shihata, 272–273n1, 301–302n14, 313n11

Siltala, Raimo, 293n6

Sindell v. Abbott Laboratories, 67–68

Singer, Joseph, 295n29

Sirks, Boudewijn, 312n5

slave societies, 87, 282n46

Snyder, Timothy, 247

socialist legality, 43

social justice, 2–3, 117–118, 148, 155, 214, 224

Solon, 216

South Africa, 58, 146

sovereignty, 147, 303n25

sports, 106–107

stability, 264. *See also* constancy

standards, 3, 6–7, 15, 18–22, 126; as avowedly indeterminate directives, 115, 136; not inchoate rules, 21, 114–115, 136–137; in relation to precedents, 297n40; self-application of, 82, 112–115; versus rules, 127, 173

standing to sue, 78

Star Chamber, 46, 88

stare decisis, 8, 18, 27–29, 179–180; based on analogical reasoning, 204–206; as central feature of common law, 184–185; in constitutional law, 28, 183; downside of, 179–180; force of, 183; justification of, 180; not in civil law systems, 294n; numerous theories of, 180; permitting overturning of precedents, 201–203; relation to rule of law, 180–181, 183–185, 206

state, 217–218; law enacted by, 218

State v. Schaeffer, 20, 121–124, 138, 140

State v. Stanko, 19

status, 76–77, 86–87, 280n5

Stephenson, Matthew, 305n61, 313n8

Stevens, John Paul, 217, 303n29

Steyn, Johan, 291n31

Stoics, 86

strains of commitment, 286n58
subjective preferences, 13–14
substantive aspects of rule of law, 5, 16, 59–60,
   148, 160, 162, 225, 228–231, 254, 290n4;
   contrasted with values underlying rule of
   law, 228–229; cynical argument for, 230;
   disagreement about, 230
Summers, Robert, 14
Sunstein, Cass, 14, 19, 313n18
super-precedents, 28
supremacy clause, 183
Supreme Court of the United Kingdom, 15–16
Supreme Court of the United States, 153, 206
systematicity, 25, 54–56, 65–66, 172

Tamanaha, Brian, 226–228, 238, 291
Tashima, Wallace, 290
taxes, 102
technology of justice, 118
telephone justice, 239
Tennessee Valley Authority v. Hill, 67–68
terror, rule by, 43, 92, 116, 230, 247–248
terrorists, 159
text, 13, 27, 67, 99, 183–184, 200
third source of government authority, 251–252
Thompson, E.P., 166, 231, 306n68
thoughtfulness, 4–5, 11–34
Tocqueville, Alexis de, 31, 176, 215
tort law, 20, 184
torture, 87, 91, 141–143; definition of, 142;
   statute concerning, 141, 288
totalitarian systems, 57
trade-offs, 3
traffic law, 6–7, 19–20, 66, 97–98, 108–109,
   121–127
transparency, 214
treating like cases alike, 181, 205, 300n70
Tribe, Laurence, 273n21
tyranny, 117

unfairness, 139–140
United Nations, 17
United States, 58, 61, 64, 243; and burden of
   history, 94; legislation in, 203
United States Constitution. *See* Constitution of
   the United States
universalizability, 297
Upham, Frank, 210, 292n37
upright stance, 93, 281–282n45
utility, 27

vagueness, 16, 139, 144; void-for-vagueness,
   19, 122
value, 77
value judgments, 19–20, 59–60; thick
   value-judgments, 21, 114, 134–135;
   upstream or downstream, 127
Vermeule, Adrian, 308
Vlastos, Gregory, 87

Waldron, Jeremy, 147
Washington Consensus, 171, 209, 230,
   300–301nn1–3
waterboarding, 142
Weber, Max, 89, 921
Wechsler, Herbert, 303
welfare state, 224
Whitman, James, 87, 282
will (testament), 100
will (volition), 55, 217, 264
Winston, Kenneth, 247–248
Wolfensohn, James, 259–260, 312–313n6
World Bank, 15, 259, 272–273, 292
World Justice Project, 242–243
worth, 78

Zakaria, Fareed, 302n16
Zimbabwe, 64
Zywicki, Todd, 224